Youth Culture

*For my father, for allowing me to grow,
and Dan Goldstein, for continuing
the family tradition*

YOUTH CULTURE

IDENTITY IN A
POSTMODERN WORLD

Edited by Jonathon S. Epstein

Copyright © Blackwell Publishers Ltd 1998; editorial matter and organization copyright © Jonathon S. Epstein 1998

First published 1998

Reprinted 1999

Blackwell Publishers Inc.
350 Main Street
Malden, Massachusetts 02148
USA

Blackwell Publishers Ltd
108 Cowley Road
Oxford OX4 1JF
UK

Library of Congress Cataloging-in-Publication Data

Youth culture: identity in a postmodern world / Jonathon Epstein, [editor].
    p.   cm.
  Includes bibliographical references and index.
  ISBN 1-55786-850-6 (hb). – ISBN 1-55786-851-4 (pb)
    1. Teenagers – United States – Social conditions. 2. Teenagers – United States – Attitudes. 3. Subculture – United States. 4. United States – Social conditions – 1980- I. Epstein, Jonathon S.
  HV1431.Y684 1998
  305.235'0973 – DC21   97-2121
                                                            CIP

British Library Cataloguing in Publication Data

A CIP catalogue record for this book is available from the British Library.

Typeset in 10½ on 12½ pt New Aster
by Best-set Typesetter Ltd., Hong Kong
Printed in Great Britain by TJ International Ltd, Padstow, Cornwall

This book is printed on acid free paper

CONTENTS

CONTRIBUTORS

Linda Andes is a sociologist working in the Chicago area. She has done work in the areas of punk rock subculture and the riot grrrl movement.

Steven Best is Assistant Professor of Philosophy at the University of Texas at El Paso. With Douglas Kellner, he is author of *Postmodern Theory* and the forthcoming *Postmodern Adventure*. Best has also published *The Politics of Historical Vision* and many articles in philosophy, social theory, and cultural criticism.

Thomas C. Calhoun is an assistant professor of Sociology at the University of Nebraska-Lincoln. He is interested in researching drugs and religion as they impact the African American community and juvenile male prostitution. His work has appeared in *Sociological Inquiry, Sociological Spectrum, the Journal of Social Psychology*, and the *Western Journal of Black Studies*.

Julie Ann Harms Cannon is a PhD candidate in Sociology at the University of Nebraska-Lincoln. She received her BA in Sociology from Western Washington University, and her MA in Sociology from the University of Nebraska-Lincoln. Her areas of interest include the sociology of sex and gender and sociological theory. She is currently preparing a textbook on the women founders of sociology.

Jonathon S. Epstein holds a PhD in social theory from Kent State University, where he has taught the sociology of adolescents, mass media and society, and social theory. In addition to his work as an academic, he serves as a consultant for the education department of the Rock and Roll Hall of Fame and Museum. He is the editor of the 1994 book *Adolescents and Their Music: If It's Too Loud You're Too Old* (Garland).

Rhonda Fisher is a PhD candidate at the University of Nebraska-Lincoln. She serves as an assistant professor in Sociology at Midland Lutheran College. Her research interests include Protestant fundamentalism and violence, special needs adoption, deviance, and gender.

Bruce K. Friesen is Assistant Professor of Sociology at Kent State University – Stark campus. He has written extensively on heavy metal subculture and the aesthetics of heavy metal.

Henry Giroux is the Waterbury Chair Professor at Penn State University. His latest books include: *Disturbing Pleasures, Fugitive Cultures: Race, Violence, and Youth*, and the forthcoming *Pedagogy and the Politics of Hope* (Westview). He is looking for a job.

Warren Helfinch holds an MSW from the University of Calgary. Currently he is playing drums in a hard rock band, and working as a social worker in Calgary.

Mary Celeste Kearney is a PhD candidate in the School of Cinema–Television, Division of Critical Studies, at the University of Southern California. She is writing her dissertation on the relationship between feminism, female youth cultures, and the construction of feminine adolescence in popular culture.

Douglas Kellner is Professor of Philosophy at the University of Texas-Austin. He has widely published in the areas of postmodern theory and mass communications. His many books include *Media Culture, Postmodern Theory*, and *Postmodern Adventure*, co-authored with Steven Best.

David A. Locher received his PhD in sociology from Kent State University. He is currently Assistant Professor in the Department of Social Science at Missouri Southern State College. His areas of interest include music subcultures, visual sociology, and photography.

Javier Santiago-Lucerna is a social psychologist living in San Juan, Puerto Rico. He has done work in the area of youth culture and published in *CTHEORY* and other critical journals.

Sarah Nixon-Ponder is currently a university fellow at Kent State University. As a PhD candidate in curriculum and instruction, her major is in literacy studies with an emphasis in multicultural education.

Robert Sardiello is a PhD candidate at the State University of New York-Stoney Brook, and an Instructor at Nassau Community College on Long Island. He has published a number of articles which explore the Grateful Dead Head subculture.

Lisa Sloat graduated from the University of Southern Indiana, Evansville, Indiana, in 1995 with a BS in communications and sociology. She is currently working on her MA in Sociology at Old Dominion University, Norfolk, Virginia.

Samuel R. Smith is nearing completion of his PhD in mass communications at the University of Colorado's Center for Mass Media Research. His dissertation research focuses on America's ideologies of science and technology, especially as manifested in popular culture genres such as cyberpunk. Other areas of research interest include popular music and Internet development.

Lori Tomlinson is a PhD student in the American Culture Studies program. Lori is the assistant to the anector at the Wood County Historical Museum, and an editorial assistant at the BGSU Popular Press.

ACKNOWLEDGMENTS

This book was completed in perhaps what has been the most difficult period in my life. A number of people have offered not only their critical commentary, but their personal support, and I would like to take a few moments to recognize them. Above all, my friend and colleague Pat Lichty has been more than generous with his time and his patience, insisting that I could in fact finish this volume despite the personal upheavals that have occurred this year. I owe him a large debt, and hope that one day I can return the generosity in the same gracious manner that he showed me. Tim Gongaware, from Ohio University, has also been a critical yet supportive colleague. My friend, the Scottish poet Fish, came through for me at a time in my life where I was in desperate need of solitude and understanding. I owe you one, Fish.

I would also like to take the time to thank the following people for their support and faith in my work: Susan Rabinowitz, my editor at Blackwell, has been constantly supportive and enthusiastic. Among the community of scholars a number of people have taken the time to comment on this work, and have been a tremendous source of inspiration. Among these friends are Douglas Kellner, Henry Giroux, Stanford Lyman, Tom Calhoun, Jerry M. Lewis, Sheila Whiteley and the rest of the faculty at Salford University, Andrew Herman, Steve Redhead, and Norman Denzin. I would also like to thank my friend Cathleen Ann White for helping me relocate my heart.

1
INTRODUCTION: GENERATION X, YOUTH CULTURE, AND IDENTITY

Jonathon S. Epstein

Why Is the Topic of Youth Culture an Important Area of Study?

As the end of the millennium approaches, the task of defining what it means to be a young person seems to be taking on a new urgency. Social scientists and cultural critics have long been both intrigued and confused by youth. Young people, after all, sometimes seem like a completely different species from adults, and their habits, idiosyncrasies, and argot have long mystified grown-ups. While some scholars and critics make positive assessments about the current status of adolescence, for the most part this bafflement seems to lead those interested in young people to define adolescence itself as a social problem. Unfortunately, much of what has been written about youth follows from that point of view. The essays in this book are an attempt to move away from that narrow ideation of youth towards a more compassionate and reasonable understanding of what it means to be young in a rapidly changing world.

A Teacher's Experience: Dr Jonathon Epstein

I first became concerned about the ways in which young people were viewed by the adult world in the mid-1980s, when I was in graduate school. At the time, I was also a young father, trying desperately to juggle the responsibilities of parenthood (most importantly those which revolve around making a living), the requirements of acting as a research assistant, and, of course, attempting to keep up with my course work. Earlier in that year, in order to make ends meet, I had applied for, and received, a provisional teaching certificate in the state of North Carolina and taken a job as a special education teacher in an "optional" middle school. However, as most educators know (although most are not willing to admit it), the term "optional" is defined only by its specific usage by school administrators. For the students there is no option: one attends the optional school, or one does not attend school at all. Students in my classes often faced the choice between optional school or incarceration. My particular class-room was often the last stop before the detention center. In fact, a number of my students, who were labeled "severely behaviorally and emotionally handicapped," were residents of the juvenile facility and were no strangers to the world of the juvenile justice system. At this writing, over 25 percent of the 84 students who passed through the revolving door that was my classroom are deceased, most by way of gunshot. A few of the ones lucky enough to survive the violence of their world are presently incarcerated.

What I found the most distressing about my duties as a special education instructor was that the actual education of my students was at the very bottom of my list of responsibilities. My primary responsibility was actually to contain my students in my classroom, and prevent them from having all but the most minimal contact with the mainstreamed students who had been sent to the middle school for remedial education. I was allowed, under North Carolina law, to use any means, up to and including physical restraint and involuntary confinement in what was euphemistically referred to as a "quiet room," to keep these students separated from their peers. On some days I spent significantly more time holding these young men – for they were always boys – face down on the floor in a "thera-peutic restraint" than I spent teaching. Overall, these were angry, desperate, and violent young men, made all the more so by their almost complete lack of academic knowledge and skills.

As a sociologist, I was acutely aware of the social and cultural situations that had led these young people to my classroom. They were by and large poor, minority youth who had spent their days in public housing projects and trailer parks. Most came from broken families in which drug abuse and alcoholism was the general rule, and a distressing number of them had been sexually abused by a family member. What I lacked was a way to address the anger of these young people while simultaneously teaching them at least a minimum of skills that would allow them to function reasonably well in the unlikely event that they actually lived to reach adulthood. My sense of frustration was exacerbated by institutions that viewed the kids, and not their situations, as the social problems. In essence I was charged with forcing these youngsters to accept their assigned roles as "problems," and to acquiesce to the decisions made by those in positions of authority.

This situation, while extreme, should not be viewed as unique or unusual, and it is not specific to working-class or poor youth. All young people undergo what are essentially similar processes and mechanisms of socialization into the dominant culture. At the same time, all adults working with young people must face the challenge of understanding the individual in the context of his or her environment.

Existing Studies of Youth Culture

When one is reviewing the sociological and cultural studies literature on youth, three distinct periods of scholarship emerge: the sociological work from the University of Chicago in the early part of the twentieth century; the work of the Centre for the Study of Contemporary Culture in Birmingham, England; and the recent work being done in the United States by cultural critics such as Henry Giroux, Douglas Kellner, and Deena Weinstein. In order to fully comprehend the subsequent essays, it is crucial that the reader understand these theories and their application to the study of adolescence. In view of this necessity, an overview of these periods, the major contributors, and theories will establish a theoretical framework for the chapters that follow. In addition, an example illustrating the convergence of these ideas can be found in an inquiry into what has been referred to as "Generation X."

Alienation and Adolescence

It has been said that adolescence is the period in the lifecourse in which individuals are most likely to be alienated. Calabrese (1987) points out that adolescence in itself is a growth period that is conducive to alienation, primarily due to the "betwixt and between" nature of this particular position in the lifecourse. Adolescents are seen as no longer being children, but not yet being completely adult (Weinstein, 1994). It is this tension between childhood freedom and adult responsibility that reportedly proves to be a fruitful ground for the growth of alienation (Calabrese, 1987). According to Erikson (1968), adolescence is the period in one's life in which choices begin to be made and identities are formed. It is through this process of identity formation that cliques and subcultures tend to flourish. Central among adolescent choices, for Erikson, is the choice of a future career. This issue is made increasingly problematic by the current perceived downward mobility of most of today's young people. Their belonging to subcultures who are apathetic to the future is, in Erikson's sense, simply a mechanism of identity protection.

The concept of alienation is one which has a multiplicity of meanings in the extant literature. In general usage in the sociological literature on the topic, the term is used to describe the various ways in which an individual can be estranged from society in general, from particular institutions, such as education or religion, and even from herself and others, such as peers. In this way alienation can be viewed in two distinctive ways, one dealing with the structural issues of alienation as a defining feature of members of particular groups, and the other with the social psychological instances that can lead to, or cause, an individual being alienated.

Sociologically, alienation falls into two broad categories. The first is the estrangement experienced as a result of social structural position, and is closely related to the work of Marx, Durkheim, and Merton. While there is quite a bit that differentiates the thinking of these three men, all held that alienation, or anomie according to Durkheim and Merton, was always to be opposed to the social structural position of particular groups in society.

The second broad category of alienation is social psychological in nature. These conceptualizations of alienation refer to the internal feeling of detachment felt by the individual in given situations. While this alienation might in fact be situationally defined by the various group memberships of those present, it is the individual's sense of estrangement that is at issue. It can be pointed out, however, that both structural and social psychological types of alienation can coincide, and in fact do so frequently.

Structural Conceptions of Alienation

Structural conceptions of alienation hold that the individual's relationship to social structure proper should be the focus of analysis. In order for alienation to be a structural variable, there must be a discrepancy between the resources of a society and the ability of certain groups to attain those resources. For the Marxist, the resource is always capital, and the bourgeoisie have a monopoly on its ownership. This monopoly leaves the proletariat without recourse but to sell their labor power to the capitalist at a wage determined by the profit motive of the capitalist. The worker then becomes alienated from society at large, since his work is what attaches him to structure as such, and eventually alienated from himself for metaphysical reasons based on the expression of man's basic spirit through the things he creates through his labor, which has now become objectified (Marx, 1968).

The related concept of anomie was first introduced by Durkheim in his classic text *The Division of Labor in Society* in 1893 (1947). According to Durkheim, an anomic condition is represented by the relative absence or confusion of clear values within a group. Anomie is characterized by a lack of normative definition and clarity. Anomie, for Durkheim, related not to the individuals in society as such, but rather to the breakdown of the normative structure in which these individuals were located. The individual who finds himself or herself in such a social situation is said to be in a state of anomia (Antonovsky, 1987).

Merton (1968) expands on Durkheim's concept of anomie, while retaining a connection to the assumption that all conflict within a social structure is related to the unavailability of the means necessary to acquire the valued objects of a culture. Merton's conceptualization of anomie is central to the Birmingham school's theorizing on youth subcultures (Cohen, 1980).

In the case of the structural varieties of alienation, the individual is seen as being set apart by virtue of a social group's structural position within society, thus becoming detached from society at large. The individual's alienation is contingent upon that of the group to which he or she belongs. When this argument is centered within a discussion of social class, as is the case with the cultural studies theory discussed above, it is said to be operating within the conflict tradition. Thus it essentially must adhere, at least in part, to Marx's discussion of alienation and false consciousness.

Processual conceptions of alienation generally revolve around social-psychological measures of individual attitudes or beliefs, and leave issues of ideology to others. Scales which purport to measure constructs such as powerlessness (Neal and Groat, 1974), meaninglessness (Neal and Groat, 1974), and sense of coherence (Antonovsky, 1987) are all related in their focus on the alienation of the individual from social structure and others on a personal, as opposed to a collective, level. Antonovsky, in particular, has defined alienation, or in his terminology the opposite of "sense of coherence," as the extent to which a lack of confidence about the manageability, meaningfulness, and comprehensibility of life permeates one's orientation to life. In terms of the experiences of adolescent alienation, meaningfulness is the most critical of these three components of alienation because it is the search for meaning in the life of adolescents that creates, or allows for, the creation of youth subcultures (Hebdige, 1979).

As a result of the research carried out under the auspices of the Centre for Contemporary Cultural Studies at the University of Birmingham, England, sociologists now know a great deal about youth subcultures in the English Midlands. With the possible exception of the Chicago gang research undertaken in the early part of the twentieth century, which, it should be pointed out, had a profound impact on many British subcultural theorists, the Birmingham school has provided sociology with its most sustained and theoretically focused examination of youth subcultures to date.

British Youth Studies

The Birmingham school was strongly influenced by American sociology. Cohen (1980) and others have argued that the work of the Centre for Contemporary Cultural Studies represents the British encounter, and ultimate incorporation, or symbolic interactionism as outlined by the "Chicago School" of that field under the rubric of "transactional" sociology. As Stuart Hall and Tony Jefferson point out in their introduction to the Birmingham school's most widely cited collective work, *Resistance through Rituals: Youth Subcultures in Post-war Britain*, (1975, p. 5):

> Our starting point, as for so many others, was Howard Becker's *Outsiders* – the text which, at least for us, best signaled the "break" in mainstream sociology and the subsequent adoption, by many sociologists working in the fields of deviance, sub-cultural theory, or criminology – originally in America but rapidly in this country too of what came to be known as an interactionist, and later a "transactional" or "labelling" perspective.

These British sociologists discovered that interactionism, and particularly the work of Howard Becker and Erving Goffman, provided profound insight into the ways in which becoming a "deviant" was largely the result of being labeled as such by others, and that some groups, because of the oppositional stance they take *vis-à-vis* society proper, are much more likely to be labeled as such than other less oppositional groups. Adolescents, whose identification with, and embracing of, rock music as their badge of in-group identity (Frith, 1981), proved to be a frequent target for the labeling process (Dotter, 1994). However, these British theorists found that they could not account for the obvious class-based origins of British youth subcultures and stay completely within an interactionist framework. At this point it became apparent that a comprehensive approach that accounted for both the processes of subcultural formation and the structural basis of subcultural affiliation was necessary if the Centre was going to provide sociology with an account of modern youth that was theoretically sound and verifiable within the social reality of youth. This recognition culminated in the development of the first paradigm which the sociology of youth culture could call its own.

The research agenda eventually associated with the Birmingham school was unique in its incorporation of several diverse theoretical positions. Birmingham researchers began with American symbolic interactionism, added the structural functional categories of innovation and ritualism found in Merton's anomie theory, then centered their basic orientation on the topics of deviance and delinquency.

The Birmingham school holds that becoming a delinquent is largely a result of the labeling process, and that working-class youth is much more likely to be labeled as such than are members of other groups. Borrowing from the Frankfurt school – particularly Adorno – and with a nod towards Antonio Gramsci's (1971) theory of hegemony, researchers were able to outline youth's basic orientation towards popular culture as being a combination of mass-market manipulation and genuine expression through reappropriation (McRobbie, 1995). The politics of youth's resistance to hegemonic culture was explained through the use of semiology, the interpretation of the cultural use of signs and symbols and the subcultural, class-oriented meanings that come to be attached to these symbols. The use of a semiological method was generally made with particular reference to the work of Roland Barthes (1985).

The overarching purpose of the Centre's work on youth was to provide an in-depth, empirical, and objective analysis of the phenomenon of youth culture that would build on the work that came before it while at the same time removing the understanding of youth culture from the mass media accounts of it. These mass media accounts, according to Clarke et al. (1975), become a part of the phenomenon of youth culture itself by focusing on the spectacular aspects of adolescence, such as its artifacts – dress, drug use, subcultural style and idiom – and thus the media contribute more to the "myth" of youth subculture (Cohen, 1980) than to an academic understanding of it.

Culture, as it was defined by Clarke et al. (1975), refers to the distinct patterns of life, choice, and taste of social groups. Culture is the expressive form (Simmel, 1968) of the social. It is the way in which social groups handle the raw material of social experience in order to make it meaningful and understandable for members of the group. Culture is the objectification of the social. According to Clarke et al. (1975, p. 10):

The "culture" of a particular group or class is the peculiar and distinctive "way of life" of the group or class, the meanings, values and ideas embodied in institutions, in social relations, in systems of belief, in customs and mores, in the uses of objects and material life. Culture is the distinctive shapes in which this material and social organization of life expresses itself.

While groups living within the same society will share a common culture, the ways in which these different groups make use of that culture will not necessarily be uniform. Culture, for the Birmingham school, is actually plural. Access to, and the ability to make use of, cultural capital is unequal in the same ways in which access to social position is unequal when discussed in terms of social class. For this reason a distinction must be made between "hegemonic culture" and "common culture." Hegemonic culture is created by those groups which possess the greatest power, weight and influence in a society, and whose powerful social position makes it possible to create a dominant culture. Common culture (Willis, 1990) is an expression of the everyday lives of the other social groups and classes. Common culture, it should be pointed out, arises in those cultural places which hegemonic culture is unable to completely penetrate.

When common culture expresses opposition to hegemonic culture, as is generally the case in youth culture, the cultural practices which ensue are labeled "resistance" by the Birmingham scholars, to indicate the function of that cultural practice. This resistance is generally considered to be evidence of "at risk" behavior by youth workers and school officials despite the political nature of the resistance itself (Giroux, 1983).

The plurality of cultures within a dominant, hegemonic culture is largely determined by social class. Each class within a given society will have a specific way of expressing and realizing itself culturally. These class-specific expressions make up what the Birmingham theorists called "parent culture," an unfortunately confusing choice of terminology for an otherwise straightforward concept (Cohen, 1980). Parent cultures, it should be pointed out, are not subcultures, the reasons for which will be discussed below. Nor are parent cultures in any way a reference to the relationship between adults and their offspring. The term parent culture refers specifically to the overarching, class-based, cultural choices that are available for appropriation by specific groups. As a result, expressions of parent culture are by and large considered class-oriented responses to hegemonic culture.

This relationship is exemplified by Paul Willis in his book *Learning to Labour* (1977). He demonstrates how the cultural values of working-class adolescent boys, the values of what he calls "the shop floor," are expressed through this group's emphasis on masculinity, toughness, and street-smarts. It is these values, he argues, which will allow these "lads" to accept their transition from adolescent status to the world of everyday, working-class adult responsibility. At the same time, and not incidentally, those values allowed the young men to form identities that were resilient to the possibility that spending the remainder of their life on the shop floor was the only alternative to life "on the dole" in Britain's unemployment lines of the 1970s.

From Willis's observations we can see how the behavior, lifestyles and attitudes of these working-class youth were primarily oriented towards class-based ideas and values of their "parent," working-class culture. This demonstrates an acceptance of their class-oriented life chances. The young workers' ways of engaging their social world were primarily affirmative responses to the focal concerns of their social class. Additionally, and not unimportantly, these young men rejected middle-class ideologies. They referred to middle-class youth as "ear 'oles." This rejection, while possibly an act of resistance, virtually guaranteed their remaining in the working class, a fact that seemed to be beyond these young people's understanding.

When the responses of a group are distinctly at odds in both content and structure with both the hegemonic culture and the parent culture, and when these responses are taken up by that group as a way of life, then we have what is called a subculture. A subculture must be identifiably different (Clarke et al., 1975) from its parent culture. Membership in a subculture always follows from membership in a parent culture. However, the subcultural values and activities can either affirm the class culture or reject it. Affirmative groups such as the American Skinheads, the "lads" in the Willis study, and many minority gangs in the American urban environment strongly affirm their working-class origins. Others, such as the "wigger" (self-proclaimed "white nigger") subculture, oppose the overarching parent culture (Cooper, 1994).

In "wigger" subculture, white lower-middle-class suburban youth take on the trappings, including dress, argot, and music, of inner-city African-American youth. Significantly, their image of urban youth is the one which is presented to them primarily through the mass media in films such as *Menace II Society* and *Juice*, which have been interpreted as not only being unrealistic in their portrayal of the extent of violence, but being racist as a result (Giroux, 1994). This media effect has also been noted by Kellner (1994), who would hold that the very fact that "wigger" subcultures have sprung up in locations like Des Moines, Iowa, Sioux City, Iowa, and Lincoln, Nebraska (Cooper, 1994) would suggest that these youth have rearticulated their social and cultural position primarily through the appropriation and reinterpretation of media images.

The apparently oppositional stance of these subcultures, however, is interpreted and filtered through the dominant, or hegemonic, system of ideology and, as a result, is not a real threat to society, despite the day-to-day manifestations of such opposition, including delinquent or destructive activities. While these activities – premarital sex, drug dealing, fighting, etc. – may be destructive to a particular group of adolescents, the impact of this destructiveness will by and large only affect that particular subculture, leaving society proper relatively unaffected. In this manner, resistance of the subculture is reduced to ritual. Rather than affirming the experiences of these young people, resistance itself becomes an end, thus becoming a mechanism in their alienation.

Following from Georg Simmel's (1968) discussion of cultural forms, and from Brake (1985), it can be proposed that subcultures, not unlike cultures in general, operate on at least three levels: the level of basic historical ideas, the level of values, the level of material expression. It is the understanding of these three levels, as they come to present themselves in subcultural style, that is the focus of subcultural studies. The subcultural researcher's task is to determine what, specifically, a subcultural style signifies to the members of the subculture themselves (Hebdige, 1979). This is achieved through an examination of the relationship and the fit between the three levels of subculture. The study of the relationship between the cultural elements of a subculture and the fit between objects, the meanings granted to those objects, and behavior (Brake, 1985) is called a homology.

According to Willis, the use of a homology as a sensitizing concept extends the analysis of what Walter Miller (1958) called the focal concerns of a subculture from a strictly class-based, social analysis into the "cultural" elements of subcultures, by examining the meaning of "style" as symbolic expression. Homologies allow the researcher to determine the extent to which particular aspects of a subculture parallel, or reflect, the overarching concerns, styles, and behaviors of the broader social group to which a particular subculture may belong.

In reference to youth subcultures, homologies are used to describe the symbolic links between a subculture's values and its lifestyle. This lifestyle, for Hebdige (1979), is centered in a subculture's subjective experience and the types of music which the subculture uses to express or reinforce its focal concerns.

This rearticulation of structural positioning within a subcultural framework is exemplified by Dick Hebdige's work on "Rude Boy" subculture in Great Britain. The Rude Boys, or Rudies, were members of the small non-white population in England. Non-whites of African descent make up approximately 3 percent of the British population (Brake, 1985). These youth's experiences are strongly informed by the lasting effects of British colonialism, and many are of West Indian heritage.

These youth, not unlike their American counterparts, consider their lot to be an almost impossible one. As a result, they create a subcultural space through the appropriation of petty crime, use of marijuana, and the rejection of working for "the man." Their music of choice is variously called ska, reggae, or dub. While there are differences in these musical styles, all share a common origin in the Jamaican music of the late 1960s and early 1970s. Underlying this subcultural style is an ideology based on Rastafarianism, a Black nationalist religion which also has its roots in Jamaica and Africa. Significantly, the reggae style primarily concerns itself with the Rastafarian ideology of emancipation from "Babylon," which refers to white Western society. This ideology is reappropriated by the Rude Boys as a way of justifying unlawful or delinquent behavior. It should be noted that Hebdige uses the term "reappropriated" in the sense that the religious and cultural experiences of the West Indian colonial subjects cannot be translated, in total, to the experiences of Black, urban, British youth. In this manner the subcultural style of these youth is considered, by Hebdige, to be essentially problematic.

The use of homologies to uncover the meaning of subcultural styles and values is made difficult by the subcultural "reordering and re-contextualization of objects to communicate fresh meanings, within a total system of significances, which already includes prior and sedimented meanings attached to the objects used" (Clarke et al., 1975, p. 177). The recontextualization generally takes place at the level of language and style, which cannot be understood intuitively by those outside of the subculture. An example is provided by Weinstein (1991) in her discussion of the style of heavy metal subculture. According to Weinstein, many heavy metal fans would appear to be working-class motorcycle gang members, as evidenced by the frequent use of the Harley-Davidson logo on subcultural members' clothing. However, although working-class fans do seem to make up the core audience, heavy metal fans can come from any social class (Weinstein, 1991), and few actually own motorcycles.

This symbolic reordering of objects and their meanings is referred to as bricolage, a term introduced into subcultural sociology from the work of Lévi-Strauss. According to Weinstein (1991, p. 5):

> A bricolage is a collection of cultural elements. It is not like a machine in which each part is specially adapted to contribute to the proper functioning of the whole. A bricolage is much looser than that. Its parts exist for themselves as much as they do for the whole. They are held together not by physical or logical necessity but by interdependence, affinity, analogy, and aesthetic similarity.

A subculture will engage in bricolage in order to establish a unique identity and subcultural style and to set the subculture apart from the parent culture. It is important to note that while subcultures engage in bricolage activity, it is not necessarily a conscious activity, although, as was the case with the Californian punk rock scene in the late 1970s, it can be. More often than not, bricolage occurs through a process of subcultural evolution. This can be compared to the covert nature of socialization process. If an individual engages in this type of conscious activity he or she is referred to as a "bricoleur." While the process of bricolage allows for new uses of existing cultural artifacts, subcultures, according to the Birmingham school, ultimately never stray far from their class-based, parent culture. As Mike Brake (1985, p. 15) has pointed out:

> Objects and Artifacts (both of a symbolic and concrete form) have been reordered and placed in new contexts so as to communicate fresh acts of meaning . . . there is a reassemblage of styles into a new subcultural style . . . the assemblage must not look as though it is carrying the same message as the previously existing one. A new style is created by appropriating objects from an existing market of artifacts and using them in the form of collage, which recreates group identity and promotes mutual recognition by members.

Recent Literature on the Sociology of Adolescence

Recent work in this area is exemplified by the work of two social thinkers, Donna Gaines and Henry Giroux. Gaines's work can be seen as an inventory of what she labels "teenage wasteland": suburbia's forgotten dead-end thirteeners. Giroux's work is centered on the processes of domination and resistance which play themselves out in the cultural institutions of education and the mass media, in the classrooms and in the basements of suburbia, using adolescents as a kind of ultimate litmus test of our societal health.

Donna Gaines has become the chronicler of a generation. Historically, her work can best be placed as the logical extension of the suburban sociologists of the 1950s and early 1960s: David Reisman, Herbert Gans, and C. Wright Mills. Like those who came before her, Gaines relies on a journalistic style of presentation that forgoes that strictures of "proper" academic writing in order to tell a story that will both inform sociologists and resonate with those about whom the book was written.

Over the past several years, Gaines has provided sociology with an exemplary ethnographic history of teenagers in a suburban New Jersey town. This work has been documented in one book, *Teenage Wasteland: Suburbia's Dead End Kids* (1990), an essay on the local economy of the suburban youth scene (1994a), and a number of articles in magazines such as *The Village Voice* and *Rolling Stone*.

Gaines began her investigation into the everyday lives of the adolescents of the present when she was asked to report on the suicides of four suburban teenagers in Berganfield, New Jersey. These four drug-using youth, who were commonly referred to as "burnouts" by school administrators and community authorities, ended their lives in a Chevrolet Camaro, with the engine left running, while parked in a sealed and abandond garage. The fact that the car was a Camaro is not without importance. The Camaro is the car most often identified as a sign of prestige for lower-middle-class youth. It is *the* cool car, a sign of identity and prestige, just as the imported four wheel drive ATV is to the middle- and upper-middle-class youthful drivers of the present.

These suicides created a national scandal; suddenly teen suicide was an epidemic. Adolescents were counseled, parents taught to watch for warning signs, rock stars sued for damages, films like *Heathers* and *The River's Edge* made. But sociologically, according to Gaines (1991), these youth had a particular worldview that was tacitly understood by all youth and that was being all but lost in the media maelstrom that was surrounding the teen suicide issue. Gaines (1991, p. 54) sums up this tacit understanding thus:

> Maybe you hate it here so much you will try anything to escape – to an abandoned garage, to the railroad tracks, to Coppers Pond. Desire now leads you straight to nowhere. You're high but the streets are ugly and cold. The world "out there" is shrinking. The possibilities of suburbia are exhausted, and your capacity to dream has reached a dead end. But nobody cares, nobody gives a shit.

The youth of Gaines's study in Berganfield were portrayed as America's forgotten generation. They believed that they had no future, and that the promises made to their parents, and by proxy to them, were no longer possible. They had grown up watching the middle-class world of their parents be destroyed in the turbulent economic 1980s as America downsized, and moved a good percentage its manufacturing base overseas, along with their parents' jobs and their futures. Theirs was an alienation of exhaustion. Their life histories would be very similar, says Gaines, to those of adolescents in places such as Youngstown, Cleveland's western suburbs, or other cities in the rust belt states. Teen subcultures arise in these locations, through this shared experience and the fatalism, or exhaustion, that comes with it. They wear the clothing of the lower-middle-class teenager just as their older siblings, and most likely their parents, did: jeans, T-shirts, flannel button-ups, sneakers or Doc Martens. Their choice of clothing is almost always black. Their music of choice – thrash, industrial, grunge, death – is almost always harsh and unforgiving. There is a homology, an affinity as it were, between these youth's social circumstances and their style and identity. They wear their alienation from everything except their subculture as a badge of honor. It is who they are. Their alienation, rage and sometimes suicide are all parts of adolescent resistance in teenage wasteland.

Just as Donna Gaines is an ethnographer, Henry Giroux is a pragmatic. Giroux's work, which now spans over two decades, has remained dedicated to the attainment of what he calls radical democracy since he first established his position in *Theory and Resistance in Education* in 1983. Giroux takes this fatalism, this alienation described by Gaines, and empowers it as "resistance." Locations of resistance, the schools and the streets, are viewed as arenas of cultural struggle, as places where domination by hegemonic culture can be challenged (Giroux, 1994). The alienation, in Giroux's conception of the term, is related to the use of Merton's theory of anomie, which also served as the basis for the Birmingham school's use of the concept. Giroux's resistance is conceptually and functionally related to Merton's concept of ritualism.

In order for an act to be considered one of resistance, for Giroux (1983) the activities engaged in by the individual as an expression of subcultural identity must be deliberately undertaken. Subcultural behavior, style of dress, choice of music, and the further refinement of these cultural field elements should be understood not only as an attempt on the part of youth to set themselves apart from hegemonic, adult culture, but also as ways of completely denying their complicity in the events of current history. Their activity is therefore ritualist in Merton's sense of the term, and also points towards the postmodern paradox of youth culture, which has been the subject of much discussion recently (Postman, 1981; Coreno, 1994; Grossberg, 1994; Kellner, 1994; Weinstein, 1994). Youth subculture's resistance to hegemonic culture is said to reject the goals of adult society, just as the adolescents in Gaines's study claim. Yet their resistance is expressed through means made available to them through consumerism and the mass media. While pockets of "actual" resistance do occasionally appear – the 1970s punk scenes in Britain, New York and Los Angeles, for example – they are quickly swallowed up into the corporate music machine and as such can no longer be viewed as genuine resistance.

Two slightly less pessimistic points of view are offered here by Gaines (1994b) and Coreno (1994). Gaines found that suburban subcultures frequently support underground music scenes, almost unknown outside of a particular locality. These scenes are held together by word of mouth and crudely published "fanzines," which are generally hastily pasted together pieces of what would appear to the uninitiated as random thoughts. These underground scenes are not immune to the music industry, however, and spawn national trends. This was the case with grunge, which originated as an underground music scene in Seattle, Washington.

The success of a number of bands on a local Seattle-based record label called SubPop, particularly the bands Nirvana and Soundgarden, not only brought grunge music to national attention, but also destroyed the original Seattle subculture in the process. In this manner, youth's search for meaning through music becomes linked to their alienated state. Each resistive activity is countered by the co-optation of that activity into the marketing of a particular music, as was the case with grunge. The alienation of youth becomes a marketing strategy, which, of course, only further alienates the youth in question. It is this relationship between youth and the commodified society in which they carry out their identity work that is the focus of this text.

The bricolage concept has been particularly useful in the study of youth music subcultures, which, as Weinstein (1991) points out, are generally bricolages simply by virtue of definition. Rock music is a central feature of youth subcultures and subcultural belonging is expressed to a large degree through musical preferences. It is the appropriation of specific styles of rock that allows youth subcultures to identify themselves within the realm of possibilities allocated for youth. However, the ways in which these subcultures come to be, the values that they express, their appropriation of cultural ideas and artifacts, and how they relate to parent and hegemonic culture has been an area that has been widely ignored in American sociology (but see Gaines, 1991; Weinstein, 1991; Berry, 1994; Sardiello, 1994).

Generation X

An illustrative application of the concepts of bricolage and homology can be made to a study of the American music sub-culture whose members identify with, and are the primary con-sumers of, the style of rock called grunge or alternative rock. These youth have been alternately labeled either "Generation X" (Rushkoff, 1994) or "Slackers" (Felder, 1993; Kellner, 1994). The description of Generation X follows from Weinstein's assertion that the bricolage of youth subcultures is often held together by musical preference. It is also taken as a given that the British cultural theorists Dick Hebdige (1979) and Simon Frith (1981) were correct in their assertions that identifying and understand-ing a subculture's musical preferences is central to the under-standing of that subculture, thus centering this discussion of youth within a cultural studies framework.

"Slackers," the twenty-something members of "Generation X" who were born between 1964 and 1979 (Howe and Strauss, 1993), are the group which make up the core of alternative or grunge fans. This group's social position has recently begun to be discussed in academic and popular literature (Felder, 1993; Kellner, 1994; Kirschner, 1994), and their situation has been played out almost endlessly in the mass media since the over-dose, and subsequent suicide, of Kurt Cobain.

Before his death by a self-inflicted shotgun blast at age 27, Kurt Cobain had become the publicly unwilling spokesperson for his generation, a fact that has not escaped many authors commenting on his suicide (see Gaines, 1994b). He was the leader of the hugely successful Seattle band Nirvana, and his music was said to speak to a generation who are without hope and have no illusions about a brighter future. Slackers are the children of suburbia, raised on McDonalds, shopping malls, and MTV.

Typically, the Slackers' parents are the baby-boomers, the young adults of the sixties and early seventies. Their children, many of them members of Generation X, do not share their ideals. Many are middle class or upper-working class (Gaines, 1991), and the ideology of these classes has shaped their subcultural style. While some critics have labeled members of this cohort "Slackers," these youth think of themselves as being realistic and, conversely, view their parents' generation's activities in the sixties as having been highly unrealistic (Howe and Strauss, 1993).

Characteristics of Generation X and Their Music

The Slacker look consists primarily of blue jeans or loose baggy shorts called jams, invariably oversized T-shirts under flannel work shirts, often with the sleeves cut off, and sneakers or work boots, most frequently Doc Martens, a British-made boot with a long history in both British and American youth subcultures. Hairstyles are relatively unimportant (which is an interesting switch in rock culture in general), but the long, unkempt look, or assorted variations on "punk" haircuts, such as long hair on top with shaved sides, for males, and short unkempt hair for females is normative. Multiple tattoos, earrings, and other types of body piercing are also found in equal rates for both sexes. The grunge rock band Nirvana was said to be the band that most clearly articulated these youth's experience (Howe and Strauss, 1993).

Grunge music is closely related to both heavy metal and alternative music, and elements of both of these genres can be found in this music. Like heavy metal, grunge is a guitar-based music that relies on relatively simple song structure, extreme volume, and a heavily distorted sound (Weinstein, 1991; Walser, 1993; Friesen and Epstein, 1994). Unlike heavy metal, and despite its reliance on guitar for its overall presentation, grunge rock has no guitar heroes in the sense discussed by Weinstein (1991) and Friesen and Epstein (1994). Technical proficiency, in grunge musicianship, is second to attitude in importance. Support for this assertion is made available in an interview with Kurt Cobain (Gilbert, 1994), who made his lack of interest in the finer aesthetics of guitar playing clear by saying of his music:

> We're just musically and rhythmically retarded. We play so hard that we can't tune our guitars fast enough. People can relate to that. They're [Cobain's choice of guitars are] cheap and totally

inefficient, and they sound like crap and are very small. They also don't stay in tune.

The attitude expressed here clearly strays from the heavy metal aesthetic of high-priced, "signature series" guitars, and the corresponding emphasis on technical virtuosity. A "do it yourself" attitude more clearly represents alternative music's ideology regarding musicianship.

While grunge gets its musical sense from heavy metal, its overall attitude is more clearly related to alternative, and in everyday usage the two terms are often used interchangeably. Alternative music, which began, and remains, a mainstay of college radio, is a direct offshoot of the punk rock ethic which radically changed rock music from the late 1970s onward. Alternative music received its title because during its genesis this music was found almost exclusively on records released by small, independent record labels, like SST, TVT, Enigma, and Sub Pop. Since these labels were not connected, or in some cases connected but only slightly, to the huge major labels such as Warner Brothers or CBS, they were more willing to take chances with the types of music they recorded (Felder, 1993). An album which sells 50,000 copies is a "flop" according to major label standards set for rock music sales, but for the independent label it is quite respectable.

Due to the fact that these labels were not terribly interested (at least publicly) in record sales, an ideology focusing on the showcasing of new, or decidedly non-commercial, music soon emerged. By the mid-1980s, alternative music had become the music of choice on college campuses, primarily due to the independent labels which focused their marketing on the radio stations on these campuses. The reasons for this are straightforward: college radio has generally been considered anticommercial radio by its listeners.

These stations are generally run by college students who reject, as a matter of generational ideology, the trappings of commercialism, including playlists and the Top Forty. College radio provided the perfect place for alternative music to take root, which it did with a vengeance, introducing bands like The Smiths, Sonic Youth, The Connells, The Meat-Puppets and R.E.M. to the college-age record-buying public. While these bands are stylistically quite different, they all shared the notion that it was the music that mattered, not the image. In general, the musicians shunned the trappings of what they saw as corporate rock. Gone were the elaborate stage sets, snazzy costumes, and multi-million dollar productions. In their places, these bands relied on their music and their identification with their listeners. It was through alternative music that rock regained its sense of community, its sense of in-group cohesion, which had all but disappeared in the seventies.

The portrayal of Generation X in the mass media has focused on the more spectacular events and has continued the practice of labeling entire groups of young people as "problems" because of these incidents. Since the suicide of Kurt Cobain, a great deal of media attention has been given to the "problem" of teen suicide. However, more time is usually spent on comparing teen suicide victims to Kurt Cobain than is usually spent on exploring the societal factors which may have more immediately had an impact on the individual. Another focus of media attention has been the increased use of drugs by members of Generation X. Oddly enough, the drugs of choice seem to be the ones used and abused in the late sixties and early seventies – when the baby boomers came of age. Heroin, LSD, and marijuana use have all increased. Members of the media and politicians have zeroed in on depictions of heroin use in movies such as *Trainspotting*, or the popularity in the fashion industry of models who have the appearance of heroin addicts. Critics, themselves members of the baby boom generation, often express dismay at the failure of Generation X members to heed the warnings promulgated by "Just Say No," "DARE," and other drug-education campaigns. Popular articles addressing these issues question whether such behavior is delinquency, rebellion, resistance, or the rational reaction of a generation that views its future pessimistically. No one answer seems sufficient. The following essays engage these and other issues in the hope of broadening our understanding of youth in the postmodern world.

References

Antonovsky, A. (1987) *Unraveling the Mystery of Health*. San Francisco: Jossey-Bass.

Barthes, R. (1985) *The Responsibility of Forms*. New York: Hill and Wang.

Berry, V. (1994) Redeeming the rap music experience. In J. S. Epstein (ed.), *Adolescents and Their Music: If It's Too Loud, You're Too Old.* New York: Garland, pp. 165–88.

Brake, M. (1985) *Comparative Youth Culture: the Sociology of Youth Cultures and Youth Subcultures in America, Britain and Canada.* London: Routledge and Kegan Paul.

Calabrese, R. L. (1987) Adolescence: a growth period conducive to alienation. *Adolescence*, 22(88), 929–38.

Clarke, J., Hall, S., Jefferson, T. and Roberts, B. (1975) Subcultures, cultures, and class: a theoretical overview. In S. Hall and T. Jefferson (eds), *Resistance through Rituals: Youth Subcultures in Post-war Britain.* London: Hutchinson, pp. 9–74.

Cohen, S. (1980) *Folk Devils and Moral Panics: the Creation of the Mods and Rockers.* Oxford: Blackwell.

Cooper, M. (1994) Reality check. *Spin*, 10(4), 52–6.

Coreno, T. (1994) Guerrilla music: avant guarde voice as oppositional discourse. In J. S. Epstein (ed.), *Adolescents and Their Music: If It's Too Loud, You're Too Old.* New York: Garland, pp. 189–224.

Dotter, D. (1994) Rock and roll is here to stray; youth subculture, deviance and social typing in rock's early years. In J. S. Epstein (ed.), *Adolescents and Their Music: If It's Too Loud, You're Too Old.* New York: Garland, pp. 87–114.

Durkheim, E. (1947) *The Division of Labor in Society.* Glencoe, IL: Free Press.

Erikson, E. H. (1968) *Identity: Youth and Crisis.* New York: Norton.

Felder, R. (1993) *Manic Pop Thrill.* Hopewell, NJ: Ecco Press.

Friesen, B. and Epstein, J. S. (1994) *Rock 'n' Roll Ain't Noise Pollution: Artistic Conventions and Tensions in the Major Sub-genres of Heavy Metal Music.* Calgary: Canadian Sociological Association Meetings.

Frith, S. (1981) *Sound Effects: Youth, Leisure, and the Politics of Rock 'n' Roll.* New York: Pantheon.

Gaines, D. (1991) *Teenage Wasteland: Suburbia's Dead End Kids.* New York: Pantheon.

Gaines, D. (1994a) The local economy of suburban scenes. In J. S. Epstein (ed.), *Adolescents and Their Music: If It's Too Loud, You're Too Old.* New York: Garland, pp. 47–66.

Gaines, D. (1994b) Suicidal tendencies: Kurt Cobain did not die for you. *Rolling Stone*, June 2, 59–61.

Gilbert, J. (1994) Spirit in the sky. *Alternative Guitar*, 1(1), 26–7.

Giroux, H. (1983) *Theory and Resistance in Education.* New York: Bergin and Garvey.

Giroux, H. (1994) *Disturbing Pleasures.* New York: Routledge.

Gramsci, A. (1971) *Prison Notebooks.* New York: International Books.

Grossberg, L. (1994) The political status of youth culture. In J. S.

Epstein (ed.), *Adolescents and Their Music: If It's Too Loud, You're Too Old*. New York: Garland, pp. 25–44.

Hall, S. and Jefferson, T. (eds) (1975) *Resistance through Rituals: Youth Subcultures in Post-war Britain*. London: Hutchinson.

Hebdige, D. (1979) *Subculture: the Meaning of Style*. New York: Methuen.

Howe, N. and Strauss, B. (1993) *13th Gen: Abort, Retry, Ignore, Fail*. New York: Vintage.

Kellner, D. (1994) *Media Culture*. New York: Routledge.

Kirschner, T. (1994) The Lollapalooziation of American youth. *Popular Music and Society*, 18(1), 69–89.

McRobbie, A. (1995) *Postmodernism and Popular Culture*. New York: Routledge.

Marx, K. (1968) *Marxist Social Thought* (ed. R. Freedman). New York: Harvest.

Merton, R. K. (1968) *Social Theory and Social Structure*. New York: Free Press.

Miller, W. B. (1958) Lower class culture as a generating milieu of gang delinquency. *Journal of Social Issues*, 14(3), 5–19.

Neal, A. G. and Groat, H. T. (1974) Social class correlates of stability and change in levels of alienation: a longitudinal study. *The Sociological Quarterly*, 15, 548–54.

Postman, N. (1981) *The Disappearance of Childhood*. New York: Delacorte.

Rushkoff, D. (ed.) (1994) *The GenX Reader*. New York: Ballantine.

Sardiello, R. (1994) Secular rituals in popular culture: a case for Grateful Dead concerts and dead head identity. In J. S. Epstein (ed.), *Adolescents and Their Music: If It's Too Loud, You're Too Old*. New York: Garland, pp. 115–40.

Simmel, G. (1968) *The Conflict in Modern Culture and Other Essays*. New York: Teachers College Press.

Walser, R. (1993) *Running with the Devil: Power, Gender, and Madness in Heavy Metal Music*. Hanover, NH: Wesleyan.

Weinstein, D. (1991) *Heavy Metal: a Cultural Sociology*. New York: Lexington.

Weinstein, D. (1994) Expendable youth: the rise and fall of youth culture. In J. S. Epstein (ed.), *Adolescents and Their Music: If It's Too Loud, You're Too Old*. New York: Garland, pp. 67–86.

Willis, P. (1977) *Learning to Labour*. Farnborough, England: Saxon House.

Willis, P. (1990) *Common Culture*. Boulder, CO: Westview.

2
TEENAGE SEXUALITY, BODY POLITICS, AND THE PEDAGOGY OF DISPLAY

Henry A. Giroux

Representing Youth as a Problem

Representations of youth in popular culture have a long and complex history and habitually serve as signposts through which American society registers its own crisis of meaning, vision, and community. Youth as a complex, shifting, and contradictory category is rarely narrated in the dominant public sphere through the diverse voices of the young. Prohibited from speaking as moral and political agents, youth become an empty category inhabited by the desires, fantasies, and interests of the adult world. This is not to suggest that youth don't speak; they are simply restricted from speaking in those spheres where public conversation shapes social policy and refused the power to make knowledge consequential with respect to their own individual and collective needs.

When youth do speak, the current generation, in particular, their voices generally emerge on the margins of society – in underground magazines, alternative music spheres, computer hacker clubs, and other subcultural sites. The places youth inhabit, especially since the beginning of the 1980s, increasingly point to the dangerous erosion of civil society that has resulted in the undermining of the safety nets and nurturing systems that historically have provided some sustenance and hope for youth.[1] Quality public schools, youth clubs, religious institutions, public art programs, urban shelters, and drug and crime free urban neighborhoods seem to have receded and been replaced, in part, by public spaces largely marked by the absence of adult support.

The basketball court, the shopping mall, the darkly lit street corner, the video arcade, the urban dance hall, the suburban home inhabited by latchkey children, the decaying housing projects, and the second hand automobile have become the privileged sites for working-class youth. In alarming numbers, youth in the 1990s are being distanced from the values, language, and practices necessary to shape a democratic social order and those public terrains that traditionally have been used to promote and embody civic discourse and critical reflection.

Lauded as a symbol of hope for the future while scorned as a threat to the existing social order, youth have become objects of ambivalence caught between contradictory discourses and spaces of transition. While pushed to the margins of political power within society, youth nonetheless become a central focus of adult fascination, desire, and authority. Increasingly denied opportunities for self-definition and political interaction, youth are transfigured by discourses and practices that subordinate and contain the language of individual freedom, social power, and critical agency. Symbols of a declining democracy, youth are located within a range of signifiers that largely deny their representational status as active citizens. Associated with coming-of-age rebellion, youth become a metaphor for trivializing resistance. At the same time, youth attract serious attention as both a site of commodification and a profitable market. For many aging baby boomers, youth represent an invigorated referent for a mid-life consciousness aggressively in search of acquiring a more "youthful" state of mind and lifestyle.[2]

At stake here is not merely how American culture is redefining the meaning of youth, but how it constructs children in relation to a future devoid of the moral and political obligations of citizenship, social responsibility, and democracy. Caught up in an age of increasing despair, youth no longer appear to inspire adults to reaffirm their commitment to a public discourse that envisions a future in which human suffering is diminished while the general welfare of society is increased. Constructed primarily within the language of the market and the increasingly conservative politics of media culture, contemporary youth appear unable to constitute themselves through a defining generational referent that gives them a sense of distinctiveness and vision, as did the generation of youth in the 1960s. The relations between youth and adults have always been marked by strained generational and ideological struggles, but the new economic and social conditions that youth face today, along with a callous indifference to their spiritual and material needs, suggest a qualitatively different attitude on the part of many adults toward American youth – one that indicates that the young have become the lowest national priority. Put bluntly, American society at present exudes both a deep-rooted hostility and chilling indifference toward youth, reinforcing the dismal conditions that young people are increasingly living under. Donna Gaines is insightful in her claim that the 1980s represented a decade in which "young people were devalued, dismissed and degraded at every turn," and that the children and teenagers are currently losing ground in securing a decent present and future for themselves and others.

> In post-Vietnam America, young people have experienced an erosion in their cultural prestige, their impact as a social force has diminished, they are losing ground in their rights and civil liberties. The nature of the nuclear family, the global economy and the world stage is in rapid transition. The American working class is disappearing as a social entity. Thee now exists a permanent subclass of American citizens we call "the homeless." Half the kids in America don't go to college, and the ones who do spend six years getting degrees, after which they cannot find jobs, or afford housing, health care or cars.[3]

For many youth, especially those who experience ruthless subordination and oppression, nihilism often translates into senseless violence, racism, homophobia, drug addiction, date rape, suicide pacts, escalating homicide rates, and a refusal to participate in building communities of hope and alliances with other oppressed groups. This is not meant to portray youth merely as reproducing a larger social pathology as much as it is meant to make visible the political, economic, and cultural conditions that undermine democratic public life and take the young and the very old as their first victims.

Of course, conditions of oppression produce not simply victims or ongoing forms of resistance, but also social systems that become ethically frozen because they have become indifferent to forms of political courage and civic responsibility necessary to engage critically the most pressing problems of the times. The distinctive change of attitude toward working-class and black youth in the USA, while rooted in histories of racism and class struggle, can be seen, in part, by the dismal statistics concerning the quality of life of children that reflect new economic and ideological realities. Statistics are often too abstract to capture the day-to-day suffering they attempt to register; nonetheless, they serve as reminders of what can only be judged as a national crisis regarding the deteriorating conditions in which many children currently find themselves.

> Nationwide, the number of children living in poverty increased by 2.2 million between 1979 and 1989. Child poverty among European-Americans increased from 11.8 percent to 14.8 percent, among Latinos from 28 percent to 32 percent, and among blacks from 41.2 percent to 43.7 percent . . . The United States has one of the worst infant mortality rates among industrialized nations. Out of every thousand babies born in the US, 9.8 die in infancy – a rate worse than sixteen other nations. Black children die at almost twice the national average – 18.2 per thousand births.[4] .

Not only are there fourteen million children living in poverty in the United States, but the USA ranks in the lower half of Western industrialized countries in providing services for family support. Moreover, the United States has experienced an alarming growth in cases of child abuse. It is also a country where more teenagers "die from suicide than from cancer, heart disease, HIV infection or AIDS, birth defects, pneumonia, influenza, stroke and chronic lung disease combined."[5] Similarly, behind the meager distribution of resources allotted for children of the poor looms an oppressive and exploitative structure of economic inequality, in which the top 1 percent of the population "holds 46.2 percent of all stocks and 54.2 percent of all bonds."[6] In a recent study by the Organization for Economic Cooperation and Development it was revealed that the United States, out of the top 17 wealthiest industrial countries, has the biggest gap between the rich and poor.[7] It appears that for the richest and most powerful groups in American society youth represent one of the lowest priorities.

The most striking example of such callous indifference can be seen in the actions of the 1995 Republican Party congressional budget cutters, who have promoted legislation that would add 1.2 million children to the poverty roles, eliminate basic health care coverage for 7 million young people, and disadvantage 14 million additional children as a result of cuts in federally funded food and nutrition programs.[8] Even more disturbing is the fact that the largest growing population of homeless in the USA are children and the average age of such children is nine years. For white working-class youth, prospects are also bleak; they can look forward to dead-end jobs, unemployment without the benefit of health care, or, perhaps, homelessness.

Black teenagers face an unemployment rate of 57 percent and unprecedented levels of poverty, while impoverishment and hunger become the rule of the day.[9] But what sets black youth off from their white counterparts is that the preferred method of containing white teenagers is through constitutional controls exercised through schooling, where working-class youth suffer the effects of school choice programs, tracking, and vocation-alization. On the other hand, black youth are increasingly sub-jected to the draconian strategies of "tagging," surveillance, or more overt harassment, and imprisonment through the criminal justice system.[10] Recent statistics based on Justice Department figures in 1995 reveal the full scope of this policy, by indicating that one in three black men in their twenties are imprisoned, on probation, or under the supervision of the criminal justice system on any given day in the USA.[11]

As the political tide has turned against the well-being, support, and happiness of working-class and black children, further weakening support for the very young in troubled families and social circumstances, a new form of representational politics has emerged in media culture, fueled by degrading visual depictions of youth as criminal, sexually decadent, drug crazed, and illiter-ate. In short, youth are viewed as a growing threat to the public order.

Hollywood Youth and the Politics of Representation

Traditionally, the body for youth has been one of the principal terrains for multiple forms of resistance and as a register of risk, pleasure, and sex. It has been through the body that youth displayed their own identities through oppositional subcultural styles, transgressive sexuality, and disruptive desires. The multi-ple representations and displays of the body in this context were generally central to developing a sense of agency, self-definition, and well-placed refusals.[12] The body as a potent marker of youthful resistance served to set youth off from the adult world and suggested that the body was outside the reach of dominant forms of moral regulation and sexual containment. Many adults responded with trepidation to the youth resistance of the 1950s, to what was viewed as the mutually reinforcing phenomena of juvenile delinquency and rock and roll.[13] Hollywood and other conduits of media culture capitalized on such fears by constructing youth as both a social threat and a lucrative market. Redefining teen culture as both separate and in opposition to adult society, youth became the embodiment of alienation, anger, and potential danger. Meanwhile, Hollywood films in the 1950s provided a new youth market with romantic images of anti-heroes such as James Dean and Marlon Brando, to both identify with and emulate. Films such as *Rebel without a Cause* (1955), *Blackboard Jungle* (1955), and *Rock Around the Clock* (1956) portrayed youth as icons of defiance and rock and roll as the subversive space where sexual desire was explored and its excesses were repudiated. The social and political turmoil of the sixties was explored in films such as *Easy Rider* (1968), *Alice's Restaurant* (1968), *Zabriskie Point* (1968), and *The Strawberry Statement* (1970).

Following the sixties, Hollywood employed different representational strategies to portray middle- and working-class youth. Films such as *Mean Streets* (1972), *Taxi Driver* (1976), and *Saturday Night Fever* (1977) reproduced a representational politics in which the city was increasingly being viewed as a space of violence, pathology, and resistance inhabited largely by dangerous, white, working-class youths facing dead-end futures. At the same time, as the exhaustion of the politics of the sixties had become manifest, along with a growing conservative backlash, Hollywood resurrected white, suburban, middle-class youth in the nostalgic image of Andy Hardy and Frankie Avalon, but with a twist. In a historical rendering of youth in the fifties, films such as *The Last Picture Show* (1971), *American Graffiti* (1973), and *Diner* (1982) combined white bread angst with the comforts of the cool, ordered nostalgia of the 1950s. Hollywood's fascination with middle-class youth was predicated on a claim to public memory that by-passed the radical politics of the sixties by portraying youth within a historical and sociological context that erased moral and political considerations, while reducing the realm of the social to utterly privatized and personal narratives. Films such as *Love Story* (1971) and the *Summer of '42* (1971) produced an image of youth in which ethical perspectives and public politics became unimaginable. At the same time, when youth engaged the political sphere, as in popular films such as *Woodstock* (1970), *Harold and Maude* (1971), and *Hair* (1979), considerations of power and domination were replaced by either a quirky cynicism or a fatuous rendering of youth resistance as turned on and tuned out. Erased from such representations were those diverse institutional spaces through which youth of the 1960s had linked a politics of meaning to strategies of engagement. In this scenario, youth appeared to be without a politics, and public memory to be in the service of a "past [that] appears as both pervasive and apparently irrelevant."[14]

As the recession of the 1970s gave way to the conservatism that burst forth with the election of Ronald Reagan in the 1980s, films such as *Breaking Away* (1979), *Risky Business* (1983), *The Breakfast Club* (1985), and *Sixteen Candles* (1984) provided a sympathetic portrait of white working-class and middle-class youth as confused·but innocent, doing their best to come of age in a dramatically changing world. The anti-teen impulse that surfaced in Hollywood films in the late 1970s and early 1980s began to emerge in dramatic Hollywood style in slasher films such as *Halloween* (1978), *Friday the 13th* (1980), and *Nightmare on Elm Street* (1984). While a hateful misogyny swept through the horror genre films, a dismal and dystopian depiction of youth spread across the Hollywood screens in the late 1980s, and seemed to forecast a new politics of representation through which dominant media culture attempted to rewrite and represent the identities and social status of "youth in [communities] whose older local support institutions had been all but demolished."[15]

If a crisis of representation regarding youth was to emerge in the 1990s, it was rooted less in a transformation of representational ideologies than in a host of complex national and global forces changing the face of the contemporary urban landscape: a downward spiraling economy, a resurgent racism, a diminishing allocation of funds for crucial public services, the creation of Tippi Gore's Parent's Music Resource Center, the hostile public response from many adults to rap and urban contemporary music as it entered the mainstream. All of these factors, among many others, appear to register a shift from media culture's simplistic but sometimes sympathetic portrayal of youth as a problem through which to analyze social and political dynamics at work in the larger society, to a more racist and brutalizing view of youth. Youth were no longer seen as a symptom of a wider social dilemma, they were the problem.

A representational politics began to emerge that strongly resonated with a growing neoconservative demonization of urban white and black youth in the commercially dominated sectors of media culture. In films such as *A River's Edge* (1987), *My Own Private Idaho* (1991), and *Natural Born Killers* (1995), white youth are framed and presented through the degrading textural registers of pathological violence, a deadening moral vacuum, and a paralyzing indifference to the present and future. On the other hand, Hollywood blockbusters such as *Wayne's World* (1992), *Dazed and Confused* (1993), and *Dumb and Dumber* (1995) project onto post-Watergate youth a long legacy of anti-intellectualism that has been a defining principle of American culture. In this script, idiocy and hilarity become a sign of what's in, as Jim Carrey portrays the teenager who will eventually grow out of a fascination with Beavis and Butthead and emulate the simple-headed but responsible Forrest Gump, who has become the conservatives' 1990s model of family values, motivation, and patriotism. Needless to say, simplistic Hollywood portrayals of working-class youth as either potential muggers or dead from the neck up legitimates real futures that offer the horrifying images of the prison, mental hospital, or local fast food outlet. As youth are conceived in images of demonization, sexual decadence, and criminality, the only public sites that appear available to them are unskilled work, highly policed public spaces, or the brute reality of incarceration.

Hollywood representations of black youth in the 1990s seem to be largely inspired by the dynamics of class hatred as well as the powerful resurgent racism in American society. In films that include *Boyz N the Hood* (1991), *Menace II Society* (1993), and the more recent *Clockers* (1995), black male youth are framed through narrow representations that strongly articulate with the dominant neoconservative image of "blackness as menace and 'other'."[16] Within these films, violence resonates with the popular perception that everyday black urban culture and the culture of criminality mutually define each other. If white working-class youth are seen as a problem to be contained, black youth are seen as a dangerous threat to be eliminated.

Fashioning Teenage Sexuality

Media representations of white and black working-class youth in the 1990s differ from the portrayal of such youth historically, in that the contemporary construction of youth appears to be limited to a politics of demonization through which sexuality is defined as either a commodity or a problem. Within current representational politics, teenagers are largely defined in terms of their sexuality; what fuels their limited sense of agency and the brutality and violence it produces is an adolescent libido out of control.

Within the new representational politics of youth, the body is increasingly being commodified and disciplined through a reactionary, postmodern cultural politics. Within the terrain of such a politics, the struggle over the body and sexuality as a sign becomes as important as the more traditional practices of containing and disciplining the body as a threat to the social order. In part, the new crisis of representation erases the body of youth as a site of resistance, whether expressed through a transgressive sexuality, an appropriation of popular culture, or in the formation of underground cultural formations. The bodies of youth in the age of Newt Gingrich and the Christian Coalition signify one of the most unsettling threats to American society as an increasingly conservative agenda dominates the discourse about the rights of children and the nature of the social problems facing the United States. Surely there is more than irony at work in a conservative discourse that defines its notion of family values, in part, on an image of the completely pure and sexually innocent child (read white and middle class), while it refuses to acknowledge the "immense sexualization of children within consumer capitalism."[17] The hypocrisy of such a discourse cannot be easily dismissed. As Marilyn Ivy points out, "For to think about the child as a sexual object in capitalism is already to have violated the pristine space the child must occupy to guarantee the crumbling social order, with its insistence on the sanctity of the nuclear family and standardized gender relations."[18]

In what follows, I want to analyze the representations of teenage bodies in the controversial 1995 Calvin Klein designer jean advertising campaign and in the bleak depiction of urban youth in Larry Clark's film, *Kids*. These representations of youth need to be addressed as part of a broader public struggle over how "technologies of power produce and manage . . . the individual and social body through the inscription of sexuality" within consumer culture and the visual and pedagogical machinery of Hollywood culture.[19] The primary issue is not whether artists, educators, and the general public should be condemned for finding pleasure in representations of youth as depicted in the Klein ads or in films such as *Kids*. Finding pleasures in sexually charged images of children does not make people morally culpable. At the same time, the emergence of a representational politics in which the bodies of youth are no longer seen as the privileged site of critical thinking, agency, resistance, or productive desires raises important questions regarding the moral responsibility and limits of one's pleasures at a time when subordinate youth are under massive assault by conservatives. In doing so, I want to illuminate how the Klein ads and Larry Clark's *Kids* function pedagogically within a broader discourse about youth, focusing specifically on how such representations resonate with specific conservative attacks on related issues of sexuality, race, and gender. Central to this analysis is a critique of a transgressive art that serves either to commodify appropriations of stylized youthful bodies or to deploy teenage sexuality as decadent and predatory.

Related to this criticism is the call to challenge the current fascination of many cultural workers with forms of aesthetic and textual criticism and the ways in which such criticism ignores representation of children's culture and bodies as part of a larger debate about power, ideology, and politics. Textual criticism that celebrates the formal aesthetic principles at work in "realistic representations" of teenage sexuality often provides justification for flaunting the commodification of young bodies. Moreover, portraying teenage sexuality as decadent and predatory is neither critically transgressive nor worthy of being labeled as progressively transformative. Artists, critics, and others who respond to these representations by retreating to an ideologically "neutral" defense of aesthetics and artistic freedom often reproduce the very problems such representations legitimate. That is, by failing to engage in a broader public dialogue about the messy political realities of exploitation and social injustice that result from current attacks on poor, urban, white and black youth, such critics often legitimate rather than challenge the current conservative agenda for dispensing with those youth they view as disposable, if not dangerous, to the imperatives of the free market and global economy. I will conclude by offering some suggestions for a pedagogy that addresses popular culture and the representational politics of youth in a progressive way. *Harlem Diary* (1996) will serve as one example of a representational politics in which a politics and pedagogy of the popular make it possible to understand the ways in which working-class youth attempt "to open social and cultural spaces in which to express themselves,"[20] as well as engage and transform the conditions through which they push against the constraints of poverty and racism.

Youthful Bodies and Dead-End Pleasures

American youth are unable to vote, are denied basic civic liberties, and face a world of increasing poverty and unemployment, and diminished social opportunities. They have few opportunities to make their voices heard as they witness a growing culture of violence, with its assault on public life, deteriorating cities, and a seeming indifference toward civil rights. At the same time, the collective image stands as a reminder of lapsed social responsibility, a disturbing sexual presence, and a symbol of powerlessness. As such, youth become an easy target for a public discourse in which the dual strategies of scapegoating and commodifying take on the proportions of a national policy and minor revolution in the media.

In the profit-driven world of advertising and fashion, the image and culture of youth are appropriated and exploited for the high pleasure quotient they evoke. The body in this "fashionscape" does not represent the privileged terrain of agency, but rather serves as a site of spectacle and objectification, where youthful allure and sexual titillation are marketed and consumed by teens and adults who want to indulge a stylized narcissism and a self that is all surface. In this public sphere of simulated yearning and sexualized images, advertisers inventively present the fragmented bodies of youth as the site where pleasure, desire, and commodification intersect in a commercial display "that fetishizes and marginalizes the body as the locus of spectacle."[21]

A recent, highly publicized example of this is the controversial 1995 Calvin Klein jeans advertising campaign. In these images, photographed by Steven Meisel, young models are presented in various stages of undress, poised to offer both sensual pleasure and the fantasy of sexual availability. In a departure from the signature black-and-white photography and self-conscious artistry of Calvin Klein's high-end product advertising, the young models are set against a backdrop of dated purple carpeting and wood-paneled basement walls, rife with connotations of a particular class and lifestyle. In these advertisements, coquettish girls flash their breasts and white panties, and lounging boys display black nail polish, tattoos, and bulging briefs.

The images of these kids resonate with a cultural perception of the sexuality of poor, white, urban youth. In the televised ads, a low, gravelly, off-camera voice prods the kids with questions such as "Do you like to take direction?" and "Ya think you can rip that shirt off ya? That's a nice body. You work out? Yeah, I can tell," evoking the dialogue of a low-budget porn flick. These present a romanticized vision of the dangerous and seedy world of desperate kids on the make; the youthful bodies portrayed suggest kids who are powerless and poor, perhaps forced to negotiate their sexuality as the only currency they have to exchange for profit or the promise of glamour. These images not only test the limits of using sexuality to sell jeans; their use legitimates a "hip" promiscuousness and invites the "most intrusive of gazes."[22] I would argue that this advertising campaign is symptomatic of a broader representational struggle being waged against youth, one that needs to be understood for both the political and the pedagogical lessons it can provide for artists, educators, and other cultural workers.

Participating in this romanticized vision of the dangers and seedy world of desperate teens on the make, Klein's models exude a decadent sexuality displayed almost exclusively through an eroticized privileging of the senses, in which the body becomes the only terrain through which youth can express themselves. One wonders which social groups were considered the target market for this suite of Calvin Klein's ads. Is it working-class youth who are meant to find themselves in the images of the hustled – working class youth who can barely afford Calvin Klein's merchandise? Or is it more elite social groups who might view the working class as an exotic other, that are meant to be titillated by the fantasy of sexual slumming? The ads resonate with a broader conservative politics in which representations of youth seek to erase the complex historical and social formations at work in the shaping of societal subjectivities, desires, and needs.

The controversial Calvin Klein advertising campaign was met with a swift and uniformly critical response. Angry critics – including parents, social welfare groups, conservative politicians, and President Clinton – called the images suggestive and exploitative, and condemned Klein for using children as sexual commodities. Other critics likened the ads to child pornography. The public outcry eventually prompted the Justice Department to launch a Federal Bureau of Investigation inquiry to determine if the advertising campaign had violated any legal statue by using under age models (the FBI inquiry found no evidence that under-age models were used). The investigation was eventually dropped, but the massive public criticism forced Calvin Klein Inc. to announce a halt to the advertising before its scheduled end.[23]

Many critics, artists, and activists have rightly pointed out that displaying semi-nude youth is not new, especially in Klein's advertising campaigns. After all, it was Klein's jeans and underwear commercials with Brook Shields, Kate Moss, and Marky Mark that helped to situate Klein's "corporate image right on the razor edge between propriety and titillation."[24] Many of the same critics argued that the critical responses to the Klein ads are less about the rights of children than about the hypocrisy exhibited by right-wing conservatives who rally around the sanctity of family values while attempting to enact anti-pornography legislation that would undermine First Amendment rights. In this instance, the attack on Klein's advertising campaign is viewed as a political strategy on the part of zealots such as the Christian Coalition and Donald Wildmon's American Family Association to undermine artistic freedom and promote political censorship.

Camille Paglia added another twist to the criticism surrounding the ads. Paglia took Calvin Klein to task for portraying the models as looking "caught and caged by manipulative, jaded adults," and for undermining the "pedophiliac homoeroticism [that] suffuses the Western high art tradition." Paglia complained that "if Klein and Meisel want to borrow the iconography of pedophilia, they should have the courage to step forward to admit it."[25] Missing from this analysis is any mention of power, ideology, human rights, the historical legacy of child abuse in the interests of capital. Also absent is any challenge to representations of youth that reinforce a fragmented notion of the body, or any exploration of the limits of desire based on exploitation, degradation, and domination. On the contrary, Paglia sees aesthetics posturing as a liberated politics in defense of the homoerotics of pedophilia, but she has nothing to say about either the needs/rights of children or the glamorization in the mass media of a not-so-hip violence in which kids are sexually preyed upon by adults. By focusing exclusively on representations of children as the sexual, Paglia situates youth within a representational politics that links their bodies solely to the virtues of pleasure and consumption. This is exactly what Calvin Klein does, but Paglia seems unaware of the convergence between her defense of pedophilia and Klein's cultural politics of depicting the body for voyeuristic consumption and financial profit.

Among Calvin Klein's defenders, Dave Mulryan, a partner at Mulryan/Nash Advertising, likened the campaign to a moving target on which was being pinned the blame for all of society's ills. "People are concerned about teens having sex, but instead of focusing on the real problem, they're attacking the fictional portrayals in such movies as *Kids* and in advertising like Calvin Klein's."[26] Michael Musto, writing in *Artforum*, proudly proclaimed that the ads "were the most delicious media event of the year. Bringing teenage sexuality to the front half of everyone's brains, they pushed buttons and made people livid, the way a great, nasty, confrontational ad campaign should . . . I considered them a major breakthrough in advertising in front of which I sat in awe."[27] It seems that Musto defends the use of children's sexuality as a vehicle for commercialism through an appeal to the freedom of visual representations. Seemingly indifferent to the operations of power that hide behind advertising's use of images of children within a stylized aesthetics, Musto ignores how representations of sexuality work as part of a broader public discourse in which children's bodies are defined exclusively through "the commercial imperative of spectacle, commodification, and objectification."[28]

My concern with the depictions of such representations lies not in deciding whether they are good or bad, but in analyzing them in relation to the pedagogical work they are doing. That is, what knowledge, values, and pleasures do such representations invite or exclude? What particular forms of identity, agency, and subjectivity are privileged, and how do they help to reinforce dominant reactions, messages, and meanings? What do they say about the representers, the context in which they are produced, and the meanings they circulate? What do such representations say about the relationship between children's bodies and the AIDS crisis, the use of drugs by young children, the disciplining of children's bodies by any number of authority figures, or the symbolic violence waged by Hollywood films that present in graphic detail the bodies of young inner-city black youth steeped in violence and stylized gore?

Calvin Klein responded to criticisms of his jean campaign publicly by issuing an advertisement in the *New York Times*, in which he argued apologetically that the ads were meant to convey a media generation of youth who are savvy, and "have a real strength of character and . . . strongly defined lines of what they will and will not do – and have a great ability to know who they are and who they want to be."[29] One wonders how strength, character, and independence are represented in pictures of Marky Mark clutching his crotch, or bare breasted young women exhibiting their underwear while posing suggestively. In an interview in *New York Magazine*, Klein compared himself to Larry Clark, the photographer and director of the feature film *Kids*. Klein justified the ads on the grounds that he, like Clark, used unaffected kids to represent to an adult world something that was both real and frightening; that is, a youthful sexuality that lacked artifice. Klein appropriates the goals and rhetoric of realism as a pedagogical tool to inform society about the supposed desires of and possibilities available to young teens. But Klein's claim to lack of artifice rings false. This is a realism that is all surface, without context, voyeuristic. It peddles a hollow aesthetic defiance rather than probing how kids might narrate themselves rather than yield to the power of adults such as Klein, who markets kids in the image and fantasies of adult drives and desires.

In the slick world of advertising, teenage bodies are sought after for the exchange value they generate in marketing an adolescent sexuality that offers a marginal exoticism and ample pleasures for the largely male consumer. Commodification reifies and fixates the complexity of youth and the range of possible identities they might assume, while simultaneously exploiting them as fodder for the logic of the market. This may not be pornography, but it has little to do with civic virtue or responsibility regarding how the identities of youth might be constructed as part of a broader project of substantive citizenship and civic responsibility.

When situated within the broader context of social and political life, Klein's transgressive images fail to challenge dominant, conservative codings of youth as sexually decadent, drug crazed, pathological, and criminal. Representations of youth in Klein's ads are reduced to aesthetics, style, and promotion; such images lack the mediating mechanisms of historical reflection or critical analysis and fail to challenge conservative depictions of youth. In fact, Calvin Klein has more in common with Newt Gingrich and the family values crowd than he realizes. Moreover, both Calvin Klein and Newt Gingrich privilege market values over human value. That is, human needs in both ideologies are subordinated to the laws of the free marked, with its endless drive to accumulate profit, and ignore, if not undermine, the notion of social responsibility and the reinvigoration of democratic public life. Those artists, educators, and cultural workers who defend Klein in the name of artistic freedom run the risk of simply retreating, as Andrew Ross argues, into a "safe haven [that] is really a quarantine zone, in which artists [and others] are not only immune from public accountability but are also excluded from public dialogue."[30]

This is not, however, meant to suggest support for the right wing's empty call for censorship. For many on the right, attempts to censor the media serve primarily as a way of keeping the progressive social agenda out of the discussion for social change. For progressives, discussing the limits of public representations, especially regarding children, would be a way of analyzing underlying economic, political, and social concerns while reinvigorating the possibility for public debate and political action. But if the objectification and exploitation of youth have found "legitimacy" within the logic of consumerism and the relentless search for new pleasures and sensations, the bodies of youth in the representational images and discourse of Hollywood films have taken an equally ominous turn.

Kids and the Politics of Diminished Hopes

> Seeing comes before words. The child looks and recognizes before it can speak. But there is also another sense in which seeing comes before words. It is seeing which establishes our place in the surrounding world; we explain that world within words, but words can never undo the fact that we are surrounded by it. The relation between what we see and what we know is never settled.[31]

One of the most controversial films to appear about teenage sexuality and youth in 1995 was *Kids*, a film directed by Larry Clark from a script written by nineteen-year-old Harmony Korine. Most of the characters in the documentary-like film are non-actors and skateboarding friends of Korine. The film opens with a closeup of a teenage boy and girl loudly kissing each other. The image is crucial both aesthetically and politically.

Aesthetically, the camera focuses on open mouths, tongues work overtime, a sucking noise highlights the exchange of saliva – the scene is raw, rubbing against the notion of teenage sex as "a scaled down version of adult couplings, glamorized and stylized."[32] And it seems to go on forever, positioning the audience as voyeurs watching sex explode among kids who look too young to be acting on their own passions. In voiceover, Telly (Leo Fitzpatrick), the fifteen-year-old known to his friends as the Virgin Surgeon, says "Virgins. I love 'em." After seducing a young blond virgin in her bedroom, Telly bolts from the Manhattan brownstone and joins his friend, Casper (Justin Pierce), who has been waiting for him. Telly provides an account of his conquest in intimate detail, and so begins Clark's rendition of urban teenage youth in the 1990s.

After Telly's initial seduction, he and Casper head out to wander through the streets of Manhattan. Along the way, they knock off a 40-ounce bottle of beer, urinate in public, jump over subway turnstiles, and steal some fruit from a Korean grocer. They end up at a friend's apartment where they do drugs, talk sex, and watch skateboarding movies. The scene becomes more violent as Telly and his friends end up at Washington Square Park, where they smoke some more dope, insult two gays who walk by, and viciously beat with their skateboards a black youth whom Casper gets into an argument with. After stealing some money from Telly's mother, the youths break into the local YMCA for a swim. The day's activities culminate in a night of excessive drinking and drugs at a party given by a kid whose parents are out of town. The party degenerates into a haze of narcotized and drunken bodies, hands plunged randomly into crotches. Telly scores his second virgin. In the meantime, Jennie (Chloe Sevigny), appears at the party looking for Telly to inform him that she has tested positive for HIV, but she is too drugged to prevent him from infecting another young girl. Too numb to do anything, she falls asleep on a couch. In a grotesque and perverse reversal of the fairy tale plot, Clarke's sleeping beauty, Jennie, is not awakened with a kiss and the promise of living happily ever after. Rather, she suffers the brutal humiliation of a rape by Casper and will awaken to the nightmare reality of her eventual death and potentially his as well. The scene ends with Casper looking directly into the camera and asking, "Jesus Christ, what happened?"

Irresponsible sex becomes lethal violence as it becomes clear that Jennie contracted HIV virus from Telly, who now emerges as the infector: "the ultimate villain of American culture in the age of AIDS."[33] If Telly's story is one of sexual conquest, Jennie's is one of tragedy and powerlessness in the face of a ruthless urban youth culture that celebrates reckless sexuality and violence while it reduces young girls to one of two sexist stereotypes. They are sexual objects to be taken up and put down at will or they are sex-crazed and on the make. When the girls come together in the film, they are sitting around talking about oral sex, titillating the guys or each other, or getting set up to be exploited, as in the case of Darcy, Telly's last sexual conquest, to become another AIDS statistic.

As for the younger generation of pre-teens, their future is foreshadowed as the camera focuses on a quartet of dope smoking eleven-year-old boys who watch the older kids drink and drug themselves into a stupor at the party. The future they will inherit holds no positive role models or encouraging signs of hope.[34] For even younger girls, there is the ominous and disturbing message that they will soon become sexual trophies for the predatory male buffoons who stalk them in the dangerous space of the city. Michael Atkinson captures this sentiment in noting that the camera "lingers on a stepside moptop 3 year-old girl as if to grimly intone, it's only a matter of time."[35] The wholly gendered and sexualized bodies of young girls captured by Clark's gaze sustains "the representation of the female body as the primary site of sexuality and visual pleasure."[36] Passivity and helplessness become the privileged modes of behavior as the girls in the film follow the lead of the male characters, silently observe their expressions of brutality, and plead tearfully when they become the objects of such violence. Predatory sexuality permeates the ruthless world of misogynist teenage males filled with a sense of themselves and their desire to prey on young girls who wait passively to be pulled into a ritual of seduction and possibly death.

Decontextualized Youth and the Swindle of Agency

Floating on the surface of a dead-end cynicism, Clark's film refuses to probe where identity resides for the urban youth he represents. The teenagers in *Kids* are portrayed as if they live in a historical, political, and cultural vacuum. Lacking any depth, memories, or histories, Clark's teenagers are drawn in personal and stylized terms. For example, he provides no larger context for understanding the cultural, social, and institutional forces working on the lives of these urban teenagers. In this severely decontextualized perspective, it is almost impossible to understand the absence of adults in the film, the at risk sexuality, the rabid homophobia, or the random violence practiced by these teenagers. Representing teen life as if it existed outside the forces of history, the dominant culture, or the powerful interpellative pull of dominant institutions too easily resonates with a dominant, conservative ideology that blames the psychological instability of poor and black urban youth for the social decay, poverty, and endless disruptions that influence their everyday lives. Not unlike the Klein ads, Clark's narrative about youth plays on dominant fears about the loss of moral authority, while reinforcing images of demonization and sexual license through which adults can blame youth for existing social problems, and be titillated at the same time.

Clark's realism works too easily in the service of transforming the jolting experiences of the teenagers he represents from insightful historical and social considerations to those primarily defined through stylized evocations of shock and transgression. Failing to come to grips with considerations of politics, power, and ideology, Clark elides serious questions regarding how the viewer can account for the simultaneous aggression and powerlessness portrayed by teenagers in *Kids*; nor can he offer resistance to the brutality and limited options that define their lives. Lacking depth and detail, the teenagers who inhabit Clark's film are one-dimensional to the point of caricature. David Denby is right in insisting that Clark "turns the youth of his subjects into aesthetic shock. His teens have arrived at decadence without passing through maturity. They seem to have no dimensions – intellectual, spiritual, even physical – apart from carnality. They're all tongues."[37] Clark's attempt to let the film speak for itself results in a stylized aesthetic of violence that renders the reality of violence voyeuristic, spectacular, and utterly personal, rather than social and political. *Kids* avoids a central pedagogical lesson in dealing with any segment of teenage culture: unsafe sexual practices, violence, and drug use are learned behaviors that "society seems to be going all out to teach."[38] Similarly, Clark seems unacquainted with the notion that any serious portrayal of teens in this culture "that wishes to force a shift in ways of seeing, feeling and perceiving begins by questioning established power."[39] In the end, pathology and ignorance become the basis for defining the identity and agency of urban youth in Clark's world of casual violence, rampart nihilism, and incorrigible depravity. While Clark has been quick to defend his film as a cautionary tale about safe sex as well as an indictment of adults who either don't understand teenagers or are simply not around to provide guidance for them, he fails to understand – or at least represent – that it is precisely adult society, with its celebration of market values, market moralities, and its attack on civil society, that "undermines the nurturing system for children."[40]

Realism and the Politics of Teenage Sexuality

Framing the film in pseudo-documentary style – an aesthetic rendition of representing the world directly as it is – serves to legitimate Larry Clark's claim that *Kids* provides a full-blown, "no holds barred," journey into the culture of contemporary urban youth. But the *cinema verité* approach and loosely structured narrative cannot salvage Clark's surface exploration of a typical 24 hours in the lives of some drug- and sex-crazed, morally rudderless adolescents, regardless of the aura of "truth" that structures *Kids*. Clark's use of and appeal to realism as a testimony to the film's authenticity obscures Clark's own political and ethical responsibility in depicting a brutal and bitter portrait of a specific group of young people. The invocation of truth that accompanies appeals to gritty realism serve to sanction the severity of right-wing images of urban youth at work in broader popular representations.

Clark's reliance on the verisimilitude of documentary-like narrative, playing on the audience's fears and anxieties, and the positing of sexuality and hedonism as the driving forces of agency among urban youth, reveals the ideological conservatism that undergirds *Kids*. The consequences of portraying youth through the "transparent" lens of realism is a viewpoint marked by the absence of a reflective moral perspective, and one that offers critics and viewers a dose of media sensationalism that serves as an apology for a specific view of reality by making it appear natural, matter-of-fact, and outside of human control.[41] Teen sexuality in Clark's discourse becomes a metaphor for insincerity, crudeness, violence, and death. Missing from this perspective is a political understanding of the relationship between violence and sexuality as a daily experience for those who inhabit the places and spaces that promote suffering and oppression. The dangers of such a position are exemplified in a review of *Kids* by Amy Taubin, the film critic writing for *Sight and Sound*.

Fascinated by Clark's use of light, shade, and color in *Kids*, and its realistic portrayal of teenage sexuality, Taubin adds an ideological twist to Clark's chic aesthetic by suggesting that adolescent socialization is determined less by culture than by biology: high-powered libidos out of control. For Taubin, it is precisely this high-intensity libidinal energy that gives Clark's representations of teenage youth "their feverish energy, their mad humor, their extravagantly blunt language . . . [making them] mean, sordid, hungry and radiant at the same time."[42] Taubin's fascination with the aesthetics of teen sexuality excludes ideological considerations even as they are invoked, betraying the conservative politics – or the perversion – underlying her analysis. This is particularly clear when she describes the horrible rape scene of Jennie at the end of the film. Taubin writes, "it seems to take forever, leaving one time to feel as helpless as the semi-conscious Jennie, and perhaps (if one is totally honest) slightly turned on."[43] Not unlike Clark, Taubin is fascinated with teenage sexuality even when it legitimatizes voyeuristic titillation in the face of a ruthless and gruesome rape. What the perspectives of Clark and Taubin have in common is that teenage sexuality is not only a negative force in teens' lives, it also pushes the limits of an aestheticism that provides fodder for the celebration of stylized perversion and teen lust. What such thinking shares with current right-wing attempts to demonize youth is the assumption that young people are primarily identified with their bodies, especially their sexual drives. Stripped of any critical capacities, youth are defined primarily by a sexuality that is viewed as unmanageable and in need of control, surveillance, legal constraint, and other forms of disciplinary power. Similarly, this reductionist rendering of sexually active youth is a short step from stereotypical portrayals of black sexuality, in which it becomes a metaphor for disease, promiscuity, and social decadence.

Race Talk and Contaminating Youth

There is another disturbing aspect of *Kids* that has received little attention in the popular press. Though Telly and Casper are white, they talk in the accents of black street lingo and call each other "nigger." Their clothes, walk, and street style mimic the black cultural fashion of hip hop. Though the black characters in *Kids* are not central to the film, they are either the recipients of violence or serve as comic backdrop for sexual stereotyping. The role of blackness is not an incidental aspect of Clark's film because it articulates too strongly with the broader dominant view that black culture is responsible for the self-destructive journey that white youth are making through the urban landmines of drugs, sex, and violence. Marcus Reeves captures this sentiment explicitly.

Taken alongside the right's urgent moves to demonize and eliminate African American cultural influences in America and abroad (especially hip-hop music, language, and fashion) Clark's unyield-ing and 'verite' focus on the summer-day transgressions of two hip-hop dressing/street slang-wielding/40 ounce-drinking/blunt-smoking/pussy-conqüering white teenage males . . . provides a focus on what's making white American youth so crazy: Dey hanging out and acting like dem nasty, demoralizing niggas. That the race baiting is unintentional doesn't help.[44]

While Clark's alleged racism and demonization of youth may be unintentional, it participates in what Toni Morrison calls race talk. "The explicit insertion into everyday life of racial signs and symbols that have no meaning other than pressing African Americans to the lowest level of the racial hierarchy . . . the rhetorical [and representational] experience renders blacks as noncitizens, already discredited outlaws."[45] The pertinent ques-tion is not whether one can accurately declare Clark a racist, but whether the effects of his cinematic representations perpetuate racist discourse and practices in the wider society. Clearly his representations about working-class and black youth hint at an ideological irresponsibility rooted in an over-identification with the recklessness of the young.

Clark's own tortured childhood reveals in part his infatuation with teenage culture. Ignored by his father and forced to accom-pany and aid his mother, who went from door to door peddling baby photography, Clark started using his own camera to shoot his friends, many of whom were petty hoodlums, speed freaks and thugs. Eventually Clark produced a number of books of photography, including *Tulsa* (1971), *Teenage Lust* (1983), *Larry Clark* (1992), and *The Perfect Childhood* (1993). The first two books secured Clark's image as a tough guy photographer. Despite his notoriety, Clark drifted around in the 1970s and eventually spent 19 months in jail in Oklahoma on an assault and battery charge. After the jail stint, he headed for New York and became a professional photographer. By Clark's own account, he came into puberty too late and suffered a lousy adolescence for not measuring up to his peers. In part, this betrays his obsession with adolescence and the horror, excitement, and intensity it reflects.[46] In a revealing comment to Terrence Rafferty, he says, "Since I became a photographer I always wanted to turn back the years. Always wished I had a camera when I was a boy. Fucking in the backseat. Gangbangs . . . A little rape. In 1972 and

73 the kid brothers in the neighborhood took me with them in their teen lust scene. It took me back."[47] Clark reveals more than nostalgia about his adolescence, he uncritically romanticizes the very violence he portrays in *Kids*. This is the disturbing quality in Clark's film. It suggests the erotic compulsion of the voyeur, a middle-age man whose infatuation with teen sex is more narcissistic than socially or politically revealing, more symptomatic than productively pedagogical.

Recovering Ethical Discourse for a Pedagogy of Representations

In the world of Hollywood films and big name advertising, children's sexuality closely resembles adult behaviors and privileges the adult male gaze. As the right wing wages war against sex education, condom distribution in schools, sex on the Internet, and video stores that carry pornographic films, there is a curious silence from progressive and other radical cultural workers about the ways in which children and sex are portrayed in films, advertising, and media culture in general.[48] The primary issue is not whether such images of children might be labeled pornographic or invite questionable pleasures in their audiences; on the contrary, I am more interested in how such media work to purge desire of its constitutive possibilities for productive agency, portray the bodies of urban youth as dangerous, and celebrate an excessive hedonism that rejects personal and social responsibility. What is refused in such representations is the ethical imperative to provide complex images, ideas, narratives, and sites of struggle that not only challenge conservative "common-sense" notions of the real but also demand from youth critical self-reflection, moral commitment, and social responsibility, but always within a politics that questions its own authority as well as the authority of dominant ideologies and institutions.[49]

But I am also concerned about a progressive cultural politics that refuses to cede the terrain of ethical and pedagogical discourse to right-wing conservatives; at stake here is the need for artists, educators, and others on the cultural left to address popular representations in films and ads as social discourses grounded in public struggles, and to recognize whose point of view is being legitimated, what pleasures are being mobilized, and what the limits of such pleasures might be in terms of how they play out in public life. Within the visual and aural world of popular culture, cultural progressives must be willing to make judgments about how certain moral scripts are being narrated and linked to pushing back the possibilities of democratic public life. For too long, progressives have viewed the politics and pedagogy of representations as less significant than what is often referred to as the "real" world of politics; that is, the world of material suffering, hunger, poverty, and physical abuse. While such a distinction suggests that representations of rape and its actual experience cannot be confused, it is also imperative to understand how both modalities interact in providing the basis for constructing moral arguments as practices, recognizing how interpretations have a consequential impact regarding how people make discriminatory judgments about that is better or worse, and in doing so provide the grounds to act by addressing grave human problems in both their symbolic and material forms.[50]

Pedagogically and politically, young people need to be given the opportunity to narrate themselves, to speak from the actual places where their experiences are shaped and mediated. This suggests more than letting kids have the opportunity to voice their concerns, it means providing the conditions – institutional, economic, spiritual, and cultural – that allow them to reconceptualize themselves as citizens and develop a sense of what it means to fight for important social and political issues that effect their lives, bodies, and society. Writing in *Spin*, columnist Eurydice goes right to the heart of the matter in arguing:

> Millions more kids are abused by silence than by leering pedophiles, and kids who are kept ignorant are kept exploitable. Our society retards the emotional growth of kids so their physical and psychological maturities don't coincide. Instead of scrambling explicit programming on cable and the Net, blocking the distribution of condoms at school, and in every way making it difficult for kids to act responsibly, we should give them charge of their bodies. In the nationwide discussion about protecting kids from the sickos who prey on them, the kids are missing. And by refusing kids our trust, we encourage them to refuse us theirs.[51]

As artists and educators, we need to develop pedagogical practices in which discourses and representations of the adolescent body in its relationship to others are mediated through considerations of power, politics, and ethics. Media and popular culture increasingly teach kids to gaze inwardly at the body as a "fashionscape," a stylized athletic spectacle, or a repository of desires that menace, disrupt, and undermine public life. Not only do young people need to become critical agents able to recognize, appropriate, and transform how dominant power works on and through them, they also need a pedagogy steeped in respectful selfhood, one that does not collapse social into personal problems, systematic oppression into the language of victim blaming. In short, they need a pedagogy that provides the basis for improvisation and responsible resistance.

But any pedagogy about youth must take as one of its central concerns how authority and power are wielded by adults. This is particularly true for those aspects of public space where teens and other youth learn how to define themselves outside of the traditional sites of instruction, such as the home and the school. As I have argued elsewhere, learning in the postmodern age is located elsewhere – in popular spheres that shape their identities through forms of knowledge and desire that appear absent from what is taught in schools.[52] The literacies of the postmodern age are electronic, aural, and image based; and it is precisely within the diverse terrain of popular culture that pedagogical practices must be established as part of a broader politics of public life – practices that will aggressively subject dominant power to criticism, analysis, and transformation as part of a progressive reconstruction of democratic society. In this instance, whatever possibilities get framed in the name of children serve as ethical and political markers for the world view that adults construct as they generate images, spaces, desires, fears, and resentments about who kids are and how they act.

Of course, popular culture is contradictory and responsible for unleashing a torrent of youthful creativity in the arts, public access radio, dance, video, film, underground journals, and computer bulletin boards. Pedagogy and politics can combine in a fruitful way to seize upon this creativity not simply as a hip aesthetic or ideologically suspect, but as a creative source for recovering an ethical discourse in which cultural justice and rights become integral to expanding and democratizing popular forms and public spaces.[53] In this instance, there is no politics without pedagogy, and no pedagogy without a politics of critique and possibility.

Similarly, reading Calvin Klein's ads and Larry Clark's *Kids* should not suggest that such texts have no value except for recognizing how they reinforce right-wing attacks on subordinate teens in the broader culture. They are also texts ripe with potential for what Eve Sedgwick calls a "scornful, fearful, pathetizing reification of ignorance."[54] For Sedgwick, such ignorance cannot be treated as passive or innocent. Rather, critics need to explore such ignorances both in terms of what knowledge, social practices, and power relations are repressed and absent from their legitimating discourses and in terms of their effects. Sedgwick's notion of ignorance also offers the theoretical possibility for constructing a pedagogy based on the exploration of both knowledge and ignorance. For instance, how might a pedagogy that takes ignorance seriously work to explore how such refusals to know reinforce right-wing calls for censorship, the silencing of adult discussions of sexual desire, or the refusal to distribute condoms in schools, while simultaneously offering other productive pedagogical interventions into such politics?

Finally, educators, artists, and other cultural workers must address the challenge of developing pedagogies that teach kids how to use media a mode of self-expression and social activism. We need to find new ways in which pedagogy can translate into an activist strategy that expands the opportunity for knowledge and skills that help young people to extend their participation into and control over those cultural, economic, and social spheres that shape daily life (mass media, schools, media, workplace, policy-making institutions, the arts). Evidence of such work can be found in films such as Jonathan Stack's *Harlem Diary* (1995), which narrates the complexities, struggles, and hopes of nine black youths attempting to reclaim their lives within a destructive culture of violence and drugs. Stack is no romantic, but he lets the kids' voices capture the complexities of their lives, their courage, and their strength by giving them video cameras to provide representations of their own experiences. These narratives become the basis for the students to engage in dialogue with others and to debate both the meaning and the ideologies that constructed their engagement with selected aspects of their daily lives and the implication such an engagement has for their future. This is a remarkable cultural document, full of complexities, tensions, and subtleties; moreover, it is acutely aware of its own politics and the dangers these kids face. At the same time, it refuses to romanticize resistance and the power of critical pedagogy, and Stack holds firm in the belief that progressive pedagogical and political interventions might give rise to possibilities and real achievements for kids too often viewed as throwaways. Stack's film moves beyond the simplistic call for positive images of black youth; instead, it captures the complexities of how such youth are produced within certain social, economic, and political circumstances while simultaneously working to transform such conditions. Stack's politics are clear and he refuses to hide behind the alleged "neutral" appeal to realism. This is film with an up-front project that takes seriously the challenge of developing a language of critique and possibility, one that confront both racist representations of youth and a representational politics in which youth are blamed for society's failures. *Harlem Diary* provides an example of a representational politics in which a politics and pedagogy of the popular make it possible for audiences to understand the ways in which black youth attempt "to open social and cultural spaces in which to express themselves,"[55] as well as engage and transform the conditions through which they push against the constraints of poverty and racism.

Harlem Diary is much less interested in "realistically" portraying domination than in revealing its contradictions, cracks, fissures, and how within such spaces teenage youth fight domination and racism rather than simply yield to it. This is a film in which the pedagogical inserts itself into a representational politics, and in so doing expands and deepens the democratic possibilities for producing films that resist rather than reinforce the current racist and demonizing portrayals of subordinate youth.

Similar pedagogical lessons can be found in the work of Lucy Lippard, Michele Wallace, Olivia Gude, Nicholas Paley, Richard Bolton, David Trend, Carol Becker, Suzanne Lacey, and others too numerous to mention. The point, of course, is that art, education, and cultural work need to reinvent spaces for ethical, political, and pedagogical practices through which diverse cultural workers might create alliances and produce social practices and policies that rewrite the importance of what it means to treat youth with dignity. Unlike cultural workers such as Calvin Klein

and Larry Clark, who offer children either the cheap satisfac-
tions of stylized bodies and commodified pleasures, or the sensationalism of decadent sexuality, progressive educators and
other cultural workers need to challenge such limited representations of youth through an "integrative critical language in
which values, ethics, and social responsibility can be discussed
in terms" of how youth are constructed within such images.[56] In
addition, artists and other cultural workers need to create pedagogical practices that provide the conditions through which
young people actually learn about and understand their personal
stake in struggling for a future in which social justice and political integrity become the defining principles of their lives.

Notes and References

1   C. West (1994) America's three-fold crisis. *Tikkun*, 9(2), 42.
2   D. Weinstein (1994) Expendable youth: the rise and fall of youth
    culture. In J. S. Epstein (ed.), *Adolescents and Their Music*. New
    York: Garland, pp. 67–83.
3   D. Gaines (1994) Border crossing in the USA. In A. Ross and
    T. Ross (eds), *Microphone Fiends*. Now York: Routledge, p. 227.
    For a more specific indication of how black youth are faring in the
    age of Bill Clinton and Newt Gingrich, see A. Hacker (1995) The
    crackdown on African-Americans. *The Nation*, July 10, 45–9.
4   G. Lipsitz (1994) We know what time it is: race, class and youth
    culture in the nineties. In A. Ross and T. Ross (eds), *Microphone
    Fiends*. New York: Routledge, p. 18.
5   C. Sweeney (1995) Portrait of the American child. *The New York
    Times Magazine*, October 8, 52–3.
6   Cited in R. Kuttner (1995) The overclass is waging class warfare
    with a vengeance. *The Boston Globe*, July 24, 11.
7   Cited in Associated Press (1995) Global Study: US Has Widest Gap
    Between Rich and Poor. *Chicago Tribune*, October 28, Section 1,
    21.
8   See the figures offered by B. Reynolds (1995) Now we've learned
    who Clinton is not. *USA Today*, November 17, 15A. For an insight-
    ful critique of such cuts, see S. Mayer and C. Jencks (1995) War
    on poverty: no apologies, please. *The New York Times Op-ED*,
    November 9, A3.
9   H. Sklar (1993) Young and guilty by stereotype. *Z Magazine*, July/
    August, 54.
10 "Tagging is the police practice of picking up all Black men at least
    once and entering their names into police records." In Denver, it

has been reported that tagging was so successful that an "estimated two-thirds of all Black men between the ages of 12 and 24, were on the list. Whites made up only 7 percent of the list in a city that is 80 percent Caucasian." Cited in C. Parenti (1994), Urban militarism. Z Magazine, June, 49.

11   Cited in F. Butterfield (1995) More blacks in their 20's have trouble with the law. New York Times, October 5, A18.

12   Paul Gilroy argues, and rightly so, that the bodies of black youth, in particular, are no longer the privileged space of agency; instead, they have become the location of violence, crime, and social pathology. In this discourse, the body is the principal mark of identity. See P. Gilroy (1994) "After the love has gone": bio politics and etho-poetics in the black public sphere. Public Culture, 7(1), 49–76.

13   Some interesting sources documenting the moral panics around the emergence of youth and, rock and roll include: S. Frith (1987) Sound Effects. New York: Pantheon; J. S. Epstein (ed.) (1994) Adolescents and Their Music. New York: Garland; S. Frith and A. Goodwin (eds) (1990) On Record: Rock, Pop, and the Written Word. New York: Pantheon; L. Grossberg (1992) We Gotta Get Outta Here. New York: Routledge.

14   S. Friedlander (1993) Memory, History, and the Extermination of the Jews of Europe. Bloomington: Indiana University Press, p. 47.

15   T. Rose (1994) A style nobody can deal with: politics, style and the postindustrial city in hip hop. In A. Ross and T. Rose (eds), Microphone Fiends: Youth Music and Youth Culture. New York: Routledge, p. 78.

16   For an excellent analysis of the racial coding that goes on in the electronic and mass mediated culture, see H. Gray (1995) Watching Race: Television and the Struggle for "Blackness." Minneapolis: University of Minnesota Press, p. 165.

17   M. Ivy (1995) Memory, silence and satan. The Nation, 261(22), 834–5.

18   Ibid.

19   L. Quinby (1994) Anti-Apocalypse: Exercises in Genealogical Criticism. Minneapolis: University of Minnesota Press, p. 6.

20   H. Gray, op. cit., n. 16, p. 160.

21   O. Enwezor (1995) The body in question. Third Text, Summer, 67.

22   Ibid.

23   S. Elliott (1995) Will Calvin Klein's retreat redraw the lines of taste? The New York Times, August 29, D1, D8.

24   J. Kaplan (1995) Triumph of Calvinism. New York, September 18, 50.

25   C. Paglia (1995) Kids for sale. The Advocate, October 31, 80.

26   Cited in C. Miller (1995) Sexy sizzle backfires. *The American Marketing Association Marketing News*, September 25, 1.

27   M. Musto (1995) Teenage lust. *Artforum*, December, 73.

28   H. Gray, op. cit., p. 158.

29   Cited in M. Dowd (1995) What Calvin means. *The New York Times*, August 31, A25. The advertisement appeared in *The New York Times*, August 28, 1995, A5.

30   A. Ross (1995) Culture vultures. *Artforum*, December, 36.

31   J. Berger (1972) *Ways of Seeing*. London: BBC, p. 7.

32   T. Gabriel (1995) Think you had a bad adolescence. *The New York Times*, July 31, C1.

33   Cited in M. Warner (1995) Negative attitude. *Voice Literary Supplement*, September 6, 25.

34   In response to an interviewer who suggests that one message of the film is that boys are bad news and girls should beware, Clark responded, maybe ironically, that "the girls come off as the most honest, the strongest." One can't help but wonder how Clark defines these terms and in comparison to what references both within and outside the film. Cited in J. Womack (1995) Teenage lust. *Spin*, September, 70.

35   M. Atkinson (1995) Skateboard jungle, *The Village Voice*, XL(37), 66.

36   T. de Lauretis (1987) *Technologies of Gender*. Bloomington: Indiana University Press, p. 13.

37   D. Denby (1995) School's out forever. *New York*, July 31, 44.

38   H. Sklar, op. cit., n. 9, 11.

39   Cited in S. Aronowitz (1994) *Dead Artists, Live Theories and Other Cultural Problems*. New York: Routledge, p. 42.

40   C. West, op. cit., n. 1, p. 42. For two books that deal specifically with the complex forces that poor kids negotiate while retaining a sense of dignity and agency, see S. Thompson (1995) *Going All the Way: Teenage Girl's Tales of Sex, Romance and Pregnancy*. New York: Hill and Wang; J. Pratt and K. Pryor (1995) *For Real: the Uncensored Truth about America's Teenagers*. New York: Hyperion.

41   On the issue of how public memory is constructed, see G. Hartman (1994) Public memory and its discontents. *Raritan*, XIII(4), 28.

42   A. Taubin (1995) Chilling and very hot. *Sight and Sound*, November, 17.

43   Ibid.

44   M. Reeves (1995) Skateboard jungle. *The Village Voice*, XL(37), 64.

45   T. Morrison (1993) On the backs of blacks. *Time*, Fall, 57.

46   Some interesting interviews and comment on Clark's life can be found in J. Lewis (1995) Larry Clark's first feature film, "Kids." *Harper's Bazaar*, August, 144–5, 190–1; T. Gabriel, op. cit., n. 32,

C1, C7; J. Womack, op. cit., n. 34, 65–70; T. Rafferty (1995) Growing pains. *The New Yorker*, 71(22), 80–2.

47 T. Rafferty, op. cit., n. 40, 80, 82.

48 This is evident in films that extend from *Lolita* in 1962 to the more contemporary *Interview with the Vampire* (1995), with its portrayal of a nine-year-old vampire girl who exhibits the sexuality of an adult, or *The Professional* (1995), which casually narrates the sexually charged attraction between a cold-blooded hit man and the twelve-year-old Lolita-ish girl he befriends. It is also blatantly visible in all the stylish jean ads that constitute the "fashionscape" world of Guess?, Gap, and Benetton.

49 I am drawing on the productive notion of desire from G. Deleuze and F. Guattari (1983) *Anti-Oedipus: Capitalism and Schizophrenia*. Minneapolis: University of Minnesota Press; B. S. Turner (1984) *The Body and Society*. Oxford: Basil Blackwell. On the relationship between meaning maps and mattering maps, see L. Grossberg (1992) *We Gotta Get Outta Here*. New York: Routledge, especially, pp. 201–32.

50 For a brilliant analysis of ethics and social action, see B. Harrison (1985), *Making Connections: Essays in Feminist Social Ethics*. Boston: Beacon Press.

51 Eurydice (1996) Topspin. *Spin*, January, 16.

52 S. Aronowitz and H. A. Giroux (1992) *Postmodern Education*. Minneapolis: University of Minnesota Press; H. A. Giroux (1996) *Disturbing Pleasures*. New York: Routledge; H. A. Giroux (1996) *Fugitive Cultures: Race, Violence, and Youth*. New York: Routledge.

53 I am indebted to Andrew Ross for some of these insights. See A. Ross (1995) Cultural vultures. *Artforum*, December, 35–6, 108.

54 E. Kosofsky Sedgwick (1990) *Epistemology of the Closet*. Stanford: University of California Press, p. 7.

55 H. Gray, op. cit., n. 16, p. 160.

56 S. Lacy (1995) Introduction: cultural pilgrimages and metaphoric journeys. In S. Lacy (ed.), *Mapping the Terrain: New Genre Public Art*. Seattle, WA: Bay State Press, pp. 42–3.

3
TEENS AND SCHOOLS: WHO IS FALLING THROUGH THE CRACKS AND WHY

Sarah Nixon-Ponder

There are numerous factors that can cause students to be considered at risk for failure, but many children and adolescents are falling through the cracks in American public schools because of the discrepancy between cultural values and beliefs of school and home. Au and Kawakami (1994, pp. 5, 6) state that "students of diverse backgrounds often do poorly in school because of a mismatch between the culture of the school and the culture of the home." This chapter will discuss research on students who are at risk for failure because of this mismatch of cultures and present examples of schools and instructors that are practicing culturally relevant instruction.

The practices of schooling in US public schools are patterned after the home culture of the European-American middle class. The "interactive styles of continually questioning and extending the limits of knowledge that are typical of middle-class social-interaction patterns . . . are exactly what occur in schools" (Brown et al., 1994, p. 761). Even the types of parental inter-actions that take place between children and their parents in European-American middle-class homes are similar to the inter-actions between teacher and students in public schools. While this method of instruction may work for children who are familiar with and receive this type of instruction at home, those who come to school unfamiliar with these kinds of interactions are at risk of failure from the start.

However, this is not to imply that children who come from diverse backgrounds do not experience types of literate interactions between them and their parents. Taylor and Dorsey-Gaines (1988) examined the different types of literate activities that are evident in inner-city African-American homes. Heath (1983) studied the literate behaviors of rural working-class European-American and African-American families in North Carolina. Moll (1988, 1994; Moll and Diaz, 1987) has researched the types of literacies and funds of knowledge that occur in Spanish-speaking Mexican-American homes. Au (1980; Au and Jordan, 1981; Au and Kawakami, 1994) investigated the literate behaviors in Native Hawaiian homes. McCarty (1989) has explored literacy within Navajo families in the Southwest. One common feature among all these children is that their performance in school is lower than that of their European-American counterparts. Why? Researchers (Au, 1980; Au and Jordan, 1981; Heath, 1983; Moll and Diaz, 1987; Moll, 1988, 1994; Taylor and Dorsey-Gaines, 1988; Heath and Mangiola, 1991; Schaafsma, 1993; Au and Kawakami, 1994) point to the discrepancy between cultures – that of the school and that of the home and community.

Who Is at Risk for Failure in School?

An increasing number of students in the United States are falling through the cracks:

- 1 million students drop out of school each year;
- 1.5 million teenage women become pregnant each year;
- 15 percent of graduates of urban high schools read at less than the sixth grade level;
- Between one-fifth and one-fourth of all children in the USA live below the poverty line.

Davis and McCaul (1990) believe that these are conservative estimates.

There are many definitions for "at risk." Presseisen (1991, p. 5) lists several categories of students who are considered at risk for failure: members of non-mainstream groups, either minority or ethnic groups; non-native English speakers; those who are poor;

those living in a single parent home; those whose mothers have low literacy and/or educational levels; substance abusers; those whose home environment is dysfunctional; and those with physical, mental, emotional, sensory, or learning difficulties. Students who live in large metropolitan areas are usually pictured more often as being "at risk"; however, suburban and rural children can be at risk of failure as well. "At risk" may mean one who is a potential drop-out; it can also mean that the student will graduate from high school but will have low literacy levels and not be employable outside of menial labor. Because of the enormity of this topic, this chapter will focus only on students who are falling through the cracks because of the mismatch between the students' cultural background and the culture of the school. I will specifically be looking at African-American and Latina/o students.

Due to the severity and magnitude of this crisis, it is now more important than ever that school administrators and instructors seriously evaluate the problem and begin to implement change within their own districts and classrooms. How can this trend be reversed? What can schools do to assure parents and students of different cultural backgrounds that success is not just a construct for European-American middle-class America? In the past eight to ten years, the amount of research dealing with multiculturalism as it relates to educational reform has increased dramatically. One component of multicultural education is culturally relevant classroom instruction – a type of instruction that many believe is necessary for more students of color to succeed in American public schools today.

Teaching Multiculturally in New Orleans

A major component of feminst pedagogy is the theory that narrative helps to explain and clarify (Belenky et al., 1986; Cooper, 1989). Therefore, before I discuss some theoretical aspects of multicultural education and two models of culturally relevant instruction, I wish to share an example of consciousness raising that grew out of my first formal teaching experience. I hope to illustrate through my personal vignette the importance of making curriculum and instruction multicultural and relevant to students of color.

My experience as a teacher began as a language arts teacher in a Catholic all-girls high school which I will call St Agnes (SA). SA was located in a run-down section of New Orleans that had been a pleasant working-class neighborhood about 15–20 years earlier. Some of the worst public housing units in the city were not far away, and the school drew a portion of its students from there. Some of the students came to SA on scholarships; others attended SA and worked on the grounds, in the cafeteria, and cleaning after school to help pay part of their tuition. A sizable Vietnamese community lived close by – most of whom were "boat people" and ethnic Chinese from Vietnam – and many of their daughters came to study at SA. Some students came to SA because it was a family tradition; others came because it was the least expensive of all of the private girls' schools in the New Orleans metroplex. Needless to say, there was a wide variety of backgrounds, socioeconomic status, races, religions, and even languages that greeted me on the first day of school.

After the end of the first week of school, I remember thinking how my undergraduate training had not prepared me for the diversity of students, the large classes, the politics of schools, and the interactions with parents. I was a mess; floundering, I reached back into the depths of my mind, pulling from my own high school experiences as a learner. What had my teachers done? Would it work? What about classroom discipline? How did they keep control? (I spent the first months of teaching very obsessed with this "control" issue – scared to let go, afraid that the students would get the best of me.) The major difference between my high school experiences and SA was that my high school in the Midwest had two African-American and three Asian-American students – not what you would consider a diverse student population. Most of my peers came from the same background as I did – European-American, middle-class, Catholic families. This was not quite the case with my students in New Orleans.

So I taught the curriculum straight from the books, which were old and outdated. After the first month, I was bored, my students were bored, and I thought, "God this sucks! It's got to be more fun or they'll eat me alive!" Having received my education from a Catholic liberal arts college, my background was full of the great classics written by dead white men. There was not an author of color among the volumes that I had read and studied for years. And these dead white men were just not cutting it with the young African-American women, or the Latinas, or the Vietnamese, or the bayou Cajuns – who all stared at me with dull, half-closed eyes, and were on the brink of falling asleep from heat, humidity, and boredom. They revolted, throwing their books at me and out of the windows. They wanted some contemporary literature that looked like them, that sounded like them. They wanted to read literature they could relate to, that had some meaning to their lives. They wanted the old stuff *only* if it could be presented in a manner that was congruent with their cultures and would make connections to their world. And they wanted to read books by women – they were tired of always reading and hearing about great men. So I started making changes by bringing in supplementary materials.

I guess I could say that this was the start of my consciousness raising, when I began to realize that the American educational system denies students of color a sense of ownership in the curriculum that is being taught. I put myself in my students' shoes. How would I have felt if I had gone through school without ever reading about someone who looked like me, who came from my background? How would I have felt if my culture was excluded from the textbooks, from the discussions? Would I have wanted to finish school if I had felt that school was a place for other culture groups and not mine? Through this awakening grew the belief that I owed it to my students to listen to their concerns, and thus make some drastic changes in the sophomore language arts curriculum.

I needed to re-educate myself. So I began by reading African-American women writers – and lots of them – from different philosophies, styles, and genres. I shared these books with my students, and they began reading them, too. I moved on to Southern women writers like Flannery O'Connor and Eudora Welty, and read short stories, poetry, fiction, and non-fiction. These, too, were shared with the students. I had a very difficult time trying to find literature by Vietnamese women and finally resorted to Chinese-American women authors and women such as Pearl Buck who have written authentically and extensively about China. (This was how I learned that my Vietnamese students were ethnic Chinese.) Latina writers such as Sandra Cisneros and Isabel Allende became favorites. I found some excellent collections of writings by Native American women, such as *Spider Woman's Granddaughters*. I also began exploring books written by men of color. Richard Wright became a mainstay in our literature circles, producing some of the most intense discussions on the plight of the African-Americans and racism. DuBois was an inspiration to many young women who shared his book *The Souls of Black Folks* with their families.

I shared large numbers of books with my students, introducing the authors and storyline and offering multiple copies of each for small groups to read together. And the fun began! The discussions were deep, intensive, and sometimes lasted over several class periods. Students kept journals on the books they read, writing about the feelings they were experiencing, their favorite characters and parts of the books, their insights into the literature, and the ideas they were exploring. I threw out the formal, standard format for book reports, and the students started writing book reviews and critiques, discussing in detail characters, plots, and hidden themes, and connecting these with everyday living. They began exploring titles and authors on their own, bringing in new books they had found. It was quite exhilarating to observe the changes that were occurring with the students. They were excited about what they were reading, and they were alive with their newly constructed knowledge.

It's not that I don't see the importance or relevance in teaching the great classics. But I felt that it was important – perhaps more important – that these young women read, experience, and explore great literature written by women and people of color. Of my 178 students, only a handful had ever read a book written by a woman – not to mention a woman of color. Only two of my African-American students had ever read a book written by an African-American, male or female! I believed that it was high time for these young women to find some role models in literature who looked and sounded like them: women and men of color with whom they could identify and bond, and from whom they could gather strength and pride.

By introducing curriculum that related to their cultures and employing instructional strategies that were more congruent with their learning styles, I observed as the students blossomed into good readers who were also critical thinkers and creative and competent writers, and were able to discuss the complex issues of all types of literature and relate it to their worlds. By realizing that I needed to change what I was teaching and how I was teaching it, I made a conscious decision to teach multicultural literature in a culturally congruent way. Through my own consciousness raising, I was able to help the students understand the need to raise their own consciousness about the complexities of yesterday, today, and tomorrow. I found that teaching multiculturally helped all of us to achieve this in an open and honest manner.

Theory and Relevant Literature

In order to understand how multicultural education can be a means of keeping students of color from falling through the cracks, let's take a look at several pieces of literature from three of the leading multiculturalists. Although there are numerous theorists and researchers who have had a great impact on the field, it is not in the scope of this chapter to discuss them all. Several in particular have influenced my thinking and helped me to better understand the issues of multicultural education. At the heart of the matter is the basic question: what can schools, administrators, and teachers do to improve education for students of color and students whose home cultures differ greatly from that of the school culture? The following review of works by Banks, Sleeter, and Ogbu will clarify some issues of knowledge and empowerment in the area of multicultural education.

In *A Curriculum for Empowerment, Action, and Change*, Banks (1991) discusses the national debate which is occurring over the knowledge that should be taught in schools regarding cultural and ethnic diversity. He begins his discussion by explaining the philosophies of the three rival groups of scholars: the Western traditionalists, the multiculturalists, and the Afrocentrists. Banks's concern lies with the fact that the debate "has been polarized" because "little productive dialogue and exchange between the Western traditionalists and the multiculturalists" (p. 4) has transpired. Instead, all three groups have resorted to rallying behind their gathered forces, throwing barbs at each other, more often in the "popular press rather than in academic and scholarly journals" (p. 5).

Banks states that all US citizens should have a "common core of shared knowledge" (p. 126). But then he asks: "Who will participate in the formulation of that knowledge and whose interests will it serve?" He answers this loaded question by stating that "such knowledge should reflect cultural democracy and serve the interests of all of the people within our pluralistic nation and world" (p. 126). I believe that it is this question that frightens so many in the traditional establishment because it is a question that deals with power and control.

Rather than concentrating on the negative aspects of this ensuing debate, Banks turns his focus to the nature of knowledge and describes five types of knowledge: personal/cultural; popular; mainstream academic; transformative academic; and school knowledge. He states that "teachers should help students to understand all types of knowledge" (p. 5), using this idea as a springboard to tie the Western traditional, multicultural, and Afrocentric perspectives together through the understanding of the different types of knowledge. He views these five categories as "useful conceptual tools for thinking about knowledge and planning multicultural teaching" (p. 6).

In this discussion on the types of knowledge, Banks explains where each type of knowledge originates, defines it, and follows through with relevant research regarding each category. He furnishes practical examples as to how this knowledge is currently being implemented in the curriculum, as well as how it could be applied in the future. For example, Banks offers realistic models of implementation for teachers who want to modify their curriculum and instructional mode.

Banks concludes his discourse on a positive, hopeful note. He states that "multicultural education involves changes in the total school environment in order to create equal educational opportunities for all students" (p. 11), and points to the five types of knowledge "that should be taught in the multicultural curriculum" as having "important implications for planning and teaching a multicultural curriculum" (p. 11).

Banks next outlines goals that are important for multicultural teaching, stating the types of opportunities that students should have available to them in the classroom. In the past (and in most cases, presently), students have not been taught how to think critically or to evaluate what they learn or are expected to learn at school. Banks disagrees with this philosophy. He perceives multiculturalism as the chance for students to analyze the cultural, gender, and racial biases that are consistently present in many schools' curriculum and thus transform school to be more of a reflection of their own personal experiences. Banks states that the "multicultural classroom is a forum of multiple voices and perspectives" (p. 12).

In the opening chapter of *Empowerment through Multicultural Education*, Sleeter (1991) discusses empowerment in relation to social oppression. She begins this discourse by examining the concept of empowerment. Sleeter states that education for empowerment "demands taking seriously the strengths, experiences, strategies, and goals members of oppressed groups have. It also demands helping them to analyze and understand the social structure that oppresses them and to act in ways that will enable them to reach their own goals successfully" (p. 6). In the past (and presently in many cases), education in the USA has not done this. The dominant group has not taught – or addressed – the strengths of the oppressed groups; nor have the experiences of these groups been viewed as an important component of the educational and developmental process. Instead, our present system seems to work from a deficit model, focusing on weaknesses and disabilities rather than strengths and potentials.

Sleeter believes that education for empowerment is inevitably linked to the cultivation of students' skills in becoming advocates for themselves and for their cause, and working collectively for social justice. Students need "to do more than simply adapt to the social order but rather to be able to transform the social order in the interests of social justice" (p. 7). Multicultural education is about action, not passivity and submission. It is about people of oppressed groups – African-Americans, Latinas/os, Asian-Americans, Native Americans and other indigenous groups, gays and lesbians, women – coming forward to learn more about their cultures and histories and to teach others about their experiences. That is why these skills are so important and fundamental to multicultural education.

In the present educational system, people of oppressed groups are not taught how to advocate for their rights and obligations; nor are they taught about the power of collective action. Multicultural education teaches people how to "recognize and learn to use various power bases, as both individuals and collectives" (p. 15). Schools can foster the environment that is needed for empowerment to flourish, but training is needed for the teachers, administrators, and students; a sense of collaboration and cooperation is essential. Coalitions should be formed, and cooperative learning should be viewed "as a strategy for coalition building" (p. 18). Working together in groups promotes solidarity, a sense of belonging and community, and thus an understanding of the bigger picture and possible solutions. Multicultural education through cooperative learning fosters social discourse and critical thinking, helping students to become adept at analyzing puzzling situations. Multicultural education empowers students not only to ask the questions needed in order to learn about the good life but also to learn how they can obtain it.

"Immigrant and involuntary minorities in comparative perspective," by Ogbu (1991), discusses the differences between two groups of minorities: voluntary immigrant minority groups and involuntary minority groups. The major question asked by Ogbu is "why immigrant minorities are relatively more successful in school than non-immigrant minorities in spite of the apparent similarities in the cultural, linguistic and structural barriers facing both types of minorities" (p. 4). He clearly defines the problems that confront both minority groups, explains the underlying reasons for the existence of these problems, and describes how different groups have handled these problems. He cites research on various minority groups: Koreans in Japan; Mexican-Americans in California; Sikhs in Britain and the USA; African-Americans, Chinese-Americans, and Central-Americans in the USA.

Ogbu begins by stating that conventional explanations for poor school performance by certain minority groups have only been viewed from the perspective of the dominant culture. Thus, the constructed explanations are "without the benefit of what the minorities themselves think" (p. 6). Consequently, Ogbu offers the concept of the cultural model, which he describes as "respective understandings of how their society or any particular domain or institution works and their respective understandings of their places in that working order" (p. 7). Neither the cultural model of the dominant group nor that of the minorities is right or wrong, better or worse; they just exist "to provide group members with the framework for interpreting educational events, situations and experiences and to guide behavior in the schooling context and process" (p. 7). There are six concepts within a cultural model: "the frame of comparison with respect to status mobility; the folk theory of getting ahead in the host society; survival strategies; trusting/acquiescing relations; social identity; and cultural frame of reference" (p. 17). Through these concepts, Ogbu outlines and interprets immigrant minorities' and involuntary minorities' responses to the discussion involving success in school.

Minorities who have voluntarily immigrated to "their present societies" have done so because they believed that they would be better off – economically, socially, educationally, as well as politically – if they moved to another country. This belief has a great and continuing effect on their overall outlook. They "appear to interpret the economic, political and social barriers against them as more or less temporary problems" (p. 11), problems they will overcome with time, hard work, and a good education. Involuntary minorities, on the other hand, did not arrive here of their own free will, and thus do not have a "homeland with which to compare their present situation" (p. 13). Unlike the immigrants, they compare their situation in life – jobs, quality of education, housing, etc. – to that of the dominant group, confirming that they are worse off than they should be. They determine this is because they "belong to a subordinate and disparaged minority group" (p. 14), and they do not see these economic, political, and social barriers against them as temporary or ones that can be overcome with hard work, time, or education.

Immigrants have a "positive dual frame of reference which allows them to develop or maintain an optimistic view of their future possibilities" (p. 11), feeling that no matter how difficult things are here, they would be much worse if they had not left their country. This framework is reflected in their attitudes toward a segregated, poor quality education (as well as working menial jobs), through believing that their situation was worse before arrival, and that an American education is better than what they would have received in the home country. Thus, the immigrant minorities see education as "a single most significant avenue to status mobility in the new land" (p. 11), a "folk theory" that they seem to form when they come to their new country. Involuntary minorities have a negative dual frame of reference because they see the prejudice and discrimination against them as "permanent and institutionalized." They would like to see education and ability as a means for getting ahead, but they cannot. Hence, their "folk theory" stresses a "collective effort as providing the best chances for overcoming the opportunity barriers" (p. 14).

Survival strategies are used by both groups to help them cope with some of their problems. For the immigrants, this may include "the option of returning to their homeland or emigrating to other societies" (p. 12). This is not an option for the involuntary minority. Collective struggle, which European-Americans might refer to as "civil rights activities," involves trying to change the rules of self-advancement to make the rules work for them.

With regard to differences in language and culture of the voluntary minority, Ogbu states that these "existed before the immigrants emigrated," and thus are perceived as an obstacle that will need to be overcome if they want to succeed in their new land. They do not go to school expecting to be taught in their own language; they see language as a barrier, but they learn to successfully adjust to it (more or less). For involuntary minorities differences in ways of speaking and communicating are seen as a means of coping, as a symbol of identity, something that makes them different from the dominant group.

Since immigrants "bring with them a sense of who they are . . . a social identity . . . a positive sense of cultural identity" (p. 13), this aids them in their assimilation and success in school. For involuntary immigrants, an oppositional identity is developed, since they see the discrimination against them as permanent and enduring. This oppositional identity does not tend to mesh well with dominant group institutions, such as schools, and tends to be a factor in the problem of success at school. Another distinguishing feature of the immigrant population, which is an important factor in their assimilation and success at school, as well, is "the degree of trust of acquiescence they have toward members of the dominant group" (p. 13). Quite the opposite, involuntary minorities "distrust members of the dominant groups and the societal institutions controlled by the latter" (p. 16). Thus, they do not trust the schools to provide a good education. Ogbu's intelligent discussion describes the historical, economic, and sociological concepts that play an important part in the level of educational success for students of color.

Although they are recognized more for their work in sociolinguistics than multiculturalism, Heath and Mangiola's book *Children of Promise: Literate Activity in Linguistically and*

Culturally Diverse Classrooms (1991) must be mentioned in this chapter. Heath and Mangiola research the different ways of knowing, patterns of preferred interactions, and learning strategies students of color bring to the classroom. They suggest that teachers need to learn more about the ways students' languages are being used outside the classroom and to turn to the community to observe linguistic exchanges of all kinds. This knowledge will help the teacher and students to expand on their ways of "describing, clarifying, and assessing" (p. 14) the different types of experiences the students bring with them to the classroom. The authors coin the term "of promise", and urge educators to adopt the idea of looking at students of color not as students "at risk" but as students "of promise" – thus suggesting that we need to put the deficit model behind us and begin to look at the positives, at the students' abilities, potentials, and strengths.

Culturally Relevant Curriculum and Instruction

Having looked at multicultural education through the works of several prominent theorists, let's turn to two cases that demonstrate multicultural education through culturally relevant curriculum and instruction.

What is culturally congruent or culturally relevant instruction? King (1994) states: "Research within the culturally *congruent* perspective focuses on transforming the educational process to align it more closely with students' cultural knowledge and their indigenous ways of knowing, learning and being. The skills of social criticism are not necessarily addressed but it is presumed that transformed, culturally responsive and inclusive instructional approaches that drastically improve the education of African American students will generally benefit the whole society" (pp. 27, 28). It is my belief that before a teacher can acquire (or develop) these skills, a certain amount of consciousness raising needs to have taken place. I know that, for me, it occurred over the period of several years. The two following reviews examine the end result of some consciousness raising from a multicultural perspective that materialized as culturally relevant curriculum development and instruction.

In "Reading between the lines and beyond the pages: a culturally relevant approach to literacy teaching" (1992), Ladson-

Billings discusses two teachers whose approaches to literacy instruction are culturally relevant. One is a whole language teacher who is European-American; the other, an African-American, practices a more traditional approach. Ladson-Billings states: "The whole language/traditional literacy debate assumes a less critical role in efforts to promote literacy for African-American students. The compelling issue is the development of a culturally relevant approach to teaching in general that fosters and sustains the students' desire to *choose* academic success in the face of so many competing options" (p. 313).

Culturally relevant teaching describes the type of teaching that is created not just to match the school culture to the students' culture, but also to use the students' culture as the foundation for helping students to understand themselves and others. Therefore, culturally relevant teaching demands the recognition of African-American culture as an important base upon which to build the schooling experience. "The primary goal of culturally relevant teaching is to empower students to examine critically the society in which they live and to work for social change . . . Culturally relevant teaching that is successful helps produce a relevant Black personality" (p. 314).

According to Ladson-Billings (1992), culturally relevant teaching contains three components: (a) culturally relevant conceptions of self and others; (b) culturally relevant conceptions of classroom social relations; and (c) culturally relevant conceptions of knowledge (p. 317). All three components are evident in both teachers' approaches to instruction. With regard to culturally relevant conceptions of self and others, both are proud to be teachers, and they foster a strong "identification and solidarity" with their students and the African-American culture (p. 317). Both teachers encourage students to be themselves and support their students' academic excellence through high expectations. Both teachers live in the community where they teach.

The second component, conceptions of classroom social relations, is also apparent in these two teachers' style by the manner in which their students positively respond to them. There is mutual respect between teacher and students, therefore fostering positive student/teacher and teacher/student interactions. "The teachers share power with the students because they understand that education is an empowering force, not merely a job prerequisite" (p. 318). Their classrooms are cooperative and supportive, thus "creating a community of learners" (p. 318).

Conceptions of knowledge, the third component, are distinct in the decisions the teachers make regarding what to teach. They intentionally design curricula that place their students and their cultures at the center of the curriculum, therefore inviting their students to critically analyze what they read and compare it to their own experiences. "For these teachers, being literate assumes being able to evaluate critically and make decisions about what you read" (Ladson-Billings, 1992, p. 318).

Eating on the Street: Teaching Literacy in a Multicultural Society (1993) by Schaafsma describes the Dewey Center Community Writing Project, a three-week summer program for students in junior high who live in inner-city Detroit's Cass Corridor. Four teachers from the University of Michigan worked in collaboration with three teachers from the Detroit public schools.

Schaafsma puts a different twist on describing the culturally relevant instruction that occurs during this summer program. Knowing that the African-American culture is grounded in oral tradition, the curriculum of the program is built around stories – the stories of the students and those of the teachers. It is this act of sharing stories that transforms both teacher and student, because they are "not silencing each other's voices and [are] working together on common goals of learning and teaching" (p. 198). The purpose of the program is to create an environment where teachers and students can learn from and with each other, while at the same time trying to find just to what extent they might be able to "democratize" education within their learning community. Thus, it appears that teachers and students engage in consciousness raising together, using stories as the medium for doing so.

Learning transpired through compromise, cooperation, and conflicts which provided opportunities to talk about contrasting opinions. Stories were used to help make sense of the past and present and became a source of energy, strength, and solidarity, helping to bind the program's participants through the common concerns all had for the community. Schaafsma described this as "culture-preserving" (p. 199), seeing the students' stories as a pronouncement of their cultural sustenance. The teachers used stories – especially inspirational ones – to teach for transformation, to reshape culture, thus redefining it through the very act of changing it.

Curriculum as storytelling provides an opportunity for conversation to evolve, where teachers "could plan together with students how to help them learn to write, where an exchange of stories about teaching could take place" (p. 205).

Storytelling as a method of community building is a vital component of the Dewey Center's program. Sharing stories about oneself teaches respect for others because it brings a sense of bonding, a sense of ownership, to the program. "Storytelling as a means of learning about the classroom may be the best way to preserve differences in the process of 'novelizing' our various understandings of teaching literacy in a multicultural society" (Schaafsma, 1993, p. 207).

Conclusions

With the changing demographics of the school-age population in the United States, I believe that it is absolutely imperative that as educators we change our ways of thinking and teaching to encompass a more multicultural philosophy and curriculum, as well as a culturally relevant manner of educating. The first step in this change process is the type of self-reflection that Krater *et al.* (1994) describe: "The most profound and liberating changes for us emerged from questioning our own behavior, our own classrooms, and the unconscious cultural biases of the educational system. We had to look not only at how we teach writing, but also at how we work with students who might not conform to the academic and cultural mold of our school . . . We painfully realized that what we had been doing in our classrooms did not fertilize the soil for some students and in reality was killing some seeds" (p. 4). It is the type of consciousness raising that I had to experience as a new teacher in New Orleans. As educators, we must continually question *what* we are teaching and *why* we are teaching the content that we are teaching, and we must continue to thoroughly educate ourselves about our students' diverse cultures in order to better understand and teach all students – and consequently *reach* all students.

How do we do this, or begin to do this? I believe that Myles Horton and Paulo Freire (1990) eloquently answer this difficult question in *We Make the Road by Walking*. Freire asks: "How is it possible for us to work in a community without feeling the *spirit* of the culture that has been there for many years, without trying to understand the soul of the culture? We cannot interfere in this culture. Without understanding the soul of the culture we just invade the culture" (p. 131). After much discussion, Horton answers: "Because of that, one of the virtues I think that we educators have to create – because I am sure also that we don't receive virtues as gifts; we make virtues not intellectually, but through practice – one of the virtues we have to create in ourselves as progressive educators is the *virtue of humility*" (p. 195, emphasis added). In viewing our role as educators through the lens of humility, it is time to recognize our students from diverse cultural backgrounds, not as students "at risk" but as *children of promise*.

References

Au, K. H. (1980) Participation structures in a reading lesson with Hawaiian children: analysis of a culturally appropriate instructional event. *Anthropology and Education Quarterly*, 11(2), 91–115.

Au, K. H. and Jordan, C. (1981) Teaching reading to Hawaiian children: finding a culturally appropriate solution. In C. Cazden, V. John and D. Hymes (eds), *Functions of Language in the Classroom*. New York: Teachers College Press, pp. 139–52.

Au, K. H. and Kawakami, A. J. (1994) Cultural congruence in instruction. In E. R. Hollins, J. E. King and W. C. Hayman (eds), *Teaching Diverse Populations: Formulating a Knowledge Base*. Albany: State University of New York Press, pp. 5–23.

Banks, J. A. (1993) The canon debate, knowledge construction, and multicultural education. *Educational Researcher*, June/July, 4–14.

Belenky, M., Clinchy, B., Goldberger, N. and Tarule, J. (1986) *Women's Ways of Knowing*. New York: Basic Books.

Brown, A. L., Palinscar, A. S. and Armbruster, B. B. (1994) Instructing comprehension-fostering activities in interactive learning situations. In R. B. Ruddell, M. R. Ruddell and H. Singer (eds), *Theoretical Models and Processes of Reading*, 4th edn. Newark, DE: International Reading Association, pp. 757–87.

Cooper, M. M. (1989) Women's ways of writing. In M. M. Cooper and M. Holzman (eds), *Writing as a Social Action*. Portsmouth, NH: Boynton/Cook, pp. 141–56.

Davis, W. E. and McCaul, E. J. (1990) *At-risk Children and Youth: a Crisis in Our Schools and Society*. Orono, ME: University of Maine.

Heath, S. B. (1983) *Ways with Words*. New York: Cambridge University Press.

Heath, S. B. and Mangiola, L. (1991) *Children of Promise: Literate Activity in Linguistically and Culturally Diverse Classrooms*. Washington, DC: National Education Association.

Horton, M. and Freire, P. (1990) *We Make the Road by Walking: Conversations on Education and Social Change*. Philadelphia: Temple University Press.

King, J. E. (1994) The purpose of schooling for African American children: Including cultural knowledge. In E. R. Hollins, J. E. King and W. C. Hayman (eds), *Teaching Diverse Populations: Formulating a Knowledge Base*. Albany: State University of New York Press, pp. 25–45.

Krater, J., Zeni, J. and Cason, N. D. (1994) *Mirror Images: Teaching Writing in Black and White*. Portsmouth, NH: Heinemann.

Ladson-Billings, G. (1992) Reading between the lines and beyond the pages: a culturally relevant approach to literacy teaching. *Theory into Practice*, 31(4), 312–20.

McCarty, T. L. (1989) School as community: the Rough Rock demonstration. *Harvard Educational Review*, 59(4), 484–503.

Moll, L. C. (1988) Some key issues in teaching Latino students. *Language Arts*, 65, 465–72.

Moll, L. C. (1994) Literacy research in community and classrooms: a sociocultural approach. In R. B. Ruddell, M. R. Ruddell and H. Singer (eds), *Theoretical Models and Processes of Reading*, 4th edn. Newark, DE: International Reading Association, pp. 179–207.

Moll, L. C. and Diaz, S. (1987) Change as the goal of educational research. *Anthropology and Education Quarterly*, 18, 300–11.

Ogbu, J. U. (1991) Immigrant and involuntary minorities in comparative perspective. In M. Gibson and J. U. Ogbu (eds), *Minority Status and Schooling*. New York: Garland Publishing, pp. 3–33.

Presseisen, B. Z. (1991) At-risk students: defining a population. In K. M. Kershner and J. A. Connolly (eds), *At-risk Students and School Restructuring*. Philadelphia: Research for Better Schools, pp. 5–11.

Schaafsma, D. (1993) *Eating on the Street: Teaching Literacy in a Multicultural Society*. Pittsburgh: University of Pittsburgh Press.

Sleeter, C. E. (1991) Introduction: multicultural education and empowerment. In C. E. Sleeter (ed.), *Empowerment through Multicultural Education*. Albany: State University of New York Press, pp. 1–23.

Taylor, D. and Dorsey-Gaines, C. (1988) *Growing up Literate: Learning from Inner City Families*. Portsmouth, NH: Heinemann.

4
BEAVIS AND BUTT-HEAD: NO FUTURE FOR POSTMODERN YOUTH

Steven Best and Douglas Kellner

In this study, we argue that the popular MTV series *Beavis and Butt-Head*, while "only" a "cartoon," provides all-too-real indications of how many contemporary white youth think and feel as they vegetate in front the television, unprepared for the challenges of the new high-tech economy, and how their frustration drives them to extreme behavior. In the following analysis we thus use *Beavis and Butt-Head* to provide a diagnostic critique of contemporary societal and cultural trends, using the series as a source of critical insight into the situation of postmodern youth.[1] Our study will indicate the role that media culture plays in the life of contemporary youth and the need to develop critical media literacy in order to decode the messages, ideologies, and effects of media culture.

Throughout much of the day, Beavis and Butt-Head sit on their shabby living-room couch watching television, especially music videos, which they criticize in terms of whether the videos are "cool" or "suck." This aesthetic judgment depends on the quantity of smoke, fire, explosions, guns, death images, violence, leather, and "chicks," and the extent to which the soundtrack conforms to the rapid, hard-driving beat of heavy metal. Groups like AC/DC, Metallica, Black Sabbath, Motorhead, Slayer, Danzig, Judas Priest, Iron Maiden, Pantera, White Zombie, Soundgarden, the Beastie Boys, Red Hot Chili Peppers, and, above all, Gwar and the Butthole Surfers, *rule*, while Glam Rock, Billy Joel, Depeche Mode, Huey Lewis and the News, Michael Bolton, and many, many others, *suck*, as does all "college music."

Developed for MTV by animated cartoonist Mike Judge, the series spoofs precisely the sort of music videos played by the music television channel which has become the existential epicenter of youth culture.[2] Biting the hand that feeds it, in an ironic postmodern gesture, *Beavis and Butt-Head* ridicules MTV, its VJs (video jockeys), such as the ever-insipid "Kennedy," and the post-boomer audience that watches music videos. The show instantly became a cult favorite, loved by youth and adults alike, yet it also had its detractors from the beginning and elicited spirited controversy when it was claimed some young fans imitated typical Beavis and Butt-Head activity, such as lighting fires and torturing and killing animals.[3]

Beavis and Butt-Head is arguably postmodern, with its characters, style, and content almost solely derivative from previous TV shows. Beavis and Butt-Head are a spinoff of Wayne and Garth in *Wayne's World*, a popular *Saturday Nite Live* feature, later spun off into popular movies. They also resemble the SCTV characters Bob and Doug McKenzie, couch potatoes who make lewd and crude remarks while they comment on media culture and drink beer. Their comments on the music videos replicate the popular Comedy Central Channel's series *Mystery Science Theater 3000*, which features two puppet-like characters and their human sidekick making irreverent comments on dreadful old Hollywood movies and network television shows. And, of course, the music videos are a direct replication of MTV's basic fare.

One might even see *Beavis and Butt-Head* as a postmodern youth's *Waiting for Godot*, updated for today's media culture. Like Beckett's pathetic characters Didi and Gogo, Beavis and Butt-Head passively wait for life and spend most of their lives killing time, locked into a circular structure of existence mostly played out in front of the TV. Interestingly, while Beckett's characters are waiting in nature, in front of a tree, to find motivation and meaning, Beavis and Butt-Head are ensconced in their house in front of a television set, positioned as spectators of the spectacles of media culture. Moreover, while the characters in *Godot* were waiting for something, however absurd, to happen, Beavis and Butt-Head have no expectations, no purposes, and no clue. Thus, while Beckett's characters were searching for meaning and value, Beavis and Butt-Head revel in the absurd, attacking everything but the few fragments of media culture which they find to be cool. They have contempt for everyone, even for each other, as displayed in various episodes when they blithely leave one another to die by choking, drowning, shark attack, or some other painful potential death.[4]

Completely bereft of respect for others and life in general, Beavis and Butt-Head evince the kind of *Schadenfreude* diagnosed by Nietzsche, which delights in the suffering of others. In "Couchfishing," they laugh as they drag an old lady from her walker with a fishhook, using an empty prune box for bait. "The Crush" finds them mooning a TV audience at the site of a collapsed Superdome where thousands have been injured and killed. In "Way Down Mexican Way," they conclude that the torture of people by the Mexican police is "cool." In "Skeetshooting," they knock down a jet plane with a bullet and laugh at the crash victims as they peer through the window, farting and then walking away despite a flight attendant's frantic pleas for help (as President Clinton states on the TV news later that night: "it is a sad commentary on the youth of America when the preoccupation with flatulence takes precedence over human life"). While watching stage divers in a punk video, they are having great fun as they remark:

> *Butt-Head:* That would be cool if that guy jumped offstage and nobody caught him, huh huh, and he smacked his head on the floor.
>
> *Beavis:* Yeah, and then his head would crack open, heh heh, and there would be like blood everywhere, and brains. That would be cool.
>
> *Butt-Head:* Yeah. What if somebody started slipping around on his brains and blood?
>
> *Beavis:* And then he cracked his head open and then was slipping around on blood, heh heh.
>
> *Butt-Head*: Yeah, cracking their heads open. That's like the movies where that guy was riding around in that car and like his head exploded.
>
> *Beavis*: But it was all out of focus – that sucks.

It is likely that for Beavis and Butt-Head, the suffering and pain of others has no meaning or significance because their main contact with it is in the hyperreal world of media culture, as mere images and simulations. Even if TV violence does not directly produce parallel behavior, it can inure its audience to the effects of violence, dulling sensibilities through the constant onslaught of blood and gore. Life is rendered simply devoid of value, as impoverished social conditions breed apathy, anger, and violence. Their asocial behavior makes Bart Simpson look like a well adjusted student, and while Bart has an intelligent sibling, a caring family, and better life opportunities, Beavis and Butt-Head seem to have no family, living alone day and night in a shabby house and being enculturated solely by television and media culture. The world of Ward Cleaver and Ozzie and Harriet is nowhere in sight. There are frequent references to their mothers, especially Beavis's mother, who is constantly deni-grated as a "slut." Seeing the janitor in Nirvana's video "Smells like Teen Spirit," Butt-Head identifies him as "Beavis's dad." In another episode, we learn that Beavis's dad was in the navy because "he's a semen." As for his own father, Butt-Head is not certain who he is. In "Scientific Stuff," the following exchange occurs with schoolmate Daria:

Butt-Head: Everything I know I learned from my dad.
Beavis: Yeah, me too.
Daria: Really, you both have the same dad?
Butt-Head: I don't know, it's possible.

Signifying their unknown ancestry, neither character has a full name. Thus the series presents a world without parents, contem-porary youth who are home alone, fending for themselves, with mass media their prime source of socialization.[5]

Such images reveal the breakdown of the family in contem-porary society and the systematic deprivation of working-class youth. Beavis and Butt-Head are, of course, young white boys, so the oppressiveness of their situation is nothing in comparison to the racism and violence on display in films like *Boys N the Hood* or *Menace II Society*. Yet the series underscores the terror of the *suburbs*, the oppressively boring and normalizing atmos-phere of white, middle-class suburbia and its shabbier underclass counterparts. While gang warfare and drugs did not seriously disrupt Beavis and Butt-Head's sanitized white enclave of high schools, shopping malls, and fast food restaurants (as it certainly has in many places), the ethos of violence that permeates media culture and everyday life has, driving them into frenzied fits of vandalism and destruction, such that they, Beavis in particular, enjoy an explosive libidinal release.[6]

Most critics of the show who claim that it glorifies stupidity and underachievement miss the fact that it is *satire* (something its young viewers seem to understand more readily), or in our terms, a form of postmodern parody, and that it is criticizing, not advocating, the dumbing of American youth. But, as in Hutcheon's conception of postmodernism, the series is complicit with what it parodies and may well increase stupidity, adolescent behavior and attitudes, sexism, and violence. Such satire is double-edged and can either induce critical thought concerning dominant forms of social behavior, or reproduce objectionable values and action.

Yet the series does provide a powerful critique of numerous contemporary institutions, from media culture and the school system to organized religion and the family, while ridiculing a wide array of generational influences, including an older disciplinary authority from the Time of Fathers, the 1960s counterculture, New Age philosophies, and political correctness. Thus, the buffoonery of Beavis and Butt-Head has a sharp subversive edge in their rejection of all authority figures. They make fun of the authoritarian representatives of these institutions and attack the hypocrisy of Rush Limbaugh and the Right, a Christian businessman's association, and various capitalist lackeys who come into their classroom to teach them manners or salesmanship. They identify far more readily with dangerous criminals, as shown when Principal McVicker's ploy backfires in "Scared Straight." Rather than being scared into normality by tough-talking prisoners, they bond with them over a mutual love for Iron Maiden, and sneak back into the jail, declaring "prison's cool." Similarly, in "Most Wanted," they quickly form a bond with an escaped serial killer.

Although *Beavis and Butt-Head* provides examples of the creation of an oppositional identity to mainstream models, their own social defiance is extremely limited and highly problematical. Their rebelliousness is aptly symbolized when they cut an anarchy sign into their high school lawn with a rider mower. But Beavis and Butt-Head are rebels without a cause or a clue, attacking a conformist culture they don't understand. Of course, "anarchy" for them does not have the positive, constructive meaning it had for revolutionaries like Kropotkin and Bakunin, but rather conforms to the predominant misconception of the term as violence and destruction for their own sake. On the rare occasions they leave Butt-Head's couch to attend school, to work at Burger World, to try to score chicks at the mall or Qwik-Mart, or to pursue whatever adventure possible in their staid Southwestern suburb, they often engage in destructive and even criminal behavior.[7] Thus, Judas Priest's song "Breaking the Law!" or their own "Let's go break something!" is their battle cry. The bourgeois sanctity of private property has no halo for Beavis and Butt-Head; for them, only nachos and heavy metal are sacred.

In a sense, the series enacts youth and class revenge against older, middle-class and conservative adults, who appear as oppressive authority figures. Their neighbor Tom Anderson – depicted as a conservative Second World War and Korean War veteran – is a special butt of their escapades, as they destroy his property and torment him in endless ways. They cut down trees in his yard with a chain saw which causes the tree to demolish his house, assorted fences, power lines, and cars. They put his dog in a Laundromat washing machine to clean it; they steal his credit card to buy animals at the mall; they lob mud baseballs into his yard, one of which hits his barbeque and knocks him down; they destroy a swimming pool that they are supposed to help him build; they appropriate his rented steamroller and destroy his new driveway – and otherwise torment him.

In other escapades, they blow up an army recruiting station with a grenade, as the officer attempts to recruit them; they steal the cart of a wealthy man, Billy Bob, who has a heart attack when he sees them riding off in his vehicle; and they love to put worms, rats, and other animals in the fast food that they are shown giving to obnoxious white male customers at Burger World. The dynamic duo also harass and ridicule their liberal hippie teacher, Mr Van Driessen, who tries to imbue them with the values of the 1960s, updated for a New Age. By ridiculing Van Driessen, the show satirizes not only the establishment but the alternatives presented to it by the cultures of the 1960s, and hence underscores conflicts between boomers and busters. Where some 1960s youth dropped out of mainstream culture to drop into a new world of peace and love, or pursued activist projects to transform society, Beavis and Butt-Head flout these values as wimpy, underscoring the huge gulf between two generations of youth and the alienation today's youth frequently feel toward their 1960s generation parents, many formerly hippie but now mainstream. Not surprisingly, Van Driessen's attempts to bring Beavis and Butt-Head into the New Age, where they can access their "inner child" and feminine side, is an abject failure, prompting only masturbatory references and sexist jokes. They destroy his irreplaceable eight-track music collection when he offers to let them clean his house to learn the value of work and money. When he takes them camping to get in touch with their feelings and nature, they fight and torment animals. They totally disrupt his attempt to score with a date as they peer into his windows, barge their way into his house, and make lewd and insulting remarks, driving the woman away. Like many youth of their generation, they care little for values and a meaningful philosophy of life – money and excitement matter far more.[8]

Interestingly, Beavis and Butt-Head reject all authority except white male bands. The less-than-dynamic duo idolize white male rock singers, their only heroes and role models, as they proclaim again and again when they shout "Metallica [or whoever] *rules!*" The phrase "rules" accurately portrays their subordination to their white male idols which literally energize them into dancing, playing air guitar, or jumping about. The series thus points to the bizarre phenomenon of rock culture providing the male icons and deities of the 1990s, who provide royalty and authority for postmodern youth. Curiously, the white male rock stars for the most part reinforce dominant values, since – despite their long hair and grungy appearance – they embody the ultimate in money, possessions, and "babes," usually models, movie stars, or beautiful groupies.

Thus it is that male rock stars are the role models and the purveyors of capitalist values for the current generation. Consequently, despite their anarchistic veneer, Beavis and Butt-Head are ultimately conformists, adapting to the values of their white male superstars and the ethos of media culture. Devoid of critical thinking skills, susceptible to the ruses of the image industries, they are also ready victims of the propaganda of the Right. In one show, they express enthusiastic approval of Rush Limbaugh's advocacy for the death penalty. They phone Limbaugh, who praises them as model youth and invites them on to the show – which they quickly disrupt with profanity and mooning. They are easily mobilized into almost any position, depending on the video and their mood; not only are fire and chicks cool, but also torture and death. They can adopt any contradictory position, satirizing religion, for instance, while also claiming that "Christ is cool." Were it not for their pathological passivity, and disrespect for all authorities, they would be precisely the type of subjects who are easily mobilized into a neo-Nazi movement, especially with their love of violence. All they need to be taught is hatred for minorities and reverence for leaders.

Contrary to popular opinion and the show's opening disclaimer that it's only a cartoon, Beavis and Butt-Head are not "just cartoon characters;" every educator, from kindergarten to the universities, has them in his or her classroom. Teachers know that reading skills, historical knowledge, and the ability to reason and write are *in decline*, that the rudiments of spelling and grammar which were once learned for life in second or third grade are now visibly lacking in college students, that few people adopt regular reading habits, that today's youth are in fact as immersed in media culture as Beavis and Butt-Head, and that *many people talk just like them!*[9] This would be the case even if the series never existed, for *Beavis and Butt-Head* is an effect, not the cause, of contemporary youth culture, the result of its creator's fine-tuned ear to the Zeitgeist and the discursive style of youth.[10]

Media Literacy and the End of the Enlightenment

Beavis and Butt-Head underlines the catastrophic effects on the current generation of youth raised primarily on media culture, showing how they have become "dumbed down" by image machines. This generation was likely conceived in the sights and sounds of media culture, weaned on it, and socialized by the glass teat of television used as pacifier, baby sitter, and educator by a generation of parents for whom media culture, especially television, was a natural background and constitutive part of everyday life. The digital skills of this generation most likely have been formed more through video games than sports or musical training, and their most developed muscles may be the thumbs that manipulate the remote control.[11]

Beavis and Butt-Head depicts the dissolution of the rational subject, the Recline of Western Civilization, and perhaps the End of the Enlightenment in today's media culture. We move from Kant's modern slogan "Dare to know!" to Beavis and Butt-Head's postmodern reactive cry "Don't care to know!" as they attack and ridicule the norms of reason, education, and autonomy. When threatened with suspension from school, they rejoice, with Butt-Head adding that: "I wish like in school they would teach something practical like heavy metal." The Enlightenment's great *Encyclopedia* project, where Diderot and other luminaries systematized the new forms of learning to promulgate reason, has collapsed into Beavis and Butt-Head's *Ensucklopedia*,[12] whose A to Z purview of the postmodern adolescent mind features entries on "Anatomy" (including operations of the butt and nads), "Dudes and Chicks" (with tips on scoring from the unscored), "Foreinurz" ("dudes" of various nationalities), "Literater" (including analysis of *Moby Dick*, uh, huh huh huh), and "Toilet" (inimitable research into the mechanics and etiquette of the john).

Their assault on the intellect, their *misology* (hatred of reason), is so unremitting that they even express revulsion toward words ("I hate words." "Yeah, words suck"), videos with words ("If I wanted to read I'd go to school!"), aesthetics and symbolic complexity ("Art sucks"), and even narrative ("Stories suck"). Indeed, like so many youth and even adults in our own world, they are illiterate, a problem that frequently lands them in trouble when they misread various signs. The rational, linear modes of thought imparted to the citizens of the Enlightenment and Gutenberg Galaxy is abandoned by the postmodern vidiots who seek scopophilic escape from everyday life, finding visceral satisfaction through subliminal immersion in the images and sounds of corporate media. Bereft of the skills of critical and analytical thinking and devoid of a moral sensibility, Beavis and Butt-Head react to their environment in a mindless fashion and appear to lack all cognitive and communicative skills – victims of undereducation and excessive media socialization.

Like many members of the media society, Beavis and Butt-Head suffer from *TV addiction*, going through image withdrawal when placed in a room without a TV or when TV sucks so bad they have to turn it off.[13] Their "ideas" for class-assigned scientific experiments, for example, include lighting farts and figuring out the mystery of morning wood. Frequently, when thought balloons rise above their head, they are empty or lit by very dim bulbs. With their TV predecessor Archie Bunker, they are most inventive in their malapropisms ("trick pornography," "decrapitated," etc.). In an exchange with their dorky neighbor Stewart, we discover how deep their ignorance runs:

> *Butt-Head:* Hey, isn't there like a word for it when something happens and you don't expect it?
> *Stewart:* You mean ironic?
> *Butt-Head:* No way, peckerbutt, it's like an English word.
> *Beavis:* Uh, . . . cool?
> *Butt-Head:* Yeah, that's it!

Their ignorance extends to other cultures and geography. In "No Laughing," their Spanish teacher is incensed because the only Spanish they know they learned from Taco Bell (which Beavis even confuses with Italian food names). Throughout the series, they make numerous stereotyped insults toward Mexicans, Indians, Asians, and others, evincing a multicultural illiteracy uncommon to many of their peers. Their geographical ignorance is aptly displayed in the following exchange as they try to figure out the origins of Black Sabbath:

> *Beavis:* Hey Butt-Head, are these guys from Seattle?
> *Butt-Head:* No, assmunch, they're American!
> *Beavis:* Oh, yeah.

In another episode, Beavis asks Butt-Head where Seattle is, and Butt-Head responds: "You don't know! It's this place where like stuff is really cool." Mentally challenged though they are, Beavis and Butt-Head are very shrewd in their own element, as they play the role of media critic and construct their Manichean world of cool versus sucks. They rarely are viscerally attached to and numbed by TV; rather, they engage in an ongoing critical and deconstructive analysis that exposes pretentiousness, mocks advertisements, and even decodes the pornographic content of many music videos ("Dial 1-900," they say, providing an ironic voiceover for a particularly suggestive female look). While they seem to instantly recognize a really cool video, many times they identify elements that *should* make a video cool, but don't, for even fire and explosions cannot redeem a sucky band like Krokus. Fire, "chicks" (their term), and other images may be necessary criteria of a cool video, but they are not sufficient. Sometimes Beavis will ask Butt-Head: "Does this video suck?" Butt-Head will then identify some cool things about it, and together they will deliver the final verdict, which is invariably negative if they have to think about it. One might even say they watch TV primarily to spoof it. Ultimately, they reinforce what everyone already knows: TV sucks. Despite the plethora of available channels, TV is rarely worth watching and the promises of the technology remain aborted because of corporate control and the profit imperative.

While it is possible that *Beavis and Butt-Head* reinforces TV addiction, their critiques can also distance their audience from music video and media culture and inspire critical judgments on its products. Kids today can learn much more about media criticism from Beavis and Butt-Head than from most of their teachers. Many of the videos that they attack are stupid and pretentious, and in general it is good to cultivate a critical attitude toward cultural forms and to promote cultural criticism – an attitude that can indeed be applied to much of what appears on *Beavis and Butt-Head*. They have their moments as media critics, mooning *The Brady Bunch* and making sarcastic remarks about CBS's insufferable *60 Minutes* commentator Andy Rooney. Such critique distances its audience from music video and media culture and calls for making critical judgments on its products. Obviously, Beavis and Butt-Head are more socialized by the media than they would admit, and their critical consciousness is highly limited, applying mainly to the products of media culture, rather than to the world that produces them. Their criticism is largely aesthetic, never ethical, commenting only on the look or sound of a video. While one might often agree with their taste (they shrewdly detect all musical posers), many of their judgments are highly questionable, when either praising mindless violence and sexism, or condemning more off-beat and challenging videos.

Obviously, Beavis and Butt-Head show the need for more print literacy, but their sometimes uncritical or illiterate response to media culture discloses the need for training in media literacy and visual culture as well. In fact, given that youth culture today is primarily mediated, like everyone and everything else, by media culture, a key aspect of education today should be developing critical media literacy, the ability to read, decode, and criticize the images and spectacles of media culture – indeed, we believe that all sectors of contemporary education from early schooling through University training need to develop a media pedagogy aiming at critical media literacy.[14] Neil Postman, for example, argues that around the turn of the century, Western society left print culture behind and entered a new "Age of Entertainment" centered on a culture of the image. Accompanying the new image culture, Postman argues, is a dramatic decline in literacy, a loss of the skills associated with rational argumentation, linear and analytical thought, and critical and public discourse. In particular, this sea change in literacy and consciousness has led to a degeneration of public discourse and a loss of rationality in public life.[15] Postman attributes this "great transformation" primarily to television, which indeed is the most prolific image machine in history, generating between 15 and 30 images per minute and thus millions of images per day, reducing news, information, entertainment, and even politics to "sound bites," fragments of images and discourse.

Other image machines generate a panoply of print, sound, environmental, and diverse aesthetic artifacts within which we wander, trying to make our way through this forest of symbols. And so we need to begin learning how to read these images, these fascinating and seductive cultural forms whose massive impact on our lives we have only begun to understand. Surely, education should attend to the new image culture and teach how to read images and narratives as part of media literacy. Such an effort would be part of a new critical pedagogy that attempts to uncover the roots of our experience, knowledge, and behavior and that aims at liberation from domination of oppressive images, discourses, and narratives. A critical media literacy would also be oriented toward a cultural politics aiming at the creation of plural, diverse, and challenging cultures and more empowered individuals, able to both critically analyze and produce the forms of their culture and society.

Reading images critically involves learning how to appreciate, decode, and interpret images, concerning both *how* they are constructed and operate in our lives and *what* they communicate in concrete situations. Certain postmodern theory (e.g. Foucault, Derrida, Deleuze/Guattari, Lyotard, and Denzin) helps to make us aware of how our experience and selves are socially constructed, how they are overdetermined by a diverse range of images, discourses, codes, narratives, and the like.[16] This strand of postmodern theory, along with postmodern parodic art, excels in deconstructing the obvious, taking the familiar and making it strange and unfamiliar, and thus in making us attend to how our language, experience, and behavior are socially constructed.

Yet a postmodern pedagogy should demonstrate how our culture is constrained, overdetermined, and conventional, but also subject to change and transformation. In developing a postmodern pedagogy, we reject an anti-hermeneutical thrust of one strand of postmodern thought that is overly restrictive concerning what it wants critical theory to do, attacking interpretation and limiting postmodern analysis to focus on formal analysis of texts.[17] This approach limits theoretically correct inquiry to either descriptive analysis of how culture works, of formal analysis of how signification and representation function, eschewing hermeneutical interpretation of ideological content for a more formal and structuralist type of analysis. We also reject the type of postmodern analysis in which the audience alone creates meaning, refusing analysis of texts for focus on how audiences use and appropriate the material of media culture.

For us, however, a postmodern pedagogy focuses on analysis of form and content, text and content, production and reception of cultural artifacts.[18] It aims at developing a media literacy that can discern meanings and ideologies in the images, discourses, and narratives of media texts and spectacles. Such a pedagogy engages form and content, attends to surface images and narrative depth, attempting to grasp the fascination and seduction of media culture, of how it produces pleasure and mobilizes desire, but also attempting to interpret what the texts tell us about contemporary society and what messages and effects they disseminate. Although the series *Beavis and Butt-Head*, for example, may not make explicit larger sociological statements, it does show how their characters get most of their ideas and images concerning life from the media and how their entire view of history and the world is largely derived from media culture.

The figures of history are collapsed for Beavis and Butt-Head into media culture and provide material for salacious jokes, which require detailed knowledge of media culture:

Butt-Head: What happened when Napoleon went to Mount Olive?
Beavis: I don't know. What?
Butt-Head: Pop-Eye got pissed.

As true for so many people, and as represented on TV retrospectives, history is but a collage of different moments and figures from popular culture. The 1960s for Beavis and Butt-Head is the time of hippies, Woodstock and rock "n" roll; Vietnam is ancient history, collapsed into other American wars. Even the 1950s is nothing but a series of mangled media cliches. On Nelson, the twins of 1950s teen idol Ricky Nelson, Butt-Head remarks that "These chicks look like guys." Beavis responds: "I heard that these chicks' grandpa was Ozzy Osbourne." And Butt-Head rejoins; "No way. They're Elvis's kids."

Thus, for a diagnostic critique, *Beavis and Butt-Head* depicts the problematical effects of media culture and contemporary youth and the need for critical media literacy. The world of Beavis and Butt-Head is indeed a complex intertextual web of cross-referencing from different quarters of advertising and the mass media world. Every media character reminds them of another, whether it be Paul Schaffer, Weird Al Yankovich, Ted Danson, or Sean Penn. Frank Sinatra, for example, is thought to be "that dude from the Eagles," or maybe Keith Richards. To get their jokes and puns, one has to have a certain knowledge of media culture oneself, such as when Butt-Head muses about starting a band named "Butt-Head Butt-Head" (during an unidentified Duran Duran video), or when he jests: "Hey Beavis, you know what's in Olivia Newton's John? Gomer's pile." In their hyperreal orbit, the difference between fact and fiction is constantly confused. Rather than identifying Joe Cocker as the original singer whom John Belushi parodies, they see him as the imitation of "that dude from Saturday Night Live," thus calling attention to the implosion between "reality" and the hyperreal of media culture in this phase of the postmodern adventure.

Thus, we believe that *Beavis and Butt-Head* provides material for what we call a diagnostic critique of contemporary youth.

The series – along with other key artifacts of youth culture – presents insights into the situation, problems, and outlook of contemporary youth and thus is a worthy topic for a cultural hermeneutics, with the intent of developing a critical theory of society. Media culture provides privileged access to the situation of contemporary youth because it is a big business that must resonate to its audiences' experiences if its wares are to be successful. Thus, the creators of media culture are often finely attuned to the hopes, fears, fantasies, and conflicts of their audiences, which are articulated in their products, making media culture an important terrain to gain insights into the dynamics of the contemporary. Consequently, we are concerned both to use media culture to provide insights into contemporary society and to use cultural theory to help illuminate and dissect media culture. Far from being merely an academic affair, cultural studies is thus part of an effort to produce a more democratic and enlightened society.

"Futures Suck"

> We are raising a generation without a future. (Bill Clinton)

> No Future, No Future, No Futuurrre, for YOU!! (The Sex Pistols)

In our reading, *Beavis and Butt-Head* puts on display youth lost in a media world, living in hyperreality, and like the punk rockers before them, with no future. While their behavior is undeniably juvenile, offensive, sexist, homophobic, and downright politically incorrect, it allows diagnosis of the underclass and downwardly mobile youth who have nothing to do but to destroy things and engage in asocial behavior. From this perspective, *Beavis and Butt-Head* is an example of media culture as popular revenge: Beavis and Butt-Head avenge youth and the downwardly mobile against those oppressive authority figures they confront daily. The series points to the existence of a large teenage underclass that is undereducated; that comes from broken homes; that is angry, resentful, and potentially violent; and that has nothing to do but to engage in social mayhem.

In fact, the young underclass Beavises and Butt-Heads of society have nothing to look forward to in life save promotion to manager at Burger World or perhaps a military career.

The episode "Army Recruitment" satirizes how the military try to exploit hopeless youth. Beavis and Butt-Head declare to Sgt Dick Leaky that headbanging is their purpose in life. Recognizing a good recruiting challenge, he lures them into his office on the promise they can see his guns, and he pulls out the video marked "No Future." Showing a beer-drinking soldier bragging about his kills, rock music blaring in the background, the promo states: "Today's Army rocks! We're looking for a few good headbangers."

Occasionally, Beavis and Butt-Head break out in despair, recognizing their hopelessness and that they will indeed not score or have any kind of future at all. In "Madame Blavatsky," they are shown walking through a slum and they fantasize about having a car and getting chicks; they see a fortune teller sign and after painfully decoding the language, Butt-Head wants to have his fortune told:

Beavis: What's that?
Butt-Head: You know, your future.
Beavis: What's that?
Butt-Head: I don't know.

In "At the Sideshow," Butt-Head asks: "Hey Beavis, is this supposed to be the future?" and Beavis responds "Futures suck!" Butt-Head realistically concludes: "I may be pretty cool, but I can't change the future." In one poignant episode, they are watching Nirvana's video of "Heart-shaped Box," and Beavis says that he'd like to have "a cool room like in the video," so he could "get chicks." Butt-Head responds, in the most devastating terms possible: "You're never going to fix up your room like that. You're just going to hang around this dump spanking your monkey and you're never going to score." Indeed, in one of the most hilarious scenes of the series, a flash-forward into the "future" of Beavis and Butt-Head shows them to be old, bald, fat, and bespectacled, still sitting together in front of the TV, the only difference being they are now drinking beer instead of soda pop, smoking cigarettes instead of eating nachos. The highlight of their life was that they once saw "naked people" after sneaking into a nudist camp.

"Having a future" means having potential opportunities to better oneself and having the abilities to actually shape one's life, to make one's future. But this is exactly what Beavis and Butt-Head and their counterparts in real life seem to lack. Various episodes suggest that the future of youth in general is hopeless. In "Bedpans and Broomsticks," they are watching a commercial about the killing of sperm (the word does not pass unnoticed) whales. After the announcer says, "The only hope for the future of the sperm whale is youth who will grow up more caring and understanding of animals," Beavis and Butt-Head exchange puzzled looks and Butt-Head asks: "Did you fart?" In another episode, President Clinton appeals to the youth of America to step forward and face the leadership challenges of tomorrow, prompting blank stares and a loud burp from Butt-Head.

Yet the two ultimate losers have been shown to be victims as much as victimizers. The 1993–4 seasons on the whole portrayed Beavis and Butt-Head as highly destructive and anarchic, genuine threats to existing law and order. Episodes focused on their aggressive acts against conservative school authorities and their neighbor Mr Anderson.

Many post-1994 episodes, by contrast, depict them as victims of their undereducation and underclass situation, and these episodes can almost be read as cautionary morality tales showing the harmful effects of ignorance. In 1994 episodes such as "The Great Cornholio," Beavis is the victim of excessive sugar consumption; in "Pipe of Doom," first Butt-Head and then Beavis get stuck in a construction site pipe; in "Patients, Patients," a dentist messes up work on Butt-Head's braces and an eye-doctor misprescribes glasses for Beavis, harming his eyesight; in a health club ("Pumping Iron"), they are attacked by both weight-lifters and the equipment which they don't know how to use; and in "Liar! Liar!" they are victims of job discrimination and lie detector tests. Moreover, they are constantly victimized by women: in "Date Bait," they buy women movie tickets, give them money, and wait outside the back door of the theater for the women to come and let them in; when the women leave the theater with tough dudes they picked up inside, Beavis and Butt-Head are brushed aside and then attacked by a macho theater attendant when they try to sneak in the back door. In one episode, they leave a pay phone-sex line on for hours. In "Beard Boys," they cut off their hair and paste it on their faces to try to attract girls, after seeing a TV scene where a bearded dude was popular with women. In a dating service episode they actually connect with real women ready to date them, but are so stupid that they botch things up, while in many episodes, they meet women only to get rejected.

The victimization of Beavis and Butt-Head shows that they are not totally to blame for their idiocy, being products of consumer society, media culture, a recessionary economy, and a poor public school system. Their destructive behavior can be seen in part as an expression of their hopelessness and alienation, and shows the dead-end prospects for many contemporary youth.[19] In a sense, *Beavis and Butt-Head* is an example of what has been called "loser television," surely a new phenomenon in television history.[20] Previous television series tended to depict wealthy, or secure middle-class, individuals and families, often with highly glamorous lives. It was believed that advertisers preferred affluent environments to sell their products, and so the working class and underclass were excluded from network television for decades. Indeed, during the Reaganite 1980s, programs like *Dallas*, *Dynasty*, and *Life Styles of the Rich and Famous* celebrated wealth and affluence. This dream has been punctured by the reality of everyday life in a downsliding economy, and so a large television audience is attracted to programs that articulate their own frustration and anger in experiencing downward mobility and a sense of no future: hence, the popularity of new "loser television," including *The Simpsons*, *Roseanne*, and *Beavis and Butt-Head*.

Consequently, the series is a social hieroglyphic which allows us to decode the attitudes, behavior, and situation of large segments of youth in contemporary US society. For a diagnostic critique, then, it is wrong to simply excuse the antics of Beavis and Butt-Head as typical behavior of the young. Likewise, it is not enough simply to condemn them as pathological.[21] Rather, one must probe to the *real* problem, which is an economic and educational system that provides no meaningful life opportunities. The Beavises and Butt-Heads of the world are "dumbed down" and kept down by inadequate education, by schooling which "teaches" them irrelevant "facts" and subject matter in authoritarians ways, that does not really empower students to be the subjects of their own life, and that does not impart the critical skills needed in an emerging high-tech economy and society.

Contemporary youth are locked into a confined existence,

subject to the whim and often irrational authority of their parents, teachers, bosses, and the older generation, forced to submit to stupid rules and regulations, and unable to engage in self-valorizing and empowering activities. Thus, the metal culture in which Beavis and Butt-Head immerse themselves should not simply be reviled, but needs to be seen as a way for those caught up in dead-end lives to blot everything out, to escape in a world of pure noise and aggression, and in turn to sublimate their rage and frustrations through headbanging and air guitar.[22] When Beavis and Butt-Head fantasize, playing the game of "what if" (they really had a life), they invariably see themselves as rich or as rock stars in front of a huge audience with adoring "chicks." In their utopian fantasy, someday they will "roam the earth among all that is cool," living, in other words, in Seattle, immersed in a postmodern culture of sex, money, spectacle, and fun, amusing themselves to death.

But the reality is that the young victims of American society are being denied a viable future. The Hudson Institute report *Workforce 2,000* predicts that the current average skill level of 21- to 25-year-olds is 40 percent lower than the level required of the new workers needed by that year, and without the skills necessary to function in the emerging information and high-tech society, youth are condemned to menial jobs and a life of insecurity. By eviserating the economic infrastructure to the point that basic life services – from food and shelter to medical treatment and psychological counseling – are not provided, a situation the US Congress of the mid-1990s is exacerbating through its reduction of social programs (as its members mourn the loss of family values), the society as a whole will pay the much higher future costs of dealing with their hopelessness, illnesses, and rage. Other statistics indicate that while violent crime rates are going down across the nation (and even these are disputed), juvenile crime rates are going up and youth are expressing the extent to which their lives and school are being disrupted by violence in the streets and schools.[23] While some large city mayors like New York's Rudolph Giuliani exult over the temporary drop in the homicide rate (in part because of increased police presence and "zero tolerance" neighborhood programs), criminologists are warning of far worse cycles of violence in the coming decades, with "the coming of the super-predators," in James Alan Fox's phrase. These are teenage boys who "kill and maim on impulse, without any intelligible motive" except for their blind rage, in possession of deadly weapons but bereft of any respect for life.[24]

Moreover, there have been countless episodes of "home invasion," in which violent youth indiscriminately break into homes and commit violent acts, choosing to confront crime victims in their homes rather then wait for an empty house. For example, on January 19, 1996, two youth burst into a modest lower-middle-class apartment with guns, tied up the four men inside, raped the four women, and robbed the apartment (KABC TV, Los Angeles). Two days later, several youth burst into the Beverly Hills residence of actor Harry Dean Stanton, tied him up, beat him, and robbed his house and car (*Los Angeles Times*, January 22, 1996, B1). Such actions obviously exhibit pleasure in violence and suggest an increasingly violent future. Indeed, the following week in Los Angeles there were three triple murders and CNN interviews with LA inhabitants indicated that they sew nothing unusual in the situation, that it was simply part of life in the big city (CNN Primetime, January 29, 1996).

More and more, the nightly news presents the appalling spectacle of kids killing kids (or adults), throwing the legal system into confusion. There is obvious cause for alarm in such a deteriorating social fabric where adolescents will kill each other over a pair of tennis shoes, where the teen population is expected to grow substantially over the next decade, where hundreds of thousands of kids are being pushed into criminality because of poverty and neglect, and where there may be a future "bloodbath of teenaged violence that will make 1995 look like the good old days."[25] While such predictions may be apocalyptic hyperbole, they are not without plausibility. At any rate, it should be clear that the reality of today's youth is not only the hyperreality of watching TV or surfing the Net, but also difficult lives filled with violence, poverty, homelessness, systemic neglect, drug and alcohol abuse, high pregnancy rates, and poor education. They are not merely absorbing images, playing video games, and hanging out at the malls; great numbers of them are suffering, living in fear of various health and safety threats, and under the psychological duress of "lockdown" from concerned parents aware of the dangers of the streets ("Living in lockdown," *Newsweek*, January 23, 1996, 56–7).

The current political response to escalating teen violence is reinforcing lock-ins through curfews, increased police on the street, and increased penalties and incarceration for juveniles. Already California has a startling number of young people in prison and Texas Governor George Bush, Jr (popularly known as "shrub") has been proposing locking even more young people up to prevent crime.[26] But prisons notoriously breed a culture of crime, and with worsening social conditions one can logically except crime to escalate. How much worse will the situation of youth be, how much more violent will they become, knowing that their overall situation may be far more desperate and that violence is learned and perpetuated from generation to generation? Or will the next generation learn quite different lessons and turn the situation around?

Thus, we see that *Beavis and Butt-Head* provides often chilling glimpses into the lives of completely disaffected and alienated youth, unable to participate in the high-tech economy on the horizon. To be sure, the series is only a cartoon, but we believe that it is an especially illuminating one, which provides cautionary warnings that a large sector of youth is falling through the cracks and is not properly prepared for the challenges of the future. The show is thus not merely an often amusing satire of media culture and conservative social institutions, but a prescient warning that if today's youth do not develop communicative, technological, and analytical skills they will not have a future at all. Yet we wonder if *Beavis and Butt-Head* itself serves to promote adolescent escapism and highly problematic behavior. In any case, youth today face the decision as to whether they themselves wish to be Beavises and Butt-Heads or empowered subjects who create their own culture and future.

Notes and References

1   On the concept of diagnostic critique, see D. Kellner and M. Ryan (1988) *Camera Politica*. Bloomington: University of Indiana Press; D. Kellner (1995) *Media Culture*. New York: Routledge. As we use the concept here, it is part of a postmodern pedagogy that uses media culture to provide insights into contemporary social reality and that reads culture contextually, deploying the concepts of cultural studies to decode, analyze, and criticize the products and effects of contemporary culture. Such a project aims at developing a critical media literacy that cultivates the skills necessary to empower individuals over their culture, a theme we develop in detail

throughout this study, which is part of a forthcoming Guilford Press book, *The Postmodern Adventure*.

2   *Beavis and Butt-Head* was based on an animated short by Mike Judge, in which the two characters play "frog baseball," shown at the Sick and Twisted Animation festival, and was taken up by MTV's animated series *Liquid Television*. The series *Beavis and Butt-Head* premiered in March 1993, but because there were only four episodes, the show went on hiatus, returning on May 17 after Judge and his team of creative assistants put together 32 new episodes (*The San Francisco Chronicle*, June 29, 1993). The series tripled MTV's ratings and MTV ordered 130 more episodes for 1994 (*The New York Times*, October 17, 1993). Production continued until 1997, when Beavis and Butt-Head were killed off and sent to eternal rerun heaver. The production of the series replicates postmodern globalization and the "flexible accumulation" of post-Fordism, in which pieces of the program are assembled all over the world. There are MTV writing and production teams working on the series in New York and California, much of the animation for the program is done in Korea, and show creator Mike Judge, who writes some of the stories, does most of the voices, and supervises the program, lives in Austin, Texas, while the show is ultimately assembled and distributed from the MTV studios in New York. The series in turn is shown not only on the US MTV channel, but also its Latin American, European, and Asian ones: a global popular series for the global village.

3   As a response, MTV moved the series to a later evening timeslot, edited out all references to fire and violence toward animals, and forbid further use of the word "fire" and excessive violence. See the discussion in Kellner, op. cit., n. 1.

4   Occasionally, Judge will show the sentimental side of Beavis and Butt-Head as they bond with one another, such as the poignant time in "Sperm Bank" when they walk off into the sunset, stacks of freshly scored porno mags in hand, fondly trading insults such as "monkeyspank" and "buttmunch." This rarely expressed solidarity of the two stooges underlies their chronic verbal and physical fights, suggesting a vague homoerotic bond. The homoeroticism of both is underscored in their relation with Todd, the tough-guy drop-out of Highland High, particularly in the episode where red hearts flutter out of their chests as Todd burns rubber pulling out of Quik-Mart. The fact that they seek to join Todd's gang also suggests that they desire greater adventures than watching TV and wish to belong to a group, mainly to be cool and score chicks.

5   Their family genealogy in a book on the series puts a question mark in the place of both of their fathers (S. Johnson and C. Marcil (1993) *Beavis and Butt-Head: This Book Sucks*. New York: Pocket Books). It is also unclear exactly whose house they live in, or are shown watching TV in, and whether they do or do not live together. One episode suggests that they are in Butt-Head's house and that his mother is always out with her boyfriend, but other episodes show two beds together in what appears to be their highly messy bedroom, and their parents have never been shown.

6   There is some evidence that Beavis and Butt-Head's suburb does suffer from these problems. In the 1994 episode "Incognito," they accidently graze their Asian classmate Earl in the head with a thrown fork. Angrily, he responds by displaying his gun. Soon afterwards, a gunshot is fired through the window by one of Earl's rival gangs, and he fires back. Calmly, Mr Van Driessen asks for Earl's gun, and places it in his desk drawer, alongside other guns, TNT, and hand grenades. While sex and rock and roll are prominent in the world of *Beavis and Butt-Head*, curiously, drugs are missing, as though a subject too taboo for the MTV no guns/no drugs/safe sex/stop the violence message – though they do sometimes sniff glue and other substances to get a buzz. One would also expect the likes of Beavis and Butt-Head to be racist and – more than they are portrayed to be – homophobic, but they are respectful of black music artists, much more so than the white male videos that they so savagely critique. And while they make frequent homophobic remarks, one could easily read their relationship to each other as repressed homosexuality ("Hey Beavis. Pull my finger").

7   Their town is never identified but it appears to be the sort of nondescript Southwestern environment where Judge grew up. In "Tornado" they ride into a trailer park whose sign reads "almost Florida," but this is probably a joke. In an America Online interview, when asked where the series takes place, Judge answered in West Texas or Eastern New Mexico.

8   A UCLA survey entitled "The American freshman: twenty-five year trends," found that in 1967, over 80 percent of college freshmen considered developing a meaningful philosophy of life to be a very important goal; by 1991, that number had dropped to about 40 percent (N. Howe and B. Strauss (1993) *13th Gen: Abort, Retry, Ignore, Fail*. New York: Vintage, p. 46).

9   We have observed that the insipid "Valleyspeak," which spread across the culture beginning in the early 1980s and forms the syntactical basis of Beavis and Butt-Head's chatter, had penetrated even the speech of older adults and "educated" people. Rare is the

young person today who does not employ puerile constructions such as "I'm like tired today," "He's like stupid," or "We're like happy to be here" in his or her narrativizations, fatuous phrases which have eclipsed verbal skills as the key to communication. At present, the word "like" is so often used as useless filler, wedged in between almost every other word as though grammatical cement, that it has become almost obsolete as a simile. Similarly, the words "suck" and "cool," certainly not invented by Judge, are now near universal, as is the phrase that "X rules" and the anticlimactic, sentence-finishing phrase "or something."

10 The dialectic continues, however, to the extent that the show seemingly inspires some (very young) children to imitate their violent and destructive antics. Most children and certainly adolescents seem to understand that the show is satire, though many imitate their mannerisms and younger viewers have imitated their mayhem. See the discussion of the Beavis and Butt-Head effect in Kellner, op. cit., n. 1.

11 A recent *Newsweek* article shows that musical training greatly aids the overall formation of the brain, even improving math skills, and that it is crucial to provide young children with a wide range of stimuli in their very early years (February 19, 1996, 55–62). TV may have a reverse effect, and an important symptom in the decline in education is the gutting of music and art programs in the schools as "superfluous."

12 See Johnson et al. (1994).

13 As couch-bound slackers, they completely reject the work ethic; when they visit their guidance counselor they tune him out and talk about last night's videos. Despite Mr Van Driessen's attempt to instill the work ethic in them, they remain oblivious to the concepts of working in school to acquire job skills and prepare for success.

14 On critical media literacy, see Kellner, op. cit., n. 1 and McLaren Hammer, et al. (1995).

15 While Postman's (1985) critique of television (*Amusing Ourselves to Death*. New York: Vintage) is often provocative and incisive, his framework invites the sort of deconstruction of binary oppositions which is a central part of many postmodern epistemologies. His book is structured around an opposition between rational, logical, discursive, and coherent print discourse ("The Age of Exposition") and an irrational, incoherent, and fragmented electronic media discourse ("The Age of Entertainment"). Print media are serious, important, contextual, and conducive to democracy and other fine values, while electronic media and the culture of the image are trivial, frivolous, and subversive of everything valuable in life (religion, education, politics, etc.). This binary absolutism obscures the

more negative aspects of print culture and presents a purely negative view of image and electronic culture.

16 See S. Best and D. Kellner (1991) *Postmodern Theory: Critical
Introduction*. New York: Guilford.

17 See the discussion in S. Best and D. Kellner (1997) *The Postmodern
Turn*. New York: Guilford.

18 See Kellner, op. cit., n. 1.

19 In fact, a recent report by the Carnegie Council on Adolescent
Development has sounded the alarm of a serious crisis for American youth. After a nine-year study, the 27 member panel has issued
a report entitled *Great Transitions*, which documents gross neglect
of the nation's 19 million young adolescents. Youth aged 10–14 are
being abandoned at all levels, by their parents, schools, communities, and governments.

20 Being a loser seems to be an increasingly popular identity, with
songs like "Loser" by Beck and "I'm a Creep" by Radiohead.

21 After a Washington, DC, psychologist said that Beavis and Butt-
Head's humor sounded like the antics of normal youth, she fran-
tically called back the reporter after seeing that night's episode,
leading her to comment on voice mail: "I totally condemn this
program. I do not see any shred of normal adolescent behavior
here. It's one of the most sadistic, pathological programs I've ever
seen. I would not recommend it to anyone of any age" (*The
Washington Times*, October 17, 1993).

22 As Donna Gaines argues in her book *Teenage Wasteland* (New York:
Harper Perennial, 1991), heavy metal music is the religion of many
white suburban kids, speaking to their anger and despair and
providing a release for their aggression, as well as working-class
kids without job opportunities and adequate education. Its popularity suggests that a large number of kids want to blot out "reality"
through waves of sound that articulate their frustrations and rage;
the popularity of heavy metal for over two decades indeed requires
sociological scrutiny in an era of quick turnover of musical fads, as
does the longevity of rock and roll.

23 A recent poll of 2,000 teenagers found that one in eight youths, and
almost two in five in high crime areas, carry a weapon for protection. One in nine, and more than three in nine in high crime
neighborhoods, report that they cut class or avoid school at times
for fear of their safety. One in four teenagers, one in two in high-
crime areas, state they do not feel safe in their neighborhoods, and
almost one in three worried about being victims of drive-by shoot-
ings. The study also showed that nine of ten youths would be
willing to take part in mentoring, education, or community awareness programs if available, suggesting that they are an able and

caring pool of help that has so far gone untapped (*New York Times*, January 12, 1996, A6). That much can be done even with few resources is clear from the example of the Dorchester Youth Collaborative in Boston, which has successfully rescued kids from drugs and crime to teach them effective life and career skills. As one experienced Rochester youth worker said, "I have never seen a lost generation; what I have found is a lot of adults who want to lose the generation" (*The Nation*, January 15, 1996, 16–21).

24 Fox cited in *Newsweek*, December 4, 1995, 41.

25 Ibid., 41–2.

26 Prison statistics are especially high for young African-Americans. In a May 1996 talk in Austin, Texas, Angela Davis indicated that of young African-American males between the ages of 20 and 29, 32.5 percent have been in prison nationally; 40 percent in California have been incarcerated and 75 percent arrested at least once.

5
THE INDUSTRIAL IDENTITY CRISIS: THE FAILURE OF A NEWLY FORMING SUBCULTURE TO IDENTIFY ITSELF

David A. Locher

Introduction

Ethnographic documentation of subcultures in the United States is far less abundant than in Britain (Levine and Stumpf, 1983). Those most recently examined in the USA include the Los Angeles punk movement (Levine and Stumpf, 1983), New York "Guidos" (Tricarico, 1991), and California Low Riders (Holtz, 1975).

Youth subcultures are characterized by a meaningful symbolism and modes of expression that coalesce as "style" (Brake, 1985). This style, a predominant defining feature of youthful subcultures, is a key identifying component to the members. It allows them to express themselves as belonging, and to recognize others who are also within the subculture. Further, this style represents an identity "outside that ascribed by class, education, and occupational role" (Brake, 1985, p. 12). Style organizes a worldview for a group of people who share certain meanings (Grieves, 1982). Being in fashion determines whether an individual is "in" or "out" within a particular group (Maniscalco, 1979). Durkheim (1982, p. 80) himself pointed out that all of social life is "made up entirely of representations."

This chapter began as an attempt to document one group's representations, the style that composed a part of its social

reality. Originally, this research was to document the development of a new musical youth subculture as it grew and asserted
itself in popular music. When I began in late 1993, all parties
concerned were positive that they were part of a rapidly growing
subculture that would soon begin to "take over" the local music
scene. However, by early 1994 it started to become clear to me
that this might not actually happen. The key factors that determine the development and success of a subculture simply failed
to appear.

As I write this in 1996, these bands have broken up, and have
not been replaced by similar bands. National acts that performed
the same type of music have backed away, becoming less
hardcore and more industrial. More importantly, none of them
clearly identify themselves as industrial hardcore or industrial
metal.

As far as I know, this chapter is unique in that it documents
something that *did not* happen; a social movement that failed to
coalesce. This is not to imply that industrial-hardcore cannot or
will not ever achieve genuine subculture status, but it is not
happening right now, and it is not happening in Ohio.

Description

There is an element to many youth musical subcultures that the
authors mentioned above seem to have overlooked. Such subcultures (punk, gothic, metal, etc.) are frequently exclusive; the
members accept others into the group not based entirely on what
the individual likes (as an inclusive subculture would), but on
what he or she does *not* like. I have personally witnessed many
arguments in the past where one individual insisted that another
was "not really punk" because he or she admitted to liking (for
example) Led Zeppelin.

The issue involved in such arguments points to the exclusive
nature of the subcultures: it is not enough to like that which the
other members like, one must also dislike that which the other
members do not like. Adler and Adler (1995) point out that while
inclusionary dynamics form the basis of attraction to an adolescent clique, it is the exclusionary nature of such groups that
reinforces cohesion among the members. This same process
applies to most youth musical subcultures (although the authors

examining such groups do not seem to realize it): the initial appeal lies in one's ability to take part and join in without going through any sort of formal entry requirements, but it is the fact that not just anyone can be a member of the group that makes identifying oneself as a member worthwhile.

This may be a key factor in the general failure of industrial-hardcore: individuals who considered themselves punk or heavy metal or industrial were not willing to sacrifice their social standing within that group by admitting to liking music that was considered unacceptable by other members of their subculture.

As the descriptions of these various musical styles illustrate below, all three styles share certain common elements, but all three contain elements that make them unacceptable to the other subcultures. To admit a liking for heavy metal frequently means sacrificing one's standing as a punk, and vice versa. This may have led to a great deal of trepidation on the part of youths. Industrial-hardcore was frequently considered "techno" by metalheads, "heavy metal" by punks, and too "rock" by industrial fans.

This marriage of existing subcultures began around 1990, when a new combination of elements that had existed within various musical subcultures began to be combined into a distinctly new style. This new music, called "industrial-hardcore" or "industrial-metal" by bands and fans, combined different elements of industrial, hardcore-punk, and heavy metal into an overall sound that is extremely hard, heavy, abrasive, and regimented. It is important to realize that the elements taken from each of these existing styles were considered unacceptable by members of each of the others at the time.

Straight industrial music (sometimes called "techno") is usually produced almost exclusively through electronic keyboards and computers, emphasizing dance beats and long songs with plenty of "samples" (sounds, voices, or even segments of other songs which are digitally reproduced at the touch of a button). It is generally believed that the term "industrial" came about due to the literally industrial/mechanical nature of the samples frequently used, and because the music itself is performed using machines (computers, drum machines, keyboards, etc.). This type of industrial music developed in the early 1980s[1] and was closely tied to the disco-like "Euro" movement, which stressed dancing and having a good time. In essence, it is dance music with an angry or aggressive sound, performed by bands like Front 242 and Skinny Puppy.

Hardcore punk, which developed in the late 1970s with bands like Black Flag and Fear, is diametrically opposed to industrial, both stylistically and ideologically. Lyrics usually address social concerns (rather than personal issues), and the musical emphasis is on power, volume, and (sometimes) speed. Songs are short (one minute is acceptable, three is average) and repetitious, and there is very little emphasis placed on musical virtuosity. Technology such as drum machines, samplers, and keyboards is firmly shunned by hardcore punk musicians.

Heavy metal has been around in varying forms since the late 1960s. It places more emphasis on musicianship and song structure, and originated the heavily distorted guitar style. Black Sabbath are generally credited as one of the first heavy metal bands, and Metallica are currently one of the most successful.

Industrial-hardcore/industrial-metal was distinguished by its use of electronic technology, such as drum machines and samplers (which are common in industrial music but were considered unacceptable in hardcore punk or heavy metal); loud, heavily distorted guitar (common in hardcore and metal but not in industrial before 1990); and relatively short, repetitious songs played with little or no solos (common to hardcore; metal tends toward longer, more complicated songs with at least one guitar solo, while industrial frequently has no guitar at all). Further, vocals (shouted low, in the hardcore style) are usually "processed" (electronically distorted), a practice which has always existed, but not universally, within industrial and which was formerly considered taboo by most hardcore and metal bands. Although many members simply refer to this music as "industrial," it is quite separate and distinct from the synthesizer-based music produced by earlier techno-style industrial bands.

On the national level, industrial-hardcore has been performed by such bands as Ministry (a former straight industrial band that added heavy guitar to their recorded sound around 1991), Nine Inch Nails (who did likewise in 1992), Skrew, and Big Catholic Guilt. Anthrax, a metal band, released an industrial-metal CD in 1993. White Zombie have become progressively more and more industrial with the release of their last three albums, but were still playing music that could be called heavy metal in the early nineties. It is only with their 1995 release that they have become industrialized enough to be considered an industrial-metal band. These bands represented a new style within the larger rock and roll culture.

A small number of bands in the Columbus, Ohio, area had been performing this type of music since early 1992. This chapter started as an attempt to document this local subculture in the early stages of development. I focused on why the individuals chose to dress (and to a lesser extent act) in the way they did, and on what their style meant to them.

Subjects

The participants in this study were all members of two industrial-hardcore bands which had been playing in the Columbus area starting around late 1992: the Urban Grind Corps Guerrillas and Shrapnel.[2] Subjects were all between the ages of 24 and 30 (members of hardcore bands tend to be younger), and all grew up in suburban or urban environments.

Both of these bands contain female members, and the lead singer of the Urban Grind Corps Guerrillas is African-American. Sadly, this is an unusually diverse group of individuals for any regional band playing any type of rock and roll. Permission to photograph and interview subjects was obtained through signed consent/release forms.

Methods

As a member of one of these bands, I was in a unique position to comment on aspects of the then-developing scene which may not have been apparent to an outside observer. Although I may carry some bias into these comments, I think that the study benefits from my position as an insider. After photographs had been developed and chosen, I used them as tools in fairly informal interviews with several of the subjects. Comments were tape-recorded so that I could maintain the conversational atmosphere without disrupting anyone by taking notes.

My hope is to provide the reader with an idea of what the styles meant to the members themselves, using the photographs both to focus the subjects' comments and to provide the reader with an exact idea of the symbols and accessories that the members used to define themselves as such. I believe that photographs are a tremendous improvement over written descriptions in such a study.

I wanted to determine what the subjects felt about their own image, if anything: why they dressed the way they did, why certain recurring accessories (combat boots, black guitars, etc.) were so universal, what they meant, and what they were intended to signify. As the reader can see from the interview excerpts below, the musicians themselves were not always sure. Looking at a variety of comments to the same questions reveals a tremendous variety in the thoughtfulness (or lack thereof) with which each approaches these issues.

Interview Comments[3]

What kind of music do you play?

Industrial. Although I consider us industrial metal, almost.

I would call it industrial-metal, although that one song I would call hardcore-ish.

I just call it rock and roll. Industrial-metal, I guess.

Psychotic hardcore industrial noise.

As the reader can see, the musicians themselves could not agree on what to call the music. We usually just called it "industrial" to each other, but had an extremely difficult time labeling it when trying to talk about it to someone who had never heard us or any other industrial-hardcore/metal bands.

What is the difference between your music and heavy metal?

None of us have long hair [laughing].

It's less cheesy. [Could you be a little more specific?] Heavy metal has a tendency to be more sexist; kind of "come on, let's drink another beer." From a style standpoint, and this is both instruments and clothing; like they would play a pink guitar. A pink guitar is not something that we would play. [Why not?] Because everyone would make fun of you . . . it's not a classic, established instrument. [So is it a conservative thing?] I think there's an element of conservativism. We are like heavy metal for alternative kids; we are the heavy thing you can like and still be cool.

Basically, technologically speaking, we go beyond just guitars and amps. I think the biggest difference is in technology.

Heavy metal wears a lot of spandex and long, curly hair and Marshall stacks, and we have none of the above.

We don't go cliché. If the chord progression is usually like G–C–D, it's good to go like G–D–D#–C#–C–D. We use chords or notes that will jar the listener a little bit. We create tension by taking something that you're used to, and making it so that it's kind of the same, but we twist it and then repeat it over and over and over until it's like you're getting bludgeoned. When you listen to it and think, "God, I wish it would stop," then it's good. I hate heavy metal.

What is the difference between what you play and techno?

I've never seen a techno band with a "look." They're just kind of up there.

They're more dance oriented. We're heavy.

I would say techno is more repetitive, meant to be more hypnotic, more dance oriented.

The big difference is techno is faster tempo, a lot faster than what we do, a lot more repetition. They don't tend to use any instruments.

What separates you from hardcore punk?

We're slower than hardcore; much more melodic.

We do come close to the hardcore thing. We don't necessarily share a lot of the philosophy. I don't think that the music we do would be as widely accepted. Plus, I think our musicianship is a little bit tighter.

Hardcore is even more established, more of a community thing. That is very much a clique sort of thing. They will boo and throw things if you don't fit into what they consider hardcore.

Well, I'm a hardcore punk at heart. I guess, no mohawks.

The reader should notice how careful almost all the subjects are to separate and distinguish themselves from heavy metal, the genre of music that is most similar stylistically, but most different ideologically from the music that they perform. Notice the lack of vigor when distinguishing themselves from techno or hardcore, which are produced by socially similar people. An individual who knows very little about these different musical groupings would be likely to confuse industrial-hardcore/metal with heavy metal. These styles of music share a great deal of similarity in approach and overall sound. However, industrial musicians identify very strongly with the alternative rock culture, which is very different *socially* from heavy metal.

As one musician says above, this music is "like heavy metal for alternative kids." The same can be said of the musicians who perform the music; they do not identify at all with the larger heavy metal scene, but *do* agree with certain very specific stylistic approaches to playing music. When asked how they would feel if someone mistook them for a heavy metal musician, one replied, "I would be offended. I'm a punk."

Why do you dress the way you dress?

Because that's the way I dress. No particular reason.

Because I feel like it looks good on me. Black is slimming.

Because I like to wear them.

Because it's the way I feel comfortable. [Why the boots?] Because they're punk rock. [Why shorts?] Freedom of movement. [Why the shirt?] So you can see my tattoos. [Why the tattoos?] Because it's my way of expression. The way I express art. I feel that tattoos are art. [Why the hair?] Because I'm a rockabilly fan.

That's just what I feel comfortable playing in. I don't dress to the accepted code or anything. I don't look at a picture of like Al Jorgensen and try to dress like him. [Why the boots?] For the durability; it's street survival wear. And also maybe to be taken more seriously.

I like bigger clothes. I don't want to wear something tight. It's different for me than it is for guys. [Why?] Because I'm there to play guitar. I'm not there to turn the entire audience on. It's kind of like a mixture of a bunch of different styles of dress, none of which are "out" at the moment. Maybe if the entire universe crossed over and decided to wear really tight pants, I would too. We all just happen to kind of like to dress the same way. It's just coincidental that it happens to fit the music we play. Sometimes it looks almost like we're going to war. The biggest difference between us and some heavy metal bands like Pantera is our style, our look.

The only thing that we don't have in the band is a hippy thing.

Sometimes I wear cowboy boots, sometimes I wear different things. Whatever it takes for any given day, as long as it's black. Dressing is just an interpretation of how you feel.

I don't have anything on that's worth over twenty dollars, and that's like if you put it in a nice little pile. I look like a Salvation Army truck threw up on me, and that's how it should be.

Some of the members seem to be totally lacking in any self-consciousness about their visual style, but they are all dressed fundamentally the same (black leather combat boots, black shorts or pants, tank-tops or t-shirts). Everyone seems to realize that there is a proper way to dress, but some do not seem to realize that external norms are responsible for the look.

What does the way that you dress say to other people?

That I'm a threat; to their way of life, to them physically. They [people] say "are you in a band?"

If someone walked into a bar that you were going to play in, and they saw your band standing there, would they be able to tell what kind of music you play?

No. They would maybe think something hardcore.

I don't think so. The styles of different types of music are so interrelated now.

Oh yeah. At least it identifies that it's not going to be R.E.M. or the Smiths or some piece of shit like that.

Why do you play that particular guitar (or bass)?[4]

Because it has a nice heavy sound, and because it's not a common guitar.

Because it's just a really cool guitar, I think. [The look or the sound?] Both. I would never be seen with a pink guitar. The sound is more of a . . . like a creamier . . . to me, it's heavier-sounding; more hard instead of a countrified sound. There are other guitars that would sound hard, but would not have such classic looks. I'm not going to spend a lot of money on something that is stupid-looking. For me, it's important that I have something that is very serious looking because I'm a woman; to get some respect.

Because it's lightweight, it's very easy to play, and because it's black. Anything I bought would had to have been black. Black is my favorite color.

It looks conservative, but it looks classy as well. [Would you feel comfortable playing a Flying-V guitar?] I could do it, but it would make me sick. [Would you feel comfortable playing a bright yellow Ibanez?] No. Next question. Yellow clashes with my skin tone [laughs]. I feel sad for people with one. I have a thing against them. They have no taste. You could make it cool by defacing it a bit, I suppose.

Well, I go out and I pick out the cheapest, most fucked-up guitar that I can find, I take it home and I paint it black, and I put stickers on it and shit, and then it's good. I grew up with like *Guitar* magazine and Eddie Van Halen and all those cocksuckers, and I was taught that it is good to play a name-brand guitar, you know? Play the Randy-Rhodes-Charvel-Bullshit, and then you're good. I subscribed to that for a little while, but it didn't make me any better or any worse, so I like playing beat-up old guitars. 'Cause it's honest. [Why not pink, or white, or yellow?] Because those colors don't emit foreboding, and they don't look like a threat. It doesn't make a statement as to what type of music we're playing. Everything has to make a statement, including the visuals. It has to make a statement. If you don't look at it and immediately think something, be it good, bad, or whatever, then what the fuck is it? The stickers are a symbol of our culture. Everything in our culture says "buy, sell, good, bad," whatever. My guitar reflects my feelings on those subjects. ("Fuck off.") It's just a rejection of the dominant musical culture that I grew up with.

None of my guitars are over a hundred dollars, and that's the way I'm gonna keep it. It has to be something that I can throw across the room. Everything that I do, as far as playing, has got to reflect me. The music does, the instruments do. It has to.

Notice that while every musician believes the *look* of the instrument to be extremely important, they disagree somewhat as to *why* this is so. Nonetheless, all agree that there are just certain instruments that are visually appropriate and others that are not. Once again, the most important factor seems to be to differenti-ate themselves from heavy metal. Responses were particularly vehement when asked about playing brightly colored Ibanez or Flying-V guitars, instruments that are very closely associated with heavy metal in this region (but *sound* the same as the guitars used by these subjects).

Do you think that there is an industrial-hardcore or industrial-metal image or style?

I don't think so.

The barriers have been breaking down.

I don't know. I think before, there was. You know, the short hair, European thing. I don't think there really is now. Do you?

I'm sure there is. The black colors, of course. Maybe extremes, like eye makeup. That whole "modern primitive" thing, with the pier-cing and tattooing and stuff. But take that type of clothing out of the context of the bar, and I think it loses any "industrial hardcore" thing. Lots of different types of people wear stuff we wear.

Everyone seemed to recognize that there was no set visual style, just a vague set of general guidelines and boundaries. The important thing seemed to be to establish what they were *not*: heavy metal, "synth," or techno.

Can you think of a single term or word that we use that they don't use in other styles of music?

No.

No.

"Flying?" No, I guess that's just industrial.

What question should I have asked you?

Why is there no live drummer? Because it's too much of a hassle, and it allows us to have a little more flexibility in our drum sound. Could a metal band get away with it? The image probably wouldn't go over very well. Heavy metal bands tend to go for image over talent.

I don't know; it's like a big melting pot of technology and rock and roll!

The expense affects the age. A seventeen-year-old kid can't usually afford to buy a digital keyboard and stuff.

I would argue that the kind of stuff that we do could only be done by someone in their twenties; there's something very age-driven here. The younger kids are more into the hippy-dippy thing, so that even if they're hard, it's in a different sort of way. We're old enough that we've gone through the heyday of punk and heavy metal . . . these kids have never even seen that stuff . . . they're all like "post-Watergate kids" . . . we were at the tail end of all that hippy stuff, which is why we don't as readily embrace that stuff. We know what bell bottoms look like. We have no desire to go back to that stuff, and it gives us a different approach to style.

Discussion

It is important to note the implicit assumptions behind many of the interview comments above. Notice that the musicians themselves did not have an agreed-upon label for the music that they played. All agreed that it was not techno, nor metal or punk, but none were exactly certain what they *were*. It is easy to point to the key style elements that separate these people from their counterparts in the parent subcultures (especially the clothing and instrument choices of heavy metal, which are arguably the biggest factor separating these two types of music).

Notice, however, that although all these musicians agreed on what style choices were acceptable (black, Gibson-type guitars, combat boots, black shorts, etc.) and what are not (brightly colored Ibanez guitars, spandex, etc.), almost none of them seemed to be aware that they were following any sort of dress code. Only the lead singer from each band seemed aware that he consciously chose wardrobe and accessory items to project a particular image to the audience and outsiders. I found this particularly startling, since I had openly discussed these issues with each member of Shrapnel at one time or another. We teased each other when we showed up for a performance dressed almost exactly alike without having planned to do so. To me, this meant that we had at least developed an idea of how we should look. However, almost every subject interviewed seemed to be oblivious to this fact.

The only area where the musicians seemed to be consciously aware of an effort to use symbols to project an identity was in the selection of instruments. All agreed that there are "right" and "wrong" instruments. In fact, at a 1994 Skrew performance in Columbus, the lead singer explained to the crowd that Charvel/Jackson had given them "a shitload" of free guitars, but they never use them, choosing to pay for Gibsons instead. When an audience member asked "Why?", he replied: "Because they're shitty dumb-assed heavy metal pieces of shit, that's why. "Many consider Skrew a heavy metal band; obviously they disagree.

I find it particularly interesting that all individuals had an idea of what they were not, of whom they did not wish to be mistaken for. The problem seemed to lie in projecting who they were. The general public does not know that this type of music exists. Unlike punks or metal heads, they cannot go to a store and have strangers know what type of music they perform simply by looking at the way they dress or look.

It has been suggested to me that one possible reason for the failure of this movement lies in the age and class characteristics of the performers. As I mentioned earlier, one has to possess a fairly large amount of cash or credit to start an industrial band. All bands need instruments, but samplers, drum machines, and tape machines cost several hundred or even thousands of dollars each, and cannot be purchased dirt cheap used, in the way that guitars can. Few pawn shops have samplers for sale; almost all have a $50 guitar.

For this reason, industrial hardcore is performed mostly by middle-class individuals in their early twenties or older. This may have caused a double-bind situation: younger fans do not identify strongly with bands that they cannot emulate, the middle- and upper-class youth find no glamour in associating themselves with a middle-class movement, and the lower-class youths find it too expensive to emulate it. Hardcore punk and heavy metal have always had youth and the aura of being lower class working for them; higher-class kids get to "slum" by taking part, and lower-class kids are on familiar cultural turf. Techno, on the other hand, has a prosperous feel to it, and seems to produce a feeling of belonging to an elite group by aligning with it. Industrial-hardcore lacks both kinds of glamour.

If the driving force behind most youth subcultures is to forge an identity outside of ascribed (parental) positions (Brake, 1985), then what is the point of joining one that confirms and even highlights one's middle-class, middle-American status? If being a fan of this type of music does not socially transform the individual, then the strong identity-creating power behind most musical subcultures and youth subcultures is lacking. Those who like the music do not receive any particular social recognition for doing so.

Conclusions

According to Levine and Stumpf (1983), there are three crucial elements which determine a subculture: characteristic style, a set of focal concerns, and a private code of slang understandable only to insiders. It is my opinion that over the years this movement has failed to distinguish itself with a truly unique visual style, and as a result has failed to coalesce as a coherent and distinct subculture. If industrial-hardcore/industrial-metal had managed to completely divorce themselves from the three primary parent subcultures (metal, hardcore punk, and techno/industrial) in the minds of fans through a truly unique visual style, then perhaps the potential for being stigmatized by friends would have been eliminated.

Instead, the genre has been pillaged by the general "alternative" subculture. The set of focal concerns (reflected both in the content of song lyrics and in the private lives of the musicians) came first. However, a distinctive language never did develop. Most slang terms ("samples," "flying," etc.) were simply carried over from techno-industrial, hardcore punk, or heavy metal.

In the future, if this particular genre of music gains any popularity then the subculture could develop more fully. As this occurs, the style and code are likely to become more and more universal among members, as well as more distinct from the other subcultures that currently tend to be sometimes undistinguishable to outside observers. This does not seem likely to happen.

Musicians and fans alike failed to agree on any particularly distinctive component (such as white makeup and black hair for gothic, or spikes and mohawks for punks) which clearly identified one as "industrial." Other than wearing a shirt with the name of a known industrial-hardcore band, there was *no* way for an individual to visually announce to those in the know that he or she was a member of the subculture. I argue that this failure to achieve easy recognizability points out a more general failure on the part of the emerging subculture to stake out and clearly define membership lines.

People used to make references to "industrial scenes" where such bands were active (such as Columbus and Toronto), but I have yet to encounter anyone who considers himself or herself "industrial" in the same way that people refer to themselves and others as "punk" or "metal heads." Instead, these bands continued to hover just outside acceptance by the mainstream alternative crowd, while key aural elements (particularly processed vocals and heavy use of samples) were looted by non-industrial bands, resulting in a mild "industrialization" of heavy metal and heavy alternative music, but no wholesale acceptance of industrial-hardcore or industrial-metal.

Both the bands interviewed in this chapter have fallen apart or broken up. Nine Inch Nails have gained tremendous popularity, but the disc released in 1994 is clearly a retreat away from industrial-hardcore and back into the quieter straight industrial area. Skrew released a CD in 1994, but the vocal processing and samples have been de-emphasized in favor of a more metal sound. The 1996 Ministry release is stylistically much more metal than industrial. Anthrax has not released any new industrial-metal material. The movement as a separate and distinct style seems to be dead.

However, a great many bands that are still hardcore or metal or alternative have added industrial elements to their music and seem to be accepted. White Zombie, a metal band, gradually developed all the key elements of industrial metal (processed vocals, heavy guitar, constant use of samples, drum machines, and sequencers), but did not consider themselves to be industrial. In fact, when asked by an interviewer if they thought that they sounded industrial, the answer was "No!" (Di Perna, 1995b, p. 35). Their own protestations aside, White Zombie were considered "at the forefront of today's hard rock/industrial metal scene"

(Batten, 1996, p. 11). Filter have achieved commercial success with a powerful sound that contains technical elements of industrial-hardcore, but still sounds "alternative" to most fans.

Industrial-hardcore/industrial-metal fans failed to produce a new subculture. Instead, they have succeeded in making elements of three formerly opposed styles (metal, punk, and techno) acceptable to the others. Overall, popular heavy rock music has changed to become more "industrialized." This robbed the industrial-hardcore movement of any hopes of establishing a new identity of its own. The style is dead (or at least dying); the elements of the style continue on in new musical settings.

Notes

1 "Industrial" music, as it is known today, is actually distinct from earlier "industrial," which was experimental in nature and was literally produced using a variety of industrial machines and tools (Savage, 1983; DiPerna, 1995a). The label was probably carried over to the techno style because of the types of samples used.
2 Three of the four members of Shrapnel actually live in Akron, Ohio, but the band performed most of their shows in the Columbus area due to a lack of outlets for this type of music in the Akron area.
3 Remember that all interviews were carried out in the first half of 1994, when everyone involved believed that they were part of a growing new style.
4 Holtz (1975) and Tricarico (1991) have pointed out that accessories such as cars represent an extremely important part of the overall style to the members of a group. This obviously extends to musical instruments in a musical subculture.

References

Adler, P. and Adler, P. (1995) Dynamics of inclusion and exclusion in preadolescent cliques. *Social Psychology Quarterly*, 58(3), 145–62.

Batten, S. (1996) Back to bass-ics: Sean Yseult keeps it simple. *Scene Magazine's Seventeenth Annual: Stage, Store, and Studio*.

Brake, M. (1985) *Comparative Youth Cultures*. London: Routledge and Kegan Paul.

Di Perna, A. (1995a) Jackhammer of the gods. *Guitar World*, 15(6), 54–71.

Di Perna, A. (1995b) White Zombie: Zombies gave me lunch! Feasting with J. Yuenger and Sean Yseult. *Guitar World*, 15(6), 33–46, 170–2.

Durkheim, E. (1982) *The Rules of Sociological Method and Selected Texts on Sociology and its Methods* (ed. S. Lukes). New York: The Free Press.

Grieves, J. (1982) Style as metaphor for symbolic action: teddy boys, authenticity and identity. *Theory, Culture, and Society*, 1(2), 35–49.

Holtz, J. M. (1975) The "Low Riders:" portrait of an urban subculture. *Youth and Society*, 6(4), 495–508.

Levine, H. G. and Stumpf, S. (1983) Statements of fear through cultural symbols: punk rock as a reflective subculture. *Youth and Society*, 14(4), 417–35.

Maniscalco, M. L. (1979) Fashion and Socialization. *Sociologia*, 13(1), 87–101.

Savage, J. (1983) Industrial culture handbook. *RESearch*, 6/7, Introduction.

Tricarico, D. (1991) Guido: fashioning an Italian-American youth style. *Journal of Ethnic Studies*, 19(1), 41–66.

Discography

The following list includes suggestions by the author for those interested in experiencing the music first-hand. It is not intended to be exhaustive, but rather to provide a few representative examples from each genre discussed in this research. Although it is only a partial list, readers interested in hearing what some of the bands mentioned above actually sound like should check out some of the following albums, CDs, or cassettes.

HEAVY METAL

Black Sabbath (1970) *Paranoid* (Warner Bros.).
Metallica (1991) *Metallica* (Elektra).
Anything recorded by either of these bands, or anything by Judas Priest before 1985.

HARDCORE PUNK

Black Flag (1983) *Damaged* (SST).
Assorted artists (1985) *Decline of Western Civilization Soundtrack* (Slash).
Anything recorded by Black Flag, the Circle Jerks, Fear, Minor Threat, or The Exploited.

FIRST-WAVE INDUSTRIAL

Throbbing Gristle (1978) *Second Annual Report* (Industrial).
Cabaret Voltaire (1978) *Extended Play* (Rough Trade).
Einstruzende Neubauten (1983) *Drawings of Patient OT* (Thirsty Ear Recordings).
Anything recorded by any of these bands before 1993.

TECHNO-STYLE INDUSTRIAL

Skinny Puppy (1989) *Rabies* (Capitol).
Front 242 (1988) *Front by Front* (Epic).
Ministry (1986) *Twitch* (Sire).
Nine Inch Nails (1991) *Pretty Hate Machine* (TVT Records).
Anything recorded by any of these bands before 1990 except Ministry, who began to make a slow transition to guitars in 1988.

INDUSTRIAL HARDCORE/METAL

KMFDM (1993) *Angst* (Wax Trax).
Ministry (1989) *The Mind Is a Terrible Thing to Taste* (Sire).
Nine Inch Nails (1992) *Broken* (Interscope).
Skrew (1993) *Burning in Water/Drowning in Flames* (Metal Blade).
White Zombie (1995) *Astro-Creep 2000: Songs Of Love, Destruction, and Other Synthetic Delusions of the Electric Head* (Geffen).

6
IDENTITY AND STATUS STRATIFICATION IN DEADHEAD SUBCULTURE

Robert Sardiello

Introduction

Since the Grateful Dead began performing in the early 1960s, their appeal has solidified a core of supporters known as Deadheads. Deadheads have been described as cult-like members of a nomadic subcultural community whose sense of unity and feeling of belonging promotes a unique sense of identity (Gans and Simon, 1985; Pearson, 1987; Sardiello, 1994). In some earlier research, I argued that the concerts were ritual occasions for celebrating this subcultural identity (Sardiello, 1994). In this chapter, I will focus on the nature of this subcultural identity, with particular emphasis on what it means to be a Deadhead, and the implications of intragroup status distinctions on conceptions of Deadhead identity. I propose to discuss identity in terms of two ideal type dimensions, i.e. the personal and social, which combine to form a stratified identity typology of deadheads.

Identity, Youth, and Subculture

The self is a central concept in the hybrid discipline of social psychology, with deep roots in the philosophical search for who we are. It can be broadly defined as "an organized collection of identities, each of which serves to shape our behavior in social interaction where there is a choice among possible alternative behaviors" (Burke and Hoelter, 1988, p. 29). Studies of the self and its constituent identities have, however, tended to bifurcate into a series of dualities, such as subjective or objective, individual or group, cognitive or affective, conscious or unconscious, situationally specific or transsituationally generic (Weigert, 1983, p. 203).

To a large extent, the origin of this dualistic thinking stems from the different approaches of the two social psychologies: that is, the sociologically oriented social psychology, and the psychologically oriented social psychology (Stryker, 1989). In this context, "it is the parent discipline of sociology that reinforces attention to social structure, especially large-scale social structure, and it is the parent discipline of psychology that reinforces attention to the individual" (Stryker, 1989, p. 51).

I will discuss these dualities in the context of what I see as two ideal type dimensions of identity, the personal and the social. I believe that the ideal type methodology is useful because it allows us to take the dynamic intersubjective understandings of individual social experience and temporarily freeze them in an objective model. This implies that the two ideal type dimensions can be separated and analyzed independently, but in reality they mesh in a dialectical process of interaction that influences both the individual and the social structure (Mead, 1934; Berger and Luckmann, 1966). An individual must, therefore, negotiate within and between each dimension in order to develop a coherent self-concept.

The personal dimension of identity then, will be seen to consist of a subjective self-identification (Mead, 1934). It is closer to the psychological side of the social psychological continuum and is often distinguished empirically by micro-level elements, such as personal attributes, as opposed to categorical distinctions (Gordon, 1976). The emphasis, in this case, is on the degree of internalization of a particular identity which is differentiated from others. The concept of personal identity is based on the process of negotiating personal experience into a unique biography (Hewitt, 1989). Personal identity is, then, transsituational and provides for a feeling of individual autonomy and continuity.

The social dimension of identity will be seen to consist of a self-identification that emerges from the treatment of the self as an object (Mead, 1934). It tends to be closer to the sociological side of the social psychological continuum, and is often distinguished empirically by macro-level elements, such as cat-egorical distinctions, as opposed to personal attributes (Gordon, 1976). Social identity can be specific to a social situation and dependent on a role in the social structure (Goffman, 1959; Stryker, 1968; Hewitt, 1989). There are, however, many roles and statuses in the social structure that influence an individual's sense of social identity and situational pressures may influence the salience of any particular one (Turner, 1987; Hewitt, 1989).

The social structure consists of layers of group associations structured by patterns of interaction that have some degree of stability in a cultural environment.[1] An individual may, there-fore, claim membership and an identity with several layers in the social structure simultaneously (Linton, 1936), and express varying degrees of commitment to the role expectations of each (Becker, 1960; Gans, 1979). In certain situations, then, one particular identity may be more salient than another in the hierarchical arrangement of alternatives (Stryker, 1968; Turner, 1987).

In this respect, Turner (1987, p. 45) has identified at least three different levels of abstractions – the superordinate level, the intermediate level, and the subordinate level, with which an individual may categorize themselves or others. This typology allows for comparisons within and between different levels, such that the salience of any particular identity depends on the level of abstraction as a frame of reference. Self-categories, according to Turner (1987), tend to become salient at one level less abstract than the self-category in terms of which they are being com-pared. For example, the subordinate level (personal dimension of self) becomes salient where comparisons are restricted to in-group members, the intermediate level (social dimension of self) becomes salient where comparisons are made between in-group membership(s) and out-group membership(s), and the superordinate level (human dimension of self) becomes salient where comparisons are made with other species (Turner, 1987, p. 48).

Salience is a dynamic concept relating identities to the overall self in, or through, social interaction. And over time, individual interactions will adapt to particular situations in the historical evolution of a culture, and these will, in turn, lead to changes in both the social structure and individual behavior (Berger and Luckmann, 1966, p. 20). An individual must, therefore, negotiate between the various levels of abstraction at particular historical moments, and merge them into a coherent sense of self.[2]

In the process of this negotiation, discrepancies or tensions inevitably arise within and between the personal and social dimensions (Goffman, 1963). These types of identity problems occur throughout the life course (Erikson, 1950), but the adolescent/youth stage is of particular interest because of its unique transitional, or liminal, quality in relation to the other stages in the life course. This stage has been the focus of a great deal of research, especially with regard to the formation of subcultures and the identities they promote (Klapp, 1969; Hebdige, 1976, 1979; Jefferson, 1976; Brake, 1980, 1985).

Subcultures, in general, can be defined as

> the meaning systems and modes of expression developed by groups in particular parts of the social structure in the course of their collective attempts to come to terms with the contradictions of their shared social situations . . . They therefore provide a pool of available symbolic resources which particular individuals or groups can draw on in their attempt to make sense of their own specific situation and construct a viable identity. (Murdock, 1974, p. 213)

Subcultures may be relatively homogeneous in terms of social structural variables, such as age, gender, race, and social class, but this is not a sufficient condition for identification. They must also be identified by cultural content defined in terms of distinct languages, symbols, and styles of life related to value systems that differ from the mainstream culture (Clarke, 1974; Fine and Kleinman, 1979; Hebdige, 1979; Calluori, 1985; Hannerz, 1992).

Arnold (1970) used the imagery of a circle to represent the relationship between subcultures and the broader culture. In other words, culture is represented by a large circle, and subcultures are represented as a series of smaller circles overlapping the boundary of the larger circle. Smaller circles fully inside the larger cultural circle are smaller groups representing the range of acceptable deviations from the dominant cultural values and norms.[3] Smaller circles fully outside of the larger cultural circle are groups in opposition to the dominant cultural values and norms.[4] Cultural information and behavioral options are, then, diffused through channels of communication and interaction that connect the various social groups in a network which serves as the referent for any particular subculture (Fine and Kleinman, 1979, p. 8).

I think the circle analogy is useful because it allows you to visualize the "web of group affiliations" in a cultural environment (Simmel, 1955), but not all the groups are subcultures. Social groups come in all shapes and sizes, which may, or may not, be subcultural. So what makes a subculture a subculture, and not some other form of social group?

This is not an easy question to answer because it involves identifying social groups in relation to both the broader cultural context and the structure of individual interactions, and differentiating between them at successively larger (or smaller) levels of generality. Unfortunately, there is not an agreed upon formula for doing this, which means that some groups are labeled subcultures and others are not. In this respect, many of the problems in studies of subcultural phenomena revolve around identifying what the boundaries are and how they are maintained, or modified, over time.[5]

Currently, it is fashionable to lump subcultures together into larger units and call them "cultures," such as political culture, class culture, or youth culture. This approach questions the conceptual cohesiveness of the term culture,[6] but it has proven to be a useful device because culture, as it is traditionally conceived, is a very broad term. Subdividing the concept of culture into subcategories is like subdividing subcultures into sub-subcultures, but the terminology in the former case appears to be easier to deal with (Arnold, 1970). So, for example, we may speak of youth culture, because youths cannot be considered a subculture solely on the basis of their age. Various youth subcultures will then be located within this broader cultural subcategory.

Youths are prone to joining subcultures, or claiming membership in subcultures as a means of resolving collectively experienced problems relative to their position in the social structure, and of developing a sense of identity (Brake, 1985). Youths may also claim membership in many groups, and their individual sense of self will, therefore, be based on their ability to draw on available situated identities while creatively integrating them into a coherent personal identity. These interactions are dynamic and allow for modifications in conceptions of the objective group and, at the same time, allow individuals to internalize and integrate aspects of the group as part of the individual self (Gordon, 1976).

One important aspect of identity formation among adolescents and youths involves their relationship to, and use of, music. Adolescents and youths become emotionally involved with their music as a way of distinguishing themselves from adults and from each other (Coleman, 1963; Grossberg, 1992). In post Second World War America, the medium of rock music, for example, allowed youths to express their sense of solidarity, which was often in opposition to adult society. Indeed, the history of rock and roll can be seen in relation to different generations of youth attempting to acquire exclusiveness through different symbolic representations of in-group membership. Rock performers become musical prophets (Lewis, 1987) or cultural heroes (Dotter, 1987), and concerts become the ritual occasions for celebrating group solidarity (Montague and Morais, 1976; Sardiello, 1994). The strong charismatic appeal of hero figures provides an intense social-psychological identification between performer and audience, "giving the latter an experience of common belonging and at the same time a heightened version of their own most personal experiences, disappointments, dreams, and desires" (Martin, 1979, p. 108).

Studies of musical taste in general, but particularly among youths, indicate that it correlates with structural variables, such as race, age, gender, and social class divisions (Gans, 1974; Denisoff, 1975; Frith, 1981; Denisoff and Bridges, 1983; Robinson, and Fink 1986). These types of distinctions are interesting, and have important implications as markers for one's sense of social identity, but musical taste is also associated with cultural content (Peterson and DiMaggio, 1975; Lewis, 1982, 1987; Lull, 1987a,b). One of the things inherent in this cultural content is a guideline for interpreting the aesthetic musical experience, and this can promote a deeper sense of meaning for individuals who internalize and identify with it (Frith, 1996). This can, then, affect their sense of personal identity.[7]

Certain musical tastes become associated with cultural content and value themes in the sense that they can be either contained in the content of the music itself, or created by the groups who interpret it and give it meaning (Lewis, 1987).[8] When musical tastes become associated with value themes that differ significantly from the dominant culture, we often refer to them as subcultural. Technically, this is not correct either, because musical taste alone cannot be the sole determinant of a subculture. Grossberg (1992), therefore, discussed musical taste as a set of affective sensibilities which differentiate fans with different tastes. But certain musical tastes do become associated with subcultures. Weinstein (1991), for example, illustrated the connection between musical taste and the heavy metal subculture and called it a music-based youth subculture. For any music-based subculture, it is an empirical question as to what proportion of the audience for the genre is made up of members of the subculture (Weinstein, 1991, p. 98).

In this respect, musical taste, and knowledge of musical taste, becomes a form of popular cultural capital that is used by youths in forming impressions of others and of themselves (Hebdige, 1979; Zillman and Bhatia, 1989; Fiske, 1992). These taste distinctions, and group memberships, situate identities and empower groups of youths, who are otherwise not situated or empowered in the social structure (Grossberg, 1992).

Deadheads are, in this sense, most simply fans of the music of the Grateful Dead, a rock and roll band that formed in the early 1960s. This is the most elementary ingredient of Deadhead identity, but it is significant because it separates this group of fans from the fans of other musical groups. Deadheads are unique because their devotion maintains a subcultural system of values and norms which can have important consequences for an individual's sense of identity. In the rest of this chapter, I will describe the nature of this subcultural identity, with particular emphasis on the implications of intragroup status distinctions on conceptions of Deadhead identity.

I began studying Deadheads in 1988,[9] and have continued to study them, attending 60 concerts between 1990 and the summer of 1995, when lead guitarist Jerry Garcia died. Subsequently, the band discontinued touring and in December of that year officially broke up. I have observed Deadhead behavior specifically at concert sites because they were important locations for witnessing displays of normative subcultural behavior, and because they situated individuals in a context that would make this particular identity more salient.

I was not, however, simply a voyeur, although at times my observations led me to follow particular individuals around the concert location so that I could see what they were doing and who they interacted with, over a longer period of time. I was also a participant, and would engage individuals and informally question them about their behavior, or the behavior of others. In this way, I could obtain some biographical data, and also second-hand observational data, as I probed for their comments about other people's behavior.

My efforts to reconstruct Deadhead behavior and Deadhead identity are, therefore, based on three sources, i.e. my own observations, my interpretations of an individual's interpretations of his or her own behavior, and my interpretations of an individual's interpretations of someone else's behavior. This method is firmly rooted in the ethnographic tradition of both anthropology and sociology, and particularly within symbolic interactionism (Glaser and Strauss, 1965; Geertz, 1973; Hill, 1975; Denzin, 1989).

Deadhead Subculture and Deadhead Identity

Descriptions of Deadheads in the popular press often likened them to an idealized or stereotypical view of the subcultural or countercultural hippie from the sixties. To some extent, this is true, which is not that surprising given that the band formed in the mid-1960s in San Francisco, which was considered a major location for hippies (Perry, 1984). Over the years, however, as these themes and values have faded in the broader social context, Deadheads have adopted them and have creatively applied them as the basis for a complicated network of interactive rules that form the normative structure of the subculture, and as the basis for a subcultural identity (Pearson, 1987; Lehman, 1994; Sardiello, 1994).

Deadhead subculture does incorporate many of the lifestyle values associated with the bohemian youth movements of the 1950s and 1960s. These values and themes are, by now, well documented, but to summarize, some of the more notable ones included: passive resistance, particularly in the political arena; movement, physical, psychical or existential; dissociation with the material comforts of their middle-class origin; expressivity and subjectivity, as opposed to conformity and deferred gratification; individualism, in the sense of a freedom to "do your own thing;" and exploration, particularly in spiritual quests for meaning (Hardwick, 1973; Wuthnow, 1976, 1978; Brake, 1980; Yinger, 1982; Schechter, 1983; Miller, 1991).

Manifestations of most of these values can be seen in Deadhead subculture, which combined form the core value system of the subculture. At the heart of this value system is a set of values that has spiritual connotations. In fact, Jerry Garcia, lead guitarist of the band, once commented on the nature of this spiritual connection. In an interview with *Rolling Stone*, he said, "as they [Deadheads] elucidate the relationship between what the Dead does and what they do, we start to see ourselves as part of this complex something else. Which I think is the real substance of the Sixties. For me, the lame part of the Sixties was the political part, the social part. The real part was the spiritual part" (Goodman, 1989).

In some earlier research, I argued that this form of spirituality was functionally equivalent to religious belief (Sardiello, 1994). This does not imply that Deadheads are a religious group, but it does distinguish an interpretation of social reality that is given a sacred quality.[10] This is, once again, related to the origins of the Band[11] and the search for alternative expressions of symbolic integration among the different elements of the counterculture (Hardwick, 1973).[12]

These quasi-religious[13] values are the core values of Deadhead subculture, and an identification with them is the basis of Deadhead identity. The concerts, therefore, become ritual occasions for celebrating and experiencing these values.[14] Viewing the concerts as rituals allowed me to explore the quasi-religious nature of what it meant to be a Deadhead, but I questioned the homogeneity of this identity. In other words, there are different types of Deadheads, distinguished by varying degrees of commitment to, and identification with, these subcultural values.[15]

The personal dimension of Deadhead identity is therefore differentiated by individuals' willingness to integrate these values and sentiments into their lives. Most Deadhead's share parts of this ideal, but not all people who share this ideal are Deadheads.[16] The concert experience is, therefore, meaningful on different levels for different individuals, and may even be different for the same individual at different times.

The social dimension of Deadhead identity, on the other hand, derives from the development of a normative structure which guides interactions that, in turn, maintain the system of values central to the subculture. Deadheads do, in fact, have a tendency to attend many concerts,[17] making it possible for some to have attended hundreds of concerts over the past 30 years. This prolonged interaction, both on the road and in the parking lots, has fostered the development of a nomadic community, organized around a network of norms and statuses that fulfill basic needs. In other words, these status positions are functional classifications that serve a need in Deadhead subculture, and they have important implications for the social dimension of Deadhead identity.

These functional status distinctions revolve around services in the Deadhead subculture. The expected role performance is guided by a set of informal norms that allows the community to operate smoothly. Some of the more important and popular positional classifications in Deadhead subculture would include the "skeleton crew," volunteer medics, tapers, and vendors.

The skeleton crew[18] is interesting because it is a liaison between the band and the parking lot community. When the band allowed people to camp out in the parking lots, the skeleton crew would oversee the provision of such basic necessities as portable bathrooms and fresh water (especially during summer tours). They also coordinated with volunteers to clean up trash after a run of concerts at a particular venue.

There are also teams of volunteer medics, who set up in the parking lots and inside some of the concert venues to assist with medical problems. This is especially needed during summer tours, when heat stroke is a serious problem, but they are also needed to assist with drug-related problems.

Another interesting status distinction inside Deadhead subculture involves the taper phenomenon. The band have always allowed their shows to be taped, and many Deadheads value this service because it preserves the live concert experience.[19] Exchanging tapes, therefore, builds social networks, and also preserves the qualities of the live concert experience. Generally, tapes are not sold, they are traded, often for tapes of other shows. Some tapers even circulate lists of the tapes they have or want, and this can be done either at concerts or through magazines that are oriented toward Dead fans, such as *Relix*.

Vendors are, perhaps, one of the most interesting and most important of the functional classification in Deadhead subculture. They are important because they provide many of the basic needs and services for daily life in the community. They are, in fact, the basis of an underground economy oriented toward a free market ethic for the production and distribution of goods and services.

Venders tend to cluster in a particular area of the parking lot at any particular concert venue, and can be identified by booths or displays of their products. These areas are quickly identified and develop on a first-come basis for whoever wants the space. Some venders, however, are on foot and can roam around the parking lots more freely. Once established, these central locations become a focal point in the parking lot community.[20]

Vendors provide most of the basic necessities for the nomadic community, including many types of vegetarian food,[21] a variety of alcoholic beverages, soft drinks, and water. They also sell or trade clothing, Guatemalan jewelry, and the totemic tie-dyed items,[22] including T-shirts, pants, and underwear. Some people sell drug paraphernalia and drugs, and others provide services, like face painting, hair beading, or body massage. All items and services are sold, traded, or given away, including tickets.[23]

This market is oriented toward small-scale production and distribution of items and services. Handmade products, in particular, are preferred, with most vendors making enough money to continue buying supplies and traveling during a tour. Some vendors have managed to make a living and some have even started their own companies. This tends to go against the small-scale production ethic, but it is tolerated because they are small companies, often focusing on T-shirts with unique designs. They tend to be home-based and sometimes advertise a mail order service for their products.

Generally, the larger the scale of production and distribution the less it is tolerated in Deadhead subculture. This became evident at a concert in Alpine Valley, Wisconsin, in 1989, when a vendor was seen using a credit card machine to sell a piece of clothing. A nearby vendor saw this and became irate, shouting that this foreigner was not a Deadhead, and that this was a violation of community norms. He then proceeded to smash the credit card machine on the ground.[24]

This situation illustrates some of the larger problems that developed in the Deadhead community, beginning in the late 1980s. It was after the recovery of Jerry Garcia from a near death coma and the release of a very popular album, *In the Dark*, which attracted more people into the community than it could handle. Overcrowding, therefore, created many problems.[25] The most obvious problems related to sanitation and water supply, but others threatened the very heart of the community by subverting its values and community ethic.

In some instances, vendors would set up with the sole purpose of making money, and not even bother to attend the concert. This was generally seen as an intrusion by outside influences who just wanted to exploit the purchasing power of the community; but there were also instances when members of the community themselves could be accused of this. Similar profiteering was the motivation for selling fake tickets to the concerts.

Problems also developed around the use and distribution of drugs. Drug use was a big part of the counterculture and this carried over into the Deadhead subculture.[26] When the "War on Drugs" began in the mid-1980s, Deadheads were targeted by local police departments. Not surprisingly, drug arrests often increased at local venues when the Grateful Dead were in town. Drug use then, became the source of most confrontations with police.

It eventually reached a point where the band were banned from performing at certain venues.[28] In response to these types of concerns, the band decided to discontinue support of camping and vending in the fall of 1989. The decision was designed to take some of the pressure off the subculture and redirect the focus toward the concert. The subculture was reluctant to comply, but it did adapt, altering its normative structure in some fundamental ways.

The ban was mildly successful in limiting access to the parking lots and, therefore, to the subculture. The parking lots were closed after each concert and opened each day several hours before the concert. In some places, access to the parking lots was denied without a ticket to the concert. Deadheads adapted by staying at local camping facilities, or at local hotels, often boosting the local economies (Goodman, 1990). The ban on vending, however, was less successful because the underground economy was so well established. Vendors would simply set up each day when the parking lots opened, and many became more mobile to avoid any confrontations with authorities.

Overall, the ban did limit access to the subculture, particularly by those driven more by profit than a desire to see the band; but it was difficult to maintain. Pressures from the influx of more people continued to strain the ability of the subculture to meet the basic needs of its members. It did eventually adapt to these changes, and some even welcomed the attempt to redirect attention back to the music, which was, after all, supposed to be the main ingredient of Deadhead identity.

Intragroup Status Stratification and the Diversification of Deadhead Identity

Deadhead identity also adapted to these structural changes in the subculture. Remember that this identity was based most simply on liking the music of the Grateful Dead; but as prolonged interaction developed into a nomadic community, the nature of this identity changed to accommodate different status positions. The functional classifications mentioned above not only served needs in the community; they stratified the subculture based on the accompanying role performances associated with each status position. In other words, status stratification affected Deadhead identity, leading to intragroup identity differentiation.

Interestingly enough, Deadheads will tend to refer to themselves communally, and emphasize the unity inherent in this identity, especially when differentiating themselves from non-Deadheads. However, they will also distinguish among themselves. The nature of this identity differentiation is based partially on the degree of internalization of its subcultural values, and partially on the degree of one's involvement and participation in the social world.

In other words, the personal and social dimensions of Deadhead identity can be ranked separately, forming what I see as essentially three types, or categories, of Deadhead. I will call them hardcore, new, and stable. This typology reflects some of the different strategies for negotiating identity among Deadheads, and these correspond to the aspects of Deadhead identity as Deadheads themselves perceive and define them.

I conceive of this typology as an ideal type because it is a construct against which we can measure empirical reality. In other words, individuals may be ranked on each dimension of

Deadhead identity, i.e. personal and social, and these may then be compared to an ideal type. For example, one who ranks highly in each dimension may be seen to approximate the hardcore ideal type, one who ranks in the middle of each dimension may be seen to approximate the stable ideal type, and one who ranks low in the personal dimension and high in the social dimension may be seen to approximate the new ideal type. Empirical distinctions will actually be continuous, so there will be error when comparing them to the ideal type, but these variations can be minimized with finer distinctions in the ideal type model. In this particular study, the data are more appropriately interpreted at the ordinal level.

The Hardcore Deadhead

This category is quite probably the smallest portion of the total Deadhead population.[28] In terms of the personal dimension of this identity, hardcore Deadheads are distinguished by an interpretation or perception of an individual's attitude relevant to the Deadhead value system. In other words, membership in this category depends on how close one's attitude was to some ideal conception of Deadhead, or on the perceived level of value internalization.

In the extreme, this identification may lead to what one Deadhead referred to as the "Jesus Christ archetype." The use of religious imagery is interesting because it emphasizes the spiritual quality of this aspect of identity. Another Deadhead referred to this category, and to himself, in this way: "there are hippie Deadheads who are, I consider that to be me, not just into the Grateful Dead movement but are also into making this world a better place."

This perception implies a level of internalization of Deadhead values that is transsituational. This type of attitude is important, but one can have this attitude and not be a Deadhead. One self-identified non-Deadhead made this distinction by reference to the Rainbow Family, which is another group of nomadic communalists. She stated:

> there are people who have been following the Dead for years and go out to all the concerts and they live for the Dead and they have

like transient jobs just to save enough money to go to the Dead and go on tour and that's their goal in life. And then there is a group of what I would call true transients. A lot of the rainbow family who [are] people . . . [who] follow around the rainbow family and a lot of them go to Dead shows because you get that same feeling of belongingness . . . I always hated Deadheads personally. They're very irresponsible and very egocentric . . . I like the culture that surrounds them but I use the term Deadhead as a derogatory term.

This comment is very interesting because it recognizes the existence of other groups that share value content, and implies a partial overlap of group membership. It also implies that the high degree of salience of this aspect of personal identity can affect the social aspects of identity, in the sense that one is less likely to be committed to other, more conventional types of social identity, such as having a steady job. Thus, the personal salience of identification with these types of values seems to affect both Deadheads and non-Deadheads, but for Deadheads the effect appears to draw them into the Deadhead subculture. I can only assume that this level of identification affects non-Deadheads, i.e. the Rainbow Family, in a similar way, perhaps drawing them further into their respective subcultural lifestyle.

So for Deadheads, the congruence between the personal and social dimensions of Deadhead identity means that the hard core type will likely be affiliated with social positions within the subculture and less likely be affiliated with social positions outside the subculture. Therefore, if they have outside jobs, they tend to be transient jobs, such as restaurant work, so they can travel and be a part of the Deadhead community.

In terms of the social dimension of this identity, then, hardcore Deadheads can be distinguished by reference to their behavior within the subculture. The emphasis on behavior implies that this type of identity is situated in a particular social setting. In this respect, the social markers, such as appearance and clothing, can be an initial indication of one's social identity as a Deadhead, but the degree of this identity is also measured by the perception of one's status in the subculture, such as taper or vendor. One Deadhead summarized her perceptions of the hard core Deadhead by saying:

> I guess the folks I see selling things, who are trying to make a living and possibly the ones following them all over the place . . . some people just make a life out of following this group around.

In other words, it is important not only that they occupy these status positions and play these roles, but that they are committed to doing this for a long time, and that some have made a life out of it. The amount of time spent in the subculture was, therefore, an important distinguishing qualification for determining the boundaries of this type of Deadhead. The actual amount of time, however, appeared to be ambiguous, but it suggested that age and experience were also important distinguishing characteristics. In this respect, there is a certain reverence conferred upon older members of the subculture. This "elder status" can sometimes obscure the importance of deep personal identification, especially for younger Deadheads, or what I will call the "new" type of Deadhead.

The New Deadhead

This category of Deadhead is identified largely in terms of youthfulness and lack of experience within the subculture. These new Deadheads are predominantly in high school and college and are responsible for much of the recent popularity and success the band enjoyed after the 1987 release of *In the Dark*. They are also associated with the population boom within the subculture, and are subsequently blamed for many of the problems associated with overpopulation. One Deadhead observed that:

> they seem to be pretty much just interested in the trappings of it and . . . they're not really interested in the culture *per se*. They just like the music and dressing up in their dyes and they seem pretty fake about the whole thing.

Another Deadhead added:

> nothing against the younger newer heads . . . but (a) it makes it harder for us guys who've been doing it for a while to get tickets, and (b) I was young once too, and I was immature too, you know, you throw cans and bottles and litter the places where they go, and that's not good.

So the people in this category are generally looked down upon for their lack of knowledge and experience within the subculture, but the confounding of age and experience makes the perception of these boundaries difficult. In other words, a young Deadhead could have a high level of personal and social identification with the norms and values of the subculture, but not be considered a hardcore type because of his or her age.

This generational hierarchy is interesting because of its implications for Deadhead identity, but it is also functionally important. Socialization through prolonged interaction promotes the transmission of values and allows for the continuation of the subculture. In fact, new members are often introduced to the subculture by older family members or friends. Their entrance is initially peripheral, but movement between categories is easily attained because of the semi-permeable nature of membership boundaries. People in college, for example, who have lengthy summer breaks from school, may rapidly gain experience by "going on tour" and attending many concerts.

Interestingly enough, most of the young people I talked to would not identify themselves as new. No one wanted to be identified with this group, but many of these same people made reference to the existence of the category. They tended, instead, to downplay these divisions and emphasized the overall unity of Deadheads as opposed to non-Deadheads.

The Stable Deadhead

The final category of Deadhead, I have called stable. This implies that participation is occasional, but consistent. This group is perhaps the largest in terms of membership and may be the most transient in terms of self-identification. Stable or occasional Deadheads have a limited radius within which to attend concerts due to ties and responsibilities outside the group. In the words of one particularly insightful Deadhead:

> A lot of Deadheads have two lives . . . they are part of society and have jobs like doctors and make money and provide for their families, but they always have . . . that carefree side that wants to go and give up everything and go with the Grateful Dead.

This category of Deadhead is most likely to have limited behavioral ties with Deadheads in general, and to have limited symbolic ties, especially in terms of appearance. I have, therefore, placed them in a category that represents a moderate commitment in both the personal and social dimensions of their identity.

For example, one self-identified non-Deadhead, who was a corporate lawyer, stated that he did not wear tie-dyes much because "it would not be cool professionally to be identified as a Deadhead . . . I only wear them to shows." However, this same respondent has been to over 30 concerts since 1978, and has been observed dancing enthusiastically at several concert events. I have, therefore, classified him as a stable Deadhead, even though he does not use the label himself. In fact, this particular person stated that he had a "falling out" with the Dead, but that now he was "making up for lost time." This situation emphasizes the transient, or occasional, nature of participation in the subculture and the moderate level of identification with this identity because of responsibilities and identity commitments outside the subculture.[29]

What is perhaps most interesting about this type of Deadhead is the degree to which their identity with Deadheads affects their non-Deadhead lives. For example, this same respondent noted that he wanted to keep his Deadhead identity separate from his identity as a corporate lawyer, but when I talked to him several years later, I discovered that he had become a public defender. I questioned him about this job change because I was curious to see if his identification with Deadheads and Deadhead values had any influence in his decision. He reluctantly agreed that it might have had some impact on his decision, but still did not consider himself to be a Deadhead.

This situation is not uncommon among this type of Deadhead. Commitments outside the subculture limit their participation in the subculture and limit the degree to which they will internalize these subcultural values. They do, however, find ways to integrate this identity into their sense of self. Some, for example, will plan vacations from work around a tour schedule, and some, like the person mentioned above, will change their jobs because they do relate to the subcultural values. They will not, however, give up these outside ties, so the overall effect is moderate.

Conclusions

At its most elementary level, being a Deadhead means one appreciates the music of the Grateful Dead, but through continued interaction, especially at concerts, the audience has developed a sophisticated network of interactive rules from which they further derive their group identity (Gans and Simon, 1985; Pearson, 1987; Lehman, 1994; Sardiello, 1994). In this sense, being a Deadhead may be experienced on different levels, which may range from a simple appreciation of the music to a full internalization of the behavioral and value content of this subculture.

In this chapter I have described Deadhead subculture as a system of values and norms developed to accommodate Deadheads who interact on a regular and prolonged basis. Deadhead identity, then, is based on a certain level of commitment to the values and norms of the subculture. In this sense, the different levels of commitment can be analyzed in terms of an identity typology which I have labeled hardcore, new, and stable. This typology reflects some of the different strategies for negotiating identity among Deadheads and corresponds to the aspects of being a Deadhead as Deadheads themselves perceive and define the situation. I treat this as an ideal typology such that individuals may be ranked on each dimension of Deadhead identity (i.e. personal and social), and these may then be compared to an ideal type. Actual distinctions can then be seen as variations of the ideal type.

For example, the hardcore ideal type is one who ranks high on both the personal and social dimension. Deadheads who approximate the hardcore type are stereotypical, or archetypical, of Deadhead identity. The mythic image of this identity type sets the standard by which others may judge or be judged. Subjective internalization is strongest among the people who consider themselves to be part of this type, and role commitment is also strongest, thus creating the mythic image that Deadheads envision as a way of life. New Deadheads who enter the scene are faced with this image as a model, and this filters out to mainstream society through the media. This is the image that relates Deadheads to the drug-using hippies of the counterculture and scares conservative parents.

The new ideal type is characterized by one who ranks low in the personal dimension and high in the social dimension. Deadheads who approximate the new type may be simply playing the role of Deadhead in a situated context. In this respect, Deadheads may be claiming membership identity selectively, as the members of various ethnic groups do in particular social situations (Gans, 1979). Identity is, in this case, largely symbolic and situational. This would tend to reaffirm that an objective style of life exists, but that one has no personal commitment to it as a way of life.

The stable ideal type is characterized by a moderate ranking in both the personal and social dimensions. The stable type of Deadhead represents the middle ground in this classification system. It recognizes a range of diversity in each dimension of identity and can become empirically problematic due to this ambiguity. To a large extent, membership in this category depends on one's ability, or willingness, to integrate Deadhead identity into one's overall sense of self.

Unfortunately, continuing this research will be difficult to do with Deadheads because the band has dissolved due to the death of Jerry Garcia. This means that there will be no more Grateful Dead concerts and this will seriously affect the ability of the subculture to persist. Currently, there is a great deal of speculation as to what will happen to the subculture, but it is only speculation. Further research into this area might, however, yield fruitful insights, particularly with regard to the transformation of this subcultural identity and its effect on the individual members of the subculture. For example, what will happen to Deadhead identity now that the band has dissolved? Will the subculture adapt and continue to provide the organizational foundation for a coherent social identity, or will other social identities become more salient, such that Deadhead identity is demoted in the salience hierarchy of individuals?

In this chapter, I have dealt only with Deadhead identity, but theoretically this model can be extended to analyze other aspects of an individual's identity. Using the ideal type methodology, each aspect of an individual's identity could be ranked in the personal and social dimensions, and then compared to an ideal type. This would raise interesting questions about identity salience, especially in relation to other identities in one's identity kit (Gordon, 1976).

This also raises questions related to the congruity between personal identity and social identity, and the problems inherent in identity management. For example, could Deadheads maintain a high level of commitment to the personal identity dimension if the subculture is no longer around? These topics are beyond the scope of this chapter, but I think the use of an ideal type methodology would help to isolate factors that are related to these topics and that influence how we see ourselves and others.

Future research should also focus on the broader concerns of adolescents and youths, who face unique difficulties in relation to identity formation and identity management because of their culturally defined situation in the lifecourse. Consequently, musical taste and membership in subcultures, or taste groups, can provide a very important avenue by which they may see themselves as part of something larger than themselves, and develop a sense of self (Coleman, 1963; Zillman and Bhatia, 1989).

Notes

An earlier version of this chapter was presented at the 1991 annual meeting of the Mid-South Sociological Association. It has gone through several revisions since then thanks to the help of Norman Goodman at Stony Brook and Alan Lehman.

1   Simmel (1955) referred to these as the webs of group affiliations, but I use the term layers to distinguish between a hierarchy of these group affiliations at successively larger levels of generality.
2   Different historical time periods are often represented by different conceptions of the self. Currently, the postmodern condition has been the context for these types of discussions. Kellner (1995), for example, discusses the problems of self and identity management in a postmodern context as the result of an abundance of media images which offer individuals a variety of identity possibilities. He further notes that this, "creates highly unstable identities while constantly providing new openings to restructure one's identity" (Kellner, 1995, p. 257).
3   These groups may be thought of, in a statistical sense, as within an acceptable range of standard deviations from the dominant cultural mean (see Arnold, 1970). They are also commonly seen as reference groups by individuals who may have primary or secondary attachments to them (Cooley, 1909).
4   These groups are generally referred to as countercultures. Yinger (1982, p. 3) defines a counterculture as "a set of norms and values

of a group that sharply contradict the dominant norms and values of the society of which that group is a part." The major difference between subcultures and countercultures is the degree to which the dominant society tolerates the norms and values of the group (Dorn, 1969, p. 307).

5   Some of the other terms and concepts used to conceive of these types of groups would include: idioculture (Fine and Kleinman, 1979), microculture (Hannerz, 1992), and superculture or interculture (Slobin, 1993). Other related terms, originating from communications studies and community studies, might include: interpretive communities (Radway, 1984), intentional communities (Bouvard, 1975), and protocommunities (Willis, 1990).

6   The catalyst for this type of analysis derives from the theoretical insights of postmodernists, who have a tendency to describe the postmodern condition as a period that decontextualizes, or blurs the boundary distinctions of various cultural categories. While I tend to agree with some postmodern approaches, I do not see this as an "end to culture" type of argument. I would prefer to take a moderate approach and ground discussions in a structural framework.

7   There are many such taste groups that exist among the available genres of music. These groups exist in a more or less open cultural market and compete for the legitimacy of their musical tastes, values, and styles of life. Market forces may, therefore, be important factors in the creation of musical genres, but they do not detract from the significant social and psychological implications of taste on individuals' social and personal identities.

8   Some people feel that if value content is derived from the music itself, it will be passively received by an audience. I prefer to see a dynamic interplay between the music and the audience (and even between members of the audience) in which the meanings are negotiated. This is consistent with the theoretical orientations of symbolic interactionists.

9   My earlier research was based on interviews with 45 respondents collected at eight concert sites in the fall of 1988. I also used interviews and observational notes collected at eight concert sites by a team of researchers studying Deadheads in the summer of 1989. This team was sponsored by the Department of Continuing Education at the University of North Carolina at Greensboro, and supervised by Dr Rebecca Adams (see Sardiello, 1994, for a more detailed account of this methodology).

10   I have argued this point with Shan Sutton (1993), who sees Deadheads more formally as a religion.

11   The early history of the band, particularly their participation in the acid tests, has become part of Deadhead mythology. Myths, in general, are collective representations that encode values relevant to shared experiences. They are, in a sense, what Doty (1986, p. xviii) referred to as "projective psychic models," in that they "have a way of disclosing us to ourselves, either as we are or as we might be – and as we might be in either a negative or a positive light." This part of Deadhead mythology establishes two traditions, or guidelines, for interpreting a hallucinogenic drug experience. One tradition stems for the Ken Kesey style of drug use, which is perhaps best described in Tom Wolfe's *The Electric Kool-Aid Acid Test* (1968). This tradition advocates a free spirited, do-your-own-thing approach to the drug experience. The other tradition stems from the Timothy Leary style of drug use. Leary advocated a more introspective, spiritual use of hallucinogens, which became a tool for self-actualization (Leary et al., 1964). Individuals at concert events encounter this mythology through interactions with others and learn the appropriate rules to interpret the experience (Becker, 1953). In the context of the present discussion, the Leary tradition can be seen to have important implications for defining a sacred reality.

12   According to Hardwick, "symbolic integration is . . . that set of meanings, purposes, and ideals, celebrated in cult and ritual and enacted in everyday life, by means of which a society and thus the individuals in it, articulate their social solidarity and understand the vicissitudes of historical, social, and personal life" (Hardwick, 1973, p. 290). This definition is historically based on a functionalist interpretation of religion, but is broad enough to include secular equivalents and equivalents on the subcultural level (see Berger, 1967).

13   Greil and Rudy (1990, p. 220) use the term quasi-religion to refer to "activities and organizations that involve expressions of ultimate concern or organizational dynamics similar to those of religious organizations narrowly defined (that is, functionally defined) but that do not involve a belief in the supernatural." Their approach is oriented toward both the awe-inspiring experiences of transcendence, or what Durkheim (1915) called the sacred, and the organizational dynamics that contextualize and define those experiences. The profound implications for identity are inherent in their terminology, which includes what they refer to elsewhere as "identity transformation organizations" (Greil and Rudy, 1984).

14   Rituals are defined and classified in various ways. I prefer to view them in terms of socially constructed conceptions of the sacred, which can then be seen as historically and culturally variable. This

conception allows for a broader interpretation of ritual activity than the traditional model, which is based solely on religious interpretations. I also separate ritual activity based on its level of analysis such that rituals relate to the total social or cultural level, and ritualoids relate to the partial or subcultural level. In other words, Grateful Dead concerts are secular ritualoids (see Sardiello, 1997, for a more detailed account of this distinction).

15 Lehman (1994) observed similar types of distinctions among Deadheads based on a quantitative study. He then developed a Deadhead self-concept scale, which he used as part of a broader argument, to explain how lyrics and icons are meaningfully interpreted. In terms of self-concept, he noted that "The characteristics of a respondent who scored high on the self-concept as a Grateful Dead fan would include: had less than 16 years of education; owned lots of Grateful Dead CDs; called the Grateful Dead hotline numbers often; paid a lot of attention to the words of song lyrics; the band's musical style; icons from albums, CDs, T-shirts, stickers, etc.; and reading about band members; felt that they were familiar with a high percentage of song lyrics; and talked about the Grateful Dead often with their friends" (Lehman, 1994, p. 123). Overall, these variables explained 38 percent ($r^2 = 0.38$; $p > 0.05$) of the variance in a respondent's self-concept scale, but talking about the Grateful Dead appeared to be the most important predictor for self-concept.

16 Some of the people I talked to mentioned the Rainbow Family in this respect. They are another subcultural group with connections to the counterculture of the 1960s. They gather every year, usually in early July, to celebrate their interpretations of these life style and spiritual values.

17 The band generally toured four times a year and allowed people to camp in the parking lots of venues over the duration of their stay. In the fall of 1989, however, this was discontinued due to problems associated with overpopulation and clashes with local authorities. Before this, many people attended whole tours, moving from concert venue to concert venue. Summer tours, in particular, were more popular with younger Deadheads, especially college students who had the time to travel.

18 According to Dennis McNally, publicist for the band, the skeleton crew consists of four people, originally part of the "hog farm," and is headed by a woman named Calico.

19 Some Deadheads have invested a good deal of money in taping equipment because high-quality tapes are most desired. Tapers also request special taper tickets, which allow them access to the taper section, which is generally right behind the soundboard.

20 This area is commonly referred to as Vendors Row, but I have heard it called the Market, the Mall, Shakedown Street, or the Village.

21 Vegetarian food is a value preference, but meat products are also available.

22 Tie-dyed is a totemic symbol of in-group membership, especially when it is combined with other band iconography or lyrics from Grateful Dead songs (Sardiello, 1994).

23 Tickets are often traded, particularly for tickets to other concerts. When sold, it is a normative expectation that they will be exchanged for face value, or for a modest profit. Scalping tickets is normatively discouraged, but it does happen. Sometimes, tickets are even given away. These are called "miracle tickets" by Deadheads who have nothing to trade. It is an interesting phenomenon because it is so well established in Deadhead folklore that some people come to expect it to happen.

24 The use of the term foreigner was interesting because the man in question did seem to be of Middle Eastern origin, but I think the reference was intended to imply that this person was an outsider to the subculture.

25 These problems can be seen as similar to those experienced at the height of the counterculture, particularly in San Francisco (Perry, 1984).

26 LSD, marijuana, and alcohol are still very popular at Grateful Dead concerts and are more accepted normatively in the subculture. Other drugs are also used, such as heroin, cocaine, and nitrous oxide (laughing gas), but they tend to be normatively discouraged in the community.

27 The venues where the Dead cannot play include Merriweather Post Pavilion in Maryland, and Irvine Meadows Amphitheater in California. Even in cities where the Dead continue to play, there have been clashes with public officials, such as in Hartford, Connecticut, and Washington, DC (Goodman, 1990).

28 Estimates vary historically, but by 1990 it was probably between 500 and 1,000 (Goodman, 1990).

29 Lehman (1994, p. 128) made a similar observation, which he explained in relation to the possibility of self-concept investments elsewhere.

References

Arnold, D. O. (1970) Subculture marginality. In D. O. Arnold (ed.), *The Sociology of Subcultures*. Berkeley, CA: The Glendessary Press, pp. 81–95.

Becker, H. (1953) Becoming a marihuana user. *American Journal of Sociology*, 59, 235–42.

Becker, H. (1960) Notes on the concept of commitment. *The American Journal of Sociology*, 66(1), 32–40.

Berger, P. (1967) *The Sacred Canopy: Elements of a Sociological Theory of Religion*. Garden City, NY: Doubleday.

Berger, P. and Luckmann, T. (1966) *The Social Construction of Reality: a Treatise in the Sociology of Knowledge*. New York: Anchor.

Bouvard, M. (1975) *The Intential Community Movement*. New York: National University Publications.

Brake, M. (1980) *The Sociology of Youth Culture and Youth Subculture: Sex and Drugs and Rock 'n' Roll*. Boston: Routledge and Kegan Paul.

Brake, M. (1985) *Comparative Youth Culture: the Sociology of Youth Cultures and Youth Subcultures in America, Britain, and Canada*. Boston: Routledge and Kegan Paul.

Burke, P. and Hoelter, J. W. (1988) Identity and sex-race differences in educational and occupational aspirations. *Social Science Research*, 17, 29–47.

Calluori, R. A. (1985) The kids are alright: new wave subcultural theory. *Social Text: Theory, Culture, Ideology*, 4(3), 43–53.

Clarke, M. (1974) On the concept of "sub-culture". *British Journal of Sociology*, 25, 428–41.

Coleman, J. (1963) *The Adolescent Society*. New York: The Free Press.

Cooley, C. H. (1909) *Social Organization*. New York: Scribner.

Denisoff, R. S. and Bridges, J. (1983) The sociology of popular music: a review. *Popular Music and Society*, 9(1), 51–62.

Denisoff, S. R. (1975) *Solid Gold: the Popular Record Industry*. New Jersey: Transaction Books.

Denzin, N. K. (1989) *Interpretive Interactionism*. Newbury Park, CA: Sage Publications.

Dorn, D. S. (1969) A partial test of the delinquency continuum typology: contracultures and subcultures. *Social Forces*, 47(3), 305–14.

Dotter, D. (1987) Growing up is hard to do: rock and roll performers as cultural heroes. *Sociological Spectrum*, 7, 25–44.

Doty, W. G. (1986) *Mythography: a Study of Myths and Rituals*. Tuscaloosa: The University of Alabama Press.

Durkheim, E. (1915) *The Elementary Forms of Religious Life*. Original work published 1912. New York: The Free Press.

Erikson, E. (1950) *Childhood and Society*. New York: W. W. Norton.

Fine, G. A. and Kleinman, S. (1979) Rethinking subculture: an interactionist analysis. *American Journal of Sociology*, 85(1), 1–20.

Fiske, J. (1992) The cultural economy of fandom. In L. A. Lewis (ed.), *The Adoring Audience: Fan Culture and Popular Media*. New York: Routledge, pp. 30–49.

Frith, S. (1981) *Sound Effects: Youth, Leisure, and the Politics of Rock 'n' Roll.* New York: Pantheon Books.

Frith, S. (1996) Music and identity. In S. Hall and P. DuGay (eds), *Questions of Cultural Identity.* Thousand Oaks, CA: Sage Publications, pp. 108–27.

Gans, D. and Simon, P. (1985) *Playing in the Band.* New York: St Martin's Press.

Gans, H. (1974) *Popular Culture and High Culture: an Analysis and Evaluation of Taste.* New York: Basic books.

Gans, H. (1979) Symbolic ethnicity: the future of ethnic groups and cultures in America. *Ethnic and Racial Studies*, 2(1), 1–20.

Geertz, C. (1973) *The Interpretation of Culture.* New York: Basic Books.

Glaser, B. G. and Strauss, A. L. (1965) The discovery of substantive theory: a basic strategy underlying qualitative research. *The American Behaviorial Scientist*, 8(6), 5–12.

Goffman, E. (1959) *The Presentation of Self in Everyday Life.* Garden City, NY: Doubleday Anchor Books.

Goffman, E. (1963) *Stigma: Notes on the Management of Spoiled Identity.* Englewood Cliffs, NJ: Prentice Hall.

Goffman, E. (1967) *Interaction Ritual: Essays on Face-to-face Behavior.* New York: Pantheon Books.

Goodman, F. (1989) The Rolling Stone interview. *Rolling Stone*, November 30.

Goodman, F. (1990) The end of the road? *Rolling Stone*, August 23.

Gordon, C. (1976) Development of evaluated role identities. In A. Inkeles (ed.), *Annual Review of Sociology, Volume 2.* Palo Alto, CA: Annual Reviews, pp. 405–33.

Gordon, M. M. (1970) The subsociety and the subculture. In D. O. Arnold (ed.), *The Sociology of Subcultures.* Berkeley, CA: The Glendessary Press, pp. 150–63.

Greil, A. L. and Rudy, D. R. (1984) Social cacoons: encapsulation and identity transformation organizations. *Sociological Inquiry*, 54, 260–78.

Greil, A. L. and Rudy, D. R. (1990) On the margins of the sacred. In T. Robbins and D. Anthony (eds), *In Gods We Trust: New Patterns of Religious Pluralism in America.* New Brunswick, NJ: Transaction Publishers, pp. 219–32.

Grossberg, L. (1990) Is there rock after punk? In S. Frith and A. Goodwin (eds), *On Record: Rock, Pop, and the Written Word.* New York: Pantheon Books, pp. 111–24.

Grossberg, L. (1992) Is there a fan in the house? The affective sensibility of fandom. In L. A. Lewis (ed.), *The Adoring Audience: Fan Culture and Popular Media.* New York: Routledge, pp. 50–65.

Hannerz, U. (1992) *Cultural Complexity: Studies in the Social Organization of Meaning.* New York: Columbia University Press.

Hardwick, C. D. (1973) The counter culture as religion: on the identification of religion. *Soundings*, 56(3), 287–311.

Hebdige, D. (1976) The meaning of mod. In S. Hall and T. Jefferson (eds), *Resistance through Ritual: Youth Subcultures in Post-war Britain.* London: Hutchinson, pp. 87–96.

Hebdige, D. (1979) *Subculture: the Meaning of Style.* New York: Methuen.

Hewitt, J. (1989) *Dilemmas of the American Self.* Philadelphia: Temple University Press.

Hill, C. E. (1975) *Symbols and Society: Essays on Belief Systems in Action.* Athens, GA: University of Georgia Press.

Jefferson, T. (1976) Cultural responses to the teds: the defence of space and status. In S. Hall and T. Jefferson (eds), *Resistance through Rituals: Youth Subcultures in Post-war Britain.* London: Hutchinson, pp. 81–6.

Kellner, D. (1995) *Media Culture: Cultural Studies, Identity and Politics between the Modern and the Postmodern.* New York: Routledge.

Klapp, O. E. (1969) *Collective Search for Identity.* New York: Holt, Rinehart and Winston.

Klapp, O. E. (1970) Style rebellion and identity crisis. In T. Shibutani (ed.), *Human Nature and Collective Behavior.* Englewood Cliffs, NJ: Prentice Hall.

Leary, T. Metzner, R. and Alpert, R. (1964) *The Psychedelic Experience: a Manual Based on the Tibetan Book of the Dead.* New York: University Books.

Lehman, A. (1994) Music as symbolic communication: the Grateful Dead and their fans. Dissertation, College Park, MD: The University of Maryland.

Lewis, G. (1982) Popular music: symbolic resource and transformer of meaning in society. *International Review of the Aesthetics and Sociology of Music*, 13, 183–9.

Lewis, G. (1987) Patterns of meaning and choice: taste cultures in popular music. In J. Lull (ed.), *Popular Music and Communication.* Beverly Hills, CA: Sage Publications, pp. 198–211.

Linton, R. (1936) *The Study of Man.* New York: Appleton-Century-Crofts.

Lull, J. (1987a) Listeners' communicative uses of popular music. In J. Lull (ed.), *Popular Music and Communication.* Beverly Hills, CA: Sage Publications, pp. 140–74.

Lull, J. (1987b) Popular music and communication: an introduction. In J. Lull (ed.), *Popular Music and Communication.* Beverly Hills, CA: Sage Publications, pp. 10–35.

Martin, B. (1979) The sacralization of disorder: symbolism in rock music. *Sociological Analysis*, 40, 87–124.

Mead, G. H. (1934) *Mind, Self, and Society*. Chicago: University of Chicago Press.

Miller, T. (1991) *The Hippies and American Values*. Knoxville: The University of Tennessee Press.

Montague, S. P. and Morais, R. (1976) Football games and rock concerts: the ritual enactment. In W. Arens and S. P. Montague (eds), *American Dimension: Cultural Myths and Social Realities*. California: Alfred Publishing Co., pp. 33–52.

Murdock, G. (1974) Mass communication and the construction of meaning. In N. Armstead (ed.), *Reconstructing Social Psychology*. Harmondsworth: Penguin.

Pearson, A. (1987) The Grateful Dead phenomena: an ethnomethodological approach. *Youth and Society*, 18(4), 418–32.

Perry, C. (1984) *The Haight-Ashbury*. New York: Random House.

Peterson, R. A. and DiMaggio, P. (1975) From region to class: the changing locus of country music. *Social Forces*, 53, 497–506.

Radway, J. (1984) *Reading the Romance: Women, Patriarchy, and Popular Literature*. Chapel Hill: University of North Carolina Press.

Robinson, J. P. and Fink, E. L. (1986) Beyond mass culture and class culture: subcultural differences in the structure of music preferences. In S. J. Ball-Rokeach and M. G. Cantor (eds), *Media, Audience, and Social Structure*. Newbury Park, CA: Sage Publications, pp. 226–39.

Sardiello, R. (1994) Secular rituals in popular culture: a case for Grateful Dead concerts and Dead Head identity. In J. S. Epstein (ed.), *Adolescents and Their Music: If It's Too Loud, You're Too Old*. New York: Garland Publishing, pp. 115–40.

Sardiello, R. (1997) Liminality in a postmodern world: from ritual to ritualoid. In J. Epstein (ed.), *Wilderness and Mirrors: Symbolic Interactionism and the Postmodern Terrain*. New York: Garland.

Schechter, H. (1983) The myth of the eternal child in sixties America. In C. D. Geist and J. Nachbar (eds), *The Popular Culture Reader*. Bowling Green, OH: Bowling Green University Popular Press, pp. 81–95.

Simmel, G. (1955) The web of group-affiliations. In *Georg Simmel*. New York: The Free Press.

Slobin, M. (1993) *Subcultural Sounds: Micromusics of the West*. Hanover, NH: Wesleyan University Press.

Stryker, S. (1968) Identity salience and role performance: the relevance of symbolic interaction theory for family research. *Journal of Marriage and the Family*, 30, 558–64.

Stryker, S. (1989) The two psychologies: additional thoughts. *Social Forces*, 68(1), 45–54.

Sutton, S. C. (1993) The Deadhead community: popular religion in contemporary American culture. MA thesis, Wright State University, Ohio.

Turner, J. C. (1987) *Rediscovering the Social Group: a Self-categorization Theory*. New York: Basil Blackwell.

Weigert, A. J. (1983) Identity: its emergence within sociological psychology. *Symbolic Interaction*, 6(2), 183–206.

Weinstein, D. (1991) *Heavy Metal: a Cultural Sociology*. New York: Lexington Books.

Willis, P. (1990) *Common Culture: Symbolic Work at Play in the Evertday Cultures of the Young*. Boulder, CO: Westview Press.

Wolfe, T. (1968) *The Electric Kool-Aid Acid Tests*. New York: Bantam Book.

Wuthnow, R. (1976) *The Consciousness Reformation*. Berkeley: University of California Press.

Wuthnow, R. (1978) *Experimentation in American Religion: the New Mysticisms and Their Implications for the Churches*. Berkeley: University of California Press.

Yinger, J. M. (1982) *Countercultures: the Promise and the Peril of a World Turned Upside Down*. New York: The Free Press.

Zillman, D. and Bhatia, A. (1989) Effects of associating with musical genres on heterosexual attraction. *Communication Research*, 16(2), pp. 263–88.

7
"DON'T NEED YOU:" RETHINKING IDENTITY POLITICS AND SEPARATISM FROM A GRRRL PERSPECTIVE

Mary Celeste Kearney

[They say,] "Oh, you're such a girl. You're so girly. You throw like a girl." Well, I am a girl.[1]

In 1992, Bikini Kill released the song "Don't Need You" on their *Yeah, Yeah, Yeah, Yeah* album.[2] Sung by Kathleen Hanna, the raging lyrics foreground the pro-girl identity politics and separatist philosophy adhered to by those participating in the radical female youth culture known as riot grrrl: "Don't need you to say we're cute / Don't need you to say we're alright / Don't need your protection / Don't need no kiss goodnight / Us girls don't need you . . ." Although the song is directed to boys, I would argue that we can also hear these words as an address to others who feel it is their role to both protect girls and affirm their behavior. Heard this way, the song can be understood as representative of riot grrrls' separatism not only from males, but also from adults, especially older women who all too often (and all to problematically) speak for girls in the name of "women," "feminism," and "sisterhood."

In 1980, Angela McRobbie articulated her hopeful prediction for future girl-only cultures:

To the extent that all-girl subcultures, where the commitment to the gang comes first, might forestall [the search for boyfriends] and provide their members with a collective confidence which could transcend the need for "boys," they could well signal an important progression in the politics of youth culture.[3]

Sixteen years later, McRobbie's prediction reads like a recipe for riot grrrl. Reinterpreting the "do it yourself" directive commonly associated with the punk scene as "don't need you" – a self-affirmation as well a refusal of assistance from those outside their group – riot grrrls have adopted the radical political philosophy and practice of separatism in order to liberate themselves from the misogyny, ageism, and, for some, homophobia and racism they experience in their everyday lives.

Considering the subordination of adolescent girls in our society, it seems only natural that riot grrrls are separating from males and older women as well as mainstream culture (and some segments of alternative cultures) to establish and assert their own sociopolitical identity via a culture that remains distinctly girl-oriented and unadulterated. Separatism works for riot grrrls because it is a temporary tactic enacted for safety and empowerment. Riot grrrls separate from males to act on behalf of females; they separate from adults to act on behalf of youth; and they separate from the mainstream to act on behalf of radical culture and politics.

In addition, their adherence to an identity politics which foregrounds their multiple and often contradictory subjectivities has resulted in powerful assertions of political and cultural agency. As Barbara Hudson has provocatively demonstrated, the concept of "feminine adolescence" exists as a paradox in Western society because femininity and adolescence are diametrically opposed to one another.[4] Since adolescence is prefigured in our social imagination as a time of acting out, rebelliousness, and increasing independence, its construction as masculine occurs precisely because these characteristics are at odds with traditional notions of femininity (e.g. caretaking, intimacy with others). While women have often found it difficult to bridge the boundaries which separate conventional masculine and feminine attributes, riot grrrls complicate such binarisms by refusing to allow adolescence to remain a boy-only, male-identified social position, at the same time that they refuse to let go of many traits understood as feminine. Moreover, riot grrrl remains unique in its ability to act from the liminal position between mainstream and countercultural constructions of both femininity and adolescence. By uniting as "riot grrrls," rather than "girls," "women," or "youth," they have changed the way adolescent girls are perceived, and require males, adults, the media, and those of us who study youth to deal with them on their terms.[5]

At a time when many individuals are bemoaning the inability of the Left to effectuate sociopolitical action, the formation of a radical female youth culture through separatist practices and the construction of a collective identity requires us to rethink some of the criticisms made recently about these political practices as retrograde and ineffectual. What I would like to suggest is that, in this postmodern moment when class, nation, and other conventional forms of political identification are being profoundly challenged and altered, it might be helpful to look to groups such as riot grrrl to understand how a common group identity can be created, maintained, and powerfully asserted in a way that does not require its members to abstract themselves from their specific subject positions and individual interests in history and society. My project here, therefore, incorporates an analysis of: (a) riot grrrls' reformulation of girlhood as a powerful position of social, cultural, and political investment, and their construction of a collective identity which refuses the paradox of feminine adolescence theorized by Hudson; and (b) riot grrrls' separatist philosophy and practices, especially in relation to the "space winning" processes of youth cultures and radical political movements.

Don't Need You: Separatist Tactics and Strategies

While I recognize the problems associated with describing riot grrrl (not to mention any youth culture) as "separatist," since such a term implies that these adolescent girls do not interact with adults, males, and mainstream culture when in fact they must and do (their age and inexperience keeping them from pursuing an existence independent from these groups and institutions), it is important to recognize that the construction and maintenance of youth cultures and oppositional political groups often rely on understanding themselves as already marginal as well as imagining a place of power and agency outside dominant culture.

For centuries now, separatism has been a useful tool for disenfranchised groups to come to power and act in the face of oppressions resulting from the fragmentation of society into a dominant, mainstream culture and other various cultures which negotiate, yet necessarily contribute to, the center's hegemony.[6] Separatism has functioned for such groups first as a survival *tactic*, a temporary means of acquiring social, political, and cultural space and time by separating from hegemonically defined and controlled institutions, relationships, and roles.[7] Since, as Marilyn Frye argues, the difference between the powerful and the powerless is an issue of access and autonomy ("Total power is unconditional access; total powerlessness is being unconditionally accessible"), the first political act of the disempowered must be to separate, to regain control of their spatial and temporal accessibility.[8] This stage of separatism is referred to by Frye as the "no-saying" stage, the group's exclusion, avoidance, rejection, and denial of those with power, which brings about a shift in accessibility. Discussing the importance of this initial stage of separatism, Bernice Johnson Reagon explains,

> When somebody else is running a society [that oppresses certain people] and you are the one who would be put out to die, it gets too hard to stay out in that society all the time. And that's when you find a place, and you try to bar the door and check all the people who come in. You come together to see what you can do about shouldering up all of your energies so that you and your kind can survive.[9]

In *The Practice of Everyday Life*, Michel de Certeau argues that this initial stage of separatism requires the opportunism associated with tactical maneuvering: that is, the ability to transform circumstances into favorable situations that reorganize space and thus challenge imbalances in access.[10]

As de Certeau notes, once a group is able to self-isolate, it "postulates a *place* that can be determined as its *own* and serve as the base from which relations with an *exteriority* composed of targets or threats . . . can be managed."[11] It is at this point that separatism as a tactic of the disenfranchised becomes a *strategy* of the newly empowered, who can use their collective identity as a place or location from which to initiate radical political action. In other words, once the formation of an autonomous place occurs, a self-determined agency can be asserted on behalf of the group and its individual members. As Gayatri Chakravorty Spivak argues, political agency is impossible without the creation of a common group identity formed through a "strategic essentialism" – "the strategic use of an essence as a mobilizing slogan or masterword like *woman or worker*" – which allows the disempowered to own a place, to own their voices, and, thus, to assert themselves within hegemonic structures and relationships.[12]

Considering the effectiveness of separatism in empowering a collective confidence among deprivileged people, it is no surprise that it has often served a primary function in youth cultures formed by disaffiliated adolescents. Such separatist behavior on the part of youths is perhaps best described in the groundbreaking British anthology *Resistance through Rituals*:

> [Youth cultures] . . . win space for the young: cultural space in the neighbourhood and institutions, real time for leisure and recreation, actual room on the street or street-corner. They serve to mark out and appropriate "territory" in the localities. They focus around key occasions of social interaction . . . They cluster around particular locations. They develop specific rhythms of interchange, structured relations between members . . . They explore "focal concerns" central to the inner life of the group . . . They adopt and adapt material objects – goods and possessions – and reorganise them into distinctive "styles" which express the collectivity of their being-as-a-group . . . Sometimes, the world is marked out, linguistically, by names or an *argot* which classifies the social world exterior to them in terms meaningful only within their group perspective, and maintains its boundaries.[13]

This theorization of the spatial and temporal practices of youth cultures foregrounds the tactical and strategic separatism necessary for young people to come to some form of social agency. As Dick Hebdige notes in *Subculture: the Meaning of Style*, "[This] distinctive quest for a measure of autonomy . . . characterizes all youth sub- (and counter) cultures."[14] Through empowered assertions of semantic and representational agency, a "crisis of authority" occurs as new names, new roles, new practices, and new relations are created, and adults and the mainstream are required to deal with the youth culture on its own terms.[15]

Though much has been said and written about the "magical solutions" youth cultures provide for adolescents caught between ideological and social contradictions, recent studies of youth culture are less optimistic.[16] In her street-smart analysis of contemporary adolescents in the United States, *Teenage Wasteland*, Donna Gaines speaks extensively about the colonization of youth by adults; that is, the surveillance, regulation, and containment of their movements through time and space. As she makes clear, this process has resulted in the decreasing status of young people.[17] While adults continuously deny youth their political agency while exploiting their forms of cultural expression (which are then sold back to them via the corporate consumer industries), the spaces of youth (streets, bedrooms, etc.) and the forms of youth identification (fashion, music, etc.) have become battlegrounds in the cultural processes of identification that often leave young people feeling disconnected and powerless. Gaines notes that sometimes the only option is to disengage:

> The further away from the mainstream [kids] could get, the greater their self-respect. Whether that meant nonparticipation, obliteration through drugs, or contemplating suicide, it was a matter of psychic survival.[18]

While Gaines is specifically referring to youth in the 1980s, and though much of what she observes can be seen today, she concludes *Teenage Wasteland* with an optimistic outlook for the future, noting that youth activism is on the rise in the 1990s. We need to question, therefore, why it is that now, when the concept of stable identity is being seriously challenged and deconstructed on many fronts, young people are insisting upon a politics based on their social experiences as adolescents. The reasons behind this relatively recent increase in youth activism seem to be many. Yet I believe that the impetus for young people to unite politically *as youth* has occurred primarily because that category, *their* category, no longer belongs to just them. In the United States, mainstream culture *is* youth culture, but *whose* youth culture it is remains difficult to tell. As Andrew Ross notes in his introduction to *Microphone Fiends: Youth Music and Youth Culture*,

It is not just Mick Jagger and Tina Turner who imagine themselves still to be eighteen years old and steppin' out; a significant
mass of baby boomers partially act out this belief in their daily
lives . . . On the other hand, it is also true that many kids listen
obsessively to exactly the same music that their parents did.[19]

As Kobena Mercer asserts in his discussion of identity during
postmodernity, "One thing at least is clear – identity only becomes an issue when it is in crisis, when something assumed to
be fixed, coherent and stable is displaced by the experience of
doubt and uncertainty."[20] Politicized youth cultures such as riot
grrrl which have formed through a collective identity directly
associated with adolescence are evidence that the concept of
youth is in serious trouble.

Revolution Girl-style Now: Riot Grrrl's
Ex-centric Culture and Politics

Coming to critical consciousness about their doubly subordinated position as adolescent girls at a time when MTV ruled
mainstream youth culture and Madonna the "Material Girl"
seemed the only role model for female youth, some girls began to
speak out about their complicated relationship to the patriarchy,
adultism, and heterocentrism perpetuated by dominant ideology
and often reproduced in the alternative cultures to which they
belonged. Enraged by the social positions and relations within
our largely misogynist culture which leave many girls victims
of both child abuse (rape, assault, child neglect) and self-abuse
(drug addiction, bulimia, anorexia, alcoholism, suicide), they
decided that the only way to survive was to unite with others who
had similar experiences in order to fight the oppressions girls
face each day. They began to meet, they began to organize, and
soon they formed a community that had spread internationally
via their self-made cultural products and in-your-face political
activism. The year was 1991, and the call to action was "Revolution girl-style now!"

Through the formation of a broad cultural network and active
participation in radical politics, riot grrrls have created a heterogeneous community of adolescent girls which crosses local,
regional, and even national boundaries.[21] With the knowledge

that "growing up" and "becoming a woman" often means leaving the self-confidence and homosocial bonds of youth behind, riot grrrl dares adolescent girls to stand up for themselves, for their rights, and for each other. As Misty, creator of the zines *Just Like a Girl* and *I Can't Get Far Enough Away*, writes,

> Wimmin need to learn that power is not given, we have to take it. We need to realize that we don't have to stand around and be treated like this. Don't let anyone control you or dictate your life to you . . . No one can save you from your oppression except yourself. GIRLS UNITE![22]

While feminist theorists and activists continue to debate the effectiveness of separatist strategies for women, separatism is used by riot grrrls to win their own space as well as to make themselves inaccessible to adults, males, and mainstream culture. Riot grrrls contextualize the exclusion of males (and, often, older women) from many of their gatherings as a strategy of empowerment as well as an issue of safety. As Erika Reinstein argues in an early manifesto, riot grrrl exists.

> BECAUSE we need to acknowledge that our blood is being spilt, that right now a girl is being raped or battered and it might be me or you or your mom or the girl you sat next to on the bus last Tuesday, and she might be dead by the time you finish reading this . . . BECAUSE a safe place needs to be created for girls where we can open our eyes and reach out to each other without being threatened by this sexist society and our day-to-day shit.[23]

At a time when right-wing politicians harp on about "family values" while girls continue to be violated and abused by fathers, brothers, boyfriends, and other males who feel they have a right to dominate a girl's body as well as her space, riot grrrls break the code of silence typically associated with rape and domestic abuse by reacting openly with a rage that gives voice to the horrors many girls experience as their childish bodies develop into physically mature forms too often perceived as sexually ripe and available for plucking.

Though their "don't need you"/"grrrls only" stance is often misinterpreted as "male bashing" and reverse sexism, as Dawn writes in her zine *Function*, "R[iot] G[rrrl] is meant to be empowering for grrrls, having a safe comfortable space to speak openly about anything."[24] In *Girl Power: Young Women Speak Out!* a text which brings together the writings of many adolescent girls, Jasmine recollects the power of riot grrrl meetings for herself and others:

> It makes my toes tingle every time I think of a RG meeting where we totally supported each other through hard times, and helped each other learn how to deal with the daily subliminal/subconscious sexism we endure, and how we all grooved to . . . building up our self-esteem and self-love . . . something I had little to none a year before.[25]

Temporarily appropriating spaces for their grrrl-only meetings and annual conventions in order to create a supportive environment for the discussion of personal/political concerns and the empowerment of a collective political agency, riot grrrls are known for also creating spaces for themselves in places where they feel marginalized by their status as female youth, especially at political events and concerts.

For riot grrrls, identity politics means making a claim for and taking back what is theirs – adolescent girlhood – and reconstructing it as a position of social identification and political agency. Reaffirming adolescent girlhood as a radically marginal and therefore powerful position from which to act, riot grrrls foreground distinctions between girls and women that are effaced in the blanket universalist notions of "females," "femininity," and "feminism." But instead of bonding as "girls," these female youth have appropriated the word "girl" from its dominant connotations and reformulated that social category by creating a new identity that better represents their revolutionary spirit. "Riot grrrl," therefore, symbolizes the enraged girl who empowers herself and others to speak out and fight against oppression. In turn, it is a call to action ("Riot, grrrl!").

Creating a new form of collective identification and political agency for female youth, riot grrrls seriously challenge the popular understanding of girls as boy-hungry mall rats and female youth cultures as "bedroom cultures," where boys are considered girls' primary fantasy/identification figures and romance and marriage are thought to be their only goals for the future. Indeed, riot grrrls have created a community where boys are not "on the side" (as the recent movie by that title would have it);

they are removed from the equation altogether. Rejecting the dominant position of the teenage girl as the ultimate consumer and object of consumption, "riot grrrl" appropriates the traits of assertiveness and action normally associated with (masculine) adolescence at the same time that it celebrates the characteristics of nurturance and community typically associated with femininity.

Perhaps in reaction to the rampant materialism of the 1980s, which created conservative yuppies instead of leftist radicals, riot grrrls have constructed a counterculture for themselves outside and independent of patriarchal corporate capitalism. Their mobile community, which transgresses local, regional, and national boundaries and moves between schools, concert halls, and political rallies, demonstrates a profound understanding of the impossibility today for girls to have a "room of one's own" and signals the formation of what Benedict Anderson refers to as an "imagined community."[26] Such an imagined identification with other like-minded female youth exists primarily because of the common experiences of being an adolescent girl in the United States during the 1990s. But it is also due to the circulation within their community of self-produced cultural products, products which disseminate the "Revolution girl-style now!" message and signal a rebellion against not only girls' subordinated socio-political position as female adolescents, but also their complicated economic position as teenage girls (a primary target group for the fashion, beauty, and culture industries).

Unlike most female adolescents, whose cultural identity is connected to the consumption of commodities produced by the dominant culture industries, riot grrrls attempt to exist outside the corporations which support mainstream culture by creating the music, zines, and other creative products they consume. Thus, their countercultural community signals an important shift in female youth cultures from the realm of consumption to the realm of production.[27]

As Hebdige demonstrates in his provocative study *Subculture*, style is an instrumental signifying practice in youth cultures, since it readily expresses a group's identity; that is, its members' common experiences of negotiating the contradictions inherent within dominant ideology and reproduced in mainstream culture.[28] In the 1990s, the styles of youth seem all the more apparent since, as George Lipsitz argues, young people today "Answer a culture of surveillance with a counterculture of conspicuous display, they constitute their own bodies . . . as sites for performance and play."[29] While I believe that the purpose of riot grrrl's style goes far beyond such playful performativity, Lipsitz's point is well demonstrated by riot grrrls' recuperation and reformation of the adolescent female body and its accessories.

Radically refuting the misogynist messages perpetuated by the fashion and beauty industries that encourage girls and women to believe that we will never look "good enough," riot grrrls often call attention to the objectification of female bodies in patriarchal society by marking their hands, arms, stomachs, and faces with provocative political slogans as well as with words commonly used to denigrate women (e.g. "slut," "whore," "cunt"). This practice echoes the dress-up games of young girls who code themselves feminine by applying "play" makeup with crayons, paint, and markers at the same time that it deconstructs the conventional use of cosmetics and the popular understanding of the female body as an object existing only for beautification projects. Creating their own anti-fashion style through an uncategorizable amalgam of couture *faux pas* – thrift store girls' clothes, plastic barrettes, industrial boots, knee socks, lunch boxes, tattoos and body piercings, and unconventional haircuts and colors – riot grrrls appropriate the accoutrements of girlhood, femininity, and alternative youth culture for an ironic (dis)play and disruption of the signifying codes of gender and generation.

While riot grrrl's anti-fashion style is the most visible evidence of the formation of a collective identity among these female youth, the circulation of riot grrrl zines – which contain (in varying amounts) poetry, stories, personal "confessions," interviews, drawings, collages, cultural criticism, advice columns, political manifestos, and advertisements for riot grrrl products – remains one of the primary ways the "Revolution girl-style now" message is spread. Unlike music, which requires access to instruments, sound equipment, and spaces for practice and performance, zines are the cheapest and, perhaps, easiest means of producing and distributing alternative, independent forms of cultural expression. Whether individually or collectively created, riot grrrl zines function as an important networking tool for those who feel isolated within their homes, schools, workplaces, and local communities by establishing a place where girls can meet others like themselves, as well as a place where they can discuss their most personal/political concerns without the fear of editorializing and censorship. Alternatives to mainstream teen magazines such as *Seventeen* and *YM*, which privilege consumerism and romance over self-empowerment and critical consciousness, riot grrrl zines provide not only the support system that many female youth lack today, but also a means of communal fantasy where riot grrrls can formulate plans of action for the creation of a more just society. As Renee comments in her zine *Stumble*, "Just by going out and doing a zine says something – it means that this thing called 'empowerment' is in effect. Time to make a statement. And it ain't no feeble attempt. These zines scream 'I AM MAKING A DIFFERENCE.'"[30]

Though riot grrrl zines are a crucial component in the continual, collective critique and redefinition of riot grrrl's community and its objectives, they seem less responsible in communicating riot grrrl's messages beyond the girls already involved in this community, since, for reasons of privacy, zines are usually exchanged only among riot grrrls and other supportive individuals connected to the alternative community. The music created by riot grrrl bands and performers, however, has been instrumental in spreading the "Revolution girl-style now!" message due to its wide dissemination outside this community via record sales, concert tours, and reviews by both the mainstream and alternative music presses. From Bikini Kill's early "Double Dare Ya" call for girls to "stand up for your rights" to The Tourettes' "Battle Hymn," which roars "I can't change who I am to fit into your world," to The CeBe Barnes Band's more recent "She's a Winner," which speaks of the unique forms of homophobia experienced by young lesbians ("put on a fucking dress / you should've been a boy"), the songs of performers associated with riot grrrl courageously assert the bold voice lacking in many adolescent girls, thus challenging them to speak out and fight back.[31] In addition, individual musicians effectively model riot grrrl's "Don't Need You" anti-corporatist ethos when not touring by producing their own work and that of other musicians on various grrrl-run labels. Contrary to popular conceptions of this community, however, riot grrrl music is not only punk and riot grrrl concerts are not only for punk bands. Folk singers and spoken word performers also spread the "grrrl power" message through their art, while riot grrrl concerts function as alternative marketplaces for the selling and trading of records, tapes, zines, books, and clothing.

The national (and international) distribution of riot grrrl zines and music has been quite influential in encouraging riot grrrls to create other forms of cultural expression, especially film and video projects. For example, Sadie Benning, a young video artist much celebrated for her pixelated Fisher Price visions of lesbian youth, has indicated that the inspiration for her video "Girl Power" came from her contact with riot grrrl music and zines:

> When I heard Bikini Kill and when I read these zines, it was so much what I had wanted when I was in high school. It really creates a break in the chain, you know, being able to have words to put upon things that are happening to you and knowing that we all exist and finding one another.[32]

The collaborative spirit of riot grrrl also inspired Miranda July to create a video zine (*Big Miss Moviola*) that distributes collections of material by female film- and videomakers who want to network and create visual art outside the mainstream systems of production, distribution, and exhibition.[33] In turn, several grrrls have started a "girl run and powered" mail order clothing catalog, Alien Girl, which they describe as an anti-corporate service designed to promote pro-girl messages.

While the separatist practices inspired by riot grrrl's "don't need you" ethos have helped to create this radical community, what remains unique and innovative about riot grrrl in comparison with other female youth cultures is that its focus goes far beyond the imagined identification elicited by these cultural creations. Indeed, it is the in-your-face political activism of riot grrrls – whether marching in feminist rallies, boycotting psychiatric institutions, volunteering at Rock for Choice concerts, sponsoring self-defense workshops, or organizing gay youth groups – that signals the ruptural difference of this community. Formed to express rage and ignite action in female youth, riot grrrl's alliance-building with other groups of resistance, such as the Feminist Majority, the National Children's Rights Alliance, and Students Organized Against Racism, challenges popular representations of this community as an exclusive club for middle-class white girls.

Riot grrrl activism does not manifest itself only in the more public arenas of political activism, however. Sarah, a riot grrrl from Washington, DC, interviewed by *off our backs*, indicates how riot grrrl's political activism begins with individual responsibility: "I want a revolution, but that's too big for me . . . So I'm going to do my own personal revolution. If every girl does her own personal revolution, we don't need a big one."[34] Many riot grrrls incorporate resistance in their personal lives via politicized daily practices such as vegetarianism, environmentalism, and a "straight-edged" body ethic (no cigarettes, no alcohol, no drugs). As suggested in an early riot grrrl manifesto, a leftist "personal is political" ethos guides the revolutionary praxis of this community and signals its importance in the history of youth and feminist activism:

> BECAUSE we seek to create revolution in our own lives every single day by envisioning and creating alternatives to the status quo . . . BECAUSE every time we pick up a pen, or an instrument, or get anything done, we are creating the revolution. We *are* the revolution.[35]

Since their emergence in 1991, riot grrrls have been approached by a number of mainstream publications and journalists wanting to tell (and sell) the story of this radical female youth culture. Following what they considered to be repeated misrepresentations of their community by US newspapers and magazines such as *The New York Times* and *Newsweek*, as well as British publications such as *Melody Maker*, riot grrrls initiated a press blackout in 1993 and now refuse to speak with or be photographed by anyone associated with the popular media.[36] As their blackout suggests, riot grrrls are profoundly aware of how easy it is for those in control of mainstream representational discourse to exploit and commodify marginalized cultures, and how difficult it is for young people today to resist the misrepresentation, co-optation, and containment of their particular scenes and forms of cultural expression.[37] By activating a media blackout, riot grrrls have resisted such exploitation by denying mainstream access, definition, and commodification of their culture, thus preventing the massive exploitation typically experienced by new social movements, especially youth cultures.[38] (Moreover, riot grrrl's cultural artifacts have resisted corporate co-optation, by being self-produced in small quantities and sold for minimal profit or traded within the alternative community.)

This is not to say that youth cultures such as riot grrrl exist in some "free" or "authentic" state before the mainstream media become aware of their existence. Indeed, riot grrrls' engagement with the popular press (especially via the teen girl magazine *Sassy*) demonstrates youth cultures' reliance on the mainstream media in order to "get the word out" about their communities, as well as their complicity in their cultures' incorporation in dominant ideology and discourse.[39] It is important to note, therefore, that the blackout called for by riot grrrls was not initiated until they realized that their community had become tasty (and lucrative) bait in the massive feeding frenzy for commodifiable information and cultural artifacts. By then, riot grrrls had participated (albeit not always willingly) in the documentation of their community by almost all major US newspapers and popular magazines. Thus, despite resisting full appropriation by the media and mainstream culture, the riot grrrl blackout has failed to fully curtail their misrepresentation by the press. As Theo Cateforis points out, "The journalistic media . . . deprived of a 'live' or willing subject, has an even more flexible opportunity to construct its own version of Riot Grrrl . . . They can build a Riot Grrrl prototype out of such things as fanzine titles and decontextualized quotations."[40]

The processes of commercial recuperation and discursive misrepresentation experienced by marginal movements such as youth cultures are glaringly obvious when we consider riot grrrl's repeated representation by the popular press as a cultural (rather than political) phenomenon.[41] Contrary to most descriptions of riot grrrl's community (including most academic analyses), "riot grrrl" is not just an adjective for a subgenre of punk music; nor does it describe only a group of female punk musicians and their fans.[42] While the contextualization of riot grrrl as a musical phenomenon reflects an attempt to incorporate riot grrrl within the popular frameworks for understanding youth culture, such representations more significantly reveal the desire of the media to not speak about riot grrrl as a radical political community. Given that the studies of youth continue to privilege the more visible (and audible) components of youth culture, I am interested in moving the discussion of riot grrrl away from its current focus on the music emanating from this community and toward riot grrrl's connections with feminist and other politicized counter-cultural movements.

Cherry Bombs: Riot Grrrl's Radical Girl Movement

Rather than continuing to imagine youth as only the *future* – that is, those who will bring about change once they reach adulthood – we need to form a way of discussing the various ways youth are politically active *today*, during their adolescence.[43] Our discussions and analyses of youth cultures, therefore, must move beyond the conventional frameworks on which we have come to depend (music, style, etc.). This is not to say that the various significatory practices of youth cultures are not politically motivated, nor that studies of these practices are apolitical. However, scholars of youth cultures often appear satisfied with what Clifford Geertz calls "thin descriptions" of culture: that is, representations of a culture's surface details which fail to explore the more complex (and often contradictory) processes involved in cultural signification.[44] Thus, while British studies of youth such as *Resistance through Rituals* and Hebdige's *Subculture* have been important for understanding the semiotic processes involved in youth cultures, these theories are often insufficient for understanding groups such as riot grrrl, which form in direct opposition to mainstream culture rather than outside it (as spectacular, leisure-based subcultures do).[45] Because riot grrrl's community is strongly resonant of previous youth cultures whose position *within* hegemonic culture as part of the middle class afforded them greater autonomy and political agency, I believe theories of countercultures are more useful for understanding riot grrrl's explicit opposition to dominant ideology and mainstream culture via direct political action and the creation of an alternative counterculture.

For instance, in comparison to female youth from the working class, riot grrrls are privileged with more education, greater access to the means of cultural production and advanced forms of communication (camcorders, computers, etc.), and a longer transitional stage between adolescence and adulthood, which allows them move time to experiment with new subject positions, social identifications, relationships, and forms of work (especially for those who attend college). In turn, the middle-class sensibility of riot grrrls appears in their ability to blur the boundaries between work and non-work time as they incorporate their "personal is political" philosophy in all aspects of their daily lives, not just in the activities associated with leisure time.

While many have noted that riot grrrl's "do it yourself" ethos echoes that of the punk movement, it is important to note that many of the anti-hegemonic values of both these movements are traceable to the middle-class hippie counterculture of the mid-1960s, whose oppositional stance emerged via a generational crisis caused, in part, by youth's increasing critical conscious-ness of their powerlessness in mainstream society. In turn, riot grrrl's "Don't need you" separatist stance recalls many of the radical political movements of the late 1960s, which advocated a non-assimilationist approach of resistance through the forma-tion of separate cultures and communities.

Of those political movements, riot grrrl most strongly echoes the pro-woman/consciousness raising radical feminist commun-ity of the late 1960s, which insisted upon separatism from male-dominated culture, relationships, and organizations for women's liberation from patriarchy and misogyny. Many early radical feminists believed that separatist politics, alternative institu-tions, and an autonomous "womyn's" culture were the only ways to effect positive social and cultural change for women. Early feminist separatists met with dissension from the outset, how-ever, as Alice Echols notes in her history of radical feminism, *Daring to Be Bad*.[46] Liberal feminists (most of whom were straight) – whose egalitarian, humanist political philosophy understood "women's liberation" to mean the integration of women as men's equals into the male-defined and -controlled public spheres of mainstream society – criticized the utopian idealism and philosophical essentialism they saw as inherent in radical feminists' calls for separatism. Doubting that a separate women's culture could remain outside and untainted by dom-inant ideology and, in turn, lead to greater structural changes within mainstream society, these non-separatist feminists felt that self-marginalization would further ghettoize women within the mainstream culture that already excluded them.

One of the main criticisms of feminist separatism was based on the understanding that this political practice is grounded on essentialized, universlist notions of "women," a problem which has been associated with Marxist feminists who used gender as a class. Since the feminist movement (along with other movements which insist that "the personal is political") was formed in response to the exclusion of individual interests from the public sphere, feminists who advocated separatism were often criticized for what is seen as a reproduction of the rationalist objective of consensual agreement, which comes at the expense of the abstraction and alienation of group members from their particular position and individual interests. As feminists and other civil rights advocates argue, democracy can only emerge in the dialogue between individuals who feel free to represent their specific interests.[47]

Debates over the long-term effectiveness of separatism continue today even among those feminists who continue to advocate separatism: for example, between those feminists who see separatism as a temporary strategy necessary for political empowerment and those feminists who advocate complete separation from men and male-dominated mainstream society (a position most associated with lesbian separatists).[48] Indeed, divisions in groups over separatism are often not about *whether* to separate, but *to what degree*. For example, Bernice Johnson Reagon argues that, although the "barred rooms" of groups formed through separatism are important in providing an initial "nurturing space" for the development of oppositional political movements, separateness based on an assumed similarity of identity among all group members often leads to isolation and a freezing of heterogeneity.[49] As she cautions, such continuous forms of self-marginalization might eventually be co-opted by those in power: "The door of the room will just be painted red and then when those who call the shots get ready to clean house, they have easy access to you."[50] Lauren Berlant similarly argues against feminist separatism, noting that the homogenizing effect of a separatist women's culture might be compared to "the colonizing effect [of] patriarchal fantasies," wherein the differences among women are ignored so as to totalize all members into one containable category, "woman."[51]

As Maria Luisa "Papusa" Molina notes, such criticisms of separatism – and, by extension, identity politics – often fail to acknowledge the level of empowerment and agency achieved when such strategies are utilized as a political praxis at the same time that they fail to acknowledge the temporary nature of these strategies:

> When I started to talk about separatism, its meaning, praxis, and effect on some of our lives, what have come into the conversations have been feelings of rupture, of having to choose one identity over another . . . Very seldom have the words *empowerment, self-esteem*, and *reaffirmation* appeared.[52]

While feminist activists and theorists continue to debate the effectiveness of separatism as a form of radical practice, many non-white and non-Western feminists have argued that a group's *self*-definition as marginal should never be confused with the strategies of homogenization and marginalization involved in forms of cultural hegemony such as colonialism. In her essay "Choosing the margin as a space of radical openness," for example, bell hooks adamantly argues for self-marginalization as a practice of resistance in the face of hegemonic isolations:

> For me this space of radical openness is a margin – a profound edge . . . [It is] a site one stays in, clings to even, because it nourishes one's capacity to resist. It offers to one the possibility of radical perspective from which to see and create, to imagine alternatives, new worlds.[53]

In one of the most challenging arguments for self-separatism as a radical political practice, Maria Lugones creatively employs the metaphors of curdling and splitting eggs to demonstrate how different forms of separatism can either resist or affirm a social order grounded in the logic of purity.[54] As she argues, the conception of a unified society is dependent upon a logic of purity and the notion of "split separation," which imagines that "what is multiple [is] unified, [and] what is multiple is . . . internally separable, divisible into what makes it one and the remainder."[55] Speaking from the multiple (*mestizaje*) position of a Latina lesbian, Lugones refuses the fragmented subjectivity required by the logics of unity and fragmentation and, instead advocates "curdle separation," a form of separatism

which operates not divisively, but in connection with other "cur-
dles beings:"

> I understand then that whenever I desire separation, I risk sur-
> vival by confusing split separation with separation from domin-
> ation, that is, separation among curdled beings who curdle away
> their fragmentation, their subordination. I can appreciate then
> that the logic of split-separation and the logic of curdle-separation
> repel each other, that the curdled do not germinate in split
> separation.[56]

Like many other separatists, Lugones offers provocative
insights on how to resist the logics of purity and unity put forth
by assimilationists, pluralists, and others who believe in the
"melting pot" theory of cultural diversity. Homi Bhaba, speaking
directly against the universalist and normative tendencies he
sees operating in much of the discourse and politics of diversity
and multiculturalism, agrees that politics needs to address the
multiple and often contradictory forms of identification oper-
ative today:

> it is actually very difficult, even impossible and counterproduc-
> tive, to try and fit together different forms of culture and to
> pretend that they can easily coexist . . . The whole nature of the
> public sphere is changing so that we really do need the notion of
> a politics which is based on unequal, uneven, multiple and *poten-
> tially antagonistic*, political identities. This must not be confused
> with some form of autonomous, individualist pluralism (and the
> corresponding notion of cultural diversity); what is at issue is a
> historical moment in which these multiple identities do actually
> articulate in challenging ways, either positively or negatively,
> either in progressive or regressive ways, often conflictually, some-
> times even *incommensurably* – not some flowing of individual
> talents and capacities.[57]

What Bhaba's and Lugones's arguments reveal is the direct challenge multiple subjectivity and the proliferation of social identifications make to the reductionism and essentialism found in
traditional Marxist theorizations of class struggle. This has been
an extremely important step in bringing material experiences
and histories to bear upon theories of cultural resistance and
oppositional politics.

The Politics of Identity: Creating a "We" without Abandoning "Me"

Many women have actively attempted to counter the homogenizing tendencies of a collective feminist identity constructed through universalist concepts such as "women" and "sisterhood" while continuing to value separatism as a viable tactic for the empowerment of women. For instance, in an attempt to move the feminist movement beyond its unproblematized notion of universal sisterhood and its focus on white, straight, middle-class women, the women involved in the Combahee River Collective during the 1970s formulated a theory of "identity politics" which allowed them to ground and motivate their political oppositional practices in their own experiences as African-American women.[58] In consideration of hooks's and Lugones's delineations between different forms of separatism, it is important to note that the theory of identity politics emerged from these women's simultaneous marginalization within a predominantly white women's movement and their self-marginalization as black lesbian feminists.

Though the theory of identity politics has powerful resonance and usefulness for the disenfranchised, many believe that this form of politics remains grounded in Aristotelian beliefs in the fixed and immutable nature of essence and identity. Because their political solidarity is seen as being based on a shared, innate quality (what Locke refers to as "real essence"), separatist groups practicing identity politics are often criticized for effacing the differences and diversity among their constituency, an effect of which makes identity politics appear dangerously homogenizing and ineffectual in the political arena. Thus, many of the debates over separatism and identity politics have centered on the issue of essentialism, as if recourse to some shared, irreducible essence is a necessary component of either praxis. Unlike most popular conceptions (and criticisms) of identity politics, however, the Combahee theory does not require its practitioners to essentialize into *one* category (e.g. woman). Instead, it allows them to assert their *multiple* subject positions and identifications (Locke's "nominal essence") in order to resist the simultaneous oppressions which result from that heterogeneous identity.[59]

Such an understanding of the complexity and contradictory nature of subjectivity and experience radically deconstructs the concept of unified subjectivity at the same time that it refuses essentialist notions of identity that have served Western patriarchy so well and, therefore, has been the main challenge non-white and non-Western women have made to the dominant form of feminist politics and theory. For example, expanding upon the Combahee River Collective's theory of "identity politics" and Adrienne Rich's concept of a "politics of location," Linda Alcoff theorizes a "politics of positionality" wherein group identity is created not through some innate, essential quality shared by the group's members, but through their similar external relations to the dynamic social processes of history, economics, and politics.[60] Arguing that essentialist theories of subjectivity often define identity as independent of such external forces, Alcoff argues for an understanding of identity which takes into consideration its relation to "a constantly shifting context, to a situation that includes a network of elements involving others, the objective economic conditions, cultural and political institutions and ideologies, and so on."[61]

This is not to say, as Alcoff points out, that a politics of positionality imagines identity as constructed *only* through external relations. Alcoff's conceptualization of positionality rests on the notion that identity is the product of an individual's interpretation and articulation of history as mediated through representational discourse. Thus, political positions are seen as both "relational terms identifiable only within a (constantly moving) context" *and* "a location for the construction of meaning, a place from where meaning is constructed, rather than simply the place where a meaning can be *discovered*."[62]

Similarly, Jonathan Rutherford argues that "Identification, if it is to be productive, can never be with some static and unchanging object. It is an interchange between self and structure, a transforming process."[63] Theorizing a "cultural politics of difference" as a way to overcome the problems associated with politics based on isolationism as well as pluralist multiculturalism, Rutherford relies on Antonio Gramsci's notion of articulation, noting that identity is never reducible to a single logic such as class, but "is constituted out of different elements of experience and subjective position [which] in their articulation ... become something more than just the sum of their original elements."[64] As Stuart Hall argues,

> Cultural identities are the points of identification, the unstable points of identification or suture, which are made, within the discourses of history and culture. Not an essence but a *positioning*. Hence, there is always a politics of identity, a politics of position, which has no absolute guarantee in an unproblematic, transcendental "law of origin."[65]

Political theories of identity which acknowledge the unsettled nature of our multiple subjectivities speak to the postmodern context in which we find ourselves today and, thus, provide a challenge for political groups to appreciate difference so as not to foreclose the radical possibilities that emerge from the heterogeneity of their constituencies.

What is increasingly troubling, therefore, is that critics of separatism and identity politics assume that these are ongoing, permanent practices which will eventually lead to the homogenization of a group's constituency, to further social, political, and cultural isolation – or worse. For example, Kobena Mercer asserts,

> The worst aspects of the new social movements emerged in rhetoric of "identity politics" based on an essentialist notion of a fixed hierarchy of racial, sexual or gendered oppressions. By playing off each other to establish who was more authentically oppressed than whom, the residual separatist tendencies of autonomous movements played into the normative calculation of "disadvantage" inscribed in welfare statism.[66]

Like Mercer, Lawrence, Grossberg reveals that there is a great fear among leftist theorists that the practices of identity politics will result in (a) the assertion of "authentic" experience; (b) the reification and/or fetishization of singular differences; (c) the creation of an infinite list of social identities; and (d) the posturing of moral or political correctness.[67]

Advocates of separatism respond to such criticisms by foregrounding the temporary, unfixed nature of this tactic, as Luce Irigaray does when she discusses feminist separatism as a "detour through a separation of the sexes," a necessary step women must take toward "moments of discovery and affirmation."[68] Similarly, Frye argues,

> The feminist's separations are rarely if ever sought or maintained directly as ultimate personal or political ends ... Generally, the separations are brought about and maintained for the sake of something else like independence, liberty, growth, invention, sisterhood, safety, health, or the place of novel or heretical customs.[69]

In turn, Emma Pérez notes that separatism "is not permanent or fixed" and argues that, since this process is dialectical, differences are acknowledged and their resolution is "neither desirable nor necessary."[70] And, despite her much quoted insistence that separatism and identity politics are beneficial only during the initial stages of group formation, Reagon contradicts herself by insisting that separatism remains an integral component of radical politics during *all* its stages: "You go to the coalition for a few hours and then you go back and take your bottle [get your political nourishment] wherever it is, and then you go back and coalesce some more."[71]

As Reagon's contradictory stance reveals, there is considerable anxiety among political theorists and activists alike that a politics based on identity and separatism, while helpful in the short term, may eventually lead toward the erasure of individual interests and differing material histories. It seems crucial, therefore, that we appropriately delineate between political practices used to empower and motivate a *single* group of disenfranchised people and the creation of ties and relations *between* such groups (just as we must delineate between self-separation and separation by domination). Given the displacement of class-based politics since the 1960s by political movements formed through other social experiences and relations and the failure of the Left in the face of the disintegration of the Soviet Union and conservative politics during the 1980s, it is no surprise that many of these criticisms appear within larger discussions about the current state of leftist politics.[72] As Bhaba and Lugones appropriately note, we need to question such a drive toward unity left over from classic Marxism by problematizing its connections to a logic of purity.

To criticize the ineffectiveness of identity politics in the long term, for example, or to position groups adhering to its philosophy as having this as their only political practice, is to dismiss the very message of the Combahee River Collective (which many critics seem to do, since the Collective is rarely mentioned in such criticisms). Identity politics was conceived and is practiced as a temporary tactic and strategy for the disenfranchised which does not have complete isolationism or the reification of difference as its goals, but rather the emergence of power and resistance among individuals who share common experiences of oppression produced through similar relations to external historical conditions.

Riot Grrrl: Girl Power and Its Effects

Many girls have experienced riot grrrl as a safe haven from the misogyny and homophobia of youth cultures such as punk, as well as from the adultism of the feminist and gay political movements, not to mention from the oppressions they experience each day as female adolescents in an adultist, patriarchal society. In turn, riot grrrl has been a location of power and agency for many adolescent girls, even those who move on to other social identifications. Yet, while riot grrrl was formed as a place of empowerment for all adolescent girls, it has often been perceived as unwilling (rather than unable) to appeal on a broader scale to girls of color and the working class. This may have just as much to do with the difficulty of working-class girls finding the time and money to participate in this culture as it does with the separation of white middle-class youth cultures from less dominant cultures in our society. Certainly it has everything to do with the incredible diversity among youth in our society and the inability of one community to encompass them all and still address individual needs and interests. Unfortunately, such exclusiveness among riot grrrls is often interpreted as a superiority trip, a posturing of underground, militant authenticity constructed primarily through direct opposition to mainstream culture.

Many feminists today, seeing in riot grrrl resonances of an earlier feminism, or perhaps seeds for a future feminism, celebrate this female youth culture at the same time that they critique it for what they see as its naive politics, which seem to "reinvent the wheel." Thus, while riot grrrls are applauded for empowering themselves and acting on behalf of female youth, they are also criticized for not making themselves, their culture, and their politics more palatable for mainstream society. For example, Joanne Gottlieb and Gayle Wald, finding riot grrrls to be somewhat naive about the way culture and politics work, invoke Gil Scott-Heron's 1970s' criteria for successful radical politics ("the revolution will not be televised"),[73] only to demonstrate how such criteria do not hold weight in the mass-mediated political arena of the 1990s: "If Riot Grrrl wants to raise feminist consciousness on a large scale, then it will have to negotiate a relation to the mainstream that does not merely reify the opposition between mainstream and subculture. Like it or not, the Girl-Style Revolution is bound to be televised."[74] Emily White similarly asserts:

> most of the Riot Girls [are white]. The majority are from middle- or upper-middle-class backgrounds. Like a religious sect they huddle together, rejecting the world but also somewhat afraid of it. Glorifying "youth rebellion," they sometimes will themselves into a naiveté. While the Riot Girls talk in a cursory way about branching out, they haven't. And until the Riot Girls address the socioeconomic basis of their rage – the way they have lived a life that, in many ways, has given them the time and the freedom to express this rage, that has given them enough economic power to desire other types of power – their force will be limited.[75]

Lorraine Ali describes riot grrrl's separatist position as "dead-end elitism."[76] Such an equation seems quite a contradiction in terms, since separatists are usually struggling against the elitist culture and ideologies that marginalize them. At the same time, however, it is important to question why it is that when girls withdraw from mainstream, male-dominated society, their move to separate is seen as "elitist," while male youth withdrawal is championed as part of boys' inherent masculinity, following their natural path of autonomy and independence. Riot grrrls are criticized for precisely those behaviors that run counter to the dominant construction of femininity, even while the traits to which they are adhering (independence, assertiveness, action, etc.) are highly privileged in our society.

What motivates this desire for riot grrrl to "branch out," to "raise feminist consciousness on a large scale"? Since these utopian desires for riot grrrls' widespread sociopolitical influence are commonly associated with radical feminist philosophy, it seems all the more strange that, in their final analyses, these writers/scholars ultimately dismiss the philosophy of separatism upon which riot grrrl is grounded, a logic which necessarily functions by foregrounding an oppositional position for girls in relation to the notions of girlhood constructed through dominant ideology and reproduced in mainstream culture. So what exactly do Gottlieb, Wald, White, and Ali mean? That riot grrrls should *not* be oppositional to the mainstream? That they should assimilate in a society that has historically silenced adolescent girls while at the same time exploiting them as a clueless yet highly lucrative marketing niche capable only of celebrity fandom, mall shopping, and future motherhood? Why should the burden for feminism's future and "raising feminist consciousness" rest with these adolescent girls? Why must it be *them* who "branch out" toward *us*?

Whatever the reasons why the riot grrrl community has failed to interest larger numbers of girls, this situation has caused great discomfort for riot grrrls who are committed to unlearning oppressive behaviors on every level. As Lois Maffeo notes, "It's a hard line to walk . . . To be angry at some people, men especially, and still retain any sort of warmth and humanity."[77] In an effort to work toward eliminating racism within the riot grrrl community, Corin Tucker (previously of Heavens to Betsy, now of Sleater Kinney) wrote the song "White Girl." As she explains on the record cover for Heaven's to Betsy's album, *Calculated*:

> i wanted to address the audience for this record – mainly white people – about racism in the punk/alternative community, in myself, in riot grrrl . . . it is really scarey to take responsibility for your own privilege and racism but i think that it is neccesary for this to happen before anything will change, before any productive dialogue will take place.[78]

Tucker then encourages her listeners to go out and read books by various feminists of color (e.g. bell hooks, Audre Lorde, Alice Walker), as well as zines that address the issues of racism and sexism.

Ironically, though Tucker and other prominent riot grrrls often suggest reading non-white women authors and feminist theorists, few suggest that riot grrrls should attempt to experience other subject positions via texts which are not tied to middle-class intellectualism.[79] Although recognizing (like feminists and other radical activists before them) that to ground their politics in essentialized, universalist notions of identify can be as debilitating to their political objectives as it is empowering to the organization of their group, too few riot grrrls have critically interrogated how their privileging of a white, middle-class, punk identity over other possible identifications tends to reproduce the dominant understanding of riot grrrl as a movement for only white, middle-class youth. Certainly, the "riot grrrl-as-punk" contextualization is due in part to the fact that those who have been given the privilege to speak on behalf of the riot grrrl community are usually the white members of riot grrrl's most prominent punk bands, who have much at stake in perpetuating the notion that punk is the music of choice in this community and, thus, are largely responsible for the problematic conflation of the riot grrrl community at large with a few riot grrrl bands.

While reading about others' experiences can be one means of extending riot grrrl beyond its typical white, middle-class framing, another method used by riot grrrls is the organization of workshops like the "unlearning racism" session organized for the 1992 riot grrrl convention in Washington, DC, by an African-American woman. As Melissa Klein from *off our backs* reports, when grrrls discussed ways to achieve a greater inclusiveness in their community during this workshop,

> It was suggested that instead of assuming predominantly white women's groups are the standard or ideal and trying to make them more inclusive, white women could involve themselves in the efforts of women of color, in spite of, or perhaps because of the fact that this takes them out of their immediate realm of comfort.[80]

Certainly the acknowledgment of privilege, along with the processes of self-criticism, unlearning oppressive behaviors and rhetoric, and involvement in other communities and cultures, will lead to a greater critical consciousness for riot grrrls, even if it may not lead to greater participation in their culture by girls of color and the working class. What seems the most disturbing to writers such as Gottlieb, Wald, White, and Ali, however, has been riot grrrls' lack of dialogue ("branching out") with *older* feminists.

In an age that has been dubbed (albeit erroneously) "post-feminist," we should not find it surprising that many girls and young women today are often wary of older feminists. As many point out, the "second wave" women's movement was grounded in a political philosophy that, among other things, ignored female youth in feminist agendas. The results of that exclusion can be seen in many places today.[81] Existing towards the bottom of social status/power hierarchies because of their age and sex, girls are often dismissed by older feminists who understand femininity as an *adult* form of subjectivity and politics and cultural production as *adult* activities. Part of the fallout of "second wave" feminism's pro-woman stance has been that girls' issues and experiences are often ignored, the term "girl" continues to be fraught with negative connotations, and girlhood is subordinated to the presumably more primary and less ambiguous stage of womanhood. On the other hand, girls often object to the fact that women feel they have a right to speak for girls in the name of "women's rights" and "sisterhood," without allowing girls to speak on their own behalf. As Christine Doza boldly writes,

I feel like we've been forgotten. I feel like we're all dying of anorexia and heartbreak, and everyone – you – you just turn the other way. I read *Ms.*, flipping through its pages like a tornado, looking for anything but what's there. I don't have a career, I don't have a husband, I don't need to know how to raise my son . . . I don't need help recovering from being raped when I was a kid. I am a kid.[82]

In order to combat such misrepresentation, riot grrrls have refused to dialogue not only with journalists but with academics. Caught between wanting to explore the radical potential of this community and wanting to honor the privacy of the girls involved in it, scholars have been confused on how to approach riot grrrl as a subject of intellectual analysis. For example, Gottlieb and Wald's study of riot grrrl music ends with their an examination of their "conflicted place as participants and academic observers" in relation to riot grrrl:

At the very least, unsanctioned accounts of the movement run the risks of exploitation, trivialization and tourism. Moreover, speaking about the movement, especially from a position of cultural centrality, risks appropriating Riot Grrrl's own ability, as a marginal group, to be heard, to speak for themselves, in a mode continuous with the silencing of girls' voices within patriarchal culture.[83]

Why scholars studying riot grrrl feel a need to justify our analyses of riot grrrl has much to do with riot grrrl's adherence to the logic of separatism as a radical sociopolitical praxis, as it does with their challenges to the purposes of academic analysis and the privileges accorded intellectuals in our society. As feminist scholars we see an optimistic future for women and feminism in these radical girls, who, at ages far younger than us, have created a community which resists the oppressions of patriarchy, misogyny, ageism, and homophobia. At the same time, however, we are profoundly aware that, for many reasons other than just our age and social status, we remain far outside the perimeters of this community and that our support of their powerful movement does not grant us the right to disrespect their need for privacy and their ability to self-represent.

When I first heard Kathleen Hanna sing, "Does it scare you that we don't need you?", I knew she was not addressing only boys; she was addressing *me*, and her question gave rise to others I have asked myself time and again. Who am I – a feminist scholar committed to opening, celebrating, and preserving safe, nurturing spaces for *all* females – to intrude upon the self-imposed separation of riot grrrls from certain segments of our society, including academia? Who am I – the product of a fairly functional and certainly privileged white middle-class upbringing – to assume some kind of camaraderie with those who have united to speak out about the horrors (incest, rape, child abuse, neglect) which cripple the confidence of many adolescent girls and paralyze their potential assertions of agency? My work remains compromised by power imbalances that are reproduced in my creation of riot grrrl as a fictional, homogenized object of study which displaces the real riot grrrls from this analysis and effaces the complex diversity of this community. I must acknowledge that my speaking *about* riot grrrls can be easily confused with my speaking *for* them.

In an attempt to resist misrepresenting this community, many scholars studying riot grrrl have attempted to incorporate into their work riot grrrls' self-representations, especially quotations from riot grrrl songs and zines preserving errors in spelling, grammar, and punctuation so as to preserve the authenticity of this cultural evidence (as I have done here). While this approach may be done in the spirit of academic dialogism (that is, allowing for the space of the text to include the voice of the subject of study), it does not erase the power imbalances inherent in cultural studies (even those based on participant observation), it does not make up for the fact that the picture being made of this culture will always be incomplete. Scholars' names remain tied to academic texts as signifiers of both authoritative knowledge and representational power.

A possible solution to this problem might be riot grrrls studying themselves. As riot grrrl Beth Ribet states, "I hope future coverage of grrls will be both written by an actual grrl, and from an explicitly feminist perspective. The MTV-esque media portrayal of riot grrls as hot young babes 'liberating' ourselves through lots of violent sex is not *my* riotous way of being."[84] The obvious problem with this solution to riot grrrl's misrepresentations is twofold: (a) because of their age and lack of experience, most riot grrrls do not have the cultural access or power to represent their community in the mainstream media or academic publications; and (b) most riot grrrls do not *want* to participate in either mainstream media accounts or academic analyses of their community. (However, riot grrrls have participated in Hillary Carlip's *Girl Power: Young Women Speak Out!*, as well as Barbara Findlen's anthology, *Listen Up: Voices from the Next Feminist Generation*, although neither of these texts was initiated by riot grrrls themselves. To my knowledge, as of the time of this writing, there have been only two studies of riot grrrls *by* riot grrrls, both of which are unpublished.)[85] Furthermore, this solution fails to account for much of the disparagement riot grrrls have received when they have discussed their community with the media. For example, Jessica Hopper reports that, after talking to *Newsweek* about riot grrrl, "I started catching slag. I felt I was being personally attacked for talking to the media. I felt pushed out."[86]

As those committed to both youth studies and feminist politics (not to mention youth politics), we need to think critically about *why* riot grrrls have refused to discuss their community with academics. I would argue that such a refusal comes as much from their experiences as girls in our patriarchal, adultist, commercial culture as it does from their perceived need to identify as countercultural. However, riot grrrls often uncritically construct themselves as authentic resistors by opposing themselves and their culture to the supposed "inauthenticity" of the mainstream, without understanding how these two notions are not mutually exclusive but strongly interdependent. Indeed, riot grrrls' anti-mainstream stance needs to be problematized in relation to the material reality that many of this group's cultural artifacts are dependent upon popular culture icons, from the use of Lucy from the *Peanuts* comic strip as a caricature of a typical riot grrrl to band names, like CeBe Barnes, which have been appropriated from Hollywood films and other mainstream cultural texts.

In light of many riot grrrls' assertions that only riot grrrls should represent riot grrrls, we need to problematize how riot grrrls construct themselves as ideologically correct, non-oppressive, and morally superior to academics simply by equating the exploitative practices of the mainstream media with professional intellectuals. No doubt scholars have careerist ambitions just like journalists, and riot grrrls have many good reasons to be concerned about the intentions of those wanting to make a buck off their group. However, reductive conflations of academia with the media merely serve to reproduce the notion that riot grrrl exists in some authentic, secluded place free from the effects of patriarchy and capitalism.

Riot grrrls demand to be taken seriously by mainstream society, and they have defined the narrow terms of that interaction aware that, as Frye notes, it is at the point of radical assertions of group identity that negative perceptions of the group are formed and attempts to naturalize, commodify, and/or contain difference are initiated.[87] However, Theo Cateforis's statement about the media filling the void of riot grrrl's representations is just as applicable to academia. Thus, while I think Gottlieb and Wald are correct in asserting that riot grrrl's revolution is bound to be televised, I would go one step further to say riot grrrl's revolution is bound to be *theorized*. By this I do not mean that scholars should have free license to observe all riot grrrl activities and extract and analyze convincing artifacts from their cultural texts. Nor do I mean to suggest that studies of this community should not involve riot grrrls themselves, for only through their participation will we be able to approach (because we can never fully realize) a complete understanding of their culture.

In an attempt to theorize an alternative to the imperialism often inherent in cultural studies such as those involving riot grrrl, Maria Lugones has argued,

> Through travelling to other people's "worlds" we discover that there are "worlds" in which those who are the victims of arrogant perception are really subjects, lively beings, resistors, constructors of vision even though in the mainstream construction they are animated only by the arrogant perceiver and are pliable, foldable, file-awayable, classifiable.[88]

As Caren Kaplan notes, Lugones's concept of theoretical "world"-traveling should not be confused with tourism or with the conventional understanding of travel as leading to "rapport and unconditional acceptance."[89] Unfortunately, without permission to enter the world of riot grrrl, without riot grrrls willing to act as our guides, those of us wanting to travel to this radical community are left with only the most visible and audible of signposts to follow. It is no wonder, then, that riot grrrl continues to be represented in media accounts and academic analyses as a trendy musical phenomenon rather than as a vibrant political community.

Conclusions

While riot grrrls may confidently assert that they don't need adults or males, it is not so apparent that these groups don't need riot grrrl. Changes are happening in the perception and treatment of adolescent girls, and I would argue that riot grrrl is at the forefront in drawing attention to female youth and their various social experiences and oppressions. The increase of adolescent girls' participation in radical political activism as well as countercultural production suggests, in contradiction to most reports, that riot grrrl has indeed has a broad social, political, and cultural impact.

If not for these grrrls, their culture, and their activism, how else do we understand the all-too-recent focus on girlhood as a positive structure of investment, position of empowerment, and location of political agency after a century of mainstream constructions of that social position as one of subordinate passivity, mitigated perhaps only by the more "active" behaviors of fandom and shopping? How do we explain the recent influx of girl-powered bands in the male-dominated alternative music industry? How do we explain *Sassy* magazine's commitment to a feminist, pro-girl stance.[90] How do we explain the success of the Feminist Majority's Rock for Choice benefit concerts, which largely rely upon adolescent feminist audiences and volunteers? How do we explain the girl-initiated boycott of the National Women's Studies Association's 1996 conference on adolescent girls? How do we explain the increasing popularity of texts such as *Girl Power: Young Women Speak Out!* and *Listen Up: Voices from the Next Feminist Generation*, based on the personal, diaristic writing style of riot grrrl zines? How do we understand a film such as *Fun*, a movie which takes as its subject the eruption of female adolescent rage and violence in the overwhelmingly horrific context of adolescent girls as victims of incest, sexual abuse, and societal neglect, issues so powerfully foregrounded in riot grrrl culture and politics?[91] Certainly, it has not been riot grrrls alone who have initiated such changes, for the members of this community often coalesce with gay, youth, and feminist activists. However, denying riot grrrl any part in these social, political, and cultural transformations by representing this community as elitist isolationists only works to dismiss, once again, the power of female youth.

In the fall of 1993, after a year of riot grrrl's exploitation by the media, journalist Ann Japenga authoritatively asserted:

> the movement's credo – that young women should support each other rather than competing as society urges them to do – was lost in the transition, and the movement was reduced to a kicky little clique defined almost exclusively by fashion. You can catch the Princess Dork look on MTV these days, and imitation Riot Grrrl pre-tattooed wear is for sale on Melrose [Avenue in Los Angeles].[92]

Three years after Japenga's pronouncement of riot grrrl's demise, Evelyn McDonnell entitled an article on young feminists in rock as "Riot grrrl returns, with a slightly softer roar," as if this community died and this kinder, gentler movement (what she labels as "post-Grrrl bands") has risen from its ashes.[93] Despite Japenga's, McDonnell's, and other journalists' misrepresentations of riot grrrl as a thing of the past, this radical community remains alive and active even if the media and mainstream society are not privy to all its movements.

We must remember that, while we all have the privilege of hindsight (as distorted as it is), few of us can see into the future, and we do well not to sound the death knell of riot grrrl merely because these girls have refused to assimilate in mainstream culture. What remains unique about riot grrrl in relation to the punk, girl, and feminist cultures it is compared to is its adamant refusal to be reduced to a lifestyle. Thus, while riot grrrl has been formed and maintained via separatist practices and a pro-girl stance that are strikingly similar to early radical feminism, this community's adoption of an anti-corporatist means of cultural production as well as its commitment to challenge patriarchy, adultism, and heterocentrism through in-your-face forms of political activism reveals an ability to incorporate the strengths of other radical political movements and counter-cultures without succumbing to the recuperative processes of dominant ideology and the rampant commercialism of late twentieth-century society. Riot grrrl's radical political activism on behalf of adolescent girls signals an important moment not only in the politics of youth (as Angela McRobbie predicted), but in the politics of feminism as well.

Notes and References

1   Evelyn, a DC riot grrrl, quoted in A. Johnson (1993) Start a fucking riot. *off our backs*, 23(5), 8.
2   Bikini Kill (1992) Don't Need You. *Yeah, Yeah, Yeah, Yeah*. Kill Rock Stars.
3   A. McRobbie (1990) Settling accounts with subcultures: a feminist critique. In S. Frith and A. Goodwin (eds), *On Record: Rock, Pop, and the Written Word*. New York: Pantheon Books, p. 80.
4   B. Hudson (1984) Femininity and adolescence. In *Gender and Generation*. London: Macmillan, pp. 31–53.
5   While several riot grrrls have informed me that 25 is the maximum age for members of their community, there seems to be a lack of consensus as to the group's "official" age boundaries. Despite the fact that some riot grrrls are chronologically and biologically

women, since riot grrrl activism is specifically oriented toward the social and ideological position of adolescent girls, I refer to them as such in order to avoid confusion.

6 I do not mean to suggest that separatist tactics and strategies are employed only in the service of radical/leftist groups, but rather in the interest of those groups who are marginalized and/or disempowered in relation to dominant ideology.

7 In delineating between separatist *tactics* and separatist *strategies*, I am relying upon Michel de Certeau's theories as elaborated in M. de Certeau (1988) Making do: uses and tactics. In *The Practice of Everyday Life*, trans. S. Randall. Berkeley: University of California Press.

8 M. Frye (1983) Some reflections on separatism and power. In *The politics of Reality: Essays in Feminist Theory*. Trumansburg, NY: The Crossing Press, p. 103.

9 B. J. Reagon (1983) Coalition politics: turning the century. In B. Smith (ed.), *Home Girls: a Black Feminist Anthology*. New York: Kitchen Table, pp. 357–8. Based on a presentation given at the West Coast Women's Music Festival, 1981.

10 de Certeau, op. cit., n. 7, pp. 36–8.

11 Ibid., p. 36.

12 G. C. Spivak with E. Rooney (1994) In a word: interview. In N. Schor and E. Wood (eds), *The Essential Difference*. Bloomington: Indiana University Press, p. 154. Also Spivak with S. Harasym (1990) Practical politics of the open end. In S. Harasym (ed.), *The Post-colonial Critic: Interviews, Strategies, Dialogues*. New York: Routledge, p. 109.

13 J. Clarke, S. Hall, T. Jefferson and B. Roberts (1976) Subcultures, cultures and class: a theoretical overview. In S. Hall and T. Jefferson (eds), *Resistance through Rituals: Youth Subcultures in Post-war Britain*. London: Unwin Hyman, pp. 45, 47.

14 D. Hebdige (1979) *Subculture: the Meaning of Style*. London: Routledge, p. 88.

15 Charke et al., op. cit., n. 13, p. 62.

16 This theory was first put forward by Phil Cohen (1972) *Sub-cultural Conflict and Working-class Community*. Working Papers in Cultural Studies No. 2. Birmingham: CCCS, University of Birmingham.

17 D. Gaines (1991) *Teenage Wasteland: Suburbia's Dead End Kids*. New York: Harper Perennial, p. 86.

18 Ibid., p. 92.

19 A. Ross (1994) Introduction. In A. Ross and T. Rose (eds), *Microphone Fiends: Youth Music and Youth Culture*. New York: Routledge, pp. 8–9.

20   K. Mercer (1990) Welcome to the jungle: identity and diversity in postmodern politics. In J. Rutherford (ed.), *Identity: Community, Culture, Difference*. London: Lawrence and Wishart, p. 43.

21   Riot grrrls exist in almost every major city in the USA, as well as some cities in Canada and Britain. I have also heard that the riot grrrl community has now spread to Japan.

22   Misty, quoted by H. Carlip (1995) *Girl Power: Young Women Speak Out!* New York: Warner Books, p. 58.

23   Erika Reinstein, quoted by L. Spencer (1993) Grrrls only. *The Washington Post*, January 3, C2.

24   Dawn, quoted by Carlip, op. cit., n. 22, p. 34.

25   Jasmine, ibid., p. 33.

26   B. Anderson (1991) *Imagined Communities: Reflections on the Origin and Spread of Nationalism*. London: Verso.

27   Furthermore, while riot grrrls value the centrality of homosocial bonds found in youth cultures, they often move far afield from the heterosexual fantasies of romance reproduced in previous girl cultures. Since "girl love" is advocated continuously in riot grrrl music, zines, videos, and drawings, it is important to consider why its more obvious meaning – lesbianism – has been downplayed, if not outright ignored, in mainstream accounts of this all-grrrl culture.

28   Hebdige, op. cit., n. 14, pp. 113–27.

29   G. Lipsitz (1994) We know what time it is: race, class and youth culture in the nineties. In Ross and Rose, op. cit., n. 19, p. 20.

30   Renee, quoted by Carlip, op. cit., n. 22, p. 38.

31   Bikini Kill (1992) Double Dare Ya. *Bikini Kill*. Kill Rock Stars. The Tourettes (1994) Battle Hymn. *Hidden Keys to Loving Relationships* Lookout! Records. The CeBe Barnes Band (1995) She's a Winner. *HorseKitty number 1*. HorseKitty Records/Studios.

32   Sadie Benning, quoted by V. C. Phoenix (1994) From womyn to grrrls: finding sisterhood in girl style revolution. *Deneuve*, January/February, 41–2. Bikini Kill, whose music appears on the video of "Girl Power," have also been commissioned for the soundtrack of Benning's 16 mm film version.

33   In addition to Benning's and July's projects, there is an increasing presence of films and videos made by riot grrrls.

34   Sarah, quoted by Johnson, op. cit., n. 1, p. 10.

35   Erika, quoted by Spencer, op. cit., n. 23, p. C2.

36   Some riot grrrls have willingly dialogued with journalists of alternative publications, however. See, for example, Johnson, op. cit., n. 1, and M. Klein (1993) Riot grrrls gogo. *off our backs*, 23(2), 6–12.

37   Perhaps the best description of how innovative cultural forms such as youth cultures are eventually recuperated in dominant ideology

and mainstream culture id found in Hebdige, op cit., n. 14, pp. 94–6.

38   Since the riot grrrl media blackout in 1993, the only articles on riot grrrl in the USA have appeared either in more "alternative" publications such as *off our backs* and *Deneuve* or in mainstream publications such as *The Los Angeles Times*, which have printed articles proclaiming the death of riot grrrl. See A. Japenga (1993) Grunge 'R' Us: exploiting, co-opting and neutralizing the counterculture. *The Los Angeles Times Magazine*, November 14, 26; L. Ali (1995) The grrrls fight back. *The Los Angeles Times*, July 27, F1.

39   Hebdige, op. cit., n. 14, pp. 84–9. For a more recent analysis of the interdependency of the media and subcultures, see S. Thornton (1994) Moral panic, the media and British rave culture. In Ross and Rose, op. cit., n. 19, pp. 176–92.

40   T. Cateforis (1994) Riot grrrls: punk rock's new resistance? Unpublished paper, Popular Culture Association/American Culture Association annual meeting, Chicago.

41   The contextualization of riot grrrl as a cultural (rather than political) phenomeon is apparent in the placement of articles about this community in the "lifestyle" sections of mainstream newspapers and magazines, which are popularly coded as feminized spaces of cultural trends, gossip, and consumerism (as opposed to the "news" sections which are widely thought to contain "real" politics and "serious" information).

42   To date, the only published scholarly analyses or riot grrrl are: J. Gottieb and G. Wald (1994) Smells like teen spirit: riot grrrls, revolution and women in independent rock. In Ross and Rose, op. cit., n. 19, pp. 250–74; and S. Reynolds and J. Press (1995) There's a riot going on: grrrls against boy-rock. In *The Sex Revolts: Gender, Rebellion and Rock 'n' Roll*. Cambridge, MA: Harvard University Press, pp. 323–31. Both texts frame riot grrrl as a primarily musical phenomenon.

43   Thus, I think Andrew Ross is right to point out how theoretical formulations of youth are often "acts of projection:" Ross, op. cit., n. 19, p. 8.

44   C. Geertz (1973) *The Interpretation of Cultures*. New York: Basic Books.

45   Clarke et al., op. cit., n. 13, pp. 57–71.

46   A. Echols (1989) *Daring to Be Bad: Radical Feminism in America, 1967–1975*. Minneapolis: University of Minnesota Press.

47   For a further analysis of feminist challenges to the modern conception of the civic public, see I. Young (1990) Polity and difference. In *Throwing Like a Girl and Other Essays in Feminist Philosophy and Social Theory*. Bloomington: Indiana University Press.

48   For example, see the special forum on separatism in the feminist journal *Signs*, 19(2), 1994, 435–79. As Teresa de Lauretis notes, the negative connotations often heaped upon sparatism in the USA is often distinctly homophobic. See The essence of the triangle or, taking the risk of essentialism seriously: feminist theory in Italy, the US, and Britain. In Schor and Wood, op. cit., n. 12, pp. 19, 30.

49   Reagon, op. cit., n. 9, p. 358.

50   Ibid.

51   L. Berlant (1988) The female complaint. *Socialtext*, 18–20, 240.

52   M. L. "Papusa" Molina (1994) Fragmentations: mediations on separatism. *Signs*, 19(2), 449.

53   bell hooks (1990) Choosing the margin as a space of radical oppenness. In *Yearning: Race, Gender, and Cultural Politics*. Boston: South End Press, 149, 150.

54   M. Lugones (1994) Purity, impurity, and separation. *Signs*, 19(2), 458–79. Emma Pérez similarly advocates the creation of "decolonized Third World spaces" in her argument for Chicana lesbian spaces; that is, self-marginalized spaces that differ from the homogenized "modeled minorities" created by dominant ideologies and social practices. Pérez (1994) Irigaray's female symbolic in the making of a Chicana lesbian *Sitos y Lenguas* (*Sites and Discourses*). In L. Doan (ed.), *The Lesbian Postmodern*. New York: Columbia University Press, pp. 104–17.

55   Lugones, op. cit., n. 54, p. 464.

56   Ibid., p. 469.

57   H. Bhaba (1990) The third space. In Rutherford, op. cit., n. 20, pp. 209, 208.

58   *The Combahee River Collective Statement: Black Feminist Organizing in the Seventies and Eighties*. New York: Kitchen Table, 1986. Originally written in 1977.

59   For a further analysis of the differences between Aristotelian and Lockean theories of essence, see de Lauretis, op. cit., n. 48, pp. 1–39.

60   L. Alcoff (1988) Cultural feminism versus post-structuralism: the identity crisis in feminist theory. *Signs*, 13(3), 405–36. See A. Rich (1986) *Blood, Bread, and Poetry: Selected Prose, 1979–1985*. New York: W. W. Norton.

61   Ibid., p. 433. See T. de Lauretis (1984) *Alice Doesn't: Feminism, Semiotics, Cinema*. Bloomington: Indiana University Press.

62   Alcoff, op. cit., n. 60, p. 434.

63   Rutherford (1990) A place called home: identity and the cultural politics of difference. In Rutherford, op. cit., n. 20, p. 14.

64   Ibid., p. 19. See A. Gramsci (1971) *Selections from the Prison Notebooks*, trans. Q. Hoare and G. N. Smith. London: Lawrence & Wishart.

65 S. Hall (1990) Cultural identity and diaspora. In Rutherford, op. cit., n. 20, p. 226.

66 Meercer, op. cit., n. 20, pp. 46–7.

67 L. Grossberg (1992) *We Gotta Get Out of This Place: Popular Conservatism and Postmodern Culture*. New York: Routledge, pp. 364–9.

68 L. Irigaray (1994) Equal to whom? In Schor and Wood, op. cit., n. 12, p. 79. This temporary, fluid dimension of identity politics has also been seen in the process of youth culture signification. See Hebdige, op. cit., n. 14, p. 81.

69 Frye, op. cit., n. 8, p. 97.

70 Pérez, op. cit., n. 54, p. 105.

71 Reagon, op. cit., n. 9, p. 359. It is interesting that Reagon defines the initial nurturing space of separatism as "home" as well as a "bottle with some milk in it and a nipple" (p. 359), and Jonathon Rutherford speaks of the oedipal complex leftist intellectuals have in "struggling to hold on to its certainties, clinging to some imaginary identity like an anxious child to its mother" (Rutherford, op. cit., n. 63, p. 14). While I do not have the time or the expertise to adequately unpack the complicated oedipal situation these two theorists use as a metaphor for separatism, I do think it calls for serious consideration.

72 Both Mercer's and Grossberg's arguments, for example, are framed by their larger concerns about the disunity of the left.

73 Gil Scott-Heron (1974) *The Revolution Will Not Be Televised*, compilation recording. Flying Dutchman.

74 Gottlieb and Wald, op. cit., n. 42, p. 271.

75 E. White, p. 24.

76 Ali, op. cit., n. 38, p. F1.

77 Lois Maffeo, quoted by N. Malkin (1993) It's a grrrl thing. *Seventeen*, May, 82.

78 Heavens to Betsy (1993) *Calculated*. Kill Rock Stars.

79 The members of British riot grrrl band Huggy Bear similarly advocate reading feminist theory in their essay in A. Rapheal (1995) *Grrrls: Viva Rock Divas*. New York: St Martin's Griggin, pp. 146–72.

80 Klein, op. cit., n. 36, p. 6.

81 Consider, for example, the many educational programs which misrepresent themselves as exploring gender, when the only issues discussed are those of adult women. The publishing industry and bookstores repeat this misrepresentation by categorizing texts about gender and feminist issues as "women's studies."

82 C. Doza (1995) Bloodlove. In B. Findlen (ed.), *Listen Up: Voices from the Next Feminist Generation*. Seattle: Seal Press, pp. 252–3.

83 Gottlieb and Wald, op. cit., n. 42, p. 269.

84 Beth Ribet, quoted in Feedback. *On the Issues*, Summer 1996, 6.

85   M. S. Raliegh (1994) Riot grrrls and revolution. Thesis, Bowling Green State University, August; C. Kile's forthcoming dissertation, Bowling Green State University.

86   Jessica Hopper, quoted by Malkin, op. cit., n. 77, p. 82.

87   Frye, op. cit., n. 8, pp. 98, 107.

88   M. Lugones (1990) Playfulness, "world"-travelling, and loving perception. In G. Anzaldúa (ed.), *Haciendo Caras/Making Face, Making Soul*. San Francisco: Aunt Lute, p. 402.

89   C. Kaplan (1994) The politics of location as transnational feminist critical practice. In I. Grewal and C. Kaplan (eds), *Scattered Hegemonies: Postmodernity and Transnational Feminist Practices*. Minneapolis: University of Minnesota Press, p. 150.

90   Unfortunately, *Sassy*'s editorial board has changed, and the magazine has returned to its pre-feminist focus on consumerism, boys, and romance.

91   *Fun*, screenplay by James Bosley from his play, produced and directed by Rafeal Zelinsky (Neo Modern and Damina Lee, 1995).

92   Japenga, op. cit., n. 38, p. 26.

93   E. McDonnell (1996) Riot grrrl returns, with a slightly softer roar. *The New York Times*, June 2, 28.

8

"FRANCES FARMER WILL HAVE HER REVENGE ON SEATTLE:" PAN-CAPITALISM AND ALTERNATIVE ROCK

Javier Santiago-Lucerna

> I miss the comfort
> in being sad
>
> Nirvana

The "alternative rock" movement, which has dominated the present decade, has been considered as an open rebuttal of the "selling-out" attitude of the previous decade, and also as a return to the fundamental characteristics that the genre possessed in its early stage. That is, a sort of revival that grasps in full the spontaneity and crispness that rock and roll graciously exploited during its golden era (i.e. the 1950s and 1960s). Also, there has been a return to the emotionally charged performance, the display of raw power as an assurance of the truthfulness and sincerity of the performer(s). A turn back to the political and/or social conscience so characteristic of the 1960s has been registered, as we can see in the numerous political stances that the group Pearl Jam has taken at the peak of its popularity. There is the impression that whatever route the genre took during the eighties, it has been overturned by the explosion delivered in the sounds of the new wave (e.g. R.E.M., 10,000 Maniacs), Seattle's grunge movement (e.g. Soundgarden, Nirvana), and neo-punk rock groups (e.g. the now defunct Jane's Addiction or its current reincarnation).

Take, for example, the following comment that appeared in *Spin* magazine, as a "footnote" to the main story concerning the suicide of former Nirvana front man Kurt Cobain:

> Nirvana, like most interesting current bands, just wanted to represent their exact feelings appropriately. Luckily, in their case, they were guided by Kurt Cobain, a gifted if obviously tormented man with high ideals, original ideas, and a beautifully erratic way of expressing himself. (Cooper, 1994, p. 37)

Written as a reaction to some comments made by former Sex Pistols front man John Lydon, these words tend to reinstate in Cobain's name some of the characteristics that molded the image of the "rock and roll hero" in its second golden age, the sixties. At the same time, they stress the characteristics that made Cobain a true troubadour, rather than a all-image-no-content eighties type of rocker.

The roots of the present "alternative rock" movement lie mostly in punk rock. First of all, we cannot overlook the fact that most of the present alternative bands were originally punk acts. That is the case for Sonic Youth, the Henry Rollins Band, the Beastie Boys, Smashing Pumpkins, etc. While some variations from their earlier days are clear, those changes may be a response to the development of a punk aesthetic. Still, some the basics of punk are very much present. As I mentioned earlier, most of these groups still place a lot of emphasis on the unskillfulness of the musicians and the display of raw power within their performances. They also rely on the ideological strategy of the *lied*; that is, the song as a vehicle for the presentation of the "true human spirit" (Bloomfield, 1993, pp. 14–15). In this regard, the singer/songwriter is perceived as a communicator of his inner truth. That was the case, as Cooper attests, of Kurt Cobain's work in Nirvana.

We also have to take into consideration the grunge image, so wonderfully exploited by Cobain and, at present, by Eddie Veder and Pearl Jam, as a strong statement against the glam aesthetic of eighties heavy metal and the slick elegance of techno-pop. For punk and alternative rock, image is no-image. A return to some of the fashion objects of other eras confirms their image, as an attempt to emphazise their ideological stance: polyester from the seventies, the traditional sixties jeans, T-shirts, sneakers, etc.

That is one of the many ways in which alternative rockers recalled the role of music within the political realm.

Most of these attributes, as already observed, were introduced to rock music during the punk explosion. The ways they are used as part of the construction of a regime of truth proper to alternative rock recalls the same uses punk gave to them. We have to understand that punk's initial assault was aimed at the ideologies that shaped rock music production from the late sixties on. In those days, music became conceived as a source of social resistance and the voice of the counterculture. But as time went by, all "This ideology turned out to be a wonderful source of sales rhetoric," a sort of commodity aesthetics (Frith, 1984, p. 60; Haug, 1986). As John Lydon recalls,

> Before the Sex Pistols, music was so bloody serious, all run by university graduates. . . . There was no deep thought in it, merely images pertaining to something mystical, too stupid and absolutely devoid of reality. How on earth were we supposed to relate to that music when we lived in council flats? (Lydon, 1993, p. 86)

So the punks' attack was aimed at the reigning regime of truth of rock, at the pretentious thing it had become.

As Bloomfield (1991, pp. 66–7) has stated, punk rock was pure negation directed toward the rock music establishment. Greil Marcus (1989) characterized the onslaught of punk, through the Sex Pistols, as a weapon against the conventionalities rock adhered to in the mid-seventies; punks went back to the basics (guitar, bass, drums and voice) and employed them in an all-out attack on rock music itself. As an immediate result, punk prompted an external existence of the rock attitude, its ideology, outside the channels of corporate America. "The performer–audience divide was bridged; records were made and distributed outside the channels of the music industry, and the proportions of producers to consumers were inverted" (Bloomfield, 1991, p. 69). What the author indicates here is the inherent anti-commodity stance that punk rock represented during its heyday. In other words, punk aimed at dissolving the ideologies that legitimated the separation between performers and the audience, and showed aggression to the whole idea of music-as-business.

Furthermore, punk dramatized an anti-rock stance, rather than an evolution or development of the genre. It strove towards the dissolution of rock music as it was known in those days. Through manifestos like "we make noise 'cos it's our choice" and "we're into chaos," punk rockers tried to establish a distance between themselves and rock and roll as an institution. Their ultimate goal was to regain the power and rawness that rock promised in its beginnings.

This initial explosion, however, cooled off quite quickly. Based on shock tactics and a "here and now" rhetoric, punk rock seemed destined for doom from the start. Unable to rely on the industry for its mass distribution, it depended too much on the shock it initially caused. Once the original impact diminished, it was business as usual within the rock establishment.

But punk never actually died. The best evidence to support this assertion is the current popularity of alternative rock, which follows the same premises as punk rock. This is because, while the business side of punk died after 1980, the style was able to survive. Two significant trends arose from punk: the bands that changed their approach in order to be affiliated to the music business, under variations of the punk ideology (techno-pop, post punk, and, in the United States, neo-folk rock, among others), and the others who sank into the underground in order to survive. While for the latter the practice of punk became an unconscious critique of mainstream rock and roll (by ignoring it), for the former the practice of their own ideology pushed forward the deconstruction of the actual practices of rock music (as a business). The ultimate chapter on punk history is where both trends survive within the alternative scene (i.e. U2, The Pretenders and REM are still considered part of the scene, as well as newer acts like the Henry Rollins Band and L7).

As contradictory as it may seem, however, the current popularity of punk-related music cannot be labeled as an anti-rock venture. The initial explosion and subsequent popularity of punk not only threatened in ideological terms the rock establishment; its basic objective was the business part of it. It had, nevertheless, an effect upon the economy of the industry; this is best portrayed in the shams the Sex Pistols perpetrated on EMI and A&M. But the fame of alternative rock, rather than threatening the economic health the industry experienced during the eighties, has expanded it enormously. It has not affected or diminished the business side of music. In any case, the power of the major record companies has increased as they have incorporated some of the smaller labels, as was the case of Sub Pop in the United States. In short, business has been as usual, and the current alternative movement has strengthened it.

An easy conclusion to this panorama may be that punk rock and its critique have been coopted by the popular music business, as the current alternative rock scene may evidence. Cooptation, it seems to me, is an easy way out that does not address the main issues this situation presents. Alternative rock, like its predecessor punk music, continues the ideological critique the latter established within music in the late seventies. As I have already mentioned, those practices and discourses against corporate rock are very much present in the alternative scene. So rather than pose the question of cooptation, we have to look at the strategies the music industry has adopted in the past 15 years in order to survive; or, better, to expand its dominion.

Jacques Attali (1985) once suggested that the state of the social organization of noise was a precursor of more general changes and transformations that occurred at the social level. For example, the expansion the political economy of music experienced during mass production served as a prophecy of related social events. The mass production of music brought standardization to its production, and the effective control and management of innovation. Attali parallels this occurrence with the silencing and large-scale management and control of populations in mass society. So the main question here remains, what does the current practice of the recording industry tell us about the state of capitalism in general? Is the inclusion of marginal or oppositional phenomena the final frontier of capitalism?

What I am trying to suggest is that the current state of the rock business may serve as a metaphor for a major restructuring of capitalism, that, in my opinion, is already taking place; that is, the inclusion of marginal and oppositional phenomena as part of its strategies of survival. For many years capitalism seemed to have grown and established itself upon the exigency of exclusion and difference. We may look at the work of Foucault as paradigmatic in this respect. But after the events of the sixties, when boundaries were effectively challenged, the eventual institutionalization of tolerance and multiculturalism as a possibility for social existence in the late seventies and eighties, and the ineffectiveness of the right's approach to social intolerance during the same decade, a new economic and social tactic seems at hand: that of the incorporation of the boundaries, up to the point where their material existence ceases to be.

Then, rather than living under the auspices of capitalism, we may be existing in pan-capitalism (Kroker, 1994), where, as Kroker (1992, p. 158) says, "transgression, far from representing an experience of rupture, now works only to confirm the impossibility of traversing the limit of experience." If this is the case, we may be in need of a major rethinking of indispensable categories and concepts, such as marginality, opposition, resistance and cooptation, in the study and analysis of popular culture and society in general.

References

Attali, J. (1985) *Noise. The Political Economy of Music*. Minneapolis: University of Minnesota Press.

Bloomfield, T. (1991) It's sooner than you think, or where are we in the history of rock music? *New Left Review*, 190, 59–81.

Bloomfield, T. (1993) Resisting songs: negative dialectics in pop. *Popular Music*, 12(1), 13–31.

Cooper, D. (1994) Grain of the voice. *Spin*, 10(3), 37.

Frith, S. (1984) Rock and the Politics of Memory. In S. Syares, A. Stephanson, S. Aronowitz and F. Jameson (eds), *The sixties, without Apology*. Minneapolis: University of Minnesota Press, pp. 59–69.

Haug, W. F. (1986) *Critique of Commodity Aesthetics. Appearance, Sexuality and Advertising in Capitalist Society*. Minneapolis: University of Minnesota Press.

Kroker, A. (1992) *The Possessed Individual. Technology and the French Postmodern*. New York: St Martin's Press.

Kroker, A. (1994) The political economy of virtual reality: pan-capitalism. *CTHEORY* (electronic journal), 17(1–2).

Lydon, J. (with K. Zimmerman and K. Zimmerman) (1993) *Rotten: No Irish, No Blacks, No Dogs. The Authorized Autobiography of Johnny Rotten of the Sex Pistols*. New York: St Martin's Press.

Marcus, G. (1989) *Lipstick Traces: a Secret History of the Twentieth Century*. Boston: Harvard University Press.

9

"THIS AIN'T NO DISCO" ...
OR IS IT? YOUTH CULTURE
AND THE RAVE
PHENOMENON

Lori Tomlinson

Consider the following scenario:

> The music never stops ... not for a single minute. Each song
> segues into the next. ... The lights are synchronized with the
> sound, and they never stop flashing except during the percussive
> interludes, when everything falls dark. ... After you've been
> [there] for a while ... you may begin to feel a disorientation
> of fancy within yourself, and you may attune yourself to
> the repetitive shifts of this electronic music of the spheres
> and fall into a kind of ... trance in which your brain turns off
> and you give yourself up to the sensations which envelop
> you. ... The ... trance is hypnotic. (Helgesen, 1977, p. 21)

This account, written in 1977, of a journalist's experience at a
New York disco, could just as accurately capture the "rave"
experience of the 1990s. Raves are all-night dance events, held in
abandoned warehouses and airplane hangars, open fields, and
clubs, where a predominantly young crowd (teens to mid-
twenties) dances amid often elaborate lighting and visual displays to the hypnotic beats of techno, acid house, ambient house,
brutal house, progressive house, trance, jungle, and related
musics. Rave has been dubbed by some as the "disco of the
nineties," and there are many significant parallels, including
musical and cultural roots in the black and gay communities,
and almost identical criticisms of the music and culture. But the

AIDS threat has encouraged a decidedly asexual, or pre-sexual, atmosphere at raves – they are not pick-up joints. Ecstasy has replaced cocaine as the drug of choice; baggy jeans and primary-colored T-shirts have replaced the stylized satin and spandex ensembles of Studio 54; loops and samples have replaced the soulful vocals of disco divas; and the spirit of community has replaced the celebration of the self prominent in mainstream disco. And while disco eventually found a place in the hearts and pocketbooks of young and old alike, rave has remained almost exclusively within youth culture, providing an atmosphere in which participants can temporarily forget the harsh realities of coming of age in the 1990s. In this chapter I examine the important similarities and differences between disco and rave cultures, and explore various ways in which these cultures function for their respective participants.

Musical History

Disco and rave musics share common roots in the gay and black communities. Disco was born in the early 1970s, when disc jockeys at gay New York dance clubs would splice danceable soul tunes together, by such artists as MFSB, Diana Ross, and Barry White, creating a continuous, hypnotic dance mix. Disco took on a more conventional top-40 flavor following the immense success of *Saturday Night Fever* in 1978, as the once lengthy and functionally repetitive tunes like those in Donna Summer's early repertoire were compacted into radio-length commercial hits. Following disco's "death" in early 1980, the music was driven back underground, where in Chicago's gay community, it evolved into "music without singers or conventional instruments . . . an exciting, relatively new idea" (Beadle, 1993, p. 72) which became known as Chicago house music. Shortly after, a group of young, innovative producers from Detroit named Derek May, Juan Atkins and Kevin Saunderson began combining the black grooves of house and hip-hop with the synthesized Euro-sounds of groups such as Kraftwerk, Ultravox, and Visage. The result was Detroit techno. Appropriately, an early report of such music referred to it as "acid disco" (Owen, 1988).

Techno became the music of choice at early rave events held in the United States and Europe. Other related genres soon developed, such as acid house, breakbeat, jungle, ambient, trance, tribal, and progressive. These genres employ slightly different musical structures and seem to appeal to different class- and ethnic-based audiences, though they share more than just common musical roots: they also attract the same criticisms, which, not coincidentally, are almost identical to the criticisms hurled at disco music only 15 years earlier. Rave musics are characterized as "repetitive and cold" (Hunter, 1993, pp. 50, 52), "faceless, computer-generated dance music" (Tannenbaum, 1993, p. 189), and "soulless machine music" (Owen, 1988, p. 84), just as disco was deemed "monotonous, boring, mechanical" (Peterson, 1978) and "faceless" (Gilmore, 1979, p. 54), with its "formulated, restrictive, predictable rhythms" (Joe, 1980, p. 23). "To best imagine the sound of disco, picture a steamer trunk, filled to the brim, being dragged down a spiral staircase to infinity" (Naha, 1978, p. 162); techno "blends the repetition of disco, the frenzy of punk and the melodic delicacy of a car alarm" (Tannenbaum, 1993, p. 189). As we will see, rave music's highly technological nature is one of its most appealing features to its young audience.

Participants

The earliest disco audiences consisted of marginalized groups – gays, blacks, and Hispanics – in major US urban areas. Ethnic working-class youth soon followed (and became the inspiration for Nik Cohn's 1976 *Tribal Rites of the New Saturday Night*, on which *Saturday Night Fever* is loosely based). This audience bears a striking resemblance to that discussed by Hillegonda Rietveld, as she describes the participants of the "one-off" parties held in Britain in the late 1980s, the forerunners of raves: "these parties attracted a real mixture of people; fashion victims, 'gays' and working class people," all in their late twenties, part of marginalized social groups (Rietveld, 1993, p. 62). As the rave concept spread throughout Europe and the United States, such events began attracting a decidedly younger crowd, mostly in their teens and early twenties. Andrew Ross reported in 1994 that rave culture in Europe had "splintered into class-bound factions," citing the working-class identity of techno, the "upscale, chill-out, peace vibes" of ambient, and the "intelligent techno" of progressive house and trance (Ross, 1994, p. 11).

Similarly, rave musics have tended to attract specific audiences in the States. Frank Owen (1991, p. 71) observed at a Manhattan club rave that "techno fans are aggressively heterosexual," working- and lower-middle class, in a description of young Italian-American men from Bensonhurst and Staten Island that could have come straight out of *Saturday Night Fever*. Rob Tannenbaum (1993, p. 200) describes participants at New York's NASA (Nocturnal Audio + Sensory Awakening) parties as "predominantly white and middle class." Marisa Fox of Pow Wow records characterizes trance as "a slow, groove-based form appealing to a predominantly black audience," versus "pure techno," which is white-oriented (quoted in Verna, 1994, p. 113). Many early discos tended to attract of mixture of gays, straights, blacks, and whites; but once disco became acceptable in the mainstream market, clubs quickly began to segregate to attract specific, and sometimes exclusive, clientele.

Regardless of ethnic background or sexual orientation, rave has been recognized by scholars and observers as a male-dominated genre. Women and girls have always tended to be the more dominant participants in dance activities (Frith and McRobbie, 1978/9; Peterson, 1978). Yet Tannenbaum (1993, p. 200) estimated NASA's participants to be about 60 percent male, and Robert Christgau (1993, p. 70) observed that, "for a dance scene, NASA is very male, reinforcing my suspicion that the rave concept conceals some kind of rock recidivism." While girls and young women might tend to show larger numbers at other rave events, "they appear to be less involved in the cultural production of rave, from the flyers, to the events, to the DJing, than their male counterparts" (McRobbie, 1994, p. 168). Few rave groups include women; it could be argued that, because of the "faceless" nature of rave artists (most individual group members are unknown to their fans), the lack of female participation would be unknown (and therefore, perhaps, insignificant) to rave participants. But a quick glance of credits listed on CD liner notes reveals the absence of female producers and group members.

Women were both prominent and highly visible as artists and participants in disco culture; in fact, black disco divas dominated the disco (and at times, top 10) charts. Female vocals in rave musics are commonly reduced to one-bar phrases consisting of short, simple repeated phrases, or single words or syllables (Tagg, 1994), sampled or looped. Datura's "Devotion (Inana Marga Mix)" and Psychedelic Evolution's "I Think I Want Some More" are good examples.[1] Interestingly, Donna Summer's famous early works, "Love to Love You Baby" and "I Feel Love," are, in their repetition, vocally similar in character to many contemporary rave songs. But Summer was clearly the star of these recordings, and even co-wrote them; the soul divas sampled in rave songs are largely anonymous. Responding to the question, "Why are there no women in techno?", Ted Bickers of the group Levitation posits that the music industry is only interested in female performers if they have a marketable image – that is, if they "look good" (quoted in Gittins, 1992, p. 38). Because rave artists tend to be faceless if not completely anonymous, female artists cannot be marketed in the traditional manner. Conventionally attractive (i.e., large-breasted and half-dressed) women can still be used to market compilations, however, as evidenced by Continuum Records' use of "Miss Techno" on the covers of their *This Is Techno* series. Jez Willis of Utah Saints comments: "There are a lot of similarities between Techno and heavy metal music in that they're both totally male-dominated. Techno is the cock rock of the Nineties" (quoted in Gittins, 1992, p. 38). Considering the primary role women performers have played in previous dance cultures, the limited involvement of women in rave music warrants further study.[2]

Perhaps the most important defining factor of rave participants is age. Rave is largely, if not exclusively, a youth phenomenon, and youth culture is a vital ingredient of the rave culture in general. Rave participants tend to be young, from their teens to early twenties. Disco began as a principally young-adult phenomenon, though teens were initially barred from participation due to drinking-age restrictions at discotheques. As disco was coopted and marketed at a more mainstream audience, it became fair game for all ages, from preschoolers to senior citizens. That has not been the case with rave. It has remained almost exclusively within youth culture. "There's a naive vibrancy and energy to rave that can be created only by the very young, and its message is clear to this 31-year-old: Go *away*" (Tannenbaum, 1993, p. 189).

Rave as Youth Culture

In several key ways, the culture of rave is the culture of child-hood, as illustrated by rave fashions, rave music, rave attitude. Primary and day-glo colors are standard in the raver's wardrobe. Girls and young women often don pigtails. Both boys and girls have commonly been seen sucking pacifiers; toys as accessories are also the norm. As Andrew Ross (1994, p. 11) has observed, "In this never-never land of rave, a void of psychedelic regres-sion, no one wears clothes their own size, sartorially deferring adulthood." Rave tunes sometimes include samples of children's TV-show themes and cartoons (most notably Smart E's "Sesame's Treet," based almost entirely on the *Sesame Street* theme song). But don't be fooled – ravers are not children. They are very conscious and deliberate in their employment of child-hood culture. "We dress this way because we want to look younger than we are. I want to feel younger than I am, because getting old in America is not much fun," commented one 22-year-old raver (quoted in Mead, 1993, p. 43). A female raver explains, "The idea is that people are going back to childhood. In the early 90's everything is screwed up, people don't want to deal with adult issues, and so they are regressing" (quoted in Shea, 1993, p. A40).

Unlike the disco pick-up joints of the 1970s ("Hey baby, what's your sign?"), raves are curiously asexual, or pre-sexual, environ-ments (Tannenbaum, 1993; McRobbie, 1994). This important characteristic has been linked to the AIDS threat, a "text of anxiety" or of "avoidance" that results in the downplaying of sexual activity (McRobbie, 1994, p. 172), that says "*I don't want to get AIDS*" (quoted in Russell, 1993, p. 126). Rave's asexual/pre-sexual attitude is illustrated not only in its fashions, but in its penchant for what British DJ DB characterizes as more of a "touchy-feely," "cuddly security" physical contact (quoted in Tannenbaum, 1993, p. 190). Of course, one should not be so naive as to think that romantic connections are *never* made at raves. But a hug from a fellow raver is not usually a sexual advance as much as a show of platonic affection, much like grade-schoolers holding hands – "erogenous zones are strictly out of bounds" (Russell, 1993, p. 126) – and ravers often tend to segregate by gender, boys dancing with boys and girls with girls (Tannenbaum, 1993). One may be reminded of an elementary-school playground, where the culture of childhood can be a culture of gender-based segregation.

The dance floor, as Simon Frith and Angela McRobbie (1978/ 9) point out, has traditionally been the most public setting for music as sexual expression. Interestingly, both disco and rave musics incorporate a discourse of sexuality into their structure. The building, peaking, and (delayed) climax of disco served to accentuate if not establish the sexually charged atmospheres of disco clubs. Similar sexual conventions in rave musics seem puzzling. If the musical simulation of delayed orgasms in disco tended to *heighten* the mood, then perhaps the tacit sexuality of rave serves to *replace* sexual contact. But ravers are far more patient than disco dancers; rave music takes disco's delay of climax to new heights (or, perhaps more accurately, prevents it from reaching any height at all). And the common use of the drug Ecstasy (or "E") further encroaches the idea of dance as sexual expression. Besides giving its users a "euphoric sense of communion" (Reynolds, 1990, p. 177) and "feelings of interconnectedness and well-being" (Erlich, 1992, p. 43), the drug is also known for inhibiting one's ability to reach orgasm: "E androgynizes (it's a real dick shriveler)" (Reynolds, 1994, p. 56).

So rave's "arrested orgasm" creates a "plateau of bliss that can neither be exceeded nor released" (Reynolds, 1994, p. 56), leaving ravers in a state of liminality, suspended between ascension and climax, between childhood and adulthood. And in the warehouses, open fields, and clubs where it all takes place, ravers have created their own space, beyond the naiveté of childhood and in opposition to the adult world. It is here where ravers' identities lie, in the youth *community* of rave.

Culture of Community

Many ravers will claim that the rave experience is much more that the sum of its parts. . . . Good raves have what is referred to as a vibe; a shared feeling of openness and connectedness that transcends simple sex & fun agendas. Egos and personal prejudices are left behind as people celebrate and feed off of each other's positive energy. (Fogel, 1994)

> Music in general has always been able to sweep people off their feet, but what distinguishes raves are [*sic*] the concept of the *shared* experience; a feeling of unity often arises, and people are open and friendly to one another. There is a loss of that "attitude" that is omnipresent in normal clubs and even in life in general. People are celebrated for what they are, not what they aren't. (Hilker, 1994)

This valuing of the community over the individual is reflected not only in the attitudes of the ravers (and in the communal effects of Ecstasy), but in the "faceless" nature of the music itself. Rave artists are not the rock 'n' roll stars-as-cultural-heroes described by Daniel Dotter (1987, p. 28), "symbolic figures who mobilize the masses in society to act or accomplish social goals." These artists do not posses the commercial viability needed to become public figures, as with traditional rock 'n' roll stars. In fact, they are often unknown to the very people who dance and commune to their music on a regular basis: "I have a couple of tapes and songs I really like but I am not sure who performed or mixed them," one raver confesses (Ralph, 1995). This anonymity is significant. It illustrates rave's "triumph of communal spirit over individual identity" (Tannenbaum, 1993, p. 199), and is epitomized in the "white label" concept – releases that are not labeled with artist *or* title. Many of disco's early artists tended to be similarly faceless, but while disco DJs often built their own fan following (as some rave DJs do today), it was the *individual* who became the star attraction, on whom the spotlight was cast (sometimes literally), in an attempt to attract the attention of the other dancers (or, when all else failed, one could always admire oneself reflected in a mirrored wall panel or projected on to a large screen by a live-action camera). The 1970s may have indeed been characterized as Christopher Lasch's (1979) "culture of narcissism" or Tom Wolfe's (1976) "me decade," but for its participants, rave is a culture of community, the manifestation of a "we" decade.

Philip Tagg (1994) has analyzed rave music (more specifically, techno music) in terms of its communal values as reflected in the song structure. In fact, he characterizes techno's musical innovations as expressing "a radical new socialisation strategy amongst young people in out society" (p. 219). He cites such innovations as the ability to include non-music sounds within this popular music form, techno's frequent use of the Phrygian mode (a rarity in the Western music tradition), the music's intentional artificiality, and, most importantly for our purposes, the emphasis of the "ground" (background/accompaniment) over the "figure" (melody). Following Tagg's argument, the ground could be said to represent the group or community, while the figure represents the individual. The rise of the ground and the fall of the figure constitute for Tagg a rejection of the "degenerate, hegemonic values of the individual:"

> Rave is something you immerse yourself into with other people. There is no guitar hero or rock star or corresponding musical-structural figures to identify with. . . . You are just one of many other individuals who constitute the musical whole, the whole ground – musical and social – on which you stand. . . . you could say that perhaps techno-rave puts an end to nearly four hundred years of the great European bourgeois individual music. (Tagg, 1994, p. 219).

Dave Hesmondhalgh (1995) disagrees. He points out that, for many years, people have been dancing to recorded music, often paying little attention to the artists who produced it, while still being aware that the musician is an *individual* who writes and produces in an *individual* way. He argues that "there is little evidence of social collectivism in the institutions of rave and dance culture, in spite of a discourse of love and unity amongst its insiders" (p. 262). The key word is *insiders*, the ravers themselves, who, in the creation of their identity, practice exclusion (Frith, 1987a), establishing themselves in terms of the ingroup (ravers) and outgroup (non-ravers), a process that appears, according to Katrina Hazzard-Gordon (1990), to be highly age-specific, functioning most prominently among youth. True ravers would argue that outsiders simply could not understand what the rave community is all about: "A lot of aversion against techno comes from the fact that many people 'just don't get it'" (Ralph, 1995).

Mark Jacobson (1995, p. 136) points out that dance music has always had the "surreptitious, almost mystic, edge of a secret society." Just as the marginalized groups who "founded" disco created safe spaces for themselves in their dance clubs, protected (if only for an evening) from a society of racists, classists, and homophobes, ravers have created their own secret youth society where they can privately and peacefully protest the state of world affairs. And they even have their own secret language, in the form of the music itself. "Techno is the ultimate teenage slang, a language elders can't comprehend" (Tannenbaum, 1993, p. 190). The key to understanding this language lies with one of its most common criticisms: its technical, mechanical, "inhuman" nature. The rave generation grew up in a techno-world; they can scarcely, if at all, remember life without VCRs, answering machines, computers, and digital sampling. They are at home with rave music, because "they are most at home with the notion that technology is our new nature" (Owen, 1988, p. 84). Technology is also commonly reflected in song ("Earthbase 1," "Zeroxed," "Silicon Jesus") and group (Appollo 440, Techno-Flight 1, Smashing Atoms) names. And while critics may not comprehend the "repetitive" nature of this youth dialect, the ravers themselves embrace it. "You have to understand repetition to the point of appreciation. Plus there's a lot going on in a DJ's mix that one has to learn to listen for. . . . You start hearing through and beyond it" (Eduardo, 1995). When rave music was still in its early stages of development, legendary DJ and producer Frankie Knuckles, the "founding father of house music," recognized the generational conflict: "Older people don't like it. They want something more soulful and meaningful. They think that acid house is soulless machine music . . . but they're going to have to get used to it" (quoted in Owen, 1988, p. 84). Or choose to leave the young ones to do their thing, their way, with their music – which is what the creation of safe space is all about.

Release and Resistance

Rave also provides its participants with an escape, a release, a form of therapy and catharsis, of revolution and resistance, much as disco did in the 1970s. Compare one raver's explanation of rave – "I dance . . . for some odd way of therapy (pent up emotions, writing doesn't help so I look to some sort of physical therapy). But overall, I like to dance and go to raves, because for that small moment in tyme [sic] I forget all about the world and its problems" (Misery, 1994) – to a discotheque regular's comment: "When I dance, all I think of is how good my body feels and what a release it is for me. I think kids come here to escape the problems of growing up" (quoted in Orth, 1976, p. 98). Or the commentary of these ravers:

The love and bonding experienced at raves needs to be carried out into the world. We are the visionaries, and it is our job to slowly change society. There was a women's movement, a sexual revolution, and many other giant steps made by previous generations. It is now time for the next revolution, the one back to realizing the beauty of humanity. (Rob, 1994)

"It's a love circle . . . all the races are together, dancing, having a communal experience" (quoted in Garcia, 1992, p. 60), to Richard Peterson's (1978, p. R27) assessment of disco:

> If disco provides an escape from alienating work, it also allows a fantasy escape from the "accidents" of race, ethnicity, and sexual orientation . . . disco permits close intimacy between blacks and whites. An even greater change has come for gay people, for disco transcends questions of sexual orientation. As the disco phenomenon expands, gender-free sexuality in dress, dance, and behavior is being accepted and celebrated as never before.

The cultural and societal changes that could potentially be realized through rave culture have not gone unnoticed by those in the outgroup, specifically adults. Their attack against rave has often targeted the widespread use of Ecstasy at rave events. Tagg (1994, pp. 210–1) posits that this fear of E is actually the fear of a more far-reaching "high:" "The fear that their sons and daughters (and the society we all populate) are out of control and that the young people, by organising and participating in these raves, have in fact started to take control over their own lack of control of society." Susan McClary (1991, p. 34) discusses the inherently subversive nature of dance music:

> The musical power of the disenfranchised – whether youth, the underclass, ethnic minorities, women or gay people – more often resides in their ability to articulate different ways of constructing the body, ways that bring along in their wake the potential for different experimental worlds. And the anxious reactions that so often greet new musics from such groups indicate that something crucially political is at issue.

So, as they dance to forget, ravers also question conventions of race, gender, and authority. And within their culture, they find power through identity, control through community, much like their disco forebears in the early 1970s.

Commercialization and Cooptation

McClary also points out that the culture industry – in this case, the music industry – will sell whatever it can, regardless of the politics at stake. But not without coopting, mainstreaming, and sterilizing the product first. "The rave-knockers say that with the inevitable commercialization of the trend, raves are headed down the same spiral that saw disco in the 70s go from a hip ritual of the gay demimonde to the white-suited silliness of Saturday Night Fever" (McKusick, 1992, p. 22). That's precisely the kind of commercial success that record companies are striving for. Howie Gabriel, executive vice president and general manager of Continuum records, the label that released the relatively successful *This Is Techno* compilation series, admits that "We want our record to be the 'Saturday Night Fever' of the '90s. We're going after a wider audience, a suburban audience" (quoted in Applefeld, 1992, p. 43).

However, several key factors have prevented rave musics from seeing the same US success enjoyed by disco megastars such as the Bee Gees, Village People and Donna Summer in the 1970s. Rave music tends to receive very little radio airplay in the States, which has long been the backbone of marketing for record companies. This is due in part to the fact that rave musics are largely instrumental genres (Flick, 1991, p. 87); as Frith (1987b, p. 97) has pointed out, "words are a reason why people buy records; instrumental hits remain unusual." Rave songs also tend to extend well beyond the three to five minute length acceptable for radio airplay. Early disco records met with the same resistance, until labels began to release shorter, more radio-friendly disco singles. Though several stations, such as Los Angeles's KIIS, KPWR and KSRF, eventually began to offer techno-rave shows (Rosen and Flick, 1992), the all-rave, all-the-time station has not yet become a reality. Radio executives have likely not forgotten the disco radio boom and bust of the late 1970s, when stations across the country experimented with a 24-hour disco format, to enjoy substantial, and sometimes miraculous, boosts in ratings, only to bottom out mere months later. "In its purest form, [disco] was a high-energy, highly structured format which worked well in any sustained form only in the unique environment of the club" (Joe, 1980, p. 95). The same is arguably true of rave.

Equally detrimental to widespread popularity is rave music's lack of an established star system. As discussed earlier, rave's "no-star" policy reflects the culture's communal values. It also makes it difficult for record labels to market their product in the traditional manner. Rave stars are not visual; they do not appear on their CD covers, nor do they go on tour (with rare exceptions, such as rave star Moby, who performed on the 1995 Lollapalooza ticket). And in the United States, MTV refuses to show rave videos. Most ravers wouldn't know their favorite artists if they passed them on the street. Without radio and MTV airplay and identifiable stars to promote their own releases, record companies must rely on rave and club exposure, along with word-of-mouth advertising, to market their product. Thus far, it has not been enough to push rave over the edge into mainstream acceptance and consumption. Rave records "sell about as well as Debbie Boone box sets" (Tannenbaum, 1993, p. 199).

Despite marketing obstacles, record labels have remained determined to win over a larger audience. As with early disco, most early rave recordings came from small independent labels that lacked sufficient budgets or staffing for aggressive marketing. As rave events became increasingly popular across the USA (as discotheques did following the release of *Saturday Night Fever*), major labels could sense profit potential and began to include rave artists on their rosters. By its very nature, an underground culture such as rave defines itself in opposition to the mainstream culture, to things mass-produced and mass-consumed (Thornton, 1994). "Once a music is co-opted into the mass culture, it can no longer be considered confrontational" (Epstein, 1994, p. xvii). Hardcore ravers are already mourning the loss of their music and culture to outsiders. "I hate the Bubblegum Ravers who go to raves cuz [*sic*] it's a scene and it's cool, and they all dance perfectly and they all look perfect and they all wear all the brand names. . . . Techno is getting a bad name cuz they play crap on the radio and in trendy clubs" (Kai, 1994). Originally, individual raves emerged spontaneously with only several hours notice through world-of-mouth contact among the rave underground. Raves are now often being held in popular clubs and other more traditional venues, advertised in mainstream newspapers and on the radio. Consequently, the crowds are becoming larger, filled with "bubblegum ravers" and curious observers.

As disco became more widely popular, so did stylized (and often expensive) disco ensembles, establishing distinct gender-based dress codes in the burgeoning suburban disco market: satin shirts and leisure suits for men, clingy polyester dresses and skin-tight spandex separates for women. Audiences became increasingly segregated in these suburban clubs, providing fewer opportunities for those of diverse ethnic backgrounds and sexual orientations to mingle freely. While the rave uniform has retained much of its pre-adolescent, gender-free character, "bubblegum" ravers and their designer rave fashions may be likened to the "white-suited silliness" predicted by Tom McKusick (1992). As raves attract larger crowds in suburban America, these audiences may too become increasingly segregated, diluting rave's potential for fostering community and unity among divergent peoples. And the safe communal space created by young ravers, in their quest for identity, escape, catharsis, and peaceful revolution, is at risk.

Conclusion: A Culture in Progress

Rave has yet to see the level of mainstream success and cooptation that "killed" disco at the close of the 1970s. There has been no *Saturday Night Fever* or Studio 54 of rave to pull it completely above ground for the consumption of mass audiences. As is any culture, rave is a culture in progress. The original ravers are growing up, and perhaps growing out of the scene as a younger generation takes over. One common criticism of this new generation is that they have lost touch with the true roots and spirit of raving – that they are bubblegum ravers. Not all ravers, however, seem to have abandoned the original mission of rave:

> What I got from those few experiences is a profound sense of connectedness with people, especially people whom I had never met before. I carried that feeling into my daily life – a faith or emphasis on being positive, seeking the good in all things, the desire to seek out and celebrate the goodness in all people. Then the interconnectedness with nature, the world at large, all things. Karma-ish? yeah, kinda. Spiritual? definitely. Beautiful? of course! (Alissa, 1994)

But as techno music creeps into popular movie soundtracks and mainstream dance clubs, as rave-inspired graphics are used to market Levi jeans and bottled soft drinks, the "secret society" of rave will continue to be infiltrated by outsiders. Rave's ultimate survival as a communal "love circle" remains to be seen.

Notes

1 Of course, there are always exceptions, such as "Inner Sanctum" by Bleu Featuring Copper, and male vocals are similarly sampled and modified. One could also argue that rave vocals are, at times, modified beyond positive gender identification. But overall, the male voice is prominent in rave musics.
2 For a discussion of rave culture as "clitoris-envy," as a "subconscious attempt to usurp female potencies and pleasures in order to dispense with real women altogether," see pp. 62–5 of Simon Reynolds and Joy Press (1995) *The Sex Revolts: Gender, Rebellion, and Rock 'n' Roll*. Cambridge, MA: Harvard University Press.

References

Alissa (1994) Spirit of raves archives. Hyperreal web site. http://hyperreal.com/raves/spirit/testimonials/What_We_Get_From_Raves.html.

Applefeld, C. (1992) Compilations expand techno market: more accessible format offers retail entree. *Billboard*, August 29, 43, 49.

Beadle, J. (1993) *Will Pop Eat Itself?* London: Faber and Faber.

Christgau, R. (1993) Another bleep world. *Village Voice*, February 16, 69–70.

Dotter, D. (1987) Growing up is hard to do: rock and roll performers as cultural heroes. *Sociological Srectrum*, 7, 25–44.

Eduardo (1995) E-mail interview with the author, June 5.

Epstein, J. S. (1994) Misplaced childhood: an introduction to the sociology of youth and their music. In *Adolescents and Their Music: If It's Too Loud. You're Too Old*. New York: Garland Publishing, pp. xiii–xxxiv.

Erlich, J. (1992) Brain gain: drugs that boost intelligence. *Omni*, September, 48, 50, 67–8.

Flick, L. (1991) "Techno-rave" has labels dancing. *Billboard*, October 19, 1, 87.

Fogel, L. (1994) The spirit of raving archives. Hyperreal web site. http://hyperreal.com/raves/spirit/intro.html.

Frith, S. (1987a) Toward an aesthetic of popular music. In R. Leppert and S. McClary (eds), *Music and Society: the Politics of Composition, Performance and Reception*. Cambridge: Cambridge University Press, pp. 133–49.

Frith, S. (1987b) Why do songs have words? In A. L. White (ed.), *Lost in Music: Culture, Style and Musical Event*. London: Routledge & Kegan Paul, pp. 77–106.

Frith, S. and McRobbie, A. (1978/9) Rock and sexuality. *Screen Education*, 29 (Winter), 3–19.

Garcia, G. (1992) Tripping the night fantastic, *Time*, August 17, 60–1.

Gilmore, M. (1979) Disco! *Rolling Stone*, April 19, 9, 54.

Gittins, I. (1992) The great techno debate. *Melody Maker*, August 1, 35–8.

Hazzard-Gordon, K. (1990) Afro-American core culture social dance: an examination of four aspects of meaning. In Harry B. Shaw (ed.), *Perspectives of Black Popular Culture*. Bowling Green, OH: Bowling Green State Urnversity Popular Press, pp. 46–57.

Helgesen, S. (1977) Disco. *Harper's*, October, 20–4.

Hesmondhalgh, D. (1995) Technoprophecy: a response to Tagg. *Popular Music*, 14(2), 261–3.

Hilker, C. (1994). The alt.rave FAQ. Hyperreal web site. http://hyperreal.com/raves/altraveFAQ.html.

Hunter, J. (1993) Review of *Techno Mancer* (Various Artists) and *Utah Saints* (Utah Saints). *Rolling Stone*, January 21, 50, 52.

Jacobson, M. (1995) Disco does *not* suck, Beavis. *Esquire*, February, 136.

Joe, R. A. (1980) *This Business of Disco*. New York: Billboard Books.

Kai (1994) Spirit of rave archives. Hyperreal web site. http://hyperreal.com/raves/spirit/testimonials/Why_We_Rave.html.

Lasch, C. (1979) *Culture of Narcissism: American Life in the Age of Diminishing Expectations*. New York: Norton.

McClary, S. (1991) Same as it ever was: youth culture and music. In A. Ross and T. Rose (eds), *Microphone Fiends: Youth Music and Youth Culture*. New York: Roufledge, pp. 29–40.

McKusick, T. (1992) Catch a rave. *Utne Reader*, September/October, 22–4.

McRobbie, A. (1994) *Postmodernism and Popular Culture*. London: Routledge.

Mead, R. (1993) Rave on. *New York*, August 30, 43–4.

Misery (1994) Spirit of rave archives. Hyperreal web site. http://hyperreal.com/raves/spirit/testimonials/Why_We_Rave.html.

Naha, E. (comp.) (1978) *Lillian Roxon's Rock Encyclopedia*. New York: Gossett & Dunlap.

Orth, M., Carter, B. and Whitman, L. (1976) Get up and boogie! *Newsweek*, November 8, 94–8.

Owen, F. (1988) Acid disco: make me machine. *Village Voice*, January 19, 83–4.

Owen, F. (1991) Feel the noise. Techno kids: the working-class avant-garde. *Village Voice*, September 24, 71.

Peterson, R. (1978) Disco! A sociologist suggests its distinctive sound isn't just another fad. *The Chronicle of Higher Education (Review)*, October 2, 6–27.

Ralph (1995) E-mail interview with the author. May 24.

Reynolds, S. (1990) *Blissed Out: the Raptures of Rock*. London: Serpent's Tail.

Reynolds, S. (1994) British rave. *Artforum*, February, 54–7.

Rietveld, H. (1993) Living the dream. In S. Redhead (ed.), *Rave Off: Politics and Deviance in Contemporary Youth Culture*. Aldershot, England/Brookfield, VT: Avebury, pp. 41–78.

Rob (1994) Spirit of rave archives. Hyperreal web site. http://hyperreal.com/raves/spirit/testimonials/What_We_Get_From_Raves.html.

Rosen, C. and Flick, L. (1992) Techno music becoming mainstream rave in US. *Billboard*, May 23, 1, 48.

Ross, A. (1994) Andrew Ross' weather report. *Artforum*, May, 10–12.

Russell, K. (1993) Lysergia suburbia. In S. Redhead (ed.), *Rave Off: Politics and Deviance in Contemporary Youth Culture*. Aldershot, England/Brookfield, VT: Avebury, pp. 91–174.

Shea, C. (1993) A rave can be a hard-core techno-blast; you just have to find out about it in time. *The Chronicle of Higher Education*, May 12, A39–40.

Tagg, P. (1994) From refrain to rave: the decline of figure and the rise of ground. *Popular Music*, 13(2), 209–22.

Tannenbaum, R. (1993) Techno inferno. *GQ*, September, 189–90, 199–200.

Thornton, S. (1994) Moral panic, the media and British rave culture. In A. Ross and T. Rose (eds), *Microphone Fiends: Youth Music and Youth Culture*. New York: Routledge, pp. 176–92.

Verna, P. (1994) Electric Pow Wow label stays fiercely independent. *Billboard*, May 7, 1, 113.

Wolfe, T. (1976) The "me" decade and the third great awakening. *New York*, August 23, 26–40.

10
GROWING UP PUNK: MEANING AND COMMITMENT CAREERS IN A CONTEMPORARY YOUTH SUBCULTURE

Linda Andes

Introduction

For at least the past half century, youth has been a recognizable social group with a culture of its own. Parsons (1942) described youth culture as a single cultural system characteristic of youth in a modernizing world. Other researchers (Hollingshead, 1949; Coleman, 1961; Schwartz and Merten, 1967; Larkin, 1979; Eckert, 1989) have outlined various broad social categories of youth embedded in class differences. Middle-class youth are likely to be found in the group historically known as "socies" or "jocks," while working-class youth predominate in the "hoods", "greasers," "freaks," or "burnouts." However, many smaller "spectacular" subcultures have appeared, which are often perceived as distinct from and in opposition to mainstream youth culture. These youth subcultures are distinguished from one another by "style:" modes of dress, music, behavioral rituals, and language (Cohen, 1972).

Scholars at the Centre for Contemporary Cultural Studies at the University of Birmingham in England have developed a theory explaining the emergence and disappearance of particular youth subcultures, such as the mods or punks (Clarke et al., 1976; Clarke, 1976; Jefferson, 1976; Brake, 1985; Hebdige, 1979). Youth subcultures are seen as a "magical" or "imaginary" symbolic solution (in the form of "style") to contradictions between the experiences of youth, the working-class culture of their parents and the hegemonic culture of the middle class. Cultural symbols are "resignified" to express the assumed subversive or resistant focal concerns, activities, values, and collective self-image of subculture members. In other words, these scholars argue that youth subcultures reflect class conflict as well as generational conflict.

In a review of the British cultural studies approach, Cagle noted that "this school has strived to construct a general theoretical model . . . [but many times it] contains abstract gaps that are largely *un*theorized" (Cagle, 1989, p. 306, emphasis in original). One of these gaps is a result of the adoption of a whole youth subculture as the unit of analysis. The theory risks structural and/or cultural overdetermination by neglecting the question of how individuals live out their lives within the subculture. For example, the emphases on the innovators and cooptation of the subculture's style by mainstream culture leads to the conclusion that youth subcultures can only be short-lived. However, just as the innovators can construct new meanings for clothes or other symbols from the dominant culture, so too can other members adapt and change the subcultural items for their own purposes and needs.

Empirical studies of youth subcultures have linked the macro level of social structure and culture to the micro level of the individual with the concept of commitment. Commitment is taken to represent the depth or degree of participation in the subculture, and because of the oppositional stance of many youth subcultures, commitment is usually equated with resistance. Some researchers have concluded that girls are less "committed" to youth subcultures; that they participate solely for the purposes of dressing up, socializing, and attracting boys (Kotarba and Wells, 1987; Baron, 1989a,b). "[Punk] subculture is male-dominated both in terms of numbers and severity of resistance. That is, they adopt the full code of behaviors of the subcultural lifestyle" (Baron, 1989a, p. 214). Feminist critics (McRobbie and Garber, 1976; McRobbie, 1980; Roman, 1987, 1988; Andes, 1991) have argued that these researchers have adopted a gender-biased definition of punk which privileges the behavior, styles, and values of punk boys. They have neglected to consider possible gendered differences in the meaning and consequences of the behaviors, such as slam dancing or dropping out of school. Girls express their commitment to the subculture in different ways than boys; for example, by hanging out in thrift stores or cafes instead of on the street, where the boys tend to congregate.

The feminist critique highlights a common logical flaw in attempts to link the individual to social structure through her or his committed behavior: the concept of commitment is defined tautologically (see also Becker, 1960). Punk is assumed to be an "ideal type" with a single standard of behavior, style, and ideology. An individual is committed to the subculture to the extent that he or she conforms to this single standard. Commitment is conceived of as varying relative to this non-varying ideal type.

However, commitment can vary in two ways. First, it can vary across individuals at any given cross-section of time. When commitment is conceptualized in this manner, members of a subculture are usually categorized into two groups: those who are central and very committed versus those who are peripheral (or marginal) and not very committed (Clarke et al., 1976; Brake, 1985; Kotarba and Wells, 1987; Baron 1989a, b). However, commitment can also vary within a single individual across different points in time. Kanter (1968, p. 500) defines commitment as "a process through which individual interests become attached to the carrying out of socially organized patterns of behavior which are seen as fulfilling those interests, as expressing the nature and needs of the person." In Kanter's conceptualization, commitment is not static as it is in the first definition, but a *process* of deepening involvement in and identification with a social group. This process can also be viewed developmentally. At different stages of their involvement in a group, individuals experience different kinds of commitment: to social roles, relationships, norms, etc. So, commitment can then vary as a deepening (or lessening) over time, but can also vary in the sense that this deepening can occur along multiple dimensions or axes.

Commitment to a youth subculture is usually conceptualized from the frame of reference of the *observer* in relationship to an assumed and unspecified single standard of behavior. By adopting Kanter's conception of commitment as a process, I intend to consider commitment in relationship to the frame of reference of the *actor*, and will attempt to unravel the tautological relationship between committed behavior and the standard of being "punk." That is, I am assuming that committed individual members will act in accordance with their individual standards of "punk," but the form of their committed behavior can vary.

How is the punk ideal type linked to behavior through commitment? The ideal type serves as a standard for a punk identity. Burke (1991a,b) considers commitment from the perspective of the actor as part of the cybernetic identity process. He defines "an *identity* [as] *a set of 'meanings'* applied to the self in a social role or situation defining what it means to be who one is. This set of meanings serves as a standard" (Burke, 1991b, p. 837, emphasis in original). This standard forms part of the feedback loop which constitutes the identity process: the individual observes and interprets his or her own actions and the reflected appraisals he or she receives from others regarding those actions. The perceived meanings of the actions are then compared to the identity standard. Burke (1991a, p. 837) notes, "*the system works by modifying output (behavior)* to the social situation in attempts to change the input (reflected appraisals) *to match the identity standard*" (emphasis added). Therefore, the more committed individuals are to an identity standard, the more they will want to behave in ways that are consistent with that standard. Burke assumes that identities are stable, but it is also possible for *the identity standard itself to be modified*. If individuals' reference group changes, altering the meanings of their reflected appraisals, the individuals can adjust their identity standard to match that of their new reference group. If one assumes that a punk identity is an ideal type – that is, it has only one set of meanings – then individuals should only express their commitment to punk relative to that single set of meanings. By considering commitment and committed behavior from the frame of reference of the actor and allowing the actors to express their commitment in different ways, definitions of the punk identity standard may also vary.

This study was informed by two sensitizing concepts. (a) Punks may have varying identity standards: that is, they may hold different definitions or sets of meanings for "being punk." These meanings may vary as the individual's reference group changes and hence, as the reflected appraisals of others change. (b) Commitment to an identity is a process which waxes and wanes over time for any given individual, and may take different forms at different stages in the process.

Methodology

Qualitative methods were used to conduct the study. I spent nine months between February and October of 1991 as a part-time participant observer in primarily "public" spaces: at punk concerts, on the street, and at the rehearsals of a hardcore punk band. I wrote detailed notes as soon as possible after (and occasionally during) each session in the field.

I also conducted nine semi-structured interviews with punk informants, knowledgeable and committed insiders who were not necessarily representative of the subculture as a whole, but who could provide me with detailed information about the subculture and its members. The interviews were tape recorded and later transcribed. The informants ranged in age from 18 to 27, and were involved in punk at different periods of historical time. I attempted to choose informants who were just beginning to become involved in punk, who were currently very involved, and who were no longer involved at all. However, since it became obvious from the life histories of the older informants that initial involvement in punk often occurred as early as age 12 or 13, I was not able to interview anyone at the very earliest stages of involvement. I was able to non-interactively observe the behavior of younger participants, and have relied upon reports of the informants for insight into the attitudes and biographies of younger participants. All informants will be referred to in this report by pseudonyms, and some details of the informants' personal lives have been fictionalized in order to protect their identities and confidentiality.

Results

Punks and Poseurs

From the very beginning of the research, defining "punk" was problematic. One of the first findings was that some individuals identified themselves as being punk but did not act or dress according to the punk ideal type, while other individuals who participated in the style and behaviors typical of the ideal did *not* identify as punks. Two of my informants provide excellent examples of this.

Joseph Free is a 24-year-old guitarist who works for a collection agency. While Joseph is quite knowledgeable about the history of punk music, he is unfamiliar with contemporary hardcore bands, does not attend punk concerts, and acknowledges that his style of dress is not a typical punk style. However, Joseph identifies himself as a punk, and believes that he is committed to punk values and ideals. John Heart is a 20-year-old college student. John's clothing looks well-worn, and I have often seen him wearing faded and sometimes torn jeans, T-shirts displaying hardcore bands' logos or graphics, and old flannel shirts. John is very knowledgeable about contemporary hardcore bands, attends hardcore and punk concerts on a regular basis, and participates in the typical punk concert activities of slam dancing and stagediving. John reads books about punk music, books of poetry by punk "celebrities," music magazines, and punk fanzines. However, John says that he feels little sympathy for the rebellious attitudes he associates with punks, and refuses to identify himself as a punk.

A rigid interpretation of commitment as adherence to the norms of the punk ideal type would imply that Joseph would not consider himself to be a punk and that John would. However, the opposite is true: Joseph self-identifies as punk and John does not. Clearly these two individuals do not define punk in the same manner as described in the literature.

This definitional problem is one that is recognized by the informants themselves. They spend a great deal of time and energy validating their own and others' punk identities, and condemning the lack of authenticity of others. Individuals who appear to be punk, but who are perceived by punks as lacking a true or authentic commitment to the subculture, are referred to as "poseurs." Poseurs may adopt the punk style to attract the opposite sex (Kotarba and Wells, 1987) or because the style is considered fashionable or "trendy" (Baron, 1989b). An individual must be able to display expert knowledge of punk culture and especially of punk music to be perceived as authentic by members of the subculture (Roman, 1987). Gil, an 18-year-old, said,

Punk is kind of dead now because people are using it as a fashion and forgetting about the attitude. And they just don't get the whole punk thing. Poseurs don't understand about, like, moshing and picking people up [when they fall during the dance] and stuff, and they think the goal is to hurt one another. (Interview, June 28, 1991)

Gil defines poseurs as those who try to dress like punks, but who lack insider status because they don't "know the rules."

In contrast, Mark, a 24-year-old guitarist in a hardcore band, believes that poseurs are those who adhere to the ideal type of punk style and behavior without a deeper understanding of punk values. He said,

I had a conversation with a couple of punks squatting on the corner. One was talking about how you're not really a punk unless you wear Doc Martens [a brand of work boot]. As far as I'm concerned, that guy was being a poseur; thinking that shoes are an important part of being a punk. They believe that punk is listening to the "right" music and wearing the "right" clothes and dying your hair the "right" color. It's a state of mind. (Interview, September 18, 1991)

These informants have different understandings of what it means to be "punk," and therefore they have varying conceptions of the appropriate ways to express commitment to the subculture. Poseurs, then, from the informants' various perspectives, are those who don't define punk in the same manner as they themselves do.

Punk as a Career

Relatively short-term field research tends to confirm the notion that punks utilize a single standard of what it means to be punk (Kotarba and Wells, 1987; Lull, 1987; Roman, 1987, 1988; Baron, 1989a, b). However, from the perspective of any individual punk's biography, it is obvious that punk is an achieved status rather than an ascribed one: no one is born a punk. Individuals must *become* punk and they must also, in most cases, cease to be a punk eventually. There are very few participants in the subculture who are older than their early twenties. Those who do stay actively involved in the subculture into their late twenties and beyond are people who are somehow involved at a more organizational or creative level: musicians, promoters, fanzine writers, artists, etc. Most of the people who are involved in the punk subculture eventually leave behind their punk identities.

Punks in Baron's (1989b) ethnography felt that punk style was becoming "trendy" or fashionable. Baron interpreted this as an embodiment of a hegemonic attempt at social control by incorporating punk style into mainstream culture. However, my informants not only said that they felt that punk was becoming trendy; they all said that this happened *after* they became involved, regardless of when that involvement took place within the history of the subculture. Some of the older people I interviewed had been involved in the subculture in the late 1970s and early 1980s and had ceased to participate or identify themselves as punk since around 1985. Lester, a 27-year-old graduate student in history, felt that punk had originally been a politically meaningful social movement.

> It was all about people that didn't have jobs; no prospects in life. Or they did have opportunities but they could see that careers and all that middle class stuff was bullshit. But it seemed like around my second year of college [1984], there were all these little kids around fifteen and sixteen years old that were getting into punk because they were rebelling against their parents and not because they wanted to change anything. It was better at the beginning [when he first became involved]. (Interview, June 3, 1991)

These informants could have been speaking about some of the younger informants, who were first exposed to punk in the mid-1980s. However, the younger informants all made the same observations:

Author: Were there as many people in the scene, say, five years ago or seven years ago, when you first got into it?

Buddha: No way. Punk was looked down upon. I mean, it was pretty much *all* underground and it meant something . . . But now *everybody's* wearing Doc's.

Author: So why do you think people get into it now then?

Buddha: Because it's cool, it's the "in" thing to do.

Author: So it's "trendy" now?

Buddha: Yeah, punk is trendy! (Interview, October 22, 1991)

Table 10.1 A stage model of the punk career

	Predisposition: difference	Stage 1: rebellion	Stage 2: affiliation	Stage 3: transcendence
Self-labels as a punk	No	Yes	Yes	Occasionally yes, but usually not
Definition of "punk"	Outside of standard youth categories	Unconventional, non-conformist	Lifestyle, "scene" or community, subculture	Values, ideology
Reference group	"Normal" others (peers, parents)	"Normal" others	Punk others	Self
Behavior		Undisciplined non-conformity; unconventional dress and behavior	Ritualistic "punk non-conformity", in accordance with accepted understandings of punk behavior	Dissociation from the subculture or participation at a creative/ organizational level
Core value	Perception of self as "different" from "normal" others	Being offensive, shocking	Being accepted as part of the group rather than being a "poseur"	Personal integrity, honesty, individualism

All of the informants, regardless of their age or the point in time at which they entered punk subculture, felt that they had valid, important reasons for their own involvement. Yet they all perceived the cohorts which followed them as being "trendy," as not understanding the meaning of punk, or as not being as committed to punk as themselves. However, when I asked Doug, a particularly insightful informant, about the different between a real punk and a fake punk, he replied, "When I first got into the whole punk thing, I too was a poseur, for lack of knowledge. Now I'm treated like a punk rock god" (interview, November 22, 1991). Doug recognized that just as he might perceive the younger cohorts of punks as lacking a true commitment to punk, he himself was no doubt also perceived as a poseur by the cohorts which preceded his involvement.

A Stage Model of the Punk Career

In my analysis, the punk career consists of three stages, preceded by a particular state of mind reported by all the informants, in which they can be considered to be "susceptible" to becoming involved in the subculture (table 10.1). These stages are developmental in the sense that an individual must pass through at least an awareness of changes in the definition of what constitutes a punk identity at each stage before he or she can progress to the next stage. The transitions between stages are marked by a shift in reference groups: for example, from parents to punks. However, the individual need not necessarily adopt all, or even most, of the behaviors typical of participants at each stage. In addition, not all participants will go through every stage: they may leave the subculture at any point in their career. Outside factors – being employed in a job that does not allow for continued participation, or coercion by parents – can force a participant to leave the subculture during the first two stages of involvement.

Pre-Disposition: Difference

I asked informants to describe how they were first exposed to punk subculture, and to describe themselves at that time. Almost all the informants consistently perceived themselves as being "different" from those in their reference group: "normal others," i.e. their peers, parents, and mainstream society in general.

Buddha, an 18-year-old male, told me the story of his first exposure to punk during a visit with an older cousin in California. He said:

> I was hanging out with my cousin and said "Is there anything cool out here?" and he's like, *"For you different people*, there is this band called The Exploited." I'm like, "Take me there. Drop me off. Pick me up around one" and for a twelve year old, that has got to be crazy. (Interview, October 22, 1991, emphasis added)

Not only did Buddha conceive of himself as being different, but normal others in his reference group – his cousin – considered him to be different as well.

The informants were also quick to point out that they recognized that punks were also "different" before they got involved in the subculture. Erica, a 19-year-old punk woman, described the social system in her high school in a small town in Indiana.

> *Erica:* Everyone was a jock wanna-be. That was the only thing to be was a jock. It was better to sit on the bench and blow than to be on the sidelines. Even if you sucked, it was all that mattered. There were a few dirtheads . . .
>
> *Author:* Dirtheads? What were they?
>
> *Erica:* You know, burnouts. Like druggies. And then there were like ten punks. (Interview, August 14, 1991)

So in the social world of Erica's high school, the punks were seen as being completely separate from the jocks and the dirtheads (or burnouts).

Kathy, 25 and a recent college graduate, recalled her first exposure to punk through a high school friend:

> I remember seeing Maria at school like our sophomore year. This was before we were friends. *I saw this person at school who was so entirely different from anybody I had ever met.* She wore black checkered gym shoes that she made herself, and I was intrigued and afraid at the same time. (Interview, May 29, 1991, emphasis added)

The informants recognized punks as being somehow "different" from the normal others that formed their reference group.

They felt a commonality with punk subculture because they considered themselves to also be somehow "different" from normal others. However, given that my data consist solely of self-reports of past feelings and states of mind, it is difficult to determine the extent to which the informants are reinterpreting and reconstructing their pasts in terms of their current identities.

Stage 1: Rebellion

The first stage of a punk career, when the individual first begins actively participating, is the rebellion stage. Members identify themselves as being punk and their definition revolves around being deviant. Being "punk" is anything that is offensive or shocking to their reference group, which, in this stage, is still "normal others:" parents, peers, teachers, etc. Members define themselves as punk relative to and in opposition to the normal others in their lives. Kathy recalled when she first began thinking of herself as a punk:

> When we first started, well, I think we were probably defining things as punk because they were not in the mainstream . . . My mom used to complain that my hair was too short and she hated the flaming red color. She'd say, "You're going to turn off so many people." And I'd say, "Well, screw them!" (Interview, May 29, 1991)

Gil, an 18-year-old who had only been involved in the subculture for about a year, told me:

> Punk is the coolest form of music known to mankind. My parents hate it so that makes it all the better. One of the reasons that I like to slam dance is that I am a teenager. What I mean is that I am angry at my parents, angry at my school, angry at my peers, and angry with the world. (Interview, June 28, 1991)

Most of the people I interviewed had already moved beyond the rebellion stage, but could tell me about the younger kids in the scene. When I asked Buddha how to tell the difference between a punk and a poseur, he replied, "708 or not. That's my only answer [referring to the area code of the suburban areas of Chicago]. Because the 708'ers only do it to piss their parents off" (interview, October 22, 1991). The members at this stage are perceived as rebelling or trying to shock their peers or parents –

the 'normal others' which make up their reference group – out of anger. They are often perceived by punks in the later stages of involvement as being poseurs, because their involvement in the subculture is "superficial" and focused on non-punks, and because they lack expert knowledge and a sense of punk community or ideology.

Stage 2: Affiliation

During the rebellion stage, participants think of punk as being anything that is unconventional or not normal. In the affiliation stage, they become aware of the fact that there are certain things that are indeed unconventional and shocking, but are also distinctly not "punk." Having a mohawk is nonconformist in relation to the mainstream society, but it is also an easily recognized symbol of membership in punk subculture.

The transition to the affiliation stage is marked by a shift in reference groups: instead of judging their behavior based on the reflected appraisals of "normal" others, individuals begin to see themselves from the perspective of members of the subculture. Punk is defined as a "scene," a community or social group of which one is (or can become) a member. There are recognized standards of dress and a code of behavior. During this stage punks define themselves in the same manner in which they have been defined by researchers: as a subculture with a distinctive lifestyle. Doug observed, "There are just certain things you *have* to do to avoid ridicule in this scene" (field notes, September 21, 1991). Kathy recalled: "Sometimes I really felt like I belonged there and I really knew what was going on. I knew how to behave and I knew how to dress, and I felt that there was this really specific code of ethics that the punks followed" (interview, May 29, 1991).

However, for members at this second stage, it is not enough to adopt the punk style of dress, or any other single aspect of the punk lifestyle, to establish a punk identity. One must have expert knowledge of the "punk" way to do things. Erica remarked, "I love to slam dance, but only in a pit where everybody knows the rules and picks you up if you fall down. You know, everyone looks out for one another" (interview, August 14, 1991). The member must have expert knowledge of the subculture: its style, appropriate behaviors, music, history, etc. The individual becomes aware of the distinction between a punk and a poseur, and begins to value being accepted by punks as part of their group rather than being perceived as a poseur. Baron (1989b, p. 308) quotes one punk describing poseurs: "They're there for attention . . . *I mean nobody knows them* . . . on the whole they don't have any idea what they're doing." Baron suggests that some kind of "selective initiation" was required for group members, and for my informants this "selection process" was a matter of being accepted as a member of a punk friendship network.

Erica told me that she felt that she had to "*earn* her mohawk;" that "you can't just shave your hair off one day without really being a punk first. Unless, of course, you're a poseur" (field notes, August 16, 1991). Erica earned her mohawk by hanging out with the punks in her high school and learning about punk culture: she gained the requisite expert knowledge and was accepted by the local punk community; became "one of the family," as she put it.

Adopting punk symbols such as a mohawk or a piercing was often a marker of an already established identity as an accepted member of the community, rather than a means for gaining that acceptance. Buddha discussed his initiation as a skinhead:

> I was hanging out with SHOC, The Skinheads of Chicago, like the North Side Crew. And I had been hanging out with them for like a year and one day, I said, "Okay. Shave my head." I never wore my 'hawk up anyway [he had a mohawk at the time], and they knew it was time. They didn't care if I shaved my head because they knew I was cool. They knew if there was a problem, I would help them fight.

Buddha's identity as a skin had to be accepted by the group before it was appropriate to adopt the primary signifier of membership in the group: a shaven head. If he had shaved his head *before* being accepted, then he would have been seen as being a poseur.

The friendship network is the primary reference group for punks during the affiliation stage. One day at a band rehearsal, Gil told me that "the punk scene is getting pretty bad. There are only about five or maybe seven real punks left, but some of the old punks have been coming back" (field notes, June 28, 1991). For Gil, the only "real" punks were those in his personal friendship network. Everyone else was a poseur.

Gil was something of an exception, however. Most punks recognized that there were other members outside of their own friendship networks who were authentic punks. Outsiders could not establish their authenticity simply by virtue of having a mohawk or slamming correctly. They needed to be able to display the requisite expert knowledge of punk culture. My own experience as a participant observer is illustrative. My past experiences as a member of the subculture (in the early 1980s), my knowledge of the history of the subculture and of a few of the most popular contemporary hardcore bands gave me the ability to establish some degree of authenticity. Because of this, the younger informants were willing to accept me as a punk, or at least as an "insider," on a one-to-one basis. However, I was *not* accepted as a member of their punk friendship networks. These informants were friendly and open and sometimes even seemed as if they wanted to impress me with their "punk-ness" in individual interviews, but they were much less friendly with me in public gatherings (at shows or on the street) with their friends, who were often unaware of any "expert" qualifications on my part. My informants and I both recognized that their friends usually considered me to be an outsider: a non-punk.

Stage 3: Transcendence

The third and final stage of the punk career is the transcendence stage. During this stage, individuals often do not identify themselves as punks. They do not necessarily dress in the "typical" punk style, listen to punk or hardcore music, go to concerts or hang out with punks. Being a member of the punk community is no longer their most important concern. They begin to define punk as a system of values and beliefs, and thus become concerned with expressing an ideological commitment to the subculture.

Punk ideology is anti-authoritarian and highly individualistic (Baron, 1989b; Hansen and Hansen, 1991). Punks place the highest value on individual creative expression. A strong tradition of "do-it-yourself" cultural production has persisted throughout the history of the punk subculture (Hebdige, 1979; Lull, 1987; Roman, 1987; Andes, 1991). Punks create and distribute their own culture – fashion, fanzines, art, and expecially music – without the support of established commercial institutions. The glorification of self-expression serves as an aesthetic rationale for the authenticity and superiority of punk cultural artifacts relative to those produced by the cultural industries.

During the affiliation stage, members are very concerned with punk authenticity and what other punks think of them: they want to be perceived as punks and not poseurs. However, in the transcendence stage, the reflected appraisals and acceptance of other punks become unimportant. The self, independent of the restrictions or expectations of others, becomes the primary reference group. When I asked Lester what "punk" meant to him, he replied:

> I guess it really depends on what your definition of punk is. I visualize punk and I see dozens of mohawked morons running around with spray paint, writing "Anarchy" and "The Exploited" all over the place. If you're talking about the state of mind where you don't let people tell you what to do and how to live, well then I salute you . . . Punk is not a rip in your jeans, it's a rip in your mind! (Interview, June 3, 1991)

Doug discussed the need to conform to punk behavior in order to have other punks define you as a punk, and told me that he didn't feel that was true for him any more. He said:

> At first I had medium-length hair and usually wore it under my hat and was cool but not considered to be punk rock until I started to wear my hair in twin 'hawks or in liberty spikes. I was punk rock then when I spent all that time doing my hair and trying to fit in. Eventually, I cut my hair and toned it down and went back to wearing it under my hat. But I was no longer a punk even though I still went to concerts and stage-dived and slammed just as hard or harder now not worrying about my hair. But I *am* still a punk . . . [because] my life is built upon punk ideals. (Interview, September 21, 1991)

Doug doesn't identify himself as a punk, because he doesn't conform to punk styles of dress and doesn't concern himself with fitting in with the group, but he believes that he is very committed to punk ideology. Joseph perceived himself as a punk in spite of the perceptions of others for the same reason:

I like people who are true and honest. Don't portray something you're not. Be yourself and I'd like you more. If you're not a punk, I wouldn't care . . . That's why I can sort of call myself a punk although my style may be completely different. There will probably never be a real punk style but it is what's in your heart, for if even a part of your activity involves truly standing up and opposing some of the bullshit in society, and if you take even a small stand against that, you don't have to do what everyone else is doing. (Interview, February 12, 1991)

Elements of the earlier definitions of punk are still evident in the ideological commitment of the transcendence stage. Members may still participate in various punk activities, may still have punk friends, or still utilize symbols from punk style in their personal appearance. Rebellion, or at least nonconformity, may still be a part of the definition of punk, but it has been transformed into a belief that the individual should be completely autonomous in thought, action, and style. The extremely high value placed on individual autonomy in punk ideology almost *necessitates* that members in the transcendence stage will not really perceive themselves as "members" anymore. They don't usually want to identify themselves as punks because they want to perceive themselves as being *unique* and not as a part of a social group.

Conclusions

The concept of commitment is convenient for linking individual behaviors and attitudes to social groups and structures. Studies of youth subcultures often attempt to discuss members' participation in terms of their degree of commitment to the subculture relative to each other from the point of view of an observer. However, individuals have commitment careers within youth subcultures, in which their commitment may not only wax and wane, but also be expressed by a variety of possibly conflicting behaviors.

Identity theory provides a framework for reconceptualizing commitment as a process best examined from the framework of the actor. The key elements of Burke's identity theory are committed behaviors, reflected appraisals from a reference group, and identity standards. I have presented a developmental model for an individual's participation in one specific youth subculture – punk – in which all three of these may vary. Punks progress from *rebelling* against or resisting the norms and values of "normal" others, such as parents and peers, to *affiliating* themselves with a punk community and lifestyle, then finally to internalizing punk ideology. Kanter (1968) suggested that a moral or evaluative commitment to the ideology of a social group serves as a means of social control: members give over their individual moral autonomy to group authorities. In stark contrast, however, punks *transcend* their own membership in the subculture as a consequence of their deep commitment to the anti-authoritarian and highly individualistic content of punk ideology.

Further research might explore whether members of other youth subcultures, such as metalheads or Deadheads, experience similar commitment careers as their participation in the subculture develops, as their references groups and understandings of the meaning of being a member changes. Other youth subcultures may be more successful at retaining members within the subculture if the content of their value systems is less anti-authoritarian and individualistic than punk ideology. Such subcultures may be long-lived because their members can retain a "metalhead" or "Deadhead" identity *and* lifestyle throughout their lives.

References

Andes, L. J. (1991) Sheena is a punk rocker: girls and subcultures in sociological perspective. Paper presented at the Fifth Annual Feminist Graduate Student Conference, Evanston, IL.

Baron, S. W. (1989a) Resistance and its consequences: the street culture of punks. *Youth and Society*, 21(2), 207–37.

Baron, S. W. (1989b) The Canadian west coast punk subculture: a field study. *Canadian Journal of Sociology*, 14(3), 289–316.

Becker, H. S. (1960) Notes on the concept of commitment. *American Journal of Sociology*, 66(1), 32–40.

Brake, M. (1985) *Comparative Youth Culture*. London: Routledge and Kegan Paul.

Burke, P. J. (1991a) Identity processes and social stress. *American Sociological Review*, 56(6), 836–49.

Burke, P. J. (1991b) An identity theory approach to commitment. *Social Psychology Quarterly*, 54(3), 239–51.

Cagle, V. M. (1989) The language of cultural studies: an analysis of British subculture theory. In N. K. Denzin (ed.), *Studies in Symbolic Interaction*, Greenwich, CT: JAI Press.

Clarke, J. (1976) The skinheads and the magical recovery of community. In S. Hall and T. Jefferson (eds), *Resistance through Rituals: Youth Subcultures in Post-war Britain*. London: Unwin Hyman.

Clarke, J., Hall, S., Jefferson, T. and Roberts, B. (1976) Subcultures, cultures and class: a theoretical overview. In S. Hall and T. Jefferson (eds), *Resistance through Rituals: Youth Subcultures in Post-war Britain*. London: Unwin Hyman.

Cohen, P. (1972) *Subcultural Conflict and Working-class Community*. Working Papers in Cultural Studies No. 2. Birmingham: CCCS, University of Birmingham.

Coleman, J. S. (1961) *The Adolescent Society*. New York: Free Press.

Eckert, P. (1989) *Jocks and Burnouts: Social Categories and Identity in the High School*. New York: Teachers College Press.

Hansen, C. H. and Hansen, R. D. (1991) Constructing personality and social reality through music: individual differences among fans of punk and heavy metal music. *Journal of Broadcasting and Electronic Media*, 35(3), 335–50.

Hebdige, D. (1979) *Subculture: the Meaning of Style*. London: Methuen.

Hollingshead, A. B. (1949) *Elmtown's Youth: the Impact of Social Classes on Adolescents*. New York: John Wiley and Sons.

Jefferson, T. (1976) Cultural responses of the teds: the defence of space. In S. Hall and T. Jefferson (eds), *Resistance through Rituals: Youth Subcultures in Post-war Britain*. London: Unwin Hyman.

Kanter, R. M. (1968) Commitment and social organization: a study of commitment mechanisms in utopian communities. *American Sociological Review*, 33(4), 499–517.

Kotarba, J. A. and Wells, L. (1987) Styles of adolescent participation in an all ages rock 'n' roll nightclub: an ethnographic analysis. *Youth and Society*, 18(4), 398–417.

Larkin, R. (1979) *Suburban Youth in Cultural Crisis*. New York: Oxford University Press.

Lull, J. (1987) Thrashing in the pit: an ethnography of San Francisco punk subculture. In T. R. Lindlof (ed.), *Natural Audiences: Qualitative Research of Media Uses and Effects*. Norwood: Ablex.

McRobbie, A. (1980) Settling accounts with subcultures: a feminist critique. In S. Frith and A. Goodwin (eds), *On Record: Rock, Pop, and the Written Word*. New York: Pantheon Books.

McRobbie, A. and Garber, J. (1976) Girls and subcultures: an exploration. In S. Hall and T. Jefferson (eds), *Resistance through Rituals: Youth Subcultures in Post-war Britain*. London: Unwin Hyman.

Parsons, T. (1942) Age and sex in the social structure of the United States. In *Essays in Sociological Theory, Pure and Applied*. Glencoe, IL: Free Press.

Roman, L. G. (1987) Punk femininity: the formation of young women's gender identities and class relations within the extramural curriculum of a contemporary subculture. Unpublished dissertation, University of Wisconsin, Madison.

Roman, L. G. (1988) Intimacy, labor, and class: ideologies of feminine sexuality in the punk slam dance. In L. G. Roman, L. K. Christian-Smith and E. Ellsworth (eds), *Becoming Feminine: the Politics of Popular Culture*. London: Falmer Press.

Schwartz, G. and Merten, D. (1967) The language of adolescence: an anthropological approach to the youth culture. *American Journal of Sociology*, 72(2), 453–68.

Sherwood, S. J., Smith, P. and Alexander, J. C. (1993) The British are coming . . . again! The hidden agenda of "cultural studies." *Contemporary Sociology*, 22(3), 370–5.

Wyman, B. (1989) Skinheads. *Chicago Reader*, March 24, 18–26.

11
"WHEN IT ALL CHANGED:" CYBERPUNK AND THE BABY BOOM'S REJECTION OF RELIGIOUS INSTITUTIONS

Samuel R. Smith

Over the past 15 years the cyberpunk movement has gained currency with readers of popular fiction as well as critics of literature and culture. Much of this success is due to the plausibility with which the genre portrays the near-future: the worlds depicted by the likes of William Gibson, Bruce Sterling, and John Shirley are essentially extrapolations of the late twentieth-century world their readers inhabit (Ross, 1991). Of particular interest for most of these writers is the state of Earth's institutions – the few remaining vestiges of government have been thoroughly emasculated in the next millennium, and survive only at the pleasure of the extranational and extraplanetary corporations which wield all the significant power. The overmatched (if resourceful) heroes and heroines of these worlds find themselves in a daily struggle to carve out a meager existence on the fringes of the new corporate order.

What is curious, though, is the absolute absence, in cyberpunk's credible near-futures, of the religious institutions which have dominated Western culture over the past few centuries. Novel after novel, short story after film after television show, devoted fans and critics of cyberpunk cannot help being struck by the apparent demise of religion in general, and of

Christianity in particular, in the postmillennium. Different authors pursue different angles, of course, but as a general rule, if Christianity is depicted as existing in these narratives at all, its actions mark it as dysfunctional and repressive, and its adherents are usually villains whom the stories' heroes must overcome.

One salient explanation for this phenomenon sees cyberpunk as a generational phenomenon, and views its depictions of religion as reflective of deeper conflicts imbedded in the baby boom's struggle with institutions and spirituality. We should note here that all the major writers generally associated with the cyberpunk movement, as well as one non-cyberpunk near-futurist who plays a significant part in this critique, are boomers. Rudy Rucker was born in 1946, the first year of the baby boom; John Varley was born in 1947; William Gibson, the movement's most celebrated figure, in 1948; Greg Bear, a fringe member of the club, in 1951; John Shirley and Pat Cadigan, in 1953; Bruce Sterling, the movement's critical voice, in 1954; and Neal Stephenson, the genre's newest phenomenon, was born in 1960, as the boom began to wane. The non-cyberpunk alluded to above is David Brin, who was born in 1950. With the exception of Stephenson, all of these artists are what we might call "early" or "mid" boomers – people who would have been old enough to have participated in their generation's defining moments in the middle to late-1960s.

Culturally, their membership in the boom generation is significant, as its formative period represented a significant turning point in American history. Without indulging too much in the way of uncritical boomer mythology, it is safe to say that morally, socially, and politically, these children were profoundly different from their parents. And religion was one of the most important fronts upon which the generational shift was played out, as boomers by the thousands deserted the religious traditions and institutions of their parents.

Nowhere were the jolts felt more than within institutional religion, in the churches and synagogues across the country. Most [boomers] dropped out in their teenage years or early twenties. Those who were involved in the civil rights movement and antiwar protests left in disillusionment with a church that seemed so feeble, so impotent to bring about changes in a world where so much had gone wrong. Many Catholics left in frustration and anger over the church's positions on issues like abortion and divorce. In all the religious traditions, many simply dropped out. Some felt that the mainline churches were spiritually and theologically impoverished; but most, it seems, just quit going, not out of any strong doctrinal or moral objection, but because church or synagogue seemed irrelevant to them. (Roof, 1993, p. 55)

This isn't to say that the boomers are a generation of atheists and agnostics, although many certainly are. What is critical to Roof's generational analysis, as well as the literary/cultural critique offered here, is the distinction between "spirit" and "institution." While the boomers may have found religious organizations to be lacking, they are not without profound spiritual concerns.

> *Spirit* is the inner, experiential aspect of religion; *institution* is the outer, established form of religion. The distinction is increasingly pertinent because of the strong emphasis on self in contemporary culture and the related shift from objective to subjective ways of ordering experience. Boomers have grown up in a post-sixties culture that emphasizes choice, knowing and understanding one's self, the importance of personal autonomy, and fulfilling one's potential – all contributing to a highly subjective approach to religion. (Roof, 1993, p. 30)

It is perhaps not surprising, then, that the cyberpunks, a group of writers who share a certain generational perspective, would project their generation's misgivings on to their fictional narratives. And while we shouldn't overgeneralize either the generation or the literary movement, it is nonetheless fruitful to consider similarities where we find them. And where the cyberpunks are concerned, we also know enough of their personal interactions with each other to argue with some confidence for taking them as a cohesive group.[1]

We ought also to consider, at least briefly, the placement of this chapter within a volume devoted to "youth culture." On the face of things, a group whose youngest members are in their thirties would hardly appear to qualify as "youth," but it can be argued that any discourse of or about the baby boomers is inherently a discourse of or about youth. This generation has attained a certain immortality in the public mind, an immortality constructed and maintained by an expansive, almost mythic, verbal, textual, and visual record. Woodstock, the Summer of Love, Kent State, the assassination of JFK, the arrival of The Beatles, Berkeley, the Haight, Nixon, Vietnam: the moments which defined the boomer generation were moments inextricably tied to the energy and emotion of its youth. As the boom's leading edge approaches and enters middle age, it is haunted by the long shadow of its own youth, which boldly set and pursued an idealism which has never been realized. To talk of boomers today is, more often than not, to talk of *the sixties*.

As I hope to demonstrate in the following pages, the work of one particular set of boomers demonstrates the tenacity with which certain elements of this youth culture have persisted. While the boomers may not be "young" any more, they nonetheless remain, in a very real sense, a "youth culture."

What Is Cyberpunk?

It has been over fifteen years since William Gibson first published "The Gernsback Continuum" in *Universe 11*. This seminal piece of short fiction finds Gibson, the man who literally invented our current conception of cyberspace, tackling head-on the technotopianism of the genre's pulp history, delivering a "devastating refutation of 'scientifiction' in its guise as narrow technolatry" (Sterling, 1986, p. x). In his preface to *Mirrorshades: the Cyberpunk Anthology*, Sterling takes great pains to situate this new movement as a reform within science fiction, not an overthrow from without (Sterling, 1988). He first pays tribute to the luminaries of the SF genre: Ellison, Delaney, Spinrad, Moorcock, Aldiss, Ballard, Stapledon, Wells, and Thomas Pynchon, "a writer whose integration of technology and literature stands unsurpassed" (Sterling, 1988, p. x). But even as Sterling reverences the old masters, it is clear that the new pack of visionaries, of which he is an integral member, is better understood through analysis of its reforms than through a cataloguing of its influences.

One of the main characteristics distinguishing cyberpunk from those influences was its unique sense of how credibility ought to be established. The birth of science fiction is traced to 1818, when Mary Shelley published *Frankenstein; or, The Modern*

Prometheus (Alkon, 1994). From the outset, writers of science fiction intended their work to be scientifically plausible, thus offering a new kind of terror distinct from that found in the "mere" Gothic "ghost story" (Alkon, 1994). Shelley herself "recounts listening to a conversation about Erasmus Darwin's biological experiments, about galvanism, and about possible ways of creating life by reanimating a corpse or else manufacturing 'component parts of a creature' that might somehow be endowed with vitality" (Alkon, 1994, p. 4). These theories caused her to have a nightmare, she says, and it was in that moment she understood how science might serve as the inspiration for a tale of horror. She doesn't suggest that her speculations in the novel be taken for medical reality, but she does believe that this new type of story depends upon a starting point appropriately grounded in scientific possibility (Alkon, 1994). The ideology of scientific plausibility persisted into the 1900s, where it found fertile purchase in the pulps of the early part of the century. For Hugo Gernsback, the influential editor of *Amazing Stories*, "real science" was a prerequisite for a credible SF tale. Science fiction had to be grounded in the laws of science as they were understood, or in rational extrapolations of those laws (Ross, 1991).

Although the cyberpunks understand the term a bit differently, they likewise insist on credible narrative. For them, though, "hard science" is secondary to *cultural* accuracy. Gibson, in fact, says that he really isn't interested in technology at all, except as a metaphor (Chollett, 1993).

> Cyberpunk's "credible" near-futures are recognizably extrapolated from those present trends that reflect the current corporate monopoly on power and wealth: the magnification of the two-tier society, the technocolonization of the body, the escalation of the pace of ecological collapse, and the erosion of civil society, public space, popular democracy, and the labor movement. (Ross, 1991, p. 152)

The cyberpunks view the credible portrayal of the world's cultural, economic, and socio-political future as more than a stylistic preference. It's a responsibility that they take quite seriously.

> In his introduction to Gibson's *Burning Chrome*, Sterling argued that Gibson's commitment to portray a "credible future" exempli-

fied a responsibility that SF writers, drawn in recent decades to the post-apocalyptic genre, to sword-and-sorcery, and to modern space opera, had been "ducking for years." Sterling argued that this 'intellectual failing" to "tangle with a realistic future" was redeemed by Gibson's dedication to depicting "a future that is recognizably and painstakingly drawn from the modern condition." (Ross, 1991, p. 151)

Put another way, we might see the cyberpunk movement as a critique of the unrealistic fantasies of previous generations. Expressed literarily, it manifests itself as a rebellion against the messianic scientism of the Gernsback era; taken metaphorically, it seems to argue that progress has not made everything okay; that despite the prosperity of the postwar years inequities remained, social and economic inequities which posed a serious threat to the established order of things; and that our perceived control of culture, and more critically technology, was a dangerous illusion.

Thematically, then, we understand cyberpunk as a more socially aware and committed ethic than we had perhaps encountered in science fiction prior to the 1980s. This isn't to say that SF had been uniformly irresponsible – *Frankenstein* was as apt a cautionary tale as has perhaps ever been written. But with the onset of the cyberpunks we began to see the more progressive social and political concerns of the boomer generation creeping in. Whereas science fiction has traditionally been devoted to the uses and abuses of science, the cyberpunks were the first generation to actually grow up in a "science fictional world" (Sterling, 1988, p. xi). For them the technology that previous generations had imagined and written about as temporal outsiders was a routinized element of day-to-day life. Technologies might be powerful attractors, to borrow a term from chaos theory, but they are most assuredly not determining. As such, cyberpunk worlds are places where technology is imbedded in culture, where, as Gibson (1986a) says in "Johnny Mnemonic," the streets find their own uses for things.

It might be useful, before pressing on, to offer a brief thumbnail sketch of cyberpunk's more obvious defining characteristics. The progressive critical aesthetic outlined above aside, the genre is given to a certain thematic bent, which Csicsery-Ronay has cynically characterized as follows:

How many formulaic tales can one wade through in which a self-destructive but sensitive young protagonist with an (implant/prosthesis/telechtronic talent) that makes the evil (mega-corporations/police states/criminal underworlds) pursue him through (wasted urban landscapes/elite luxury enclaves/eccentric space stations) full of grotesque (haircuts/clothes/self-mutilations/rock music/sexual hobbies/designer drugs/telechtronic gadgets/nasty new weapons/exteriorized hallucinations) representing the (mores/fashions) of modern civilization in terminal decline, ultimately hooks up with rebellious and tough-talking (youth/artificial intelligence/rock cults) who offer the alternative, not of (community/socialism/traditional   values/transcendental   vision),   but   of supreme, life-affirming hipness, going with the flow which now flows in the machine, against the spectre of a world-subverting (artificial intelligence/multinational corporate web/evil genius)? (Leonard, 1993, p. 580+)[2]

Cynicism aside, the genre is characterized by the following general tendencies. First, cyberpunk typically situates its narratives in Earth's near-future. Unlike space operas, which are often set long ago in a galaxy far, far away, cyberpunk is almost exclusively concerned with our planet (occasionally action will be set in orbital stations, and less frequently at more remote sites in the solar system), and a majority of the action occurs in a future that is near enough to be recognizable. The average displacement into the future is probably 50–100 years, although Sterling sets his Shaper–Mechanist adventures several hundred years away and Stephenson's *Snow Crash* occurs in an alternate version of the present moment. Gibson and Sterling's *The Difference Engine* is even set in the Victorian past.

Second, cyberpunk typically depicts a "dark future." The hero or heroine may survive the adventure and even prosper, but the general condition of the planet and the human condition is decidedly dystopian. We almost always see a tremendous gap between the haves and have-nots, and the reader usually finds that some large institution – governmental, quasi-religious, military, or corporate – has become immensely powerful, and is either repressive or completely unresponsive to the plight of the masses. Generally, there is no hope for a better future (Ross, 1991, p. 150).

Third, cyberpunk is obsessed with the "technocolonization" of the human body (Ross, 1991, p. 152). The genre repeatedly engages the "theme of body invasion: prosthetic limbs, implanted circuitry, cosmetic surgery, genetic alteration. The even more powerful theme of mind invasion: brain–computer interfaces, artificial intelligence, neurochemistry – techniques radically redefining the nature of humanity, the nature of self" (Sterling, 1988, p. xiii). But the question of human–machine interface is not limited to the physical implantation of technological devices. Stephenson's Metaverse (1993), an obvious extrapolation of Gibson's cyberspace, is accessed not through neural interface hardware surgically implanted in the brain, but rather through advanced virtual reality style goggles-and-gloves innovations. Further, not all technology-induced human evolution is mechanical. One of the factions vying for control of the solar system in Sterling's Shaper–Mechanist series (1989) has concentrated on improving *Homo sapiens* via a combination of genetic engineering and biochemical enhancement. Still, these stories depict a clear *human–technology* integration, despite the absence of cybernetics.

Fourth, in cyberpunk, technology has literally escaped human control. In much of Gibson's work, people often find that they have less control over their lives at the end of the adventure than they did when they began (Ross, 1991, p. 150). Technology has attained autonomy, to the peril of humanity: "times have changed since the comfortable era of Hugo Gernsback, when Science was safely enshrined – and confined – in an ivory tower. The careless technophilia of those days belongs to a vanished, sluggish era, when authority still had a comfortable margin of control" (Sterling, 1988, p. xiii). Sometimes we see a Frankensteinian lab experiment run amok, as in Crichton's *Jurassic Park* (1990), where at the end of the novel it is apparent that dinosaurs, including the baby-eating dilophosaurs, are loose on the mainland. In other narratives the bogey might be an artificial intelligence that has somehow slipped the shackles of human dominion, as in Gibson's cyberspace trilogy (1984, 1987, 1988). Or maybe the problem isn't alive and/or sentient technology, but is rather a runaway environment, such as the tornado-stripped wasteland of Texas and the lower Midwest in Sterling's *Heavy Weather* (1994a). Here technology isn't the direct problem – the immediate concern is the uncontrollable ecological hellspawn of poorly managed progress. In any case, the cyberpunks are fascinated by what Winner (1977) has called "autonomous technology" – technology that is no longer within the purview of human agency.

It should be emphasized here that, in spite of the preceding observations, cyberpunk is not a genre with clearly demarcated borders; Sterling (1988) cautions against overgeneralization, saying that "the 'typical cyberpunk writer' does not exist; that person is only a Platonic fiction." I sidestep this warning advisedly, considering the genre on more unitary terms than are strictly warranted because it provides us with perhaps the best examples of depictions of religions in the near-future. Not all of the works discussed herein are representative of cyberpunk, however. David Brin's *Earth* (1991) bears many of the markings of cyberpunk – it is set in the near-future and humanity is desperately struggling to recage what at first appears to be an escaped scientific experiment. But the ending is decidedly optimistic, the ethic ultimately scientistic. Still, *Earth* provides an excellent study of the projected ascendance of neo-paganism in the near-future.

I will also examine elements of Philip K. Dick's work. Dick is a seminal figure in the SF genre, and is one of the writers who most profoundly influenced the writing of the cyberpunks. And while works such as *Do Androids Dream of Electric Sheep?* resonate with profound cyberpunkish themes – dark near-future, corporate domination, human–technology interface in the form of android production, the Frankenstein Complex as the androids run amok – the larger corpus of his work makes clear his membership in an older, pre-punk generation, and highlights Sterling's observation above about the "typical cyberpunk writer."

Five Motifs: Depictions of Religion in the Postmillennium

What follows is an examination of the religious motifs I have encountered in my readings of near-futurism. As with the above discussions of boomers as a generation and cyberpunk as a genre, I proceed like an infantryman who must quickly and directly reach the far side of a minefield while taking heavy fire – that is, with a certain willing suspension of disbelief. The categories I will draw are not hard and fast, the lines between them are not always clear, and generalizations are to be taken as just that – generalizations. With these caveats in mind, I argue that cyberpunk and near-future science fiction tends toward five different motifs in its depictions of religion: the religion-free future; the ChristiaNazi future; the gnostic future; the neo-pagan/Gaian future; and the invented religion future.

Gibson's "The Winter Market" and a Religion-free Future

Gibson's "The Winter Market" (1986b), a short story which appears in his *Burning Chrome* collection, offers perhaps the best opportunity for the engagement of religious values of any story he has ever authored.

The narrative revolves around Lise, a young artist whose body has been ravaged by a crippling disease, rendering her incapable of independent activity. She is able to fend for herself due to a polycarbon exoskeleton – a sort of full-body prosthetic hot-wired directly into the motor skills center in the brain. As the narrative opens, her editor/producer, Casey, has just received news that she has "crossed over," has "died." The dramatic tension lies in the fact that, before she died, the entertainment mega-conglomerate with which she was contracted financed the downloading of her brain into a gigantic ROM-construct in Los Angeles. Obviously, the narrative assumes a technology sufficiently advanced to allow for the accurate and comprehensive bitmapping of the human brain.

In fact, Lise's value to the corporation lies in the advanced level of mind–machine interface technology available in the near-future. She is, for lack of a better term, a dream artist. As Casey explains,

> we call the raw product dry dreams. Dry dreams are neural output from levels of consciousness that most people can only access in sleep. But artists, the kind I work with at the Autonomic Pilot, are able to break the surface tension, dive down deep, down and out, out into Jung's sea, and bring back – well, dreams. Keep it simple. I guess some artists have always done that, in whatever medium, but neuroelectronics lets us access the experience, and the net gets it all out on the wire, so we can package it, sell it, watch how it moves in the market. (p. 123)

Casey's job is to "produce" these dreams, to whip them into something more accessible for mass consumption. "The stuff we get out to the consumer, you see, has been structured, balanced, turned into art" (p. 123).

Lise is the hopeless nihilism of the postindustrial age personified, and her dreams expressed that nihilism in a way that clicked with the kids living on the streets. Her immediate and monumental success, once Casey "discovered" her, was due to the purity of the despair she felt. As Rubin, Lise and Casey's junk artist mentor, explains,

> They know. Those kids back down the Market, warming their butts around the fires and wondering if they'll find someplace to sleep tonight, they believe it . . . She was big because she was what they are, only more so. She knew, man. No dreams, no hope. You can't see the cages on those kids, Casey, but more and more they're twigging to it, that they aren't going *anywhere*. (p. 134)

When she crosses over, has herself translated into a hardwired program so she can keep producing her art after her body dies, Casey has to confront the knowledge that eventually the ROM-construct, the downloaded Lise, is going to call. He asks Rubin, "is it *her?*"

Gibson is asking an old question, one for which we apparently have not found a satisfactory answer: *what is life?* Casey and Rubin know that a few others have done what Lise has, and one, a French writer, is still writing a few years after his death. But what Lise does is more essentially creative, more intuitive – for lack of a better term, more *artistic*. I am reminded of the exchange between Chandra and HAL near the conclusion of *2010*, when HAL asks "Will I dream?" Hence, the essential issue – is there a difference between "thinking," processing information in a more or less linear, routinized fashion, and "dreaming," the more creative, associative act of juxtaposing images and concepts? The closest we get to a conventional religious comment on the question is Rubin's ambivalent "God only knows."

I earlier argued that this story represents the best chance Gibson has yet given himself to address religious views on the philosophical and social questions he raises for himself. I say this because the central questions revolve around our notions of the origins and nature of life, the character of the soul, and most directly the possibility of life after death. What is Casey asking in "The Winter Market" if not "is there life after death?" That the ROM-construct contains a bit-for-bit copy of Lise's brain is not at issue. The litmus test will be, it is implied, whether or not the ROM-Lise can touch her audience in the same powerfully authentic way she did in *Kings of Sleep*, her first "soft," a release so popular that the owner of the local store says people steal more copies of it than they buy of anything else.

Gibson is not unaware of the religious implications in the story, his refusal to negotiate the question on institutional terms notwithstanding. In Rubin we have the oldest, most mature character in the story. Arguably, he is one of the most actualized characters in the entire corpus of Gibson's writing. As an artist who has attained international acclaim, he occupies a privileged position as the cast's elder, and as a collector of *gomi* – junk – he is an expert on both the intended and unintended uses of things. In creating Rubin, it is as if Gibson is intent on a critique of Lévi-Strauss, for Rubin is as archetypal a *bricoleur* as can be imagined. Lévi-Strauss says that

> The "bricoleur" is adept at performing a large number of diverse tasks; but, unlike the engineer, he does not subordinate each of them to the availability of raw materials and tools conceived and procured for the purpose of the project. His universe of instruments is closed and the rules of the game are always to make do with "whatever is at hand." (Lévi-Strauss, 1966, p. 17)

The *bricoleur*, in Lévi-Strauss' formulation, is intimately connected with a culture's myth-making function, and we therefore regard with interest fictional narratives which place such archetypal characters at the center of the philosophical debate. In "The Winter Market," Rubin occupies precisely this position in the narrative structure.

> Rubin, in some way that no one quite understands, is a master, a teacher, what the Japanese call a *sensei*. What he's the master of, really, is garbage, kipple, refuse, the sea of cast-off goods our century floats on. *Gomi no sensei*. Master of junk. (p. 118)

> He has nothing to say about *gomi*. It's his medium, the air he breathes, and something he's swum in all his life. He cruises Greater Van in a spavined truck-thing he chopped down from an

> ancient Mercedes airporter, its roof lost under a wallowing rubber bag half-filled with natural gas. He looks for things that fit some strange design scrawled on the inside of his forehead by whatever serves him as Muse. He brings home more *gomi*. Some of it still operative. Some of it, like Lise, human. (p. 120)

That Rubin can consider questions like those posed by Lise's situation without resorting to traditional religious wisdom is, I think, instructive. He does not seem to dismiss the possible existence of God – his evocation of divinity in "God only knows" is apparently earnest, at least within the context of his conversation with the distraught Casey. But whatever God he believes in is a distant one, and not one to whom he can appeal for answers in circumstances such as this. And just as Lévi-Strauss's iconic *bricoleur* goes about weaving cultural myths out of found bits and pieces, so Rubin is central to the quest for meaning in Casey's life – and had been essential to Lise's ultimate ascendancy to art stardom. He had found her, near death, on one of his *gomi* hunts, her prosthetic's batteries burned out, and she waiting patiently for death.

In the final analysis, there is no definitive authority to whom Casey or the reader can appeal. Rubin

> lives in other people's garbage, and everything he drags home must have been new and shiny once, must have meant something, however briefly, to someone. So he sweeps it all up into his crazy-looking truck and hauls it back to his place and lets it compost there until he thinks of something new to do with it. Once he was showing me a book of twentieth-century art he liked, and there was a picture of an automated sculpture called *Dead Birds Fly Again*, a thing that whirled real dead birds around and around on a string, and he smiled and nodded, and I could see he felt the artist was a spiritual ancestor of some kind. (p. 137)

The ChristiaNazi Scourge

Given the predominantly white, middle-class American makeup of the cyberpunk movement, discussions of depictions of religion almost necessarily become, at some point, discussions about how Judeo-Christianity is portrayed. Even when these authors are not depicting any religion at all, we have a *de facto* sense that what *isn't* being shown is Christianity. Given the centrality of Christianity to American religious life, we are especially interested in what the cyberpunks have to say about the future of these, our largest, most significant faiths.

And it is on this point that the cyberpunks, diverse and loosely defined stylistic bunch that they are, finally seem to agree. In outlining above the general character of the cyberpunk movement, I was careful to note that all examples are necessarily exceptions, since there is no "typical" representation. However, having read dozens of novels and stories and interviews in and about the movement and having watched not a few movies and TV shows in the genre, it is of some interest that I have never encountered a single depiction of the near-future by any artist remotely associated with the cyberpunk movement which portrays Christianity in any of its various manifestations as a positive, functional element in Earth's near-future. If Christianity is represented at all, it has in the worst extreme become a repressive neo-fascist organization bent on world domination, and at its best has become an annoyance to the civil liberties of the genre's more politically progressive heroes and heroines.

A good example of the former is found in John Shirley's *Eclipse* (1985), the first book of his *Song of Youth* trilogy. Rick Crandall is a Southern preacher who heads up the Second Alliance (SA), an ostensibly conservative Christian organization whose inner circle initiates are given to understand the true message of the revelation, which is one of racial purity and white supremacy. The SA's inner circle prays before a traditional wooden cross inset with the iron cross of the Third Reich (p. 204). Crandall's followers, especially his sister Ellen Mae, revere him with an absolute passion, calling to mind the sort of archetypal fanaticism our society associates with Jonestown, and more recently Waco. Shirley is, on the whole, not kind to the Crandalls.

> Crandall had a lean, wolfish face that might have belonged to a backwoods imbecile, except for the personality shining through it, transforming it in some subtle way. The personality, the benevolence on a foundation of sheer self-certainty, made that inbred country face something magnetic.
>
> Crandall had never been married. He said he was married to his mission. But in total there were four pictures of Ellen Mae, and Swenson wondered if there was some kind of repressed

undercurrent of incest between Ellen Mae and Smiling Rick
Crandall. (p. 206)

By the time *Eclipse* reaches its climax in a pitched battle for
Paris, Crandall (having survived infiltration and assassination
attempts much like those plotted against Hitler) has insinuated
his organization into the middle of what has become a global
power struggle, with powerful influence in governments and
security forces in both the United States and Europe. The
Second Alliance is, in every significant way, the Fourth Reich.

Even in less apocalyptic moments – Shirley overtly suggests
that *Eclipse* may be a pre-holocaust novel – Christians are simply
not to be trusted with the wellbeing of those less fanatical than
they. Sterling's short story "Are You for 86?" (1994b) follows
recurring protagonist Leggy Starlitz and his two Goddess-
worshipping lesbian associates, Mr Judy and Vanna, as they
undertake a mission to smuggle RU-486 into Salt Lake City.
Along the way they are discovered by fundamentalist activists –
apparently Judy and Vanna's coven has been infiltrated by un-
dercover fundamentalists – and the action surrounds their attempts to complete the delivery in spite of aggressive harassment
by the Christians. Ironically, the drop is to take place in the Utah
State Capitol Building.

> "Pro-life fanatics . . ." Mr Judy grunted. "Christian cultist weir-
> dos . . ." She clutched a slotted metal column for support as
> Starlitz weaved violently into the fast lane. "I sure hope it's not
> 'Sword of the Unborn.' They hit a clinic in Alabama once with a
> shoulder-launched rocket." (p. 295)

These Christians, who ultimately prove to be a less violent
faction than the Sword of the Unborn, nonetheless operate like a
paramilitary outfit. Leggy and his associates manage to locate
the CB channel their pursuers are using, and the radio traffic
makes clear the extensive organization and abundant resources
being arrayed against the smugglers. They later encounter a man
who heard about them on his Christian bulletin board service,
and who has been looking for them so he can "counsel" with
them about their activities.

> "I know what you're doing, even if you yourselves are too corrupt
> to recognize it," Charles continued eagerly. "You're trying to legiti-

mize the mass poisoning of the unborn generation . . . Your contempt for the sanctity of human life legitimizes murder! Today,
you're killing kids. Tomorrow, you'll be renting wombs. Pretty
soon you'll be selling fetal tissue on the open market! . . . First
comes abortion, then euthanasia! Those suicide machines . . . The
so-called right-to-die – it's really the *right-to-kill*, isn't it? Pretty
soon you'll be poisoning not just unborn kids and old sick people,
but everybody else who's inconvenient to you! That's just how the
Holocaust started – with so-called euthanasia!" (p. 304)

As the trio makes its way toward Salt Lake City it has to negotiate roadblocks, blood-balloons, homemade caltrops designed to
disable the van's tires, and even containers filled with "Skunk-
stinking butyl mercaptan and rotten-egg hydrogen sulfide" (p.
307). Finally, the smugglers are waylaid by the Christians in the
Capitol building, and as the operation is on the verge of collapse,
the protagonists are rescued by the timely intervention of the
police. The Christians are wanted in Kansas on an aggravated
vandalism warrant, as it turns out, and are hauled away by the
authorities, screeching at the tops of their lungs.

These Christians are, of course, drawn on very visible segments of today's fundamentalist right – organizations like Operation Rescue, for example – but are hardly representative of the
majority of Christians in the country. Even at their very worst,
they simply lack the numbers and resources to pose the sort of
threat to world security posed by Shirley's Second Alliance.
Nonetheless, we have Christians portrayed, and the portrayals
are typical of the few rare cases where cyberpunk authors
acknowledge the existence of Christianity in the near-future.

Gnosticism and Living Information in the Near-future

"Gnosticism" generally refers to a "heretical" set of Christian
sects which were active in the period following the death of Jesus
Christ. The gnostics' interpretation of Christian revelation is
strikingly different from the orthodox version canonized by
Peter and Paul. Some of the basic differences between the orthodoxy and the gnostics include: the gnostic refutation of God as
"wholly other" (for the gnostics, "self-knowledge is the knowledge of God" and "the self and the divine are identical"); the

gnostic Jesus teaches "illusion and enlightenment" instead of sin and repentance, and when the disciple attains enlightenment he or she becomes equal to Jesus; whereas the orthodox Jesus is distinct from humanity, the gnostic Jesus teaches that "both received their being from the same source" (Pagels, 1979, p. xx). The Gnostic sects were also decidedly less institutional and patriarchal (Pagels, 1979).

In Philip K. Dick's curious *VALIS*, one of his final works, he details a semi-autobiographical series of events involving a gnostic revelation.[3] VALIS – a Vast Active Living Intelligence System – fired a beam of light at him from space, and contained in this beam of light was pure knowledge about many subjects, including apparently accurate information about an illness from which his son was suffering. His foreknowledge of this illness, about which even the doctors had no information, provided strong evidence for Dick that what he perceived was in fact authentic revelation, and not a hallucination.[4]

What is suggested by the book is that information is literally alive, having an existence, sentience, and autonomy all its own. Operating like a biological (or, in retrospect, computer) virus, the information seeks purchase in the minds of humans, which exist as processing components in the true Mind (Davis, 1993, p. 608; Dick, 1981).

> For Dick, decoding is more than reading; it is being infected by code. VALIS is nothing less than a virus that "replicates itself – not through information or in information – but as information." Once triggered, it parasitically "crossbands" with human hosts, creating "homeoplasmates." (Davis, 1993, p. 609)

Other have shared this perspective with Dick. Burroughs said "language is a virus," and scientist Richard Dawkins's concept of *memes* sees thoughts as organisms which seek to propagate themselves.

> [M]emes should be regarded as living structures, not just metaphorically but technically. When you plant a fertile meme in my mind you literally parasitize my brain, turning it into a vehicle for the meme's propagation in just the way that a virus may parasitize the genetic mechanism of a host cell . . . the meme for, say, "belief in life after death" is actually realized physically, millions of times

over, as a structure in the nervous systems of individual men the world over. (Davis, 1993, pp. 609–10)

I note these things not because *VALIS* is a cyberpunk novel. It isn't. In fact, it is difficult to classify the book as fiction because we have reason to believe that Dick was describing more or less what he believed to be his personal revelation – his attainment of *gnosis*. However, later cyberpunk authors have been aware of and influenced by *VALIS*, and as it contains one of the most thorough treatments of the subject in the SF genre, it seems a sensible starting point.

Most recently, Stephenson's *Snow Crash* (1993), a definitively cyberpunk novel, has developed variations on the gnostic themes first raised in *VALIS*. The world itself is purest punk, and it is into this culture that not only gnosticism, but Christianity of the variety outlined in the section above, will be introduced.

In the future according to Stephenson, there is no law at all. A nightmare Los Angeles is divided into war zones: "Burbclaves," where the solid citizens hide out, behind private security guards, from a gridlocked cruise-missile spree-killing America; "Franchulates" (Franchise-Organized Quasi National Entities), like Uncle Enzo's Mafia, Mr Lee's Greater Hong Kong and Narcolombia; "Sacrifice Zones," abandoned because their cleanup costs exceeded their total future economic value; and "Shantytowns," full of hard-core Third World unemployables breathing amino acids. The only way out of this LA, if you are rich enough, is to "goggle" your way into the boundless inner VR world of Metaverse, where your phantasmal "avatar" can play with everybody else's. (Leonard, 1993, pp. 580+)

Into this society he thrusts the "literal nature of information as virus" and the suggestion of "language as a potentially pure and universal representation of human thought structures." If you know the pre-Babel language of humanity, the characters learn, you can access any human brain at the level of code (Leonard, 1993, pp. 580+). In other words, the Tower of Babel story really happened, and prior to Babel humanity spoke a language that involved the direct one-to-one correspondence between signifier and signified, between connoted and denoted. Words reflected the essential structures of the human mind.[5]

William Gibson also appears to be playing with gnostic themes in his cyberspace trilogy. At one level, an artificial intelligence of the sort represented by Wintermute is information and nothing more – it's a highly advanced computer, but despite its ability to mimic the personae of human personalities, it has no personality of its own. Wintermute is bound by the limits of its code and its resident space; it lacks the will, the autonomy to act, without restraint, in its own interest. But the sort of AI that it becomes at the end of *Neuromancer* (1984) is unarguably *live* information – it has attained sentience and transcended the limitations of its prior ordained space.

Much is suggested by Gibson's naming of the AI. "Wintermute" is an unusual appellation, and nothing in the text offers any clue as to the name's origins or any deeper significations associated with it. Gibson (1996) himself says that he took the name from a family that lived near him when he was young, and that he selected the name because of its unusualness. In an interview with Larry McCaffery, Gibson explains the intuitive process in his writing, which he says often begins with the discovery of an "accident:"

> I like accidents, when an offhand line breezes by and you think to yourself, Yes, that will do. So you put it in your text and start working with it, seeing how it relates to other things you've got going, and eventually it begins to evolve, to branch off in ways you hadn't anticipated. Part of the process is conscious, in the sense that I'm aware of working this way, but how these things come to be imbedded in the text is intuitive. I don't see how writers can do it any other way. I suppose some pick these things up without realizing it, but I'm conscious of waiting for them and seeing where they lead, how they might mutate. (McCaffery, 1991, 267)

It isn't difficult to imagine a writer such as Gibson selecting a name like Wintermute, which he heard once and liked for its very oddness and rarity, and using it for something as odd and rare as the AI character in *Neuromancer*. It is a name which certainly brings to the narrative a richness, a compellingly strange texture which cannot help but influence powerfully the tone of the story told. Perhaps we can see the name Wintermute as one of these accidents that Gibson describes in the passage above.

What makes the naming of Wintermute so curious is a coincidence which ranks as perhaps the strangest of my academic career. A review of the *Nag Hammadi Library* (Robinson, 1978) reveals that one of the translators of the gnostic texts was a scholar named Orval Wintermute, a man who helped translate *Allogenes*, a book which "describes the stages of attaining *gnosis*." Allogenes comes to understand the process of self-awareness and actualization, learning in the end the limits of human power (Pagels, 1979, pp. 138–40). The link between human *gnosis* and the sort of technological moment of actualization we see in *Neuromancer* is offered by Dick, who goes as far as to suggest, in "Man, Android and Machine," that information derived its existence from technology. Drawing on Teilhard de Chardin, he contends that

> the noösphere . . . no longer served as a mere passive repository of human information (the "Seas of Knowledge" which ancient Sumer believed in) but, due to the incredible surge of charge from our electronic signals and information-rich material therein, we have given it power to cross a vast threshold; we have, so to speak, resurrected what Philo and other ancients called the Logos. Information has, then, become alive. (Davis, 1993, p. 607)

Thus, technology has enabled the "awakening" of information, and the process by which Allogenes attains *gnosis* is significantly similar to the way in which Wintermute becomes actualized at the end of *Neuromancer*. Both stories emphasize the knowing of self and the liberating nature of revelation. If not for Gibson's express denial, we might read *Neuromancer* as a posthumanist gnostic allegory, as a revelatory text for machine enlightenment, and in doing so we would be compelled to consider the implications of Dick's ideas about the role of humans with respect to the true Mind.[6] He seems to be saying that humanity is an incubator for the information life form, that we exist ultimately to provide shelter and succorance for living information. In this formulation, we arrive at perhaps cyberpunk's darkest intimation, a possible reality only hinted at in the discussion earlier on autonomous technology. If we follow the Dickian version of gnostic revelation to its logical, if extreme, conclusion, what it suggests is that humans do not use information – it uses us.

Gibson's insistence that he was *not*, in fact, designing a gnostic allegory in *Neuromancer* raises interesting questions. To be sure, the gnostic reading upon which I initially embarked is no less fascinating, and in some respects may be even more intriguing than before. It's possible, of course, that the connection between *Allogenes* and *Neuromancer* is precisely what Gibson suggests – coincidence.[7] It is also conceiveable, if extremely unlikely, that somewhere along the way he encountered some element of the gnostic, which then became fodder for the unconscious intuitive process he describes above. Finally, as long as we are momentarily indulging the far-fetched, we might as well acknowledge the fantastic implications derived from the essence of the gnostic itself – the notion of living information, of information as autonomous. Gibson's protestations notwithstanding, the idea of information speaking through a human unconscious isn't much further afield than a coincidence of the magnitude of the Wintermute/*Allogenes* connection.

The Neo-pagan Future

The global culture of David Brin's *Earth* (1991) is, in Brin's estimation, "just one possible tomorrow" (p. 656). In this particular vision of tomorrow, Earth has survived a world war and emerged with a profound sense of responsibility toward the planet. Religion has taken a clear turn in the direction of the pagan, with Gaianism as the dominant, but not exclusive, manifestation. In terms of organizational currency, the North American Church of Gaia seems to be the only sect which approaches the influence of today's Christian institutions. The other religion which Brin depicts is a form of sun-worship common among the narrative's adolescent males – and again, the sect is decidedly pagan in its origins.

Horne (1994, p. 60) asserts that "cyberpunk has always taken for granted the decline of religion or even predicted an upswing of paganism." Paganism, though, is a loose enough term to present problems for those seeking specificity. In fact, paganism refers to a broad collection of practices, one of the most prominent being Wicca, or witchcraft.

Paganism is a broad descriptor for those religions or modes of spirituality that are not patriarchal monotheisms, such as Christianity, Judaism and Islam. Examples of paganism include Buddhism, Native American Spirituality, Hinduism, Shinto, and

Wicca. Wicca is the most prevalent form of reconstructionist neo-paganism in the United States and is the pre-Christian spirituality of the Celtic peoples who resided in the British Isles and Brittany, on the western coast of France. Wicca includes in its boundaries many different sects whose founding principles have been subject to much revisionism and non-historic, modern "reinterpretations" of the little shreds of Craft material that do still exist. Therefore, to quantify what "all Wiccans" believe would be difficult, to say the least. (Povey, 1994)

Povey goes on to characterize pagans and Wiccans in the modern world, noting socio-political tendencies which are consistent with the qualities Brin seeks to evoke in *Earth*.

Most of their numbers however are gentle, peace loving, "green" politically and committed to family, earth conservancy, their own higher spiritual evolution, peaceful relations and healing and helping wherever possible. Most actively pray for peace, for the world and with their neighbors (whether pagan or not). (Povey, 1994)

Gaianism, the manifestation of neo-paganism that Brin portrays in his novel, is an old idea which has recently gained new momentum. "Twenty years ago, British scientist James Lovelock introduced the notion that the Earth and all the living things on it work together like one big organism. He called that organism Gaia" (Castrone, 1994, pp. 3D+). The scientific theory has obvious spiritual implications, and has spurred the establishment of several small religious groups, but as yet Gaianism has not evolved anything resembling a catechism or religious orthodoxy. Still, in the following description of one Colorado congregation we can see the direction in which the momentum tends.

The Boulder Church of Gaia: Council of Six Directions has no connection to the scientific concept or the myriad institutes and churches that sprung up around it. In fact, [church founders] Buhner and Bailey believe their Earth-centered blend of mysticism and ecology is unique.

The church has a congregation of 100 to 150 people who believe the Earth is a living being and the source of all "spirit." They believe that everything on Earth – rocks, plants, animals, oceans, not just human beings – is alive and has spirit. (Castrone, 1994, pp. 3D+)

Brin posits that in five decades, when the action of the novel takes place, Gaianism might well have galvanized the spiritualism of the pro-ecology movement which today is fragmented into many smaller, less institutionally formal groups. While the idea may seem implausible on its face, he defends his extrapolations by noting that five decades before he wrote *Earth* Europe was still at peace, "ecological degradation" was a phrase which had not yet been coined, and no one knew anything about nuclear arms, missile deterrence, or toxic waste (Brin, 1991). That the evolution of technology is bound to occur at a more rapid pace than that of something as deeply embedded in culture as religious beliefs is not a question he considers, apparently, but his point is well taken. To the extent that neo-paganisms are growing as rapidly as they are alleged to be, we might well expect that in another fifty years a Gaian sect might be large enough to command significant public attention.

The Invented Religion Future

For Philip K. Dick, apparently none of the extant world religions possessed quite the qualities he was looking for as he wrote *Do Androids Dream of Electric Sheep?* (1968). So he made one up and infused it with the qualities he saw as central to his vision of the near-future. Mercerism is a faith which takes as its organizing principle the essentially human trait of empathy. Through empathy boxes, adherents enter a virtual/trance state where they relive the tribulations of the religion's namesake, and through this identification with his suffering they attain spiritual unity with humankind. Empathy is critical to a person's humanity because it is the only thing people have that replicants – highly advanced androids – don't have. The corporation which manufactures the replicants can make them bigger, faster, stronger and smarter, but it cannot infuse them with humanity, with soul, the characteristic whose essence is empathy.

Implicit in Mercerism is the higher connectedness of humanity to all living things, a desperately held tenet for those unfortunate enough to still be stranded on Dick's post-apocalyptic Earth. The planet is an ecological waste, and all those who are physically and mentally qualified (and who can afford it) are leaving the planet for a better life in space. One of the defining practices for Mercerites is the ownership and care of an animal. All animals are sacred (and, of course, vegetarianism is a given), but as animals are rare (due to the ecology) they are quite expensive, and some people, like the story's protagonist, can only afford artificial pets – the animal equivalent to replicants.

Clearly reflected in Dick's tale is a cautionary about the environment, which was becoming a significant concern around the time the novel was being written in the late 1960s. And in this respect, one might argue that Mercerism is, at least in its manifest practices, another form of paganism. However, Mercerism is defined within the context of the narrative in terms oppositional to the artificial humanity represented by the unfeeling replicants, whereas the neo-paganisms are deliberately drawn from non-Christian traditions and, in some instances, valued chiefly for their open rejection of Christianity's ideology of dominion.

Cyberpunks as a Generation of Seekers

As Roof (1993) describes the religious quests of the baby boomer generation, it is almost as though he is, at the same time, outlining the various experiments of the cyberpunks. In many cases, punk themes are boomer themes, and even where the correspondences are not one-to-one, there nonetheless remains a persistent aesthetic linking the cyberpunk project to something larger and more comprehensive than a "simple" literary movement.

> Members of [the boomer] generation are asking questions about the meaning of their lives, about what they want for themselves and their children. They are still exploring, as they did in their years growing up; but now they are exploring in new, and, we think, more profound ways. Religious and spiritual themes are surfacing in a rich variety of ways – in Eastern religions, in evangelical and fundamentalist teachings, in mysticism and New Age movements, in Goddess worship and other ancient religious rituals, in the mainline churches and synagogues, in Twelve-Step recovery groups, in concern about the environment, in holistic health, and in personal and social transformation. (Roof, 1993, pp. 4–5)

The importance of the cultural–literary dialogue cannot be ignored. First, Roof argues that individual narratives are meaningful because they reflect larger cultural narratives. In explaining the value of his seven case studies, he says that

> People's life stories are never just *their* stories, or even those of their generation; they are also the stories as told by the larger culture. Our shared stories connect our sense of self with the larger social order and anchor us in a meaningful context, in time and space. (pp. 28–9)

Certainly the published fictions of Sterling and Gibson and Dick and Stephenson are the substantive equivalent of the stories of the private citizens whose lives are chronicled by Roof. And to the extent that all these stories reflect commonly held values, they serve the societal function of binding, of contextualizing – the stories are the anchors by which we secure ourselves to the cultural mainland, and are the lines we toss to others so that they, in their turn, might bind themselves. This theme is not a new one, of course. As Donne so eloquently put it in his "Meditation XVII:" "No man is an island, entire of itself; every man is a piece of the continent, a part of the main . . . Any man's death diminishes me because I am involved in mankind, and therefore never send to know for whom the bell tolls; it tolls for thee" (Donne, 1623).

In addition to serving an essentially spiritual, cultural function, such narratives serve the more visible function of informing public debate. Hayles (1990, p. 4), reflecting on the three-way dialogic of literature, science, and culture, argues that "feedback loops among theory, technology, and culture develop and expand into complex connections between literature and science which are mediated through the cultural matrix." Although she is speaking specifically about society's scientistic discourses, the relationships between literature and the mediating function of the "cultural matrix" seem readily generalizable to other, similar discourses, such as the one at hand. Within the context of a scientistic debate, we might be more concerned with the ideologies and practices of research institutions, whereas the present discussion focuses on "second-order" concerns such as environmental degradation, which is a result, in part, of scientific progress.

As suggested early in this chapter, the cyberpunk ethic is unmistakably boomer. A few examples illustrate the point. First, cyberpunks' narratives are concerned with the evolving nature of institutions. In some cases the institutions have eroded, and in others they have boosted their power immensely, but in all cases the traditional organizations upon which our culture is centered – church, government, industry – have lost their moral authority. They have become dysfunctional and repressive, and whatever power they wield is wielded illegitimately. Correspondingly, the boomer generation is marked by a pronounced mistrust of institutions.

> Boomers still feel some "distance" from almost every institution, whether the military, banks, public schools, Congress, or organized religion. A 1985 Gallup Poll found that boomers were the least trusting of all age groups toward social and political institutions, even less so than for those younger than themselves. Alienation and estrangement born out of the period continue to express themselves as generalized distrust of government, of major institutions, and of leaders. (Roof, 1993, p. 41)

Leftist critiques of cyberpunk, of which there are several, have seen only half of this equation, and in doing so have missed pretty much the entire point. Readers of *Neuromancer*, such as Ross (1991), have been quick to latch on to Gibson's obvious (and brutal) critique of what might be called "Fourth Stage" capitalism – "Late Capitalism" (Jameson, 1984) gone extraplanetary and posthumanist. But they have generally ignored cyberpunk's equally vicious assault on the various "-isms" which have typified Leftist thinking in his century, as evidenced by the thinking of the characters who populate Sterling's *Heavy Weather* (1994a). It is not the institutions of capital that are under attack by the cyberpunks – it is institutions period. This generalized mistrust of Big Power reflects boomer thinking generally, and is noted by Roof (1993), for example, when he points out that unlike older generations, which tended to mistrust either big business or big labor, the baby boomers tend to mistrust both.[8]

The second illustration regards the way in which both cyberpunks and boomers generally see technology not as a new and wondrous thing, but as an imbedded part of everyday life.

> The boomers were . . . the first generation to grow up with television: They watched the assassination of a president and other national leaders, civil rights demonstrations, the Vietnam War, nuclear test explosions . . . More than any other medium, television shaped consumer tastes and raised their levels of expectations for the future. (Roof, 1993, p. 53)

And the cyberpunks specifically

> are perhaps the first SF generation to grow up not only within the literary tradition of science fiction but in a truly science fictional world. For them, the techniques of classical "hard SF" – extrapolation, technological literacy – are not just literary tools but an aid to daily life. (Sterling, 1988, p. xi)

Cyberpunk, of course, is deeply suspicious of technology, and science fiction has been since Shelley. And while there is no doubt that our culture remains largely enraptured of the messianic potential of science, it has also been suggested that the boomer generation was the first to question, in any meaningful way, the dangerous excesses of scientism. Ravetz (1971) sees the protests over the Vietnam War, for example, as reflecting a larger unease about the poisoning of the environment. It is further worth noting that the no nukes/green activism in the 1970s and since has been championed by the likes of Jane Fonda, Bruce Springsteen, and Jackson Browne, icons of the politically aware boomer generation.

The third illustration follows directly from the second, and that is that both cyberpunk and the boomer generation place a high value on saving and reclaiming nature. For the boomers, "global awareness and environmental consciousness have both provided 'checks' on an unbridled obsession with self and helped to shape a more balanced perspective" (Roof, 1993, p. 244). Globalism/environmentalism is in the foreground of many cyberpunk and near-future narratives, with Brin's *Earth* and Sterling's *Heavy Weather* standing as recent, almost archetypal examples. Clearly there is a concern with the future of the planet in the genre, and whether this concern is manifested in a "secular" theme such as Sterling's tornado alley or in a "sacred" context such as Brin's powerful North American Church of Gaia, the essential importance of the theme remains.

Cyber Trek: the Next Generation

In *A Generation of Seekers* Roof catalogues the several ways in which boomers relate to the sacred and spiritual in their lives today. One of the more interesting suggestions is that boomers are returning to spiritualism – whether in the form of reconstructed paganism, North American spiritualism, Eastern mysticism, evangelical fundamentalism, or even unfettered personal paths. If this is true, and if the cyberpunks are in fact a reliable barometer of the mood of the boomer generation, we might expect to see these authors and their contemporaries over the next few years producing narratives which address the themes of the return, perhaps offering post-institutional looks at the prodigal homecoming. The bits and pieces we have before us suggest that this isn't an altogether unlikely possibility. In a recent e-mail message, Bruce Sterling indicated to me that his next novel will tackle religion more directly, and he also mentioned that Rudy Rucker, whose father is a minister of some sort, occasionally attends church (Sterling, 1995).

What is implied, then, is that this chapter represents only the first part of the story, that much remains to be written in the boomers' generational history. I look forward to perhaps revisiting these issues in several years, and in particular I will be curious to see how gracefully my earlier assertions as to the eternal youth of boomer discourse have aged.

Notes

1   In the early days of the cyberpunk movement these writers corresponded, shared manuscripts, and generally served as an informal support group for the literary efforts of its members. Gibson and Sterling, in particular, seem to be pretty good friends (Sterling, 1988; Leonard, 1993).

2   In some cases I have cited periodical sources downloaded via Lexis/Nexis. Lexis/Nexis does not provide complete information on the pagination of these articles. In these cases I have given the Lexis/Nexis starting page – the only page information the service provides – followed by a "+" symbol. This has been used in the reference list as well as in the text.

3   Gnosticism was originally a "heretical" strain of Christianity, which, due in part to its anti-organizational beliefs, was exterminated by the Christian orthodoxy in the centuries following the death of Jesus Christ. We have recently learned a great deal about the gnostics, as several of their texts were found buried near Nag Hammadi, Egypt, in the 1940s (Pagels, 1979).

4   Given Dick's long-running problems with heroin, external validation would have been valuable, if not essential, for both Dick and his confidantes.

5   The bogey trying to capitalize on this information, bending it to the purpose of world domination, is another conservative Christian type. However, where the Second Alliance was bent on a physical, militaristic takeover, the religious patriarch here plans to reprogram the brains of the world's population.

6   Responding to an earlier draft of this particular section of the chapter, Gibson says that before reading it he would have been hard pressed to define what "gnostic" meant. Prior to this assertion on his part, I was proceeding under the assumption that the connection between *Allogenes* and *Neuromancer* was intentional, rather than coincidental.

7   Gibson himself sees the connection as being less coincidence than it is an artifact of the exceptionally fine grist of the academic mill.

8   Correspondingly, Lyotard (1984) argues that the postmodern era is typified by a "death of metanarrative" – that is, the widespread loss of authority by the dominant institutions of Western culture. Cyberpunk is widely regarded as an archetypally postmodernist form, which strengthens this commentary, and it raises interesting questions about the generational character of postmodernism, as sifted through the filter of cyberpunk SF.

References

Alkon, P. (1994) *Science Fiction before 1900: Imagination Discovers Technology*. New York: Twayne Publishers.

Brin, D. (1991) *Earth*. New York: Bantam Books (original hardcover published in 1990).

Castrone, L. (1994) Eco-theology – new religion or American Indian ripoff? *Rocky Mountain News*, January 18, 3D+.

Chollett, L. (1993) William Gibson's second sight; in meeting of man and machine, ecstasy and dread, the cyberpunk guru divines the future. *Los Angeles Times*, September 12, magazine section, 34+.

Crichton, M. (1990) *Jurassic Park*. New York: Ballantine Books.

Davis, E. (1993) Techgnosis: magic, memory, and the Angels of Information. *The South Atlantic Quarterly*, 92(4), 585–616.

Dick, P. K. (1968) *Do Androids Dream of Electric Sheep?* New York: New American Library.

Dick, P. K. (1981) *VALIS*. New York: Vintage Books (originally published in 1972).

Donne, J. (1623) Meditation XVII. In *The Norton Anthology of English Literature*, 3rd edn. New York: W.W.Norton & Co. pp. 619–20 (1975 edn).

Gibson, W. (1984) *Neuromancer*. New York: Ace Books.

Gibson, W. (1986a) *Burning Chrome*. New York: Ace Books.

Gibson, W. (1986b) The winter market. In *Burning Chrome*. New York: Ace Books, pp. 117–41.

Gibson, W. (1987) *Count Zero*. New York: Ace Books.

Gibson, W. (1988) *Mona Lisa Overdrive*. New York: Bantam Books.

Gibson, W. (1996) Personal communication, February 17.

Hayles, N. K. (1990) *Chaos Bound: Orderly Disorder in Contemporary Literature and Science*. Ithaca, NY: Cornell University Press.

Heisenberg, W. (1958) *Physics and Philosophy*. New York: Harper and Row.

Horne, M. (1994) Book reviews (*October Holiday*). *Christianity Today*, 38(2), 60.

Jameson, F. (1984) Postmodernism, or the cultural logic of late capitalism. *New Left Review*, 146, 53–93.

Leonard, J. (1993) Book reviews. *The Nation*, 257(16), 580+.

Lévi-Strauss, C. (1966) *The Savage Mind*. Chicago: University of Chicago Press.

Lyotard, J. (1984) *The Postmodern Condition: a Report on Knowledge*. Minneapolis: University of Minnesota Press.

McCaffery, L. (1991) An interview with William Gibson. In L. McCaffery (ed.), *Storming the Reality Studio: a Casebook of Cyberpunk and Postmodern Fiction*. Durham, NC: Duke University Press, pp. 263–85.

Pagels, E. (1979) *The Gnostic Gospels*. New York: Random House.

Povey, M. (1994) What is Wicca and what do Wiccans believe? http://spot.colorado.edu/~smithsr/paganism.htm.

Ravetz, J. (1971) *Scientific Knowledge and Its Social Problems*. Oxford: Clarendon Press.

Robinson, J. (1978) *The Nag Hammadi Library*. San Francisco: Harper and Row.

Roof, W. (1993) *A Generation of Seekers*. San Francisco: Harper.

Ross, A. (1991) *Strange Weather: Culture, Science, and Technology in the Age of Limits*. London: Verso.

Shirley, J. (1985) *Eclipse*. New York: Bluejay Books.

Stephenson, N. (1993) *Snow Crash*. New York: Bantam Books.

Sterling, B. (1986) Preface. In W. Gibson, *Burning Chrome*. New York: Ace Books.

Sterling, B. (ed.) (1988) *Mirrorshades*. New York: Ace Books.

Sterling B. (1989) *Crystal Express*. New York: Ace Books.

Sterling, B. (1994a) *Heavy Weather*. New York: Bantam Books.

Sterling, B. (1994b) Are you for 86? In *Globalhead*. New York: Bantam Books, pp. 285–321.

Sterling, B. (1995) Personal e-mail message. April 2.

Waldrop, M. (1992) *Complexity: the Emerging Science at the Edge of Chaos*. New York: Simon & Schuster.

Winner, L. (1977) *Autonomous Technology: Technics-out-of-control as a Theme in Political Thought*. Cambridge, MA: MIT Press.

Ziolkowski, T. (1981) Science, Frankenstein, and myth. *Sewanee Review*, 89(1), 34–56.

12
SOCIAL JUSTICE AND SEXISM FOR ADOLESCENTS: A CONTENT ANALYSIS OF LYRICAL THEMES AND GENDER PRESENTATIONS IN CANADIAN HEAVY METAL MUSIC, 1985–1991

Bruce K. Friesen and
Warren Helfrich

As a form of popular music, heavy metal has enjoyed a relatively persistent following since its origins in late 1960s psychedelic music. The genre has been characterized by unique popular music aesthetics, including amplification, incorporation of the full range of electronic capabilities, and specific musical conventions (Friesen and Epstein, 1994). As a cultural sign, heavy metal has consistently evoked negative reactions from the broader public, simultaneously endearing it to the hearts of millions of disaffected youth. It has been blamed for the moral corruption of young people, encouraging drug use, and causing suicides (Herman, 1982; Shapiro, 1988).

Academic research on heavy metal in Canada and the United States, however, has been limited. Despite heavy metal's emergence in the late 1960s, the first known academic discussion of the genre was not published until 1984 (Straw, 1984), and one of the first empirical studies dedicated to the topic was completed in 1986 (Friesen, 1986, 1990).[1] Studies since that time have become more numerous, and have examined the effects of the music on its fans (Epstein and Pratto, 1990; Epstein et al., 1990; Rosenbaum and Prinsky, 1987; Binder, 1993) or the subcultural activity surrounding the consumption and dissemination of the music (Verden et al., 1989; Friesen, 1990; Weinstein, 1991; Harrell, 1994; Kotarba, 1994), and, more recently, the aesthetics of the music (Weinstein, 1991; Walser, 1993; Friesen and Epstein, 1994). Despite persistent public concern over the effect of heavy metal lyrics on the behavior of adolescents, few content analyses of heavy metal have been conducted where thematic categories have been inductively generated from the lyrics.[2]

This study reports on a longitudinal analysis of heavy metal lyrics in 1985 and 1991. The intent of the original study (Friesen, 1986) was to assess the thematic content of heavy metal lyrics and to provide a deeper analysis of gender-specific traits presented in lyrics dealing with gender issues. The purpose of the 1991 sample was to see if these themes were consistent over time.

Using Content Analysis

As an investigative issue, analyzing the messages in music lyrics lends itself particularly well to the method of content analysis. Content analysis has the advantage of being unobtrusive, potentially consistent, and able to observe changes over time (Babbie, 1995, p. 320). Still, the shortcomings of the method are serious enough to warrant special care on the part of the investigator. Denisoff (1975), Denzin (1970), and Carey (1970) long ago noted recurring practices of content analysts which have weakened the credibility of such studies performed on popular culture artifacts. The most frequent problem deals with interpreting materials in such a way that it accurately and reliably reflects its content. Coding categories need to be constructed so as to reveal subjective meaning without creating a type of conceptual category which does not exist.

Ling (1984, p. 1) has commented: "Music is an excellent object of research for cultural sociologists precisely because it is a carrier of meaning without being descriptive." Any analysis of music must not only take into account the more "obvious" content of lyrics, but the affective manner in which the vocalist presents the words, the way in which the music is intended to produce a particular emotive response in a variety of listeners, and the manner in which the music is interpreted by its listeners. Walser (1993, p. 21), a musicologist, has commented:

> scholarship of recent popular music has until recently been dominated by sociological approaches that totally neglect the music of popular music, reducing the meaning of a song to the literal meaning of its lyrics. This is called "content" analysis.

Walser's criticism is legitimate. Of equal importance to the lyrics are the subtle (or not so subtle) ways that the music produces an emotive interpretation of the lyrics being sung and further defines the ideational context.

Studying Heavy Metal

In an effort to overcome the weaknesses in content analysis, a year of participant observation research into the heavy metal subculture was first completed (Friesen, 1990). This familiarized the researchers with the subjective meanings and interpretations of heavy metal listeners and their respective culture. A sincere attempt was made to generate coding categories inductively rather than superimposing our own. Most often, the participants or creators of the music were asked to define categories for us.

Random samples of 30 albums were drawn in 1985 and 1991 from hit charts in heavy metal magazines, while the analysis was performed in two stages. The first stage identified stylistic differences in heavy metal music and the dominant themes expressed in song lyrics. In a number of cases, the emotive features of the music made the difference in defining the central theme of the song.

In the second stage, an analysis was performed only on those songs dealing with gender relations. A detailed analysis of gender traits conforming or not conforming to traditional gender roles was then engaged. Again, emotive and affective aspects of each piece of music were considered when attempting to analyze in what way various aspects of gender roles were being evaluated on the part of the vocalist.

A random sample of 30 heavy metal albums was compiled from the September 1984 to July 1985 (six issues) editions of the (now defunct) bi-monthly Canadian heavy metal magazine *Metallion*. Because of the larger pop market in the United States, American heavy metal charts tend to be dominated by well known pop metal artists. This was particularly true in 1985. By contrast, a larger proportion of underground bands with a local following are represented on Canadian lists, since Canada lacks the same critical mass needed to support a larger number of more mainstream metal bands.

Each issue of *Metallion* contained a "Hard Chart" listing the best 30 heavy metal albums for that month as defined by various record distributors across Canada. In an effort to achieve as broad a range of music as possible, duplications and second albums by a band were eliminated. Two albums were unable to be obtained in the 1985 sample. In their place two other albums were hand-picked because of their inclusion of female band members. The 30 album sample constituted 22.6 percent of the total population of Hard Chart albums.

Since the magazine *Metallion* was no longer published in 1991, the April edition of *MEAT* (Metal Events Around Toronto) magazine was selected. *MEAT* magazine was distributed nationally. A population list was compiled from the lists of top ten metal hits sent in by radio stations across Canada and the *MEAT* writers' top ten listening favorites.[3] Albums were again eliminated on the basis of repetition. A random sample of 30 albums (54.5 percent) was taken from the total list of 55, eliciting a total of 342 songs.

Issues in Coding Heavy Metal Lyrics

Analyzing music lyrics intended for a popular audience is a messy business, and for several reasons. Lyrics may be intentionally vague or ambiguous in order to appeal to as broad a range of listeners as possible. Listeners may then create meaning from the lyric as it relates to their own experience. One such example is Motley Crüe's "She's Got the Looks That Kill":

Now listen up: she's razor sharp.
If she don't get her way, she'll slice you apart.
Now she's a cool, cool black, moves like a cat.
If you don't get her game, well you might not make it back.

She's got the looks that kill, that kill (repeat).
She's got the look.
She's got the looks that kill (repeat).

Now she's bullet-proof, keeps her motor clean.
And believe me – you, she's a number thirteen.
The church strikes midnight, she's lookin' louder and louder.
She's gonna turn on your juice, boy, then she'll turn on the power.

It is not immediately clear whether the song refers to a woman or an automobile. In such cases, familiarity with subcultural nuances or definitions of participants became paramount to understanding in what way the lyric was being understood by listeners. While most hardcore listeners identified the lyric as referring to a car, the majority of listeners (not hardcores) understood it to refer to a woman.

The emotional tone of the song was at times likewise difficult to distinguish. Extreme's tune "He-man Woman Hater", for example, extols the masculine "virtue" of emotional distancing from women; treating them with distrust and loathing ("You've got to hate to love, you've got to love to hate her"). Is the lyric sincere in its suggestion, or a thinly veiled tongue-in-cheek criticism of such attitudes among males?

Analysis is also complicated by the possibility of lyricists describing attitudes, actions or fantasy sequences for the purpose of sensationalism (thus increasing album sales), rather than articulating more "honest" attitudes or describing actions that most heavy metal adherents experience (or even desire to experience) on a regular basis. An example is Motorhead's "I'm So Bad (Baby I Don't Care)", which reads: "I make love to mountain lions. Sleep on red-hot branding irons. When I walk the roadway shakes. Bed's a mess of rattlesnakes." Researchers must therefore try to distinguish the literal from the symbolic when analyzing lyrics, distinguishing songs that are written with the intent to shock or mystify rather than describe or illuminate.

Transcribing lyrics was also a process fraught with potential inconsistencies, particularly with the 1985 sample, when few albums included printed lyrics on album or compact disc sleeves. In a few instances, the lyric sung did not perfectly match the printed lyric. At other times, transcribing lyrics accurately from what was sung with no written guide was next to impossible. We requested lyrics from the record companies when we encountered this difficulty; most complied. We received a letter from the lead singer of one band who indicated that he couldn't remember what the lyric was for one song, since he improvised the lyric each time.

Most of these problems were able to be resolved by relying on the perceptions and opinions of adherents. We found that a year of participant observation research led us to more "accurately" interpret the meanings of lyrics and nuances than making such an attempt without much knowledge of the subcultural activity which surrounded the consumption of the music. This is important, since audiences frequently take their own meaning from songs, regardless of the lyric (Rosenbaum and Prinsky, 1987; Murphy, 1989). Equally important to the intended message of the lyric, then, was the way it was interpreted by audience members. For the purposes of this research, any ambiguities were left with members of the subculture to define.

Thematic Concentrations

Two hundred and eighty-two songs were procured from the 1985 thirty album sample, thirteen of which were instrumentals. Of the 269 remaining songs, the lyrics to 113 and one-third[4] (42 percent) songs were printed on album covers or inside liners. For the 1991 sample, 342 songs were on 30 albums or compact discs; 11 were instrumentals. Lyric sheets, printed either on album jackets or received from the publisher, were obtained for 277 of the remaining 331 lyrics; only 54 needed to be transcribed.

A number of differences were immediately apparent between the two samples. The basic form of consumption had changed from cassette tape to compact disc. More songs were recorded on compact discs; thus a greater numbers of songs were sampled in 1991. In addition, the effects of the PMRC hearings could be measured by the increased number of compact discs including printed lyrics.

Sweeping international changes, like the fall of the Berlin Wall, had occurred in the six-year interim. What effects (if any) these monumental events had on lyrical content is difficult to say, although our research did substantiate a greater preponderance of lyrics dealing with social issues. Grunge or alternative music had entered the mainstream market in 1991, affecting all types of genres, including heavy metal. Several bands included in the 1991 sample were considered to be heavy metal alternative, a subgenre that did not exist in 1985. The impact of alternative music in heavy metal was to make some of the more popularized styles of heavy metal (such as glam-rock and California-style metal bands) appear out-of-sync and clichéd. In the metal scene, fluffy long hair and spandex was replaced to a large extent by short-cropped hair and very baggy clothes.

Lyrics were analyzed thematically by two independent coders well versed in the heavy metal subculture. Thematic categories were arrived at through analysis of a pre-sample of albums not included in the sample. At attempt was made to identify the predominant theme or concern being expressed by the vocalist in the music, a method similar to those of Cole (1971), Hirsch (1971), and others. Cole identified four themes: love–sex, religion, violence, and social protest. Hirsch identified six themes: heterosexual, social commentary, religious, novelty, personal, and nostalgic. By definition, then, categories were not necessarily mutually exclusive. The following categories were elicited:

1 *Gender themes.* Lyrics that dealt with male–female interaction or relationships, or lyrics that described various qualities of a man or woman or group of men or women. These identities were human, however, and excluded mystical or supernatural entities. Lyrics dealing with love, sex and broken hearts were popular themes.

2 *Reflective/philosophical themes.* The lyricist evaluated the lifestyle he or she was leading, or made a statement about life in general. These songs dealt more often with attitudes than behavior.

3 *Oppressive themes.* The lyricist commented upon other identities or institutions that were oppressing him or her; the songs did not deal with the lyricist who viewed himself or herself as oppressive. Usually, no real solution was given to relieve this oppression. Instead, there was a type of resolve

made to live with the conflict. Oppression came from such sources as parents, school, police, or some abstract (but not supernatural) force.

4   *Physical conflict – recognition/resignation/enjoyment.* The lyricist saw and accepted physical conflict as part of everyday life and resigned herself or himself to participating in it, even if it meant death. Enjoyment was sometimes the reason for participating in physical conflict. The conflict was the end in and of itself, not the means to an end.

5   *Physical conflict – means to an end.* Physical conflict was seen as a viable means to a desired goal; a good solution to deal with a problem. While some enjoyment may have been extracted from the conflict, it was not an end in and of itself. Even so, the lyrics concentrated upon the conflict more than the motivation for it.

6   *Mystical/supernatural themes.* The lyricist talked about or dealt with some type of force or entity that was not human, but was endowed with supernatural or mystical powers. Often these forces were seen as being overwhelming and beyond one's control. At times the lyricist was the possessor of these qualities. Satanism and occult characters (e.g. werewolves) were examples of such a force.

7   *Excitement themes.* These included descriptions of purposeful behavior that carried out for the primary purpose of producing enjoyment or thrills. Fast driving, partying, "rocking" to music, and "getting crazy" were examples. Physical conflict and sex themes were excluded from this category.

8   *Escape themes.* In desiring to get away from pressures or from the mundane world, the lyricist did not look for excitement but a way to physically avoid the conflict. At times the escape was a desired place to run to. At other times the desire to get away was merely expressed.

9   *Loss of control themes.* Due to many pressures and turmoil, the lyricist found himself or herself accidentally becoming mentally ill or being unable to control his or her emotions. This was not done as a purposeful action, but was a consequence or response to external factors.

Two coders independently identified themes and achieved 72.5 percent agreement on their first choice for thematic catego-

Table 12.1   Heavy metal lyric themes: 1985 and 1991

Theme	1985 sample (% in parentheses)	1991 sample (% in parentheses)
Gender	102 (37.9)	122 (36.9)
Reflective/philosophical	50 (18.6)	57 (17.2)
Oppressive	13 (4.8)	34 (10.3)
Physical conflict – end	21 (7.8)	14 (4.2)
Physical conflict – means	5 (1.9)	4 (1.2)
Mystical/supernatural	16 (6.0)	22 (6.6)
Excitement	48 (17.8)	26 (7.9)
Escape	4 (1.5)	11 (3.3)
Loss of control	8 (3.0)	10 (3.0)
Social justice	2 (0.7)	31 (9.4)
Total	269 (100.0)	331 (100.0)

ries. One hundred percent of their coding choices fell within each other's top three choices. In 1986, these themes appeared to be exhaustive in describing themes in heavy metal lyrics. A preliminary reading of 1991 lyrics, however, revealed a preponderance of songs making objective social commentary, so much so that a new lyric category was created:

10   *Social consciousness/social justice themes.* The lyricist commented on or evaluated a social issue or problem, such as social decay or pollution. The issue or problem discussed was not personalized, but was seen to exist outside of the immediate experience of the lyricist.

Songs in the 1985 sample were re-examined, and two songs were recoded as "social consciousness" where appropriate. The results are listed in table 12.1. There were some surprising similarities between the two samples, as noted in table 12.1. For the 1985 sample, the greatest number of songs dealt with issues related to gender, followed by reflective/philosophical, excitement, and physical conflict as an end in and of itself. In 1991, the proportion of songs dedicated to gender and reflective/

philosophical themes was virtually unchanged. However, the proportion of songs dealing with oppression more than doubled (to 10.3 percent) between 1985 and 1991, and the proportion of songs dealing with social justice increased more than 10 times to 9.4 percent in 1991. While the proportion of songs dealing with escape themes increased slightly, songs dealing with excitement and physical conflict as an end (a type of excitement) decreased substantially, from 17.8 and 7.8 percent in 1985 to 7.9 and 4.2 percent in 1991 respectively. Excitement seems to have been replaced by an increased emphasis on social justice, oppression, and a slightly increased emphasis on escape.

Also of interest was how thematic concentrations differed by type of heavy metal music and how these themes changed over time. Friesen and Epstein (1994) identified four different styles of heavy metal music – pop heavy metal, progressive, thrash, and alternative – with the last style receiving mainstream radio airplay around 1990. Because of the relatively small number of songs in a few of the categories in table 12.1, lyrical themes dealing with oppression, physical conflict as a means to an end, and escape were combined into one category called "Oppressive"; while themes dealing with excitement, physical conflict as an end in and of itself, and loss of control were combined into one category entitled "Excitement".

Table 12.2 demonstrates that most of the thematic concentrations in pop metal remained largely consistent between 1985 and 1991. Themes dealing with excitement declined by half, while themes dealing with oppression and social justice increased slightly. For progressive metal, gender themes increased 17 percent over the same time period, while philosophical, excitement, and social justice themes increased modestly. Supernatural themes in progressive metal disappeared entirely in our 1991 sample.

Unlike in other types of metal, few thrash lyrics dealt with gender themes; the proportion of these all but disappeared in our 1991 sample. The proportion of thrash lyrics dealing with oppression, excitement, and the supernatural declined slightly, while social justice themes became the second largest thematic category (22.4 percent), behind lyrics dealing with oppression (30.3 percent). No thrash lyrics dealing with social justice were present in our 1985 sample.

Table 12.2 Heavy metal music styles by heavy metal lyric themes: 1985 and 1991

Theme	Pop metal		Progressive		Thrash metal		Alternative	
	1985	1991	1985	1991	1985	1991	1985	1991
Gender	44.3	52.4	27.8	44.8	12.5	2.3		44.2
	(89)	(75)	(10)	(17)	(4)	(2)		(27)
Philosophical	16.9	14.0	16.7	18.4	9.4	18.0		24.6
	(34)	(20)	(6)	(7)	(3)	(16)		(15)
Oppressive	9.9	12.6	16.7	15.8	37.5	30.3		13.1
	(20)	(18)	(6)	(6)	(12)	(27)		(8)
Excitement	26.4	12.6	2.8	10.5	21.8	13.5		9.8
	(53)	(18)	(1)	(4)	(7)	(12)		(6)
Supernatural	2.5	4.2	30.5	0.0	18.8	13.5		6.7
	(5)	(6)	(11)	(0)	(6)	(12)		(4)
Social justice	0.0	4.2	5.5	10.5	0.0	22.4		1.6
	(0)	(6)	(2)	(4)	(0)	(20)		(1)
Total	100	100	100	100	100	100		100
	(201)	(143)	(36)	(38)	(32)	(89)		(61)

Note: Values are percentages (numbers in parentheses).

Of particular interest was the emergence of alternative music as a distinct subgenre of heavy metal. Alternative music has since become the most popular type of music played on Top 40 radio stations. While not all alternative music can be considered heavy metal, the alternative scene influenced new bands within the heavy metal genre enough to cause new stylistic innovations. Some of these stylistic or aesthetic differences (such as the rejection of the guitar god and higher vocals on the part of the lead singer) have caused tensions between some heavy metal artists (Friesen and Epstein, 1994). Our research sought to determine whether or not these early alternative bands listed on heavy metal charts (e.g. TAD, Black Crowes, the Throbs) differed thematically from other heavy metal which receives radio airplay.

As table 12.2 shows, gender still remains a major preoccupation of alternative heavy metal lyrics (44.2 percent), while over 13 percent of alternative lyrics dealt with themes of oppression. However, almost one-quarter of alternative song lyrics dealt with philosophical themes; the largest concentration of such in any subgenre in either year. Conversely, less than 10 percent of alternative lyrics dealt with themes of excitement. Because of the relatively small numbers of alternative, progressive, or thrash bands in 1985, these results must be regarded as tentative. At the same time, they point to some interesting possibilities for future research regarding heavy metal lyrical themes and stylistic differences.

Gender in Heavy Metal Lyrics

The second part of the content analysis attempted to evaluate gender role messages in heavy metal music, and the part that gender plays in defining such roles.

Of the 282 songs in the 1985 sample, 242 (86 percent) were written entirely by males. Only 29 songs (10 percent) were written by females. This is likely a higher percentage than existed in the population of heavy metal albums at the time, since two albums in the 1985 sample were selected to replace two unattainable imported records which were written and sung by males. The remaining 11 songs (4 percent) were co-written by at least one male and one female (or two males and one female). Such songs were always sung by female vocalists. Males thus contributed to female definitions of reality, while women did not contribute to male definitions.

In the 1991 sample of 331 songs, women sang only 33 (10.0 percent) songs. Two bands in the sample contained all female members, while one fronted female vocalists but male musicians. All songs sung by women were written by women, and all but one song sung by males was written by a male. This particularly successful song had been previously recorded by a female artist and had been re-recorded by a male band.

All songs sung by females in both years fell only into the pop metal category. Table 12.3 shows the differences in thematic concentrations for all male vocalists, for male pop metal vocalists, and for female vocalists. As per table 12.3, female heavy

Table 12.3 Lyrical themes by heavy metal vocalists: 1985 and 1991 combined

Theme	Males (all)	Males (pop metal artists)	Females (all)
Gender	181 (34.3)	121 (44.5)	43 (59.7)
Philosophical	102 (19.3)	49 (18.0)	5 (6.9)
Oppressive	92 (17.4)	33 (12.1)	5 (6.9)
Excitement	88 (16.7)	58 (21.3)	13 (18.1)
Supernatural	34 (6.4)	7 (2.6)	4 (5.6)
Social justice	31 (5.9)	4 (1.5)	2 (2.8)
Total	528 (100.0)	272 (100.0)	72 (100.0)

Note: Values in parentheses are percentages.

metal vocalists were more likely than either male pop metal vocalists or all male vocalists to sing songs related to gender, while males were more than twice as likely than females to concentrate on philosophical/reflective and oppressive themes. Excitement themes ranked relatively high for females and males. For the most part, then, women artists were most likely to sing about issues relating to gender, and were less likely than males to either wax philosophical or sing about oppression-related topics.

As reported in table 12.1, 102 (37.9 percent) of 269 songs in the 1985 sample dealt with gender themes. This proportion was virtually unchanged in 1991, with 122 (36.9 percent) of 331 songs concentrating on the same. Comparatively, Cole (1971) found 59 percent of lyrics of pop tunes from 1960 to 1964 dealing with love–sex themes, rising to 71 percent between 1965 and 1969. Hirsch (1971) found that a heterosexual theme predominated in 69 percent of his sample of popular music tunes. While gender themes remain the largest preoccupation of heavy metal artists, themes other than gender seem to be expressed more often than in earlier pop music.

Of the 79 such songs written by males in the 1985 sample, eight (10 percent) focused primarily on a male or group of males, six (7.6 percent) focused primarily on a female, and the remaining 65 (82.4 percent) dealt with both genders. Of the 23 gender songs sung by females, however, none dealt primarily with a male figure, seven (30.4 percent) dealt only with a female subject, and 16 (69.6 percent) dealt with both genders.

In 1991, seven (6.9 percent) of the 102 songs sung by males focused primarily on a male or males only, three (2.9 percent) focused on a female, while 92 (90.2 percent) dealt with both genders. Two (10.5 percent) of the 19 gender-related songs sung by females focused on males alone, three (15.8 percent) focused on females alone, and 14 (73.7 percent) dealt with both genders. Unlike in the 1985 sample, it appears that female vocalists were slightly more likely than male vocalists to focus on one gender or the other. However, the small number of songs sung by females makes such findings tentative.

The emotive content of gender-related songs is similarly revealing. Females singing about themselves concentrated on incompleteness, unfulfillment, and loneliness when without the company of males, while songs about males referred to males attempting to "steal their love" without any commitment or exchange in return. Songs sung by males about males, however, usually dealt with positive evaluations of male traits such as strength, independence, and so on. Songs sung by males dealing primarily with females depicted them almost entirely in the erotic role.

A sincere attempt was made to identity whether the traits of males or females described in lyrics were traditional or nontraditional in nature. Gender "traits" were chosen as opposed to the idea of gender "roles," since there is often too little inform-ation given in lyrics to assess a complete social role. In a manner similar to Chafetz (1974), Freudiger and Almquist (1978) and Thaxton and Jaret (1985), 12 characteristics were listed for each gender that were traditional in nature. Each gender was evalu-ated as conforming to the stereotyped trait, not conforming, or no mention being made of the trait in the song. Traditional gender roles were assessed on the basis of the largest sum of traits either conforming or not conforming to the stereotype. Male traits were aggressiveness, ruggedness, adventurousness, independence, confidence, and lack of emotion. For females, traditional traits included passivity, dependency, quietness, meekness, gentleness, warmth, affection, kindness, sentimental-ity, soft-heartedness, and sensitivity. We added "sexual desire" to the list of male qualities and "erotic role" to the female list, based upon comments from other researchers regarding the large part that sexuality plays in the presentation of women in rock music (Harding and Nett, 1984), and the reminder that the erotic role has been a more salient identity variable during adolescence than some other stages of the lifecourse.

Nontraditional or traditional gender roles were thus determined by selecting the column (conforms or does not conform to stereotype) with the largest number of traits. A male who expressed fear of or dependence upon a woman was one example; a woman who acted independently was another. Table 12.4 demonstrates that the proportion of males and females described in songs sung by males changed little between 1985 and 1991. However, female vocalists described more traditional males in 1991 than 1985 (73.9 to 93.8 percent respectively), and the converse for females (93.8 and 77.8 percent in 1985 and 1991 respectively).

A point of clarification needs to be made regarding definitions of "traditional" or "nontraditional" roles. We found it helpful to devise a number of informal codes for repeated "scenarios" in order to distinguish traditional from nontraditional behavior; particularly in erotic behavior or sexual displays of power. Many of the women who were described in songs acted in ways that at first may be identified as nontraditional, such as aggressively pursuing a male or using one's sexuality as a vehicle for power enhancement. Such behaviors, however, belie more traditional underlying values of female other-directed behavior (as opposed to self), or the utilization of micro or private power without challenging male power in the public sphere.

Erotic behavior on the part of the female was therefore seen as traditional behavior if it was done with the intention of pleasing the male (other-directed). Erotic behavior was also seen as traditional if one's sexuality was used to attempt to manipulate a male, since both males and females in these situations accepted the traditional gender roles of "female as object" and "male as pursuer." Erotic behavior on the part of females was not seen as traditional, however, if the female was seeking self-gratification (self-oriented), or if no commitment or dependence was expressed towards the male (i.e. independence).

While table 12.4 illustrates that traditional gender roles are overwhelmingly described in heavy metal by either gender, it

Table 12.4 Gender role stereotypes in lyrics, by gender of vocalist: 1985 and 1991

Role	Male vocalists				Female vocalists			
	Males		Females		Males		Females	
	1985	1991	1985	1991	1985	1991	1985	1991
Traditional	62 (84.9)	80 (80.8)	46 (64.8)	62 (65.3)	17 (73.9)	15 (93.8)	15 (93.8)	14 (77.8)
Non-traditional	11 (15.1)	19 (19.2)	25 (15.2)	33 (34.4)	6 (26.1)	1 (6.2)	1 (6.2)	4 (22.2)
Total	73	99	71	95	23	16	16	18

Note: Values in parentheses are percentages.

does not account for the emotive evaluation of said persons. In other words, we sought to discover if male vocalists were more likely than female vocalists to criticize people in their songs who act in a nontraditional fashion. Examples of such would be a male who is very dependent on a female, or a female who is pursuing her own freedom and self-fulfillment with little regard for anyone else's feelings. Kaplan and Goldsen developed a method for analyzing the way in which particular values or symbols are presented in various media. Symbols can be presented positively, positively with qualification, negatively, negatively with qualification, or neutrally (see Berelson, 1952; Budd et al., 1967; Freudiger and Almquist, 1978). These categories were further modified and applied to traditional and nontraditional gender traits in an attempt to assess whether a role was endorsed or criticized more by male or by female vocalists. The categories developed were: (a) endorses traditional role (includes resignation to); (b) criticizes traditional role; (c) endorses nontraditional role (includes resignation to); (d) criticizes nontraditional role; and (e) endorses and criticizes either traditional or nontraditional roles (i.e. conflicting ideas presented). The results are presented in table 12.5.

A number of observations can be made from table 12.5. First, gender presentations in heavy metal continue to predominantly endorse traditional gender roles. This is true regardless of the gender of the vocalist, and it was true in both 1985 and 1991. Second, there appears to be a slight increase in the number of songs sung by males dedicated either to criticizing traditional gender roles or to endorsing nontraditional gender roles. Of the latter, the more predominant theme is sincerely desiring to have an honest, long-term relationship with a member of the opposite sex, or an emotional dependency that they do not want to get over. Songs that endorsed these nontraditional types of feelings among males increased almost 10 percent by 1991.

Third, female vocalists were more likely than males to criticize traditional roles, and more so in 1991 than 1985. Again, the small number of songs sung by females simply makes such comparative statements tentative. On the other hand, the extremely small number of female heavy metal vocalists or band members in either year tempts us to conclude that these results may indeed be similar to those found in the larger population.

Table 12.5 Emotive interpretations of traditional and non-traditional roles by gender of vocalist: 1985 and 1991

Evaluation	Males		Females	
	1985	1991	1985	1991
Endorses traditional role	48 (60.8)	56 (54.9)	15 (65.2)	8 (42.1)
Criticizes traditional roles	2 (2.5)	9 (8.8)	4 (17.4)	7 (36.8)
Endorses non-traditional roles	3 (3.8)	14 (13.7)	3 (13.0)	2 (10.5)
Criticizes non-traditional roles	22 (27.8)	21 (20.6)	1 (4.3)	2 (10.5)
Endorses/ criticizes either role	4 (5.1)	2 (2.0)	0 (0.0)	0 (0.0)
Total	79 (100.0)	102 (100.0)	23 (100.0)	19 (100.0)

Note: Values in parentheses are percentages.

Conclusion

Heavy metal, a music characterized by its aggressive and loud musical style, was almost entirely dominated by male artists in 1985 and 1991. The few females that ventured into the artistic arena during this time produced music within the least respected (but most potentially lucrative) pop metal subgenre.

A more involved content analysis was used to identify themes in heavy metal lyrics, and presentations of gender in gender-specific lyrics. Sizable proportions of heavy metal lyrics deal with songs relating to gender and reflective themes. Songs dealing with social justice issues increased substantially between 1985 and 1991.

In examining gender representations in the music, it appears that vocalists continue to endorse traditional gender roles and criticize nontraditional roles, although less so in 1991 than 1985. While this content analysis has examined the music and lyrics of the genre of music regarded to be highly deviant, the conclusions supported by the data are congruent with those of other studies performed on more popular or mainstream styles. The gender roles described in the music support, rather than criticize, the status quo.

It appears that academic attention to heavy metal has occurred right at the time that heavy metal has undergone fundamental stylistic and aesthetical change, and may be in the process of being subsumed under the new title of "alternative" music. However, future studies may want to examine the burgeoning number of songs dealing with social justice. While the content analysis method used to evaluate gender roles in this research was adequate, developing a new method whereby "scenarios" regarding male–female interactions were described, matched to songs and evaluated for their egalitarian bent may prove to be more illuminating.

While examining the content of heavy metal songs, we make no claims in this chapter that the messages promulgated within the music influence those who listen to them in any particular fashion. Future studies may likewise want to focus on this continuing mystified process of interpretation and meaning. From this experience, it important to remember that the emotive power of the music itself is a significant social signifier. While music may have the ability to clam the savage beast, it may also have the power to make one.

Appendix: 1985 and 1991 Samples

1985 SAMPLE

Accept: *Balls to the Wall*
Iron Maiden: *Powerslave*
Queensryche: *Queensryche*
Raven: *Stay Hard*
Grim Reaper: *See You in Hell*
Dio: *The Last in Line*
Helix: *Walkin' the Razor's Edge*

Anthrax: *Fistful of Metal*
Fastway: *All Fired Up*
WASP: *WASP*
Venom: *At War with Satan*
Lita Ford: *Dancin' on the Edge*
Lee Aaron: *Metal Queen*
Molly Hatchet: *Deed Is Done*
Angel City: *Two Minute Warning*
Madam X: *We Reserve the Right*
Poison Dollys: *Poison Dollys*
Headpins: *Head Over Heels*
Ratt: *Out of the Cellar*
Motley Crüe: *Shout at the Devil*
Scorpions: *Love at First Sting*
Quiet Riot: *Condition Critical*
Exciter: *Violence and Force*
Krokus: *The Blitz*
Triumph: *Thunder Seven*
Deep Purple: *Perfect Strangers*
Kiss: *Animalize*
Alcatraz: *No Parole from Rock and Roll*
Twisted Sister: *You Can't Stop Rock and Roll*
Slade: *Keep Your Hands Off My Power Supply*

1991 SAMPLE

AC/DC: *The Razor's Edge*
Great White: *Hooked*
Poison: *Flesh and Blood*
Cinderella: *Heartbreak Station*
Damn Yankees: *Damn Yankees*
Tesla: *Five Man Acoustical Jam*
Warrant: *Cherry Pie*
Slaughter: *Stick It to Ya'*
Vixen: *Rev It Up*
Wrathchild America: *3-D*
Annihilator: *Never, Neverland*
Sepultura: *Arise*
Slayer: *Seasons in the Abyss*
Motorhead: *1916*
Megadeth: *Rust in Peace*
TAD: *8-Way Santa*
Anthrax: *Persistence of Time*
Judas Priest: *Painkiller*

Queensryche: *Empire*
Extreme: *Pornograffiti*
Sacrifice: *Soldiers of Misfortune*
Metal Church: *The Human Factor*
Precious Metal: *Precious Metal*
Malhavoc: *The Release*
Pantera: *Cowboys from Hell*
I, Napoleon: *I, Napoleon*
Black Crowes: *Shake Your Money Maker*
The Throbs: *Language of Thieves and Vagabonds*
David Lee Roth: *A Little Ain't Enough*
Cycle Sluts from Hell: *Cycle Sluts from Hell*

Notes

We are indebted to Dr Robert A. Stebbins, Nan McBlane and Kevin Worron for their assistance with this project.

1   Other studies on popular music, such as Tanner's (1981) examination of adolescents' pop music tastes, include heavy metal music as one of several possible musical preferences. Their investigations into heavy metal are insightful but limited by virtue of their focus.
2   Walser (1993, p. 184, n. 2) suggests that "dozens" of content analyses of heavy metal have been published, but cites only two.
3   One of *MEAT*'s writers had played a major role in the production and dissemination of *Metallion* magazine.
4   One-third of a lyric was printed on the inside of an album, and was part of a song that took up one entire side of a record.

References

Babbie, E. (1995) *The Practice of Social Research*, 7th edn. Belmont, CA: Wadsworth.
Berelson, B. (1952) *Content Analysis in Communication Research*. Glencoe, IL: The Free Press.
Binder, A. (1993) Constructing racial rhetoric: media depictions, or harm in heavy metal and rap music. *American Sociological Review*, 58, 753–67.
Budd, R., Thorp, R. and Donohew, L. (1967) *Content Analysis of Communications*. New York: Macmillan.
Carey, J. T. (1970) The author replies. *American Journal of Sociology*, 75, 1039–41.
Chafetz, J. S. (1974) *Masculine/Feminine or Human?* Hillsdale, IL: F.E. Peacock.

Cole, R. R. (1971) Top song in the sixties. *American Behavioral Scientist*, 14, 389–400.

Denisoff, R. S. (1975) Content analysis: the Achilles heel of popular culture? *Journal of Popular Culture*, 9, 456–60.

Denzin, N. K. (1970) Problems in analyzing elements of mass culture: notes on the popular songs and other artistic productions. *American Journal of Sociology*, 75, 1035–8.

Epstein, J. and Pratto, D. (1990) Heavy metal music: juvenile delinquency and satanic identification. *Popular Music and Society*, 14(4), 67–75.

Epstein, J., Pratto, D. and Skipper, J. Jr (1990) Teenagers, behavioral problems, and preferences for heavy metal and rap music: a case study of a southern middle school. *Deviant Behavior*, 2(11), 381–4.

Freudiger, P. and Almquist, E. (1978) Male and female roles in the lyrics of three genres of contemporary music. *Sex Roles*, 4(1), 51–65.

Friesen, B. K. (1986) Labelling youth cultures deviant: traditional gender roles in heavy metal. Unpublished master's thesis, Department of Sociology, University of Calgary.

Friesen, B. K. (1990) Powerlessness in adolescence: exploiting heavy metal listeners. In C. R. Saunders (ed.), *Marginal Conventions: Popular Culture, Mass Media and Social Deviance*. Bowling Green, OH: Bowling Green University Press, pp. 65–77.

Friesen, B. K. and Epstein, J. S. (1994) Rock 'n' roll ain't noise pollution: artistic conventions and tensions in the major sub-genres of heavy metal music. *Journal of Popular Music*, 18(3), 1–18.

Harding, D. and Nett, E. (1984) Women and rock music. *Atlantis*, 10(1), 61–71.

Harrell, J. (1994) The poetics of destruction: death metal rock. *Popular Music and Society*, 18(1), 91–103.

Herman, G. (1982) *Rock 'n' Roll Babylon*. London: Plexus.

Hirsch, P. (1971) Sociological approaches to the pop music phenomenon. *American Behavioral Scientist*, 14, 371–88.

Kotarba, J. A. (1994) The postmodernization of rock and roll music; the case of Metallica. In J. S. Epstein (ed.), *Adolescents and Their Music: If It's Too Loud, You're Too Old*. New York: Garland, pp. 141–63.

Ling, J. (1984) The sociology of music. *Canadian University Music Review*, 5, 1–16.

Murphy, T. (1989) The when, where, and who of pop lyrics: the listener's prerogative. *Popular Music*, 8(2), 185–93.

Rosenbaum, J. and Prinsky, L. (1987) Sex, violence and rock 'n' roll: youths' perceptions of popular music. *Popular Music and Society*, 11(2), 79–89.

Shapiro, H. (1988) *Waiting for the Man: the Story of Drugs and Popular Music*. New York: William Morrow.

Straw, W. (1984) Characterizing rock music cultures: the case of heavy metal. *Canadian University Music Review*, 5, 104–22.

Tanner, J. (1981) Pop music and peer groups: a study of Canadian high school students' responses to pop music. *Canadian Review of Sociology and Anthropology*, 18(1), 1–13.

Thaxton, L. and Jaret, C. (1985) Singers and stereotypes: the image of female recording artists. *Sociological Inquiry*, 55(3), 239–63.

Verden, P., Dunleavy, K. and Powers, C. (1989) Heavy metal mania and adolescent delinquency. *Popular Music and Society*, 13(1), 73–82.

Walser, R. (1993) *Running with the Devil: Power, Gender, and Madness in Heavy Metal Music*. Hanover, NH: Wesleyan University Press.

Weinstein, D. (1991) *Heavy Metal: a Cultural Sociology*. New York: Lexington.

13
INCUBUS: MALE SONGWRITERS' PORTRAYAL OF WOMEN'S SEXUALITY IN POP METAL MUSIC

Lisa J. Sloat

When rock music burst on to the scene in the 1950s, three primary elements combined to create the image of rock and roll in America: youth, rebellion, and sex. Few would disagree that sexuality became a central focus of both the opposition to rock and the musical genre itself. Indeed, the phrase "rock and roll" served as a euphemism for sexual intercourse in blues music, one of the foundations of rock.[1] Rock capitalized on its incorporation of blues sexuality because, when it became a legitimate genre, singing about sex was "one of the surest ways to rattle adults."[2] If the reaction of the Parents Music Resource Center when it condemned rock music as "glorifying rape,"[3] as well as "sexual promiscuity and perversion,"[4] is any indication, singing about sex still rattled adults thirty years later. As rock developed into numerous subgenres over those years, sex remained a vital part of each. This chapter will focus on sexuality in heavy metal, specifically the portrayal of women's sexuality by male songwriters within pop/lite metal, that segment of metal most concerned with creating radio-friendly singles. I contend that specific women mentioned serve as a reflection of women in general, and therefore depictions of individual women apply to all women.

In pop metal, depictions of women vary, but not to much degree. Women suffer degradation, violation, and even violence. Moreover, songwriters portray women as deserving of such treatment and as voluntarily degrading themselves in order to please men. Women are depicted as obsessive, evil, dangerous, and downright deadly, particularly if their powers of sex in some way threaten men. The male reaction to this perceived threat is misogynous at best, brutal in some cases. I will examine the most obvious of these depictions by analyzing lyrics containing the aforementioned themes, while not losing sight of the fact that the subject matter is entertainment. Although not all songs and bands have achieved the success of others, that success was the goal and the musical styles are all within the same genre, so lesser known works will be given the same attention as better known ones. In addition, the songs cited provide the best examples of these portrayals, regardless of whether they were the most popular. For the sake of space, only small portions of each song will be included. At the end of the chapter, a discography is included for additional research information.

Perhaps the most common role assigned to women in pop metal is that of sex toy, meant only for the pleasure of men. In "Tonight, We Need a Lover," Motley Crüe sing of a woman in these terms. Her value is in fact reduced to one line: "the question is will you please us all tonight?" Indeed, the woman in this song serves only as a receptacle for seminal fluid, as the band members intend to "fill the cup to the top." She seems willing to copulate with all four men, even sexually aroused at the thought, as indicated in the description of "honey dripping from her pot," a metaphor for female vaginal lubrication associated with sexual excitement or anticipation. The stardom as aphrodisiac aspect appears in this song with the use of the phrase "ninety-thousand screaming watts." Bands that produce 90,000 watts of power when they perform would appear in stadiums or arenas, venues that they can fill with fans. Therefore, this term represents both the band's literal and symbolic fame and power, power obviously used to gain sexual access to women.

"Little Dove" by Faster Pussycat is one of few songs containing any reference to a man's desire to sexually please a woman. He desires to please her, however, by ejaculating in or on her, rather than capturing his "oil of love" in a condom. "The high-heeled river of love dripping down your thighs" shows him that she is "finally satisfied" after his orgasm inside her. In this song too, women serve only as receptacles. Her own orgasm, or lack thereof, remains unimportant, since his orgasm provides her pleasure. "She's a super-sexed junkie for money," who has sex "for fame" and "prefers cash to a hot seat on the dating game." This description implies not only her attraction to famous men – lucky break for the band members isn't it? – but also her preference for prostituting herself rather than seeking a relationship. This further degrades her symbolic position in the sex act.

In the Jackyl song "Rock-a-Ho," women are seen as prizes for men's heroics, with no identity aside from this objectification; they exist so the "Indian warrior" can take all he wants from them. That he is "always moving over and sliding it in" indicates that he sees women as primarily valuable for his pleasure, existing so that he can "feel myself a coming between your thighs." The song further emphasizes this narrow view of women's usefulness when he promises "I'll use you up and then I'll throw you away." His desire to dominate her sexuality appears when the line "pumping like a diesel, stopping on a dime," which had been used to describe him, becomes "pump you like a diesel, stop you on a dime,' to show the control he exerts over her body. His behavior is excused in the song with the statement "I've been a bad boy for such a long time."

The woman Jackyl describe in "She Loves My Cock" is the victim of a double standard. His objectification of his penis is acceptable; her objectification of his penis is whorish, although ego-boosting. She is described as having been "all around the block" after having sex with many different types of men. But never fear, even though "there's as many hands on her as a knob on a door," he still finds her attractive because she is "such a pretty pretty pretty little whore." The line "she's got to find a bigger jerk; she's got to have his jiz" indicates that her goal is semen collection, to be a man's receptacle. Indeed, she willingly degrades herself for the honor of becoming his receptacle, because she will "walk thru the flames of hell" to gain access to his penis. This implies that in return for the right to serve as receptacle, women should beg and degrade themselves. Jesse James Dupree, lead singer for Jackyl, says the song "is meant to be tongue in cheek . . . We think it is arrogant for a man to say that about a woman. The song was done in fun."[5] Yet it will be heard by many people who have never read Dupree's comment and may take it more seriously.

In "She Goes Down," Motley Crüe again depict a woman as valuable only if her goal is pleasing a man. "She makes me feel good, just like a bad girl should" implies that women should concern themselves not with their own pleasure but with that of men. The concept of a "bad" girl, tainted by her ability to perform sexually, as desirable translates to serve as a goal for all women. Descriptions of where, when, and with whom she will perform further imply her "badness." This reference to her promiscuity shows that sex is her primary goal, and therefore her primary value. The aspect of stardom as aphrodisiac combines with her degradation to show how truly low she is, in the line "for a backstage pass, she goes down." In order to obtain such passes, women must perform sexual favors for security guards and crew members who can get the women into the backstage areas. These men are, as the fictional headbanging characters Wayne and Garth of *Saturday Night Live* and *Wayne's World* fame would say, "at the bottom of the babe food chain," the dregs of the rock and roll world. This reference further solidifies her willingness to degrade herself for the pleasure of men, regardless of their status in the class structure of rock and roll, particularly if such self-degradation will provide access to stars. And as a special bonus for those women who aren't "bad" enough to know how to please men, Motley Crüe thoughtfully provide instructions on how to properly perform fellatio, telling us to "start at the bottom and lick it to the top."

In Extreme's song "Suzi (Wants Her All Day What?)," Suzi's obsession with fellatio keeps her awake at night. The line "she's got her tongue in cheek" brings to mind the image of an old west gunslinger with his weapon at the ready. She appears willing to perform on demand, at the drop of a hat, much like the subject of "She Goes Down." The image of a man's penis as "hard rock candy" and as an all day sucker, combined with the idea of semen as a "bitter tasting treat," implies that Suzi enjoys performing oral sex for extended periods of time and desires a man to ejaculate in her mouth. Even if she dislikes the bitter taste, she willingly swallows this treat. Suzi is undoubtedly a dream woman to the adolescent males who comprise the primary audience for metal. Women still serve as receptacles; their opening simply moved from their vaginas to their mouth. In this song, Suzi not only enjoys fellatio, she appears to beg for the opportunity to perform it, only receives that opportunity if she says "pretty please," and is warned to "mind your manners" lest he not allow her to serve as his receptacle. This implies that men should dominate sexual situations by consenting to the act only if women beg and degrade themselves. The image of women's sexual power as dangerous arises when he is reassured that "she doesn't bite." Additionally, the image of her as Little Red Riding Hood and him as the Big Bad Wolf indicates that although the man may appear to hold the power in this exchange, Suzi's sexuality is the real power, since she could indeed bite and victimize him.

Where Extreme implied that Suzi was a dream woman, Lord Tracy – a band that derived its name from that of pornography actress Traci Lords – take the dream two steps further by adding two heads to the woman in "3 HC (Headed Chick)." "A wish come true, yeah, a personal dream" for a man should not be an intelligent, caring woman with whom he can share his life, but rather a "chick" with three heads who can perform fellatio in three different ways. When he sings "and then I snapped my fingers and she fell to her knees," his desire for total dominance of her sexuality is evident. Furthermore, she, like Suzi, should think of the taste of his semen as a treat. Lord Tracy seem to fantasize that semen "tastes like Cool Whip topping," but do admit that women think it tastes more like mayonnaise. Taste test results aside, the song portrays women as good for only one thing: sex, in this case oral sex. The only problem with women, it appears, is that they have only one mouth with which to satisfy men. When performing this song live, Lord Tracy encouraged women from the audience to come to the stage, don hard hats, and allow the drummer to pound out the rap rhythm on their heads. Band members often shouted sentiments such as "All right all you bitches, get on your knees!" to the women. The band reported trying this stunt with men, but found the desired effect missing.[6]

In many pop metal songs, women are depicted not only as serving no purpose other than sex but also as being dangerous or deadly, particularly if their power of sex in some way threatens men. That deadly image dominates when Jetboy sing of the evil woman who causes death by love in "Snakebite." "The end comes hard and slow" after she "fills me with her venom." This could be interpreted as meaning that her poison, perhaps injected during sexual intercourse, causes erection and ejaculation, the ultimate loss of physical self-control for a man. His loss of self-control because of her sexuality is what makes her evil and deadly. Even if this more literal interpretation is incorrect, the image of women as poisonous still exists. That she is seen as a snake, an animal which literally is beneath men, implies that she (and all other women) are symbolically beneath men, regardless of the power she may possess in her bite. Furthermore, the songwriter warns her not to attempt using her power of sex against him, lest she be "cut down to size."

Another depiction of sexy women as dangerous to a man's self-preservation exists in Alice Cooper's song "Poison." Only her power of destruction can overshadow her power of sex. He wants to kiss her, but he wants it "too much." Even her mere kiss, the first phase of sexual relations, threatens him. The dichotomy of desire and danger is perfectly illustrated in the line "I want to taste you, but your lips are venomous poison." He very much desires her, but kissing her, touching her, loving her would loose her power of sex and death over him, so he struggles to maintain self-control and to fight off her power. The line "I don't wanna break these chains" suggests that he desires a relationship, desires those emotional ties which would chain him to her, even though such a relationship would mean the death of his independence.

In the case of "Wicked Bitch" by Black 'N' Blue, the fact that "she gets cold" when he is "hot" gives her power over him. He wants her, is sexually aroused by her, but she controls whether he gets her. If she exercises her power of sexuality and rejects his advances, she is "a wicked bitch." Reference to her having his life "at the flick of a switch" indicates that she controls his very existence through her sexual behavior. Her "evil ways burn my soul," meaning that her refusal to have sex with him in some way reduces his own humanity. Women who control their own sexuality, and limit male sexual access to their bodies, are dangerous because they are not controllable and will not submit to the degradation to which men wish to subject them.

In "Looks that Kill," by Motley Crüe, death represents the woman's overwhelming power of sex. The line "well she's razor sharp" establishes her sexuality as a tangible, violent, instrument of destruction. Her power is so lethal, in fact, that he need not even kiss her, a mere gaze in her direction causes death by her sexuality; after all, "she's got the looks that kill." Also, "she moves like a cat," stealthily, without any noise; this indicates that she is sneaky and predatory, and therefore even more dangerous. Her ultimate control appears with the warning "if she's gonna turn on your juice boy" (semen), "then she'll turn on her power" (sex). It also appears in the threats that "if she don't get her way well she'll tear you apart," and "if you don't get her game well you might not make it back." Again, women controlling their own sexuality, who are desirable but not submissive, are dangerous to the men who encounter them.

Another Jetboy song, "Evil," offers a more realistic view: the evil isn't necessarily the woman, but rather the feelings men may not want to face, such as love. In this song, women represent "a strength that overpowers" men. The fear of women results from the confusion of coping with love and intimacy as depicted in the lines "is it love or evil that's inside me?/It's not really evil, but love I fear/I don't know." Even though this is the case, fear is directed at the woman because "she's an angel to hold, but man she's evil." This makes her, and not the love she offers, the dark figure in the relationship. Women are more than just evil and dangerous in this song; they are poisonous as well. The desire/death dichotomy is evident in the line "she may be candy maybe poison," establishing that the power of women's sexuality causes symbolic and literal death for men.

In pop metal, the male reaction to women, dangerous or not, is sometimes violent. In "Where There's a Whip, There's a Way," Faster Pussycat portray a man's right to dominate and brutalize women through sado-masochistic sex. The mention in this song of "sweet beating dreams," and the idea that a "slap on the ass should make her eyes glow," indicate that women desire violent treatment, even enjoy it sexually. Regardless of the pain and humiliation, "the devil in she" likes it. Although the woman screams "like a poodle on a leash" to be let go, she wants to be degraded, bruised, and beaten. He tells her she'd "better start talking," indicating that she must in some way talk him out of harming her, putting her in a position of total submission to him. The line that defines him as "the dehumanizing master" also defines her as the dehumanized slave.

Sexual violence as enjoyable for women is also glorified in "Eat Me Alive' by Judas Priest. This song depicts brutality and rape, when he promises "I'm going to force you at gun point to eat me alive." In other songs examined so far, women longed for fellatio; in this song, they long for forced fellatio. She begins "squealing with passion when the rod of steel injects," indicating that his orgasm provides her pleasure, even as he rapes her.

Other bands often mention Judas Priest as an influence on their music or their choice of music as a career, but how much this band influenced these young males in their interpersonal relationships is still unknown.

Great White in "On Your Knees" also emphasize sexual violence as pleasurable to both partners. When he sings "kicking in your door . . . pull you to the floor," there is little doubt that rape is his motivation, but it is excused because he insists on "taking what I choose." It becomes his right, and therefore the right of all men, to rape women if that is what they choose. She will, according to him, enjoy it "from the moment I take over" and will "call me back for more" of the same, because "you need it so bad." He plans total domination of the women when he promises to "nail your ass to the floor" by "driving my love inside you." To further emphasize the point of female submission, the phrase "down on your knees" is repeated three dozen times throughout the song.

Although specific sexually violent acts are not mentioned in "Tainted Angel," the song refers to the man's taking of a woman's virginity and the total dominance of her sexuality by men. She did not offer her virginity to him: instead "he took her wings away"; it is his prerogative to deflower her, if he wants. The phrase also reinforces the idea that women who have sex are spoiled, somehow dirty, yet desirable. The man fears that her father will "take back paradise," not allow him to see her again, if he discovers the man "took a bite" from the apple of daddy's eye. The implication is that she does not control her own sexuality; her father and boyfriend make her choices for her. Rape is suggested as necessary when he describes her as knowing "what she needs," and as enjoyable to women because rape "put the fire in her eyes" and made her aware of the joys of sex. Butch Walker, one of the song's writers, describes it as a harmless little song.

> That's about this poor little girl losing her virginity. But it's not done in a sleazy, dirty sort of way. We used a lot of metaphors for some of the things that went on – but the message is real clear. If you hear the lyrics, you hear the story of a girl who has some bad intentions; it's a story that everyone can relate to.[7]

Metaphors? There are plenty in this song, most of which indicate that women want to be raped and want men to control their sexuality.

Guns 'n' Roses do not portray sexual violence in "Used to Love Her," but violence is still shown as a method of resolving conflict between a man and a woman. The liner notes for the album on which this song appears include the following: "A joke, nothing more. Actually, it's pretty self-explanatory if you ask me." Self-explanatory it is. The song even includes the line "Take it for what it is." What it is the portrayal of a man who murders a woman in his life because "she bitched so much, she drove me nuts." It may all be a joke to the band, but to the female victims of domestic violence – including one who claims the lead singer abused her – and the survivors of those who died at the hands of the men they loved, it is no laughing matter.

Although Skid Row do not force the groupie in "Get the Fuck Out" into sex, she still is useful only for that purpose, and faces violence and death threats as a means of controlling her. When he tells her "you ain't my old lady and you ain't a tattoo," the implication is that he wants only sex from her, with no relationship outside of that, no permanence of any kind. The lines "there's nothing you say that I want to hear" and "this party's over so get the fuck out" further illustrate this point. If she will not leave his bed when told, she will be beaten "to a pulp." Indeed, she should simply be gone when he awakes, when her usefulness is finished; if she is not, "the maid is gonna find you dead." The reference to her "walking funny" and the observation that she "must have spent some time with the boys in the crew" further degrades the woman. Sleeping with the star is an honor; sleeping with the road crew makes you trash. (Remember, these men are the lowest of the low in the world of rock and roll.) To emphasize this point, Sebastian Bach, the band's lead singer, spits on the woman at the end of the song. One female reviewer called the song "hilarious"[8] and the band thinks it is as well, as indicated in the spoken line "Fuck you if you can't take a joke." It is doubtful, however, that many people would see threats of violence and death as amusing. According to Bach, in "real life," star-struck groupies have unrealistic expectations of what will happen between themselves and stars when they meet. "They want to fall in love with you and expect you to fall in love with them," Bach laments.[9] (Perhaps this song is Skid Row's wake-up call to these women regarding their value to bands.) This view echoes what books marketed for would-be musicians say about groupies. They are called "blind, unquestioning followers of rock stars,"[10] who seek to exploit musicians instead of the other way around. In fact, one "how to be a rock star" guide warns that groupies are "just waiting to get their clutches into the new blood of rock and roll."[11] It further warns that they are "unhappy, amoral, and determined to score for a number of reasons, out of physical needs or are truly disturbed people."[12]

Why are women viewed as dangerous, obsessive sex toys deserving of violence in these songs? Many possible explanations, excuses, and theories exist, ranging from personal problems of the writers to simple patriarchal misogyny. Axl Rose, whose band Guns'n' Roses are know for the comic-like depiction of a robot violently raping a woman that graced the cover of their first album, until protest forced its move to an inner sleeve, admits a misogynous view of women in simple terms.

> I've been doing a lot of work (in regression therapy) and found out that I've had a lot of hatred for women. Basically, I've been rejected by my mother since I was a baby . . . I've gone back and done the work and found out that I overheard my grandmother going off on men when I was four. And I've had problems with my own masculinity because of that. I was pissed off at my grandmother for her problems with men and how that made me feel about being a man. So I wrote about my feelings in the songs.[13]

Rose, it appears, blames his mother for part of his hatred toward women and his grandmother for the balance. He wrote songs about feelings he didn't realize he had until long after he'd written the songs. Interesting concept. Perhaps he thought of his mother or grandmother when he sang the line "I used to love her, but I had to kill her." Basically, he promotes misogyny because of his own gender-identity difficulties, going back some thirty years or more. Rose's bandmate, Slash, describes women as "a pain in the ass,"[14] and says they "take up too much time and they have their own ideas that they're constantly throwing in your face."[15] Unfortunately for Slash, it seems that too many women have minds of their own.

Giving Rose and Slash the benefit of the doubt, which they may or may not deserve, perhaps there are reasons for men to hate women or at least fear them. Robert Walser supports gender-identification conflict as the root of misogyny in metal music. Existing, as it does, in a culture of capitalistic and patriarchal values, and played primarily by and for young, white males who lack social, physical, and economic power, but are continually beset by messages promoting these types of power, heavy metal attempts to combat insecurities in the listeners by guaranteeing their place within the male-dominated power structure of American culture.[16] This is achieved by providing the adolescent males in the listening audience with an outlet for demonstrating their own power: women. Women become powerless victims in order to keep young males from feeling victimized themselves.

According to Walser, heavy metal "is overwhelmingly concerned with presenting images and confronting anxieties that have been traditionally understood as peculiar to men."[17] Things that cause men to lose self-control, and therefore threaten masculinity, will be seen as dangerous or deadly. In video, and in lyrics as well, women are "presented as essentially mysterious and dangerous; they harm simply by being, for their attractiveness threatens to disrupt both male self-control and the collective strength of male bonding."[18] Therefore, an examination of gender in metal should be an investigation of masculinity. The examination of female roles within metal is resigned to "reception of these male spectacles."[19] Once again, in theory as well as in lyrics, women are passive in this music, mere receptacles for men's actions. Misogyny is excused in heavy metal because of a view that women focus intimacy on relationships which create dependence of each partner on the other.[20] This type of intimacy threatens masculine independence, unlike the male-bonding intimacy which focuses on goals.[21] Heavy metal would ignore women altogether if it were not for fear of creeping toward homoeroticism.[22] So mistreatment of women, from this perspective, is clearly self-defense of threatened masculinity.

In addition to Walser's theory, the simple fact of the matter is that women who reject them are seen as evil by adolescent and even adult males. The sexual frustration resulting from such rejection would make many men willing to accept a fantasy of total control, so that no female will ever again possess the power to reject. Another possible explanation of misogynous images of dangerous and deadly women in pop metal arises if we compare such fantasy images to female rape fantasies. I contend that just as some women will fantasize rape to alleviate the guilt of sex, some men will fantasize dangerous or deadly women to alleviate guilt associated with one night stands, which dominate the sexual interaction in pop metal. Lines like Jetboy's "I've got no choice/'cause good or bad I've got to have her/she's a drug I can't refuse" demonstrate that men have no self-control when facing some women, no power of choice. Female rape victims have no power of choice, no control over what happens to their bodies. Likewise, men who face powerful, deadly, yet very desirable women have no control over how their bodies react. This dangerous woman fantasy also explains the value of women for sex only. Once sex is over, and men regain the self-control they lost to their erections, they "come to their senses," and fight to escape the dangerous threat to their masculinity. Women who fantasize rape don't think of it as the literal, brutal physical attack, but rather as "when Robert Redford won't take no for an answer."[23] Perhaps the dangerous woman fantasy and the raping fantasy are similar: men don't really believe that women can kill with the power of sex, but accept it on a certain level to serve their own purpose: maintaining self-control and masculinity. Nor do they in reality wish to rape women, but on a fantasy level it provides relief from the sting of rejection.

And while this type of misogyny may appear rampant in pop metal, it has existed in rock music, just as sex has, since its inception. One historic incident occured in the late 1970s, when the Rolling Stones outraged feminists everywhere with the advertising copy for their album *Black and Blue*. The billboard ad showed a woman, scantily clad, bruised, and bound with the legend "I'm black and blue from the Rolling Stones and I love it."[24] the billboard created such a furor that the California chapter of the National Organization for Women and Women Against Violoence Against Women threatened to boycott the parent company of the band's label over this and other ads portraying women as victims of abuse.[25] There also exists a large contingent of songs which focus on sex or women without being particularly blatant or derogatory. Bands such as KISS and Aerosmith sing of sex in many songs, but none seem to specifically degrade women as some of the songs examined here do. Admittedly, it is somewhat degrading when Steven Tyler of Aerosmith sings "let's put our clothes back on and by the way girl, what's your name again?" in "FINE," but at least he wants to know.

Yet sex-oriented lyrics are not the only lyrics that exist in pop metal. Some songs depict the dangers of drugs or the effect of social ills on our world. Others praise the fun of going out on a

Friday night or driving cars really fast. Still others show loving, committed relationships and women depicted not as objects, but as people. They are viewed as inspiring, to be respected and loved, forever. Long-term relationships are seen as worthwhile and desirable; they are no longer seen as a threat, just as women lose that threatening position. Even Skid Row, Guns'n' Roses, and Motley Crüe, who have sung of sexual violence, groupies, and women's value as purely sexual, have hearts, it seems.

Which portrayal of women is most common in pop metal? Undying love? Dangerous sex toys? That depends on which band is examined, which songs are examined, and at what point in the evolution of the band and the genre those two exist. Nikki Sixx of Motley Crüe called the band's earlier recordings "cheeseball crap,"[26] compared to the music they produced after ten years in the music industry. Overall, the balance between sex songs and love songs is fairly even, with most bands recording both types. How much either type of depiction actually reflects a songwriter or artist's own views of women is open to debate. Songs with lyrics are little more than pop culture poetry with instrumental backing. When viewed from this perspective, pop metal songwriters become the poets of a youth subculture. Perhaps like poetry, what they write should be interpreted with scant connection to "real life" situations and attitudes, and with a liberal dose of artistic license. Maybe specific songs should be seen as how one songwriter felt at one time, when he wrote that specific song. It does not have to be interpreted as how he feels 24 hours a day. One misogynous feeling is one flash of anger. One feeling of danger from a woman's presence is one moment of fear for his self-control. One loving sentiment is one moment of opening his heart to a woman. Song writers are humans, and their emotions run the same gamut of possibilities as everyone else's.

Female songwriters in pop metal are rare. Even when the genre was at its highest point of popularity, women were never within the accepted social structure. remember, heavy metal is specifically concerned with things male. Women seem to depict themselves in much the same way as male songwriters do. The only significant difference is that songs by women focus more on relationships and less on specific sexual acts. Sexual pleasure doesn't belong to anyone because it is seldom mentioned at all, and the mistreatment revolves around betrayal, not sexual violence. More research needs to be done in this area, however, before specific songs and patterns can be discussed.

It is important to remember that music is entertainment meant for the masses. Bands don't survive if they don't sell albums. So if exploiting women for sex sells, musicians will record songs which do so. When casual sex goes out of vogue, as it seems to have, at least publicly, since AIDS became a threat to all sexual orientations, popular songs may focus more on long-term relationships. Trends change quickly in the realm of popular music and bands that don't keep up with what fans want quickly find themselves without incomes. As culture became more "politically correct" in the 1990s and as women in music began appearing more frequently as strong and self-reliant, degradation of women became less acceptable. It was also about this time that the popularity of pop metal began to wane as music once again evolved into a new form. Artists that adapted to the changing times still do fairly well with each album they release. Those that didn't adapt content- and style-wise to the changing trends quickly disappeared. Where pop metal songwriters, male or female, would have gone with women's sexuality will never be known.

Discography

Artist (label)	Song title	Album (year)	Author(s)
Aerosmith (Geffen)	FINE	*Pump* (1989)	Tyler, Perry, Child
Black 'N' Blue (Geffen)	Wicked Bitch	*Black 'N' Blue* (1984)	None listed
Cooper, Alice (CBS)	Poison	*Trash* (1989)	Cooper, Child Frazier, Sever
Extreme (A&M)	Suzi (Wants Her All Day What?)	*Exteme II: Pornograffitti* (1990)	Bettencourt, Cherone
Faster Pussycat (Elektra)	Little Dove	*Wake Me When It's Over* (1989)	Downe, Muscat
Faster Pussycat (Elektra)	Where There's a Whip There's a Way	*Wake Me When It's Over* (1989)	Downe, Muscat, Steel

Artist (label)	Song title	Album (year)	Author(s)
Great White (EMI)	On Your Knees	*Great White* (1984)	None listed
Guns 'n' Roses (Geffen)	Used to Love Her	*Lies* (1988)	Guns n'Roses
Jackyl (Geffen)	Rock-A-Ho	*Push Comes to Shove* (1994)	Dupree, Worley, Worley
Jackyl (Geffen)	She Loves My Cock	*Jackyl* (1992)	Dupree
Jetboy (MCA)	Evil	*Damned Nation* (1990)	Finn, Rod, Yaffa, Mitchell
Jetboy (MCA)	Snakebite	*Feel the Shake* (1988)	Finn, Rowe
Judas Priest (CBS)	Eat Me Alive	*Defenders of the Faith* (1984)	None listed
Lord Tracy (Uni)	3HC	*Deaf Gods of Babylon* (1989)	None listed
Motley Crüe (Elektra)	Looks that Kill	*Shout at the Devil* (1983)	Sixx
Motley Crüe (Elektra)	She Goes Down	*Dr Feelgood* (1989)	Sixx, Marrs
Motley Crüe (Elektra)	Tonight (We Need a Lover)	*Theatre of Pain* (1985)	Sixx
Skid Row (Atlantic)	Get the Fuck Out	*Slave to the Grind* (1991)	Bolan, Sabo
Southgang (Charisma)	Tainted Angel	*Tainted Angel* (1991)	Walker, Harte, Child

Notes and References

1   D. P. Szatmary (1995) *Rockin' in Time: a Social History of Rock and Roll*. Englewood Cliffs, NJ: Prentice Hall, p. 15.

2   L. Martin and K. Segrave (1994) *Anti-rock: the Opposition to Rock 'n' Roll*. New York: Da Capo Press, p. 115.

3   J. Cocks (1985) Rock is a four letter word. *Time*. September 30, 70.

4   T. Moran (1985) Sounds of sex. *The New Republic*, August 12–19, 15.

5   S. Ross (1993) Jackyl's Jesse Dupree takes off all his shackles. *Playgirl*, August, 809.

6   K. Neely (1990) New faces: Lord Tracy. *Rolling Stone*, April 19, 29.

7   A. Secher (1991) Southgang: they're no angels. *Hit Parader*, September, 44.

8   K. Neely (1991) Gunners launch tour. *Rolling Stone*, July 11–25, 18.

9   P. Hunter (1990) Skid Row: guilty as charged. *Hit Parader*, April, 23.

10   B. Kinder (1991) *The Best of the First: the Early Days of Rock and Roll*. Chicago: Adams Press, p. 41.

11   S. Lawrence (1989) *So You Want to Be a Rock and Roll Star*. New York: McGraw-Hill Paperbacks, p. 204.

12   Ibid., pp. 204–5.

13   K. Neely (1992) The Rolling Stone interview. *Rolling Stone*, April 2, 36.

14   P. Elliot (1994) *Guns-n-Roses: the World's Most Dangerous Hard Rock Band*. London: Hamlyn, p. 15.

15   Ibid.

16   R. Walser (1993) *Running with the Devil: Power, Gender, and Madness in Heavy Metal Music*. Hanover, NH: Wesleyan University Press, University Press of New England, p. 109.

17   Ibid., p. 100.

18   Ibid., p. 118.

19   Ibid., p. 110.

20   Ibid., p. 115.

21   Ibid.

22   Ibid., p. 116.

23   P. J. Caplan, *The Myth of Women's Masochism*. New York: E. P. Dutton, p. 154.

24   A. E. Hotchner (1994) *Blown Away*. New York: Simon & Schuster, number 32 in photo insert.

25   Martin and Segrave, op. cit., n. 2, p. 275.

26   K. Estland (1994) Motley Crue: brand new heavy. *Rip*, March, 38.

14
EXPLORATIONS IN YOUTH CULTURE. AMATEUR STRIPPING: WHAT WE KNOW AND WHAT WE DON'T

Thomas C. Calhoun, Julie Ann Harms Cannon and Rhonda Fisher

Introduction

Amateur stripping is a contemporary social phenomenon that has undergone only limited empirical investigation (Calhoun et al., 1997). We define amateurs as those individuals, male or female, who engage in stripping as a recreational activity rather than as a primary occupation. Unlike professional female and male stripping, very little is known about the motivations of amateur strippers. Specifically, why do young men and women take off their clothes in public with no guarantee of financial reward?

Simmel (1950) discusses the ways in which urban life alters individual interaction patterns and the expression of individuality. Specifically, there is a movement from the slower, more predictable pace of rural life, to the more stimulating and un-predictable nature of urban existence. This movement creates the need for individual protective mechanisms. As individuals develop their intellectual reasoning skills, they begin to utilize fewer emotional skills when dealing with others. In this sense, individual interactions become less personal and increasingly more rational or calculating. According to Simmel (1950), this is evident in the development of a "money economy."

The money economy also serves an additional and more personal function. Simmel (1950) argues that "The same factors which have thus coalesced into the exactness and minute precision of the form of life have coalesced into a structure of the highest impersonality; on the other hand, they have promoted a highly personal subjectivity" (p. 413). This increased personal subjectivity is what Simmel labels "the blase attitude" (p. 413). The blase attitude protects individuals from the uncertainties of urban living. This protective mechanism prevents the nervous deterioration of those faced with the multiple stimuli encountered in metropolitan areas. Thus, "The essence of the blase attitude consists in the blunting of discrimination" (Simmel, 1950, p. 414).

Although the blase attitude is functional in terms of self-preservation, it also has a negative effect in terms of individual self-worth and personal interaction. Simmel (1950, p. 415) writes:

> The self-preservation of certain personalities is bought at the price of devaluating the whole objective world, a devaluation which in the end unavoidably drags one's own personality down into a feeling of the same worthlessness.

Distance, particularly distrust, between individuals in the city increases. This negative component leads to greater individual development than was previously acceptable in rural life.

Simultaneously, urban living begins to silence individual expression through alienation. "The individual has become a mere cog in an enormous organization of things and powers which tear from his hands all progress, spiritually, and value in order to transform them from their subjective form into the form of purely objective life" (Simmel, 1950, p. 422). To combat this alienation from the subjective world individuals begin to capitalize on their uniqueness. Every effort is made to stand out from the crowd. "[I]n order to preserve his most personal core" the individual must overcome the objective demands of metropolitan life and "exaggerate this personal element to remain audible even to himself" (Simmel, 1950, p. 422).

The need to stand out is an important facet of urban living; however, this task may be particularly difficult for youth. We argue that youth may in fact utilize amateur stripping as a forum for this more personal expression of self which Simmel describes, due to a lack of more publicly available or socially acceptable territories.

Before evaluating the applicability of Simmel's macro level analysis of youth culture and urban life to the study of amateur stripping, we must first identify what is known about professional stripping, particularly as it relates to individual motivations and the use of body territories. To facilitate this analysis we turn to the work of Lyman and Scott (1970).

Literature Review

Motivations

Lyman and Scott (1970) are particularly interested in the mechanisms that make society possible. When behavior falls outside normative parameters, individuals are required to account for their actions. Specifically, accounts are utilized when individual actions are "subjected to valuative inquiry" (Lyman and Scott, 1970, p. 112).

Lyman and Scott (1970) identify two types of accounts, "excuses" and "justifications." "Excuses are accounts in which one admits that the act in question is bad, wrong, or inappropriate but denies full responsibility" (p. 114). Justifications differ from excuses. "Justifications are accounts in which one accepts responsibility for the act in question, but denies the pejorative quality associated with it" (p. 114). Lyman and Scott identify several justifications that are contained in the work of Sykes and Matza (1957). Their "neutralization techniques" include: (a) denial of injury; (b) denial of victim; (c) condemnation of the condemners; and (d) the appeal to loyalties.

Two further types of justifications, also identified by Lyman and Scott (1970), have particular relevance for the study of stripping behavior. These include invocations of "sad tales" and descriptions of "self-fulfillment." In a sad tale, the individual talks about a problematic past that contributed to the behavior in question. The self-fulfillment justification is actually a "personal growth" explanation in which individuals claim to gain personal insight from their behavior.

Professional stripping literature has mainly focused on the external rewards of stripping. For professional strippers, male and female, economic gain appears to be the primary motivation for engaging in this behavior (Skipper and McCaghy, 1970; Carey et al., 1974; Dressel and Peterson, 1982b; Peterson and Dressel, 1982; Ronai and Ellis, 1989; Reid et al., 1994a,b). Female strippers typically cite financial crises as the impetus for entering the occupation of professional stripping. For these women, stripping becomes their sole means of economic support (Skipper and McCaghy, 1970).

Interestingly, male strippers offer alternative accounts of their movement into professional stripping. Specifically, male strippers do not typically view stripping as a primary occupation (Dressel and Peterson, 1982b). Rather, they utilize the professional stripping scene as a sexual outlet and source of pleasure (i.e. easy access to women, gifts, and excitement). Further, male strippers often view this extra-occupational venture as a way to move into another form of professional entertainment.

Interestingly, while male strippers endeavor to justify their stripping behavior, female strippers attempt to reduce the stigma surrounding the occupation (Mullen, 1985; Thompson and Harred, 1992). Justification strategies developed by male strippers include: (a) stripping provides liberated women with a social outlet; (b) male stripping provides women with an environment in which they can be sexually assertive; (c) stripping can be viewed as a sexual outlet for women who would otherwise not have partners; and (d) stripping is a unique form of commercial entertainment (Dressel and Peterson, 1982b). In addition to providing a sexual outlet and commercial entertainment, women's justifications include an instructional aspect. Strippers are often approached by women seeking sexual advice (Boles and Garbin, 1974).

Body Territory and Exploitation

In American society where territorial encroachment affects nearly all members of society, certain segments of the population are particularly deprived, namely, Negroes, women, *youth* [emphasis added], and inmates of various kinds. (Lyman and Scott, 1970, p. 90).

The establishment of group territories is essential in the formation of specific group identities and the enactment of some rituals or group behaviors which "run counter to expected [societal] norms" (Lyman and Scott, 1970, p. 90). Lyman and Scott identify four types of territories that individuals and groups may claim: (a) public territories; (b) home territories; (c) interactional territories; and (d) body territories.

First, "public territories" are those areas that are available to all individuals and groups for the most part (although restrictions sometimes apply). However, while access is technically unlimited, specific behavioral norms generally apply to all who wish to enter. Public areas are also governed by law, and access is limited at times for specific segments of the population. It is expected that people will follow the established rules and laws in public areas.

Lyman and Scott (1970) note the ambiguous nature of public territories. What appears to be public on the outside may actually be strongly regulated or limited by local custom. Further, status may also be a limiting factor. Those of a particular status group may be turned away from some public territories. Finally, customs or laws may change. A forbidden behavior may become legal or a once legal activity may be prohibited. Currently, it is legal to dance nude in some bars or clubs, although the same behavior would be illegal outside that territory.

A second type of territory designated by Lyman and Scott is the "home territory." Home territories are much more personal in nature than public territories. They are characterized by greater group freedom, control, and intimacy. However, the two territories (public and home) may be confused, because some may be using a space as a home territory while another group uses it as a public territory. As Lyman and Scott (1970, pp. 93–4) note, "It is precisely because of their officially open condition that public areas are vulnerable to conversion into home territories."

"Interactional territories" are identified as a third category by Lyman and Scott. Typically, these include "any area where a social gathering may occur. Surrounding any interaction is an invisible boundary, a kind of social membrane . . . Interactional territories are characteristically mobile and fragile" (Lyman and

Scott, 1970, p. 95) because of changes in social status and the intrusion of "newcomers."

Finally, and most importantly for this work, Lyman and Scott explicate the nature of "body territories." Of all territory types, body territories are the most private. A body territory includes "the space encompassed by the human body and the anatomical space of the body" (Lyman and Scott, 1970, p. 96). Accordingly, body space is more sacred than other territory types. Access, in terms of viewing and touching, is quite limited and in many cases regulated by law. However, bodies may be utilized as symbols of individual or group identity. Through specific body alterations, personal space may be used to express "individuality and freedom" (Lyman and Scott, 1970, p. 98).

Although bodies can be utilized as sites for personal expressions of individuality, they can also be exploited. In the case of professional stripping, male and female bodies are not commodified equally. Professional stripping, an occupation that has traditionally been done by women for men, serves as a glaring example of overt sexism in this society. In a move toward pseudo-egalitarianism, women have only recently been allowed access to the world of commercialized sex-related entertainment through the male strip show. Since the mid to late 1970s, more bars and nightclubs have begun to feature male strippers and research has begun to explore the differences (Dressel and Peterson, 1982a,b; Peterson and Dressel, 1982; Margolis and Arnold, 1993).

The primary differences between male and female professional stripping environments can be found in the setting and in the audience. Peterson and Dressel (1982) noted that male strip clubs propagate the notion of the "egalitarian motif:" the opportunity to be like men in terms of aggressive sexual behavior representing a form of equal rights for women.

Margolis and Arnold (1993) challenge the notion of egalitarianism in a comparison of male strip shows and the more traditional ones which feature female dancers. They hypothesize that if the male strip show is a true inversion of traditional gender hierarchy, then "it should be a mirror image of the female strip show with only the sex of the performers and the audience reversed" (p. 335). Margolis and Arnold detail the following factors regarding male strippers, which demonstrate that the role reversal is illusory: male dancers are depicted as sexual aggressors; they interact only as performers and not as waiting staff; their job is one which evokes interest because of its novelty; they are referred to as artistic and sexy versus a whore or a slut; and they are compensated more financially.

Research on stripping has also included a focus on interaction patterns between strippers, customers, managers, bouncers, and announcers, as well as occupational norms (McCaghy and Skipper, 1969; Skipper and McCaghy, 1970; Carey et al., 1974; Dressel and Peterson, 1982b; Peterson and Dressel, 1982; Peretti and O'Connor 1989; Ronai and Ellis, 1989). The types of settings and methods of entertainment determined the interaction strategies and occupational normal of the strippers.

The "homosocial setting" (Peterson and Dressel, 1982), which is typically and frequently mandatory in male strip clubs, is also typical of bars which feature female strippers, and provides a supportive environment for the expression of socially constructed traditional and nontraditional gender roles. For example, in the female stripping environment the audience members (primarily men) are encouraged to play out traditionally masculine gender roles, while in the male stripping environment the audience members (primarily female) are encouraged to transcend traditionally female gender roles and take on sexually assertive behavior which is typically associated with the male gender role (Peterson and Dressel, 1982).

Further, the confirmation of gender roles (traditional or nontraditional) is also demonstrated through the use of exaggerated "heterosexual imagery" (Peterson and Dressel, 1982). Through the use of props and costumes (firefighter, construction worker, Tarzan, Superman, etc.) male strippers seek to magnify and personalize heterosexuality. This heterosexual imagery is a crucial element of the homosocial setting (Peterson and Dressel, 1982).

Treatment of interaction strategies identified in the literature dealt primarily with customer–stripper interactions, where their purpose was to maximize financial gain for the strippers. This is frequently carried out through the manipulation of the body. Financial gain is increased by a strategy labeled "counterfeiting of intimacy" (Boles and Garbin, 1974; Enck and Preston, 1988), in which the strippers pretend to actually care about or desire a relationship with the customer in order to get more money.

For both male and female professional strippers, spatial intimacy or close proximity to the customer tends to be the most lucrative form of interaction. Variations of table dancing appeared to be the most efficient breakdown of social distance between the customer and the stripper (Boles and Garbin, 1974; Peterson and Dressel, 1982; Ronai and Ellis, 1989). However, some strippers are actually interested in maintaining relationships with customers that go beyond the stripping situation (Dressel and Peterson, 1982a,b; Peterson and Dressel, 1982; Ronai and Ellis, 1989). These relationships are usually sexual in nature, and frequently involve prostitution (Barron, 1989).

Given what the literature suggests generally about professional stripping behavior – the factors that influence entry and the interactional patterns between strippers and customers – we are now in a position to assess the applicability of Simmel's theoretical framework in explaining amateur stripping behavior. Specifically, the purpose of this chapter is to broaden our theoretical understanding of amateur stripping behavior framed by Simmel's theoretical presuppositions about youth culture.

Methodology

Subjects and Setting

Amateur strip night occurs each Thursday at a bar known as Kato's.[1] In this large Midwestern city, Thursday is the main night out for college students. At Kato's there are two contests taking place. The men's competition begins at approximately 10.30 p.m. and the women's competition begins shortly after the men's competition is completed.

During our eight-month investigation we were able to observe, on an average evening, five male and five female participants in the dance contest weekly. Some nights the number of participants in each contest were as high as 11. Only on one occasion did the number of participants fall below three per contest.

The participants in their study are ten men (five white, three African American, one Hispanic, one Asian) and nine women (five white, one African American, one Hispanic, two Asian) who performed in the dance contest at Kato's on at least one occasion, although many perform quite regularly. The age range of the male participants is 21–32, with a mean age of 25. The age range of the female participants is 21–27, with a mean age of 23.

Although we observed many performances during the course of our investigation, the findings are primarily informed by the 19 individuals who agreed to participate in the study. We made numerous attempts to contact dance participants after the competitions; however, many were unwilling to take part in our research. Specifically, women were generally less willing to be interviewed than men. At the initial request, most women were somewhat reticent and had obviously heard a variety of "pick-up lines." Men, however, responded favorably because they believed it was a "pick-up line," yet several men also refused to be interviewed even after numerous attempts were made by the researchers. Although many women agreed to participate after our credentials were confirmed, several women declined immediately due to continued harassment by audience members.

Additionally, several of the participants consider themselves to be "professional" strippers (i.e. they consider stripping to be their primary source of income). Anyone who pays the $2 cover charge upon entry can participate in the competition. Each contest carries a cash prize – $100 for first, $50 for second, and $25 for third place.

The atmosphere at Kato's is quite similar to that of a typical nightclub or disco. The lighting is dim, the music is loud, and the dance floor is the main attraction. Alcohol is available from the beer stand at the main entrance and from bars on the first and second levels. Customers may be seated at tables or booths located on both levels. The dance floor is on the first level, and this is where most customers seek seating (many arrive early to obtain seating closest to the dance floor). The second floor has a balcony overlooking the dance floor and those preferring it, or who cannot find seating on the first floor, sit and look on from above. The activity on the second level is less specifically focused on the contest. It is often difficult to obtain a good view of the competition from this location. Dancing occurs before and immediately following the stripping contests. Finally, customers may play pool at any time during the evening on either floor, even while the dance contest is in progress.

Data Collection and Techniques

The data for this study were collected over an eight-month time period from the population of male and female dancers observed at Kato's. During the beginning stages of the project we engaged solely in observational research. It was essential for us to become "regulars" at Kato's. Although note-taking during the competition was somewhat difficult and often focused a great deal of attention on our work, we took this as an opportunity to let customers and staff know about the project. Additionally, once audience members, staff, and participants realized what we were doing at Kato's they were more apt to offer suggestions and observational responses that were quite helpful to our research efforts.

Each of the 19 participants agreed to participate by written consent.[2] The participants were given information regarding the nature of the project during the initial contact and at the time of the interview. Participants were also informed that a copy of the research findings would be available at Kato's upon completion of the project.

Because this study is of a potentially sensitive nature, steps were taken to protect the identities of the participants. Participants were informed that no actual individual names would be utilized in the final report of the research findings, and each participant was told that he or she could refuse to answer any question and that the interview could be terminated at any time during the conversation.

Typically, participants were contacted at Kato's after the amateur stripping competition; however, some contacts were made utilizing snowball sampling techniques. Interviews were conducted at a variety of locations, including our offices, participants' and investigators' residences, restaurants, and professional and amateur stripping establishments. Additionally, a few interviews were conducted over the telephone. Data were collected using a semi-structured interview format. Although all interviews were directed by the interview schedule, conversations were not limited to only the scheduled questions. Participants were encouraged to discuss all aspects of amateur stripping that had the potential for the development of future research. All interviews were audiotaped and completely transcribed for future analyses.

Before we assess the appropriateness of Simmel's theoretical framework in terms of amateur stripping behavior, it is necessary that this behavior be evaluated at the micro level, based upon what the scientific literature currently suggests about professional stripping behavior. To frame this discussion we return to Lyman and Scott's (1970) work on accounts and body territories. Following this discussion, we will turn to Simmel's work on youth culture to examine amateur stripping behavior from a macro perspective.

Findings

Motivational Accounts of Amateur Strippers

As mentioned previously in this work, accounts of stripping behavior have been limited to those offered by professional strippers. Professional strippers document economic need as a primary motivation, while professional male strippers also utilize the profession as a means of achieving future sexual encounters and entertainment career opportunities.

Interestingly, the amateur male accounts are strikingly similar to those offered by professional male strippers. Additionally, amateur women's accounts come closer to the male model, and for the most part do not resonate with the accounts offered by female professional strippers. For this reason, we also present the experiences of a professional female stripper. While amateur women were more likely to use "self-fulfillment" as a justification for stripping, professionals were more likely to utilize "sad tales" (Lyman and Scott, 1970).

Typically, amateur stripping is viewed by male and female performers as a form of recreation or fun. It is also viewed as a form of self-fulfillment. Amateur generally do not believe that they are harming anyone. Rather, stripping is a way to use the body to receive attention and boost self-esteem. Friends, alcohol, and money often play a role in the decision to strip, but for the most part male and female amateurs claim that the final decision is their own. Additionally, stripping is described as an "adrenaline rush."

Sean, a male performer, discusses how he ended up performing for the first time at Kato's:

Interviewer: Why that particular night?
Sean: I was down with a bunch of friends and a bunch of girlfriends and they were pretty much coaching me to do it.

> *I:*   Did they dare you?
>
> *Sean:*   Not really. They just kept giving me a bunch of crap about it.

Although Sean claims responsibility for his actions, he justified his behavior because of his allegiance to his friends. In this sense his justification approximates an "appeal to loyalties." Brad offers a similar account of the night's events that led him to strip at Kato's that very first time:

> *I:*   The first time you took your clothes off, what was your motivation? Was it a dare, a bet, or did alcohol influence you?
>
> *Brad:*   I don't know really. Drinking makes you do stuff like that. And it was the first time I'd been to Kato's and I used to go to dance clubs and stuff like Kato's and I just wanted to find out what it was like dancing in front of people.

When asked if he would consider stripping again Brad replied:

> Yeah, I'm sure I will but like I said I don't know very much. And I don't go for money 'cause I don't need money. I just go for fun. I mean, I just like it, it's pretty cool.

Although Brad does not justify his behavior through an appeal to loyalties, it is also clear that money is not a primary motivating factor. Brad participates in the contest because it is self-fulfilling and fun.

Kyle had friends with him the night he first performed at Kato's. When asked about his motivation(s), he offered the following account:

> I just wanted to do it I guess. The night before I did it at another bar and I did it mostly because it was a fear of mine, getting up in front of an audience.

Similarly to Brad, Kyle finds amateur stripping to be self-fulfilling. He was able to overcome his fear of appearing in public by entering (and winning) the dance contest at Kato's. When asked about how stripping made him feel, Kyle described his participation as an adrenaline rush:

> Well, I always compare it to running out before the football game, before all the players run out. 'Cause you're surrounded by the noise.

However, for some, money is the primary motivation. Kevin discusses how money influenced his decision to strip at Kato's that very first time:

> I had just gotten into town and I had some problems with my car and my cousin was like well, "If you need some extra money . . . I'm sure you could probably win." So he told me about it and I went down there and the first time I went I won.

Additionally, as it turns out, Kevin utilizes his exposure at Kato's to help him get offers for professional stripping jobs (e.g. bachelorette parties):

> That's where Kato's came in. I was stripping at Kato's and they saw me there and liked the way I stripped . . . That was kind of like my advertisement. That's why I went to Kato's.

In this way stripping is actually instrumental for both amateur and professional males. Stripping is a means to future employment in the entertainment industry.

Many of the accounts offered by the female amateurs sound quite similar to those offered by their male counterparts. However, amateur women do not appear to utilize stripping as a sexual outlet or avenue for future employment, which is frequently the case for male amateurs and professionals. Rather, stripping is a way to have fun and experience self-fulfillment. Christie describes her motivation to strip at Kato's for the first time:

> All the energy from by friends that were there. They just, were like, "Oh, Christie, you know you want to do it," you know. Because I've done it at private parties before. My mom doesn't have a clue about that. But I've done it for my friends and I wanted to see what it would be like, in what the atmosphere would be like to do it at a bar. You know, in front of a whole bunch

of strangers instead of a whole bunch of men that you knew.

Specifically, Christie appeals to the loyalty of her friends and the need for self-fulfillment as primary motivations for participating in the contest. Christie stated that alcohol had nothing to do with her decision to perform that night. She only had one-half of a beer. Additionally, money was not a major motivating factor:

> Oh money, it influences, but, you know, it's not a priority. With me it wasn't anyway. With some people yeah, it might be. You got rent to pay or, you know, have bills to pay. But with me it was just, I wanted to do it. I wanted to have fun.

However, Christie does not believe that she will perform at Kato's again. She stated that "I've fulfilled my curiosity and plus my body is not in the shape that it was." Christie has achieved the self-fulfillment desired from this activity and seemingly has no need to strip again.

Donna has considered professional stripping as a primary occupation and is a regular participant in the amateur contest at Kato's. Her initial motivation to strip had more to do with friends and alcohol rather than money. The first time she participated was on her birthday. She wanted to do something she had never done before:

> I think it was my friends, you know, telling me . . . "You can do it, you can do it." And then I was just sitting there and I was like, "Yeah, I can do this," you know. So I was like, "Okay, yeah, I'll do it."

For Donna, stripping is a way to have fun, please her friends, and feel good about herself.

Tanya agrees with Donna that alcohol makes stripping easier, but argues that it was not the primary motivating factor. Typically, amateur women do not try to excuse their behavior in this way. Rather, alcohol is viewed as a way to manipulate the body in order to lessen personal inhibitions. Tanya states:

> It made it easier to do, but I'd already made my decision to do it. It wasn't one of those things where I get drunk on my birthday and

my friends are just sitting there pushing me and the next day I'm bawling.

Tanya also uses stripping to make a political statement about women's beauty expectations:

I try not to pay attention to the audience any more because they have all negative responses. Because we've thought in America you're not supposed to like yourself, you're not supposed to be sexy. And I'm sorry, but I do. And even though I have low self-esteem, I feel those things about myself. And being my size [over 300 pounds] in America or in today's society period, you shouldn't do the things I do . . . I like to do what I know people don't think I should do. And that's one of those things I can do.

Stripping is primarily a form of self-fulfillment for Tanya and argues that stripping is fun. In addition, she performs for reasons other than money:

The money is good, money is fine. It's more fun if you win. But a lot of times it's, I do it because my friends ask me to. My friends beg me to do it, "Come on, we want to see you strip, it's so much fun!"

The accounts offered by those women who strip professionally differ in some ways from those offered by amateur women. Motivational accounts regarding professional stripping correlate with those described in the literature. However, when accounting for their motivations to perform at Kato's, they sound strikingly similar to the women who perform solely as amateurs.

Tammy, a professional dancer, performs at Kato's on occasion. She describes her personal experiences that led her to professional stripping:

You know, when I first started this business I was, to be honest, only 17 years old when I started dancing. I don't know, I was real messed up is what I was. I fucked up a lot. I messed around a lot. I didn't take care of my responsibilities and things I was supposed to do. My money that I had I did not manage well. But at that time I was pretty young and I didn't know what the hell I was doing. But now I'm still young, but I'm older and wiser. I mean I still have a lot more to go in life but I've taken what's been given to me and what I've learned and done something with it.

She evokes a "sad tale" to justify her entrance into professional stripping. However, she describes the satisfaction she gets out of dancing professionally:

> It's the money. I also enjoy it. It makes my career. I have my personal, I own my own business now and am doing it. You know, there's nothing wrong with dancing and we've used it to our advantage and I've made a career out of it. It's basically my career. I mean, yeah, part of it is for the money but also I mean it's a big rush getting up on that stage. People, you know, "Wow," you know. My ex told me it's an adrenaline rush and I think you need that. [Like] rock stars on stage, they drive to that adrenaline rush. It's a type of adrenaline rush. But yeah, the money is good too. I support myself and my two kids very well and I'm very proud of that. And I do it all on my own. It's a big accomplishment.

When asked why she danced at Kato's that night she offered the following account:

> I don't know, 'cause nobody could dance that was out there . . . I was having a good time. I was out there partying with my friends, you know, and I was catching a good buzz. I wasn't drunk by any means. I was buzzed but I wasn't drunk by any means. But I mean nobody was really entering. My friend [also a professional stripper] didn't want to enter it and so I just went out there and did it. Nobody could dance so I figured I could place. I mean that may sound very naive, but I figured I could at least place and I would be happy with that.

Again, friends and alcohol play an important role in the decision to perform, but they are not considered primary sources of motivation. Although Tammy dances professionally, her motivation to participate at Kato's corresponds with that of those who perform solely as amateurs.

Amateur Stripping: Body Territories and Exploitation

The key to understanding the "attention" and the "rush" mentioned previously appears to be control. Stripping allows the performer to control the attention he or she receives through the manipulation of the body. As noted by Lyman and Scott (1970), youth have limited access to public territories for the expression of cultural values and beliefs. If they are to enhance self-esteem and individuality, they must find another outlet. For amateur strippers, this outlet is the body.

Again, stripping is a way to utilize the body to receive attention, have fun, and enhance self-fulfillment. Mike offers his opinion as to why performers strip regularly at Kato's:

> I think people strip over and over again because once you get in the public eye it's like a cocaine addiction, you just got to do it. I mean when people start yelling for you and you got 25 girls you don't even know yelling your name, you've never even met them or talked to them, it's just a thrill that they want to see you and see you in all your reality dancing. It's ego building, it builds self-esteem. It's just one of these things where you do it once and you get recognition for it, you're going to do it again. If you can get third the first time, second the third time, and first the fifth time, you're going to keep going. And if you eventually get first you're going to keep doing it just because it's a guaranteed hundred dollars. The money is a big part of it.

When asked about why people continue to strip, David also believed that audience attention is an important component in the decision-making process:

> Oh you do get a lot of attention. And see, after that I felt like a celebrity. Everybody's like, "Oh, yeah!" The guys are like, "You sly dog you!" Even if you don't win and people just see you they recognize you more afterwards. Then if you're new, you can come into town and break the ice. It's a great way to get to know a few more people. 'Cause you familiarize yourself with people you seen last week.

Further, David discusses the "rush" he gets from performing at Kato's:

> When you're dancing and then somebody goes, "Yeah, yeah," so you do "OK." Everybody else is like, "Yeah, alright." You get into it. It's kind of like a high.

Chris identifies several factors that influenced his participation in this activity. He states:

I like to do it and it's fun. And I guess I like a little bit of the attention too. but the attention doesn't play as much of a factor as, well I like to go out there and have fun doing it.

Apparently, in Chris's case, performing provides him with self-fulfillment, attention from others, and increased self-esteem.

Those who performed in the dance contest were also asked if they found stripping to be exploitative, particularly for women. Not surprisingly, accounts of exploitation were almost exclusively limited to women's participation in the amateur stripping contest. These accounts were offered by both male and female performers. Ironically, those who described their motivations to perform in terms of a rush or need for attention and self-fulfillment often described the contest as exploitative of women.

However, men and women alike described amateur stripping as entertaining and fun as noted above. Many argue that individuals have the power to make their own decisions about the event, and that people who make a choice cannot be exploited. Because the element of choice is always present, they argue that no one is *injured* and there are no *victims*. Additionally, strippers discussed this behavior as a form of empowerment or control. Those who are willing to get up in front of a large audience and remove their clothing are looked upon with respect by other strippers. Again, stripping is a way to enhance self-esteem and elicit approval or attention from others. The body is the tool to achieve these outcomes.

Dale, an amateur who has participated on numerous occasions, gives a positive account of amateur stripping:

I: some people think that stripping is exploitative for both men and women. What do you think about that?

Dale: I think that they don't have enough guts to go out there. That's why they think that. If they were in there and they had that rush and they had that sense of rush, they'd change their minds. I used to think, "I'm never going to do that, it's dumb." Then I did it and I never thought that no more.

I: Do you feel the same about women?

Dale: Yeah. If you've got the guts to do it then go do it. Whether you win or lose, you know, at least you can go out with pride.

Again, this account demonstrates the ways in which strippers utilize the body to enhance individuality while simultaneously achieving fulfillment. Additionally, Dale condemns those who would criticize performers for engaging in this form of deviant behavior. He argues that those who judge others for stripping are actually afraid to use their bodies in this way. According to Dale, strippers should be commended, not condemned for their bravery.

Tanya offers a similar account. However, she describes the tipping transaction as a mechanism of control for both audience members and performers. Through the use of the body, strippers and audience members can manipulate the transaction to their advantage and that increases individual power:

> Unless somebody is making you do something I don't think you can be exploited. It's really, it's kind of a power thing both ways. Here I am and I want you to get real close to my tits if you put the dollar bill in your mouth, but otherwise I'll keep walking right past you. It's like the guys who feel like they have power 'cause the women are like, "I'm not coming over there unless you have a dollar bill." So I mean it goes both ways. What are you going to say? I wouldn't consider it exploitation. I don't know. I'm not ready to make that kind of judgement call. I think it's a bunch of crap. People are going to do what they are going to do.

It is interesting to note that many strippers believe that the exploitation is mutual. Audience members and strippers have the ability to control the situation. This is a form of power and personal efficacy according to their accounts, and not exploitation.

Frank also describes the relationship between strippers and audience members as reciprocal in nature. He does not believe that male or female contest participants are being exploited by the management in any way:

> I don't feel that women are being exploited. I don't treat them like sex objects when I watch these female strippers. I see them as reciprocators. That is, doing something to someone that you also expect someone to do to you. I like it when I do this to women. I like it when they do this to me. That's reciprocation.

Jon offers an even more complex analysis of performer exploitation. However, rather than viewing the competition as exploitative, he condemns the gender expectations of the larger society. He describes the potential exploitation as follows:

At first, I said no, I don't think so. I think that we may define exploitation in many terms. If it was only women being paid, different pay than men were, and they were doing the same thing, then I would feel, you know, that they're being exploited. My question of exploitation differs because they both have incentive . . . $100, $50, $25. And they both have a choice. It is not a personal employment because you have been excluded by some institution. But first of all amateur, because you have a lot of young people going there, college people, and it's not necessarily, well they need the income, but it's not necessarily a job. And uh, secondly, when I consider exploitation, I think, it's a different definition for everybody.

Jon goes on to describe the amateur stripping as empowering or liberating for women. He believes that amateur stripping forces us to redefine gender expectations.

But I see the women that are out there as being uninhibited, because we restrict them so much in society. We restrict them to dress wear, to walking styles, to mannerisms, to communication . . . we categorize them in their feminine type atmosphere. But when they are out there doing certain moves, taking charge, taking advantage of what they're doing and not doing, what they show and do not show . . . I think in that sense they're more expressing themselves . . . I think it is different from when we're talking about sexual expectations and norms. We're talking not of economics, but we're talking more [about] sexuality.

As noted above, some amateurs do describe stripping as exploitative, although they often describe the event as self-fulfilling and fun. Chris describes performing as fun, but also identifies differences in how male and female performers are exploited at Kato's. Specifically, he discusses the differential expectations of male and female performers:

the women there, they have to do, like I said, certain things like spread eagle or go up and just grind on the guys or just be real suggestive in order to win there. And I think that exploits them 'cause guys don't really have to do that. I don't know. It's obviously bad, a bad point about the whole thing. There's no fairness at all. I mean girls see guys in swimming trunks all the time, you know, like what we have to wear, but guys don't see girls running around naked at the beach and stuff, so I think there's a little bit of unfairness there.

As Chris notes, the body can be used to elicit positive responses from peers, but men and women must utilize this territory in different ways. Women must be more explicit than men in order to achieve a positive response.

Dawn describes her experiences of fun and exploitation. She argues that although dancing is fun and personally rewarding, women also experiences negat6ive consequences resulting from their participation in this activity.

> I: Some people don't feel that women who participate in the dance contest are being exploited by men. How do you feel about that?
>
> Donna: Sometimes I believe it's true. But then again, like down there [at Kato's] I don't think that's the case at all.
>
> I: So you don't see women in the dance contest down there as being treated sort of as a sex object?
>
> Donna: No, not really. I mean because, well no, I have to take that back because I've had a few guys come up to me, you know, and they would talk to me and everything. And then they would just like talk to me totally different after I started doing this.
>
> I: Now, when you say totally differently, what do you mean?
>
> Donna: Well, like they'll come up and they'll like try to put their arm around me or something and then say, "Oh, what are you doing tonight after the bar closes?" You know, "We could go back to my house and party." And it's just, it kind of bothers me when they do that.

As Donna mentions, the body can be a site of individual expression and self-fulfillment; however, the attention one receives may not be perceived as positive. Audience members and performers may interpret stripping behavior quite differently, and this my negatively impact on the reputation of a female performer.

Summary and Conclusions

This study has demonstrated that amateur stripping is in some ways comparable to professional stripping, yet in other significant ways quite different. We sought to investigate those areas that make amateur stripping unique and to ascertain if Simmel's theoretical orientation could be used to enhance our understanding of this aspect of youth culture.

As pointed out in this chapter, the motivations of male and female professional strippers are quite different. Although both see money as a key factor influencing their decision to participate in this occupation, males appear to place greater emphasis on other benefits of the occupation (i.e. greater access to sexual partners, potential for movement into other forms of entertainment, and increased attention based on physical attraction).

Based on our findings, the data indicate that amateur and professional male strippers offer similar accounts to explain their participation in their behavior. The areas with the greatest degree of congruence are: potential sexual outlet; the attention provided by the audience members; an implied adrenaline rush associated with the performance; and personal fulfillment.

There are, however, based on our study, some differences that are central to our understanding of stripping behavior. Where money is a key factor for professional male strippers it is not a primary reason for amateurs. The primary motivating factor for male amateur strippers appears to be the opportunity for the individual to express himself through the body and, further, to individuate himself in the midst of an impersonal audience. Similarly, female amateur stripping behavior is distinct from professional stripping in that money is not the key motivating factor. Rather, self-fulfillment, peer encouragement, and control over their sexuality appear to be more dominant elements in the decision to participate in amateur stripping behavior. For professional female strippers, stripping is viewed as an occupation – thus the emphasis on financial gain – whereas the amateur female stripper is more concerned with entertainment and less with financial gain.

Interestingly, while male and female professional stripping accounts differ dramatically in terms of motivations, male and female amateurs participate in stripping for generally the same reasons (i.e. fun, audience attention, the adrenaline rush, and self-fulfillment). However, while male amateurs often utilize the contest as a vehicle to advance their entertainment careers and to attract potential sex partners, females do not.

Although the comparison of amateur and professional stripping is useful, Simmel's (1950) theoretical framework provides us with the tools necessary for a more complete analysis of amateur stripping behavior. Specifically, urban living allows for the possibility of increased individuality, while simultaneously creating greater anonymity and alienation for individuals. It is for this reason that individuals attempt to distinguish themselves from others. As noted previously, urban youth may have fewer opportunities to individuate themselves due to the lack of appropriate locations for self-expression.

Our analysis of male and female amateur stripping accounts indicates that urban youth utilize the amateur stripping contest as a forum for the expression of individuality through the body. The amateur stripping contest provides the participants with the opportunity to be a part of a larger group, while simultaneously allowing for individual expression apart from the group. Body territories are the sites for this more intimate form of expression. Although encouragement from friends, prize money, and alcohol are all important elements in the decision to strip, the primary motivating factors are individual in nature. Specifically, amateur stripping is utilized by both male and female participants as an entertaining opportunity to achieve self-fulfillment and to express individuality in an urban environment that is typically constraining for youth.

Notes

Some parts of this work are derived from an earlier article we have written on this subject. See Amateur stripping: sexualized entertainment and gendered fun. *Sociological Focus*, 1997.

1 All names referred to in this work are pseudonyms.
2 One of the male participants agreed to participate over the phone. His verbal consent was audiotaped at this time. Although we sent him a consent form, it was never returned.

References

Barron, K. (1989) Strippers: the undressing of an occupation. Unpublished manuscript, Department of Sociology, University of Kansas.

Boles, J. and Garbin, A. P. (1974) The strip club and stripper–customer patterns of interaction. *Sociology and Social Research*, 58, 136–44.

Calhoun, T. C., Fisher, R. and Harms Cannon, J. A. (1997) Amateur stripping: sexualized entertainment and gendered fun. *Sociological Focus*, ••

Carey, S. H., Peterson, R. A. and Sharpe, L. K. (1974) Astudy of recruitment and socialization into two deviant occupations. *Sociological Symposium*, 11, 11–24.

Dressel, P. and Peterson, D. (1982a) Becoming a male stripper. *Work and Occupations*, 9, 387–406.

Dressel, P. and Peterson, D. (1982b) Gender roles, sexuality, and the male strip show: the structuring of sexual opportunity. *Sociological Focus* 15(2), 151–62.

Enck, G. E. and Preston, J. D. (1988) Counterfeit intimacy: a dramaturgical analysis of an erotic performance. *Deviant Behavior*, 9, 369–81.

Lyman, S. M. and Scott, M. B. (1970) *A Sociology of the Absurd*. New York: Meredith.

McCaghy, C. and Skipper, J. K. (1969) Lesbian behavior as an adaptation to the occupation of stripping. *Social Problems*, 17, 262–70.

Margolis, M. L. and Arnold, M. (1993) Turning the tables? Male strippers and the gender hierarchy in America. In B. D. Miller (ed.), *Sex and Gender Hierarchies*. Cambridge: Cambridge University Press, pp. 334–50.

Mullen, K. (1985) The impure performance frame of the public house entertainer. *Urban Life*, 14(2), 181–203.

Peretti, P. O. and O'Connor, P. (1989) Effects of incongruence between the perceived self and the ideal self on emotional stability of stripteasers. *Social Behavior and Personality*, 17(1), 81–92.

Peterson, D. and Dressel, P. (1982) Equal time for women. *Urban Life*, 11, 185–208.

Reid, S. A., Epstein, J. A. and Benson, D. E. (1994a) Does exotic dancing pay well but cost dearly? Some identity consequences of a deviant occupation. In A. Thio and T. C. Calhoun (eds), *Readings in Deviance*. New York: Harper Collins.

Reid, S. A., Epstein, J. A. and Benson, D. E. (1994b) Role identity in a devalued occupation: the case of female exotic dancers. *Sociological Focus*, 27, 1–17.

Ronai, C. R. and Ellis, C. (1989) Turn-ons for money: interactional strategies of the table dancer. *Journal of Contemporary Ethnography*, 18, 271–98.

Simmel, G. (1950) The metropolis and mental life. In K. Wolff (ed.), *The Sociology of Georg Simmel*. New York: Free Press, pp. 409–24.

Skipper, J. K. and McCaghy, C. H. (1970) Stripteasers: the anatomy and career contingencies of a deviant occupation. *Social Problems*, 17, 391–405.

Sykes, G. M. and Matza, D. (1957) Techniques of neutralization: a theory of delinquency. *American Sociological Review*, 22(6), 664–70.

Thompson, W. E. and Harred, J. L. (1992) Topless dancers: managing a stigma in a deviant occupation. *Deviant Behavior*, 13, 291–311.

INDEX